TOKYO on Foot

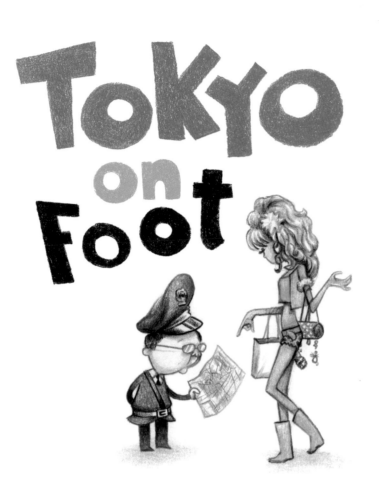

TOKYO on Foot

東京散歩

Travels in the city's most colorful neighborhoods

TEXT AND ILLUSTRATIONS BY

FLORENT CHAVOUET

TUTTLE Publishing

Tokyo | Rutland, Vermont | Singapore

Published by Tuttle Publishing, an imprint of Periplus Editions (HK) Ltd.

www.tuttlepublishing.com

Library of Congress Cataloging-in-Publication Data
Chavouet, Florent.
 [Tokyo sanpo. English]
 Tokyo on foot : travels in the city's most colorful neighborhoods/text and
illustrations by Florent Chavouet.—1st English language ed.
    p. cm.
 ISBN 978-4-8053-1137-0 (pbk.)
1. Tokyo (Japan)—Description and travel. 2. Chavouet, Florent—
Travel—Japan—Tokyo. 3. Tokyo (Japan)—Social life and customs.
4. City and town life—Japan—Tokyo. 5. Neighborhoods—Japan—Tokyo. 6.
Walking—Japan—Tokyo. 7. Cycling—Japan—Tokyo. 8. Tokyo (Japan)—Pictorial
works. 9. Tokyo (Japan)—Guidebooks. I. Title.
 DS896.35.C4413 2011
 915.2'135045—dc22
                              2010033405

ISBN 978-4-8053-1137-0

Distributed by

North America, Latin America & Europe
Tuttle Publishing
364 Innovation Drive
North Clarendon, VT 05759-9436 U.S.A.
Tel: 1 (802) 773-8930; Fax: 1 (802) 773-6993
info@tuttlepublishing.com
www.tuttlepublishing.com

Japan
Tuttle Publishing
Yaekari Building, 3rd Floor
5-4-12 Osaki, Shinagawa-ku
Tokyo 141 0032
Tel: (81) 3 5437-0171; Fax: (81) 3 5437-0755
sales@tuttle.co.jp
www.tuttle.co.jp

Asia Pacific
Berkeley Books Pte. Ltd.
61 Tai Seng Avenue #02-12
Singapore 534167
Tel: (65) 6280-1330; Fax: (65) 6280-6290
inquiries@periplus.com.sg
www.periplus.com

First English-language edition
15 14 13 12 11   10 9 8 7 6 5 4 3 2 1   1104TW

Printed in Singapore

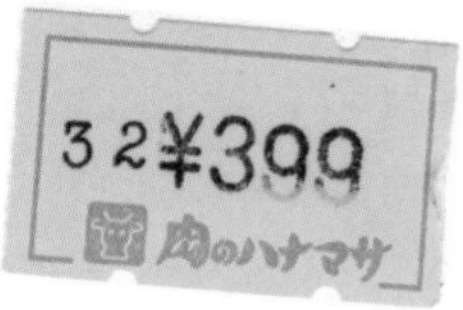
32 ¥399
肉のハナマサ

Tokyo is said to be the most beautiful of ugly cities. Those seeking old stone buildings won't find their quota of medieval streets and historical districts there, but they will still leave with the satisfied feeling of having filled their eyes (while having emptied their wallets).

There are, of course, many things to see in Tokyo. For me to say which to visit would be to predigest part of the trip for you; and besides, curiosity is much too individual a trait to take directions.

Which suits me just fine. I wouldn't know how to squeeze a glimpse of the city's many characteristics into the space of a preface. At best I would offer this thought, that it's better to be amused by the little things than to walk away from them. In Tokyo, and in Japan in general, the disoriented feeling of being in a foreign land comes from the slightly silly state of awareness that makes us admire a road sign just because it's different from the ones we're familiar with, or a fruit label because we can't understand what's written on it.

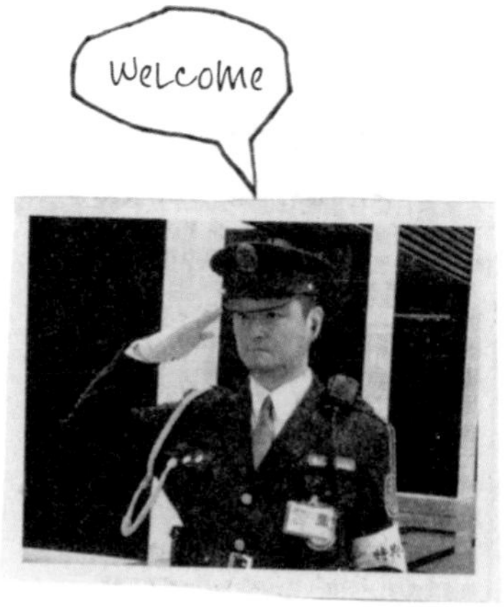
Welcome

So this is a book about Japan. About a trip to Tokyo, to be precise. It's neither a guide nor an adventure story, but that doesn't mean you'll avoid the out-of-date addresses of the one or the digressive confidences of the other. I stayed in Tokyo from June to December 2006, which corresponded

exactly to the duration of my partner Claire's internship there, the primary reason for this trip.

Since I really didn't have much to do and was reluctant to earn my keep taking on any number of meaningless jobs, I started to draw, with no particular goal in mind. Accompanied by my two most faithful friends, a lady's bicycle and a folding chair, I went scouring the streets to see what my new surroundings looked like.

One thing for sure, it's a known fact that a bike is the best means for exploring a city, and it doesn't lead to sore feet. You can befriend taxi drivers with hand gestures, and you benefit from better views than from the window of a Yamanote train. So the only advice I would give to future eager visitors is to pack your bike in your bag—though on foot you see a lot too.

However, no matter how hard I pedaled or how willing my pencils were, I wasn't able to cover all the streets of Tokyo, one more way in which I resembled the local taxi drivers. The Tokyo depicted here is strongly

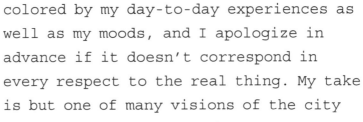 colored by my day-to-day experiences as well as my moods, and I apologize in advance if it doesn't correspond in every respect to the real thing. My take is but one of many visions of the city that travelers can turn to.

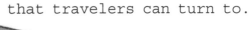

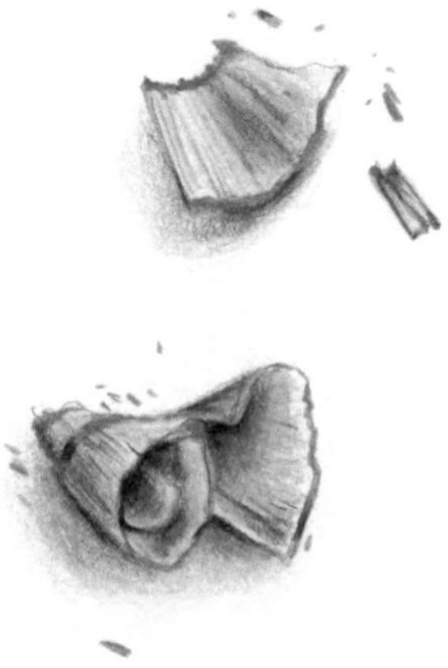

The book in your hands is organized as follows. Each chapter corresponds to a neighborhood I visited. The respective lengths of the chapters in no way indicate the relative importance of the neighborhoods in the life of the city but rather my familiarity with them.

Hand-drawn maps that are admittedly quite personal in their details introduce the neighborhoods, and on them I've marked the chapter's illustrations. I leave it to the sticklers out there to confirm whether my drawings do justice to their subjects. Finally, each chapter is announced by a koban, the local police branch station. Again, a very personal choice.

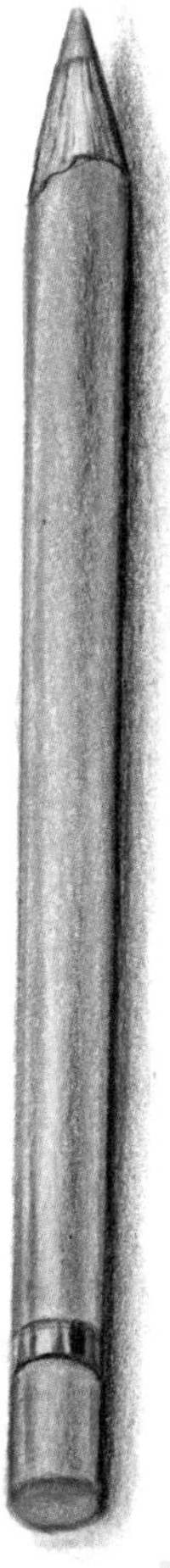

The koban is to Japanese architecture what the monuments of World War One were to French artists: a large source of commissions in which the deciding criteria were considerably more lenient than usual. For this reason, kobans offer a range of more or less recent, more or less studied styles and genres, which dot the landscape of Tokyo. The interior of the koban is, however, unvarying: the chipped furniture, the neighborhood map, the portrait gallery of most-wanted criminals, and the fine team of policemen handing out directions to passersby.

Given their usual pastime, these good officers won't mind if I use them here to introduce chapters.

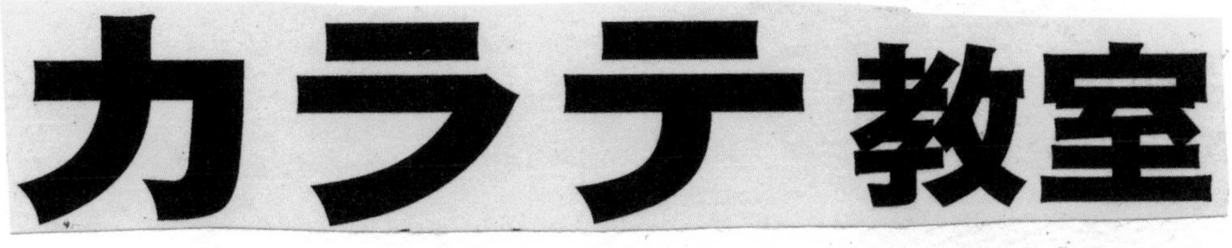
カラテ教室

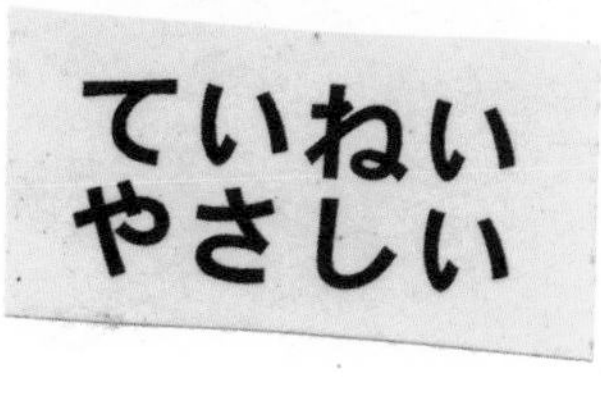
ていねい
やさしい

As for the rest, I leave it to you to discover for yourself.

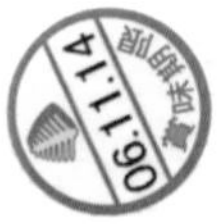
06.11.14

During the six months that I spent in Tokyo trying to absorb and understand a bit of the world around me, I remained a tourist nonetheless. With the constant feeling of not quite “getting” everything I didn’t know, and the odd habit of pasting fruit labels everywhere, because I had no idea what was written on them.

On my return to France, people asked me if China was nice. To which I responded that, in any case, the Japanese there were very friendly.

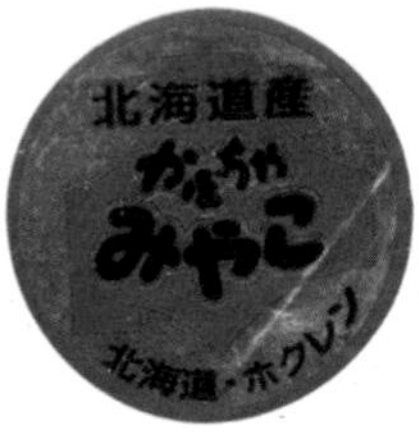
北海道産
かぼちゃ
みやこ
北海道・ホクレン

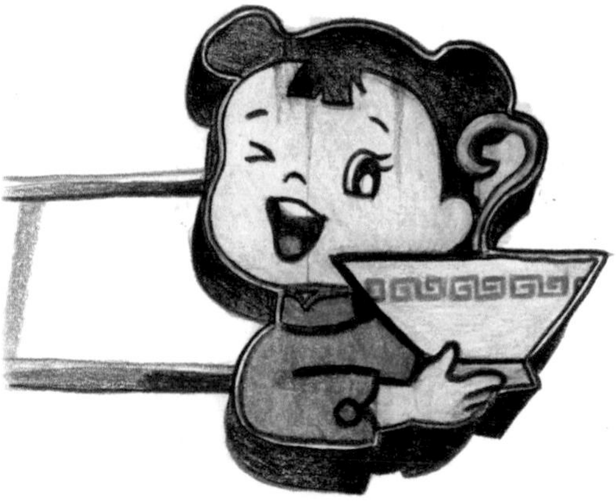

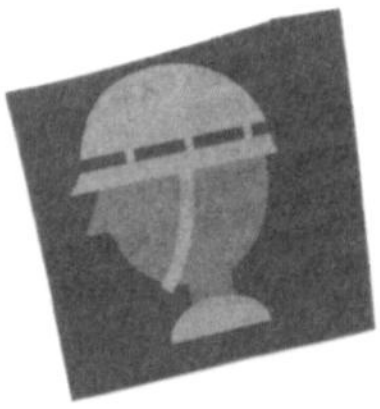

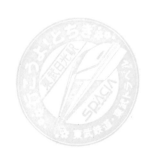

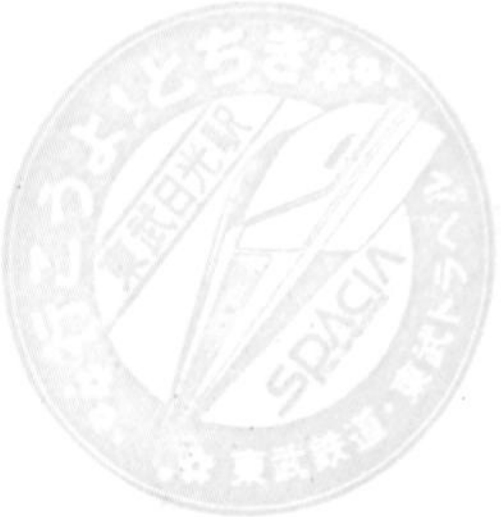

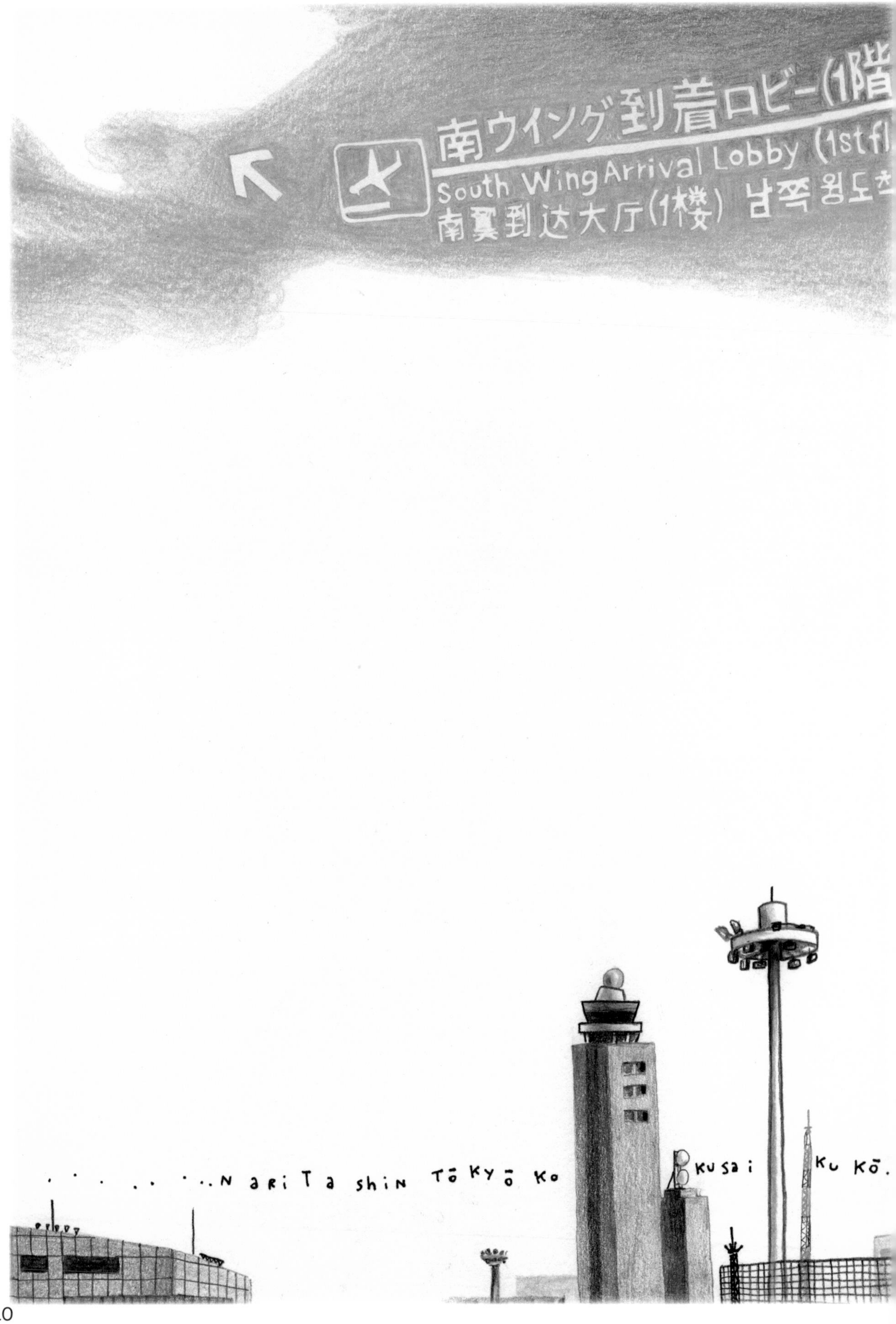
南ウイング到着ロビー(1階
South Wing Arrival Lobby (1st fl
南翼到达大厅(1楼)
남쪽 윙도
. . . .NaRiTa shiN TōKyō Ko KuSai KuKō.

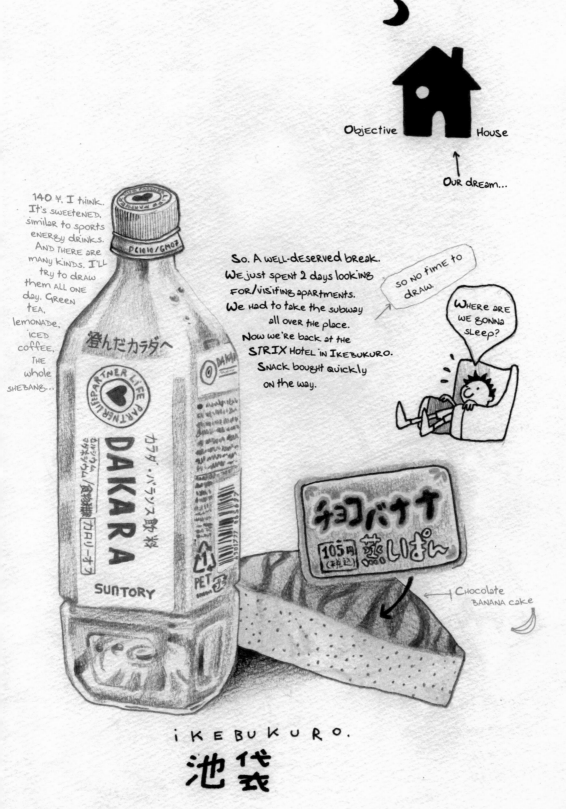

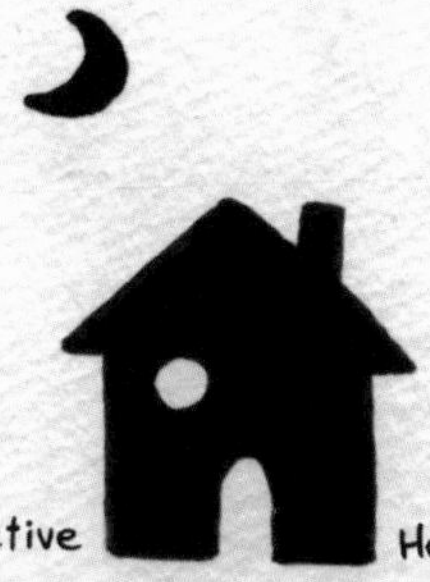
Objective
House
Our dream...

140 ¥, I think. It's sweetened, similar to sports energy drinks. And there are many kinds. I'll try to draw them all one day. Green tea, lemonade, iced coffee, the whole shebang...

So. A well-deserved break. We just spent 2 days looking for/visiting apartments. We had to take the subway all over the place. Now we're back at the STRIX Hotel in Ikebukuro. Snack bought quickly on the way.

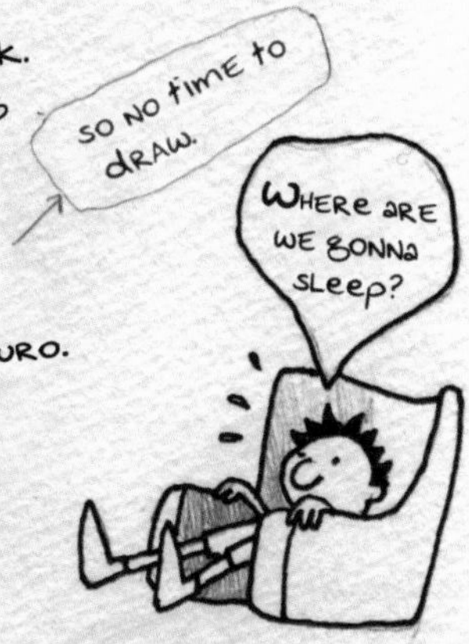
so no time to draw.
Where are we gonna sleep?

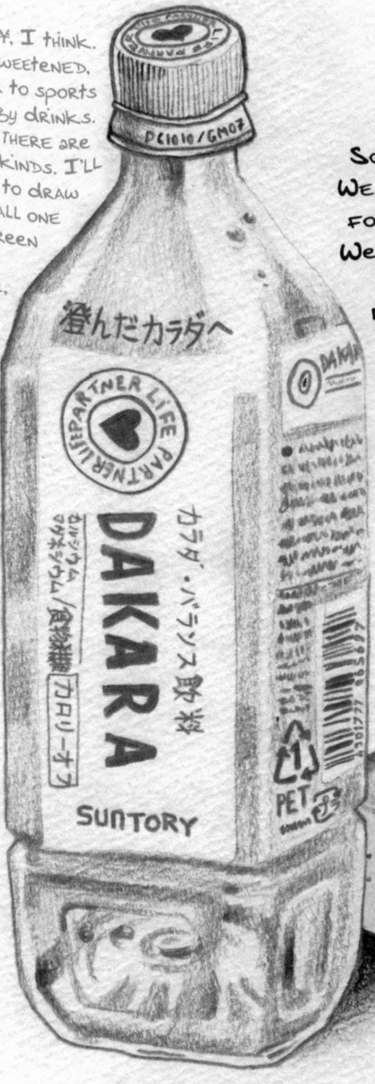
澄んだカラダへ
PARTNER LIFE
DAKARA
カラダ・バランス飲料
カロリーオフ
SUNTORY
PET

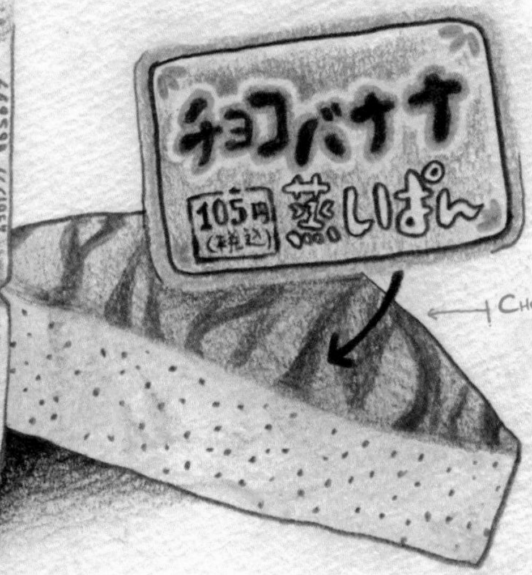
チョコバナナ
105円
(税込)
蒸しぱん

Chocolate banana cake

IKEBUKURO.

池袋

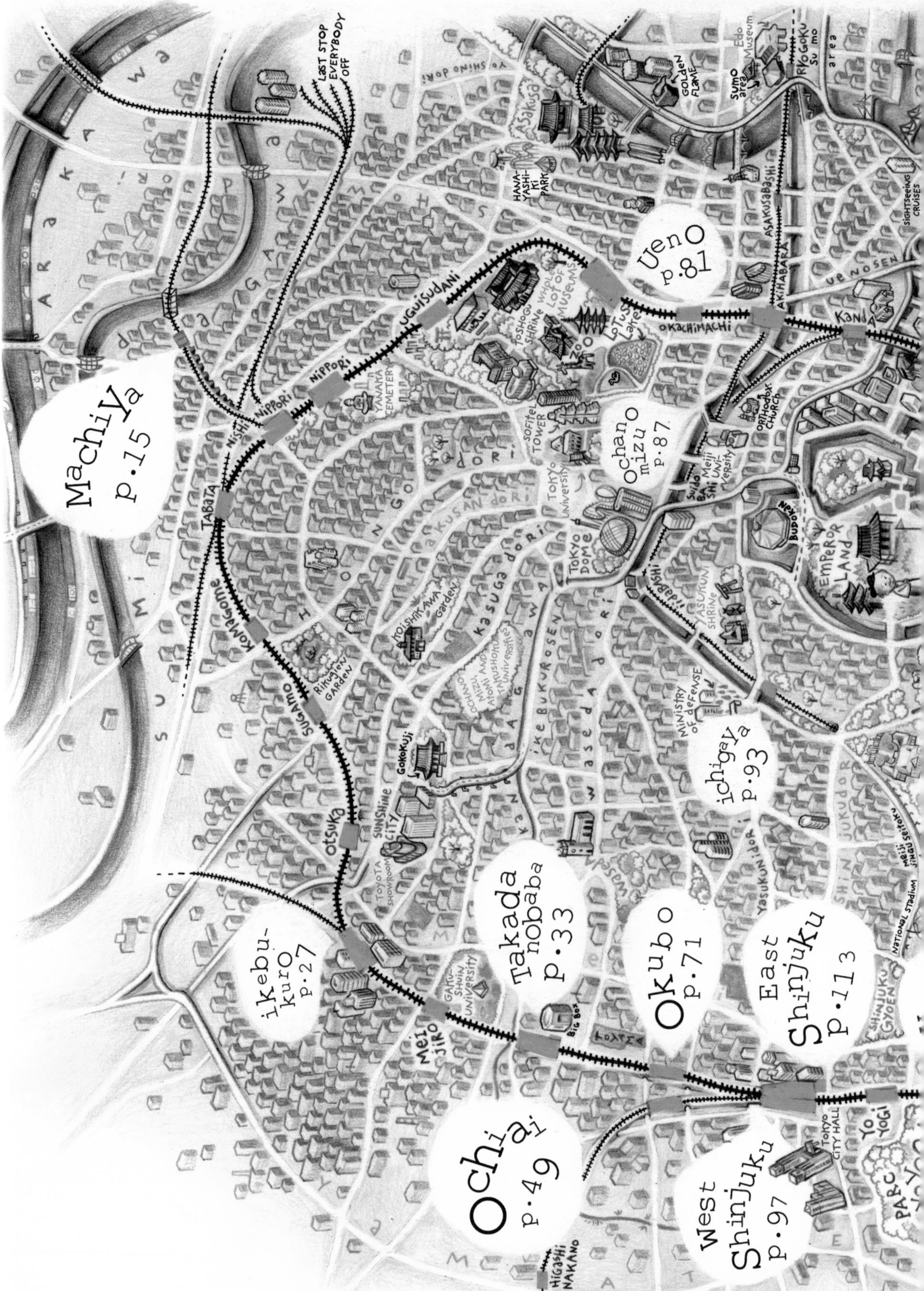

Machiya p.15
Ueno p.81
ochanomizu p.87
ichigaya p.93
Takadanobaba p.33
ikebukuro p.27
Okubo p.71
East Shinjuku p.113
Ochiai p.49
West Shinjuku p.97
LAST STOP EVERYBODY OFF
TABATA
NISHI NIPPORI
NIPPORI
UGUISUDANI
OKACHIMACHI
AKIHABARA
KANDA
KOMAGOME
SUGAMO
OTSUKA
MEJIRO
HIGASHI NAKANO
YOYOGI
SUIDOBASHI
IIDABASHI
YOSHINO DORI
ASAKUSA
GOLDEN FLAME
Edo Museum
Sumo area
RYOGOKU
HANA-YASHIKI PARK
ASAKUSABASHI
SIGHTSEEING CRUISES
UENOSEN
TOSHOGU SHRINE
WHOLE LOT OF MUSEUMS
ZOO
LOTUS Lake
YANAKA CEMETERY
SOFITEL TOWER
TOKYO UNIVERSITY
ORTHODOX CHURCH
MEIJI UNIVERSITY
BUDOKAN
EMPEROR LAND
TOKYO DOME
YASUKUNI SHRINE
KOISHIKAWA GARDEN
RIKUGIEN GARDEN
GOKOKUJI
SUNSHINE CITY
TOYOTA SHOWROOM
MINISTRY OF DEFENSE
GAKUSHUIN UNIVERSITY
BIG BOX
TOKYO CITY HALL
SHINJUKU GYOEN
NATIONAL STADIUM
MEIJI JINGU
YASUKUNI DORI
SHINJUKU DORI
IKEBUKURO SEN
kasuga dori
HAKUSAN DORI
ARAKAWA
SUMIDAGAWA

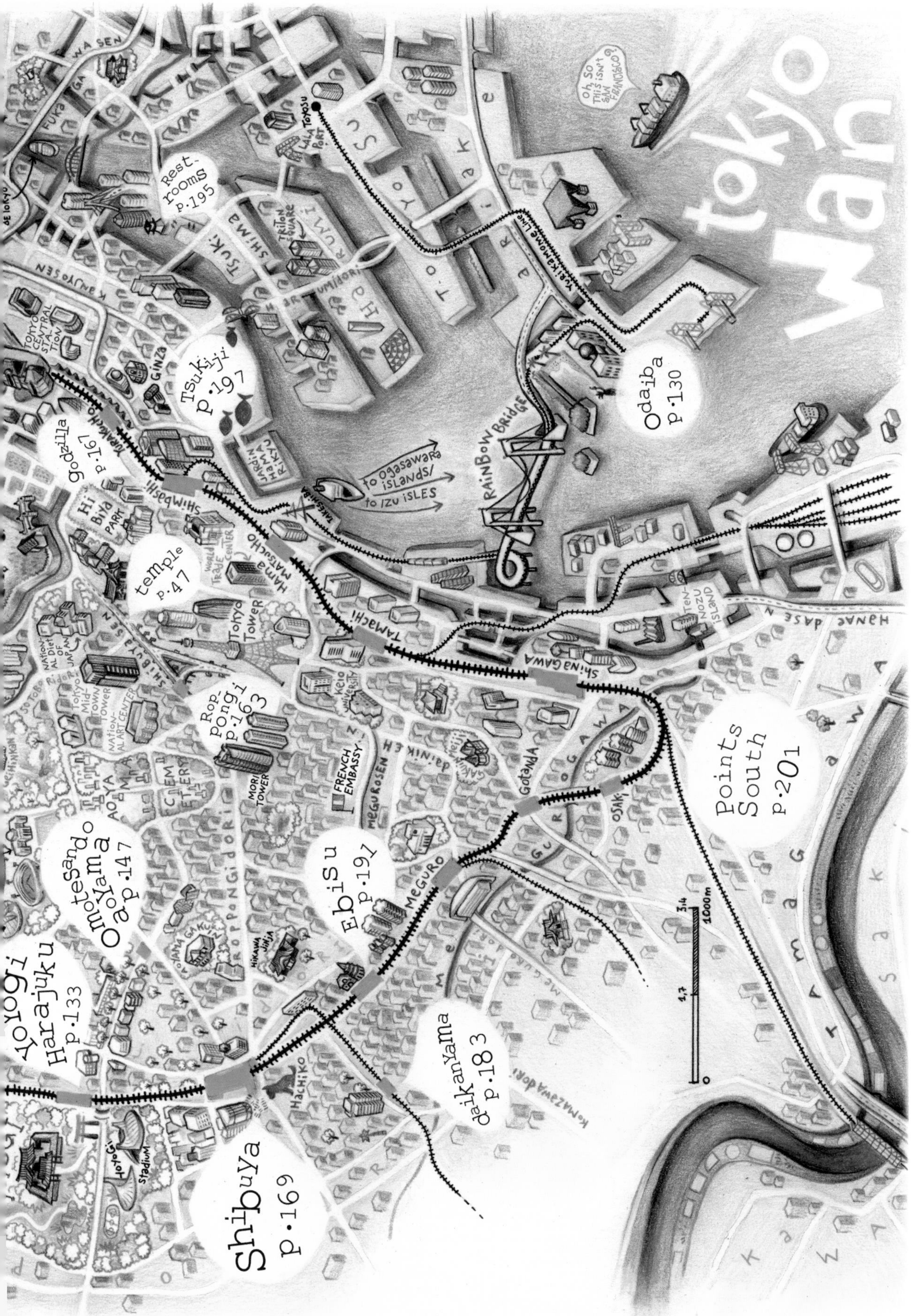

Tokyo Wan
Oh, so this isn't San Francisco?
Odaiba p.130
Rainbow Bridge
Yurikamome Line
to Ogasawara Islands/
to Izu Isles
Takeshiba
Tsukiji p.197
Rest-rooms p.195
Lala Toyosu Port
Triton Square
Jardin Hama Rikyu
Ginza
Tokyo Central Station
Yurakucho
Godzilla p.167
Hibiya Park
Shimbashi
Hamamatsucho
World Trade Center
Temple p.47
Tokyo Tower
National Diet of Japan
Tamachi
Shinagawa
Ten-nozu Island
Haneda Sen
Keio University
Roppongi p.163
Tokyo Mid-town Tower
National Art Center
Mori Tower
French Embassy
Omotesando Aoyama p.147
Yoyogi Harajuku p.133
Yoyogi Stadium
Shibuya p.169
Hachiko
Daikanyama p.183
Ebisu p.191
Hikawa Jinja
Meguro
Gotanda
Osaki
Points South p.201
1000m

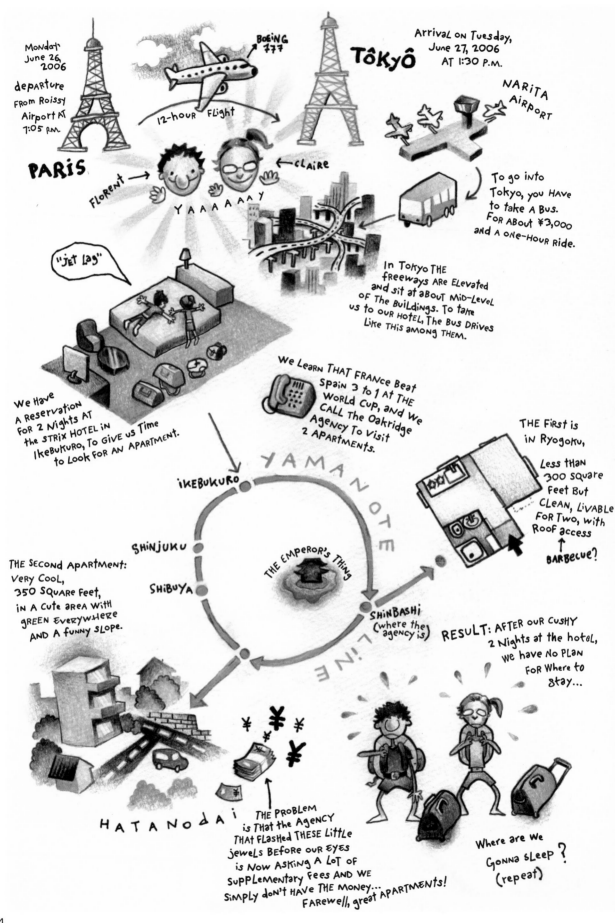

Monday, June 26, 2006

departure from Roissy Airport at 7:05 p.m.

PARIS

BOEING 777

12-hour Flight

Arrival on Tuesday, June 27, 2006 at 1:30 p.m.

TÔKYÔ

NARITA AIRPORT

Florent → ← Claire

YAAAAAAY

To go into Tokyo, you have to take a bus. For about ¥3,000 and a one-hour ride.

In Tokyo the freeways are elevated and sit at about mid-level of the buildings. To take us to our hotel, the bus drives like this among them.

"Jet lag"

We have a reservation for 2 nights at the STRIX HOTEL in Ikebukuro, to give us time to look for an apartment.

We learn that France beat Spain 3 to 1 at the World Cup, and we call the Oakridge Agency to visit 2 apartments.

THE FIRST is in Ryogoku,

Less than 300 square feet but clean, livable for two, with roof access

BARBECUE?

YAMANOTE LINE

IKEBUKURO

SHINJUKU

SHIBUYA

THE EMPEROR'S thing

SHINBASHI (where the agency is)

THE SECOND APARTMENT: Very cool, 350 square feet, in a cute area with green everywhere and a funny slope.

RESULT: AFTER OUR CUSHY 2 nights at the hotel, we have no plan for where to stay...

HATANODAI

THE PROBLEM is that the Agency that flashed these little jewels before our eyes is now asking a lot of supplementary fees and we simply don't have the money... FAREWELL, great APARTMENTS!

Where are we gonna sleep? (repeat)

machiya

machiya (NORTHERN SUBURB)

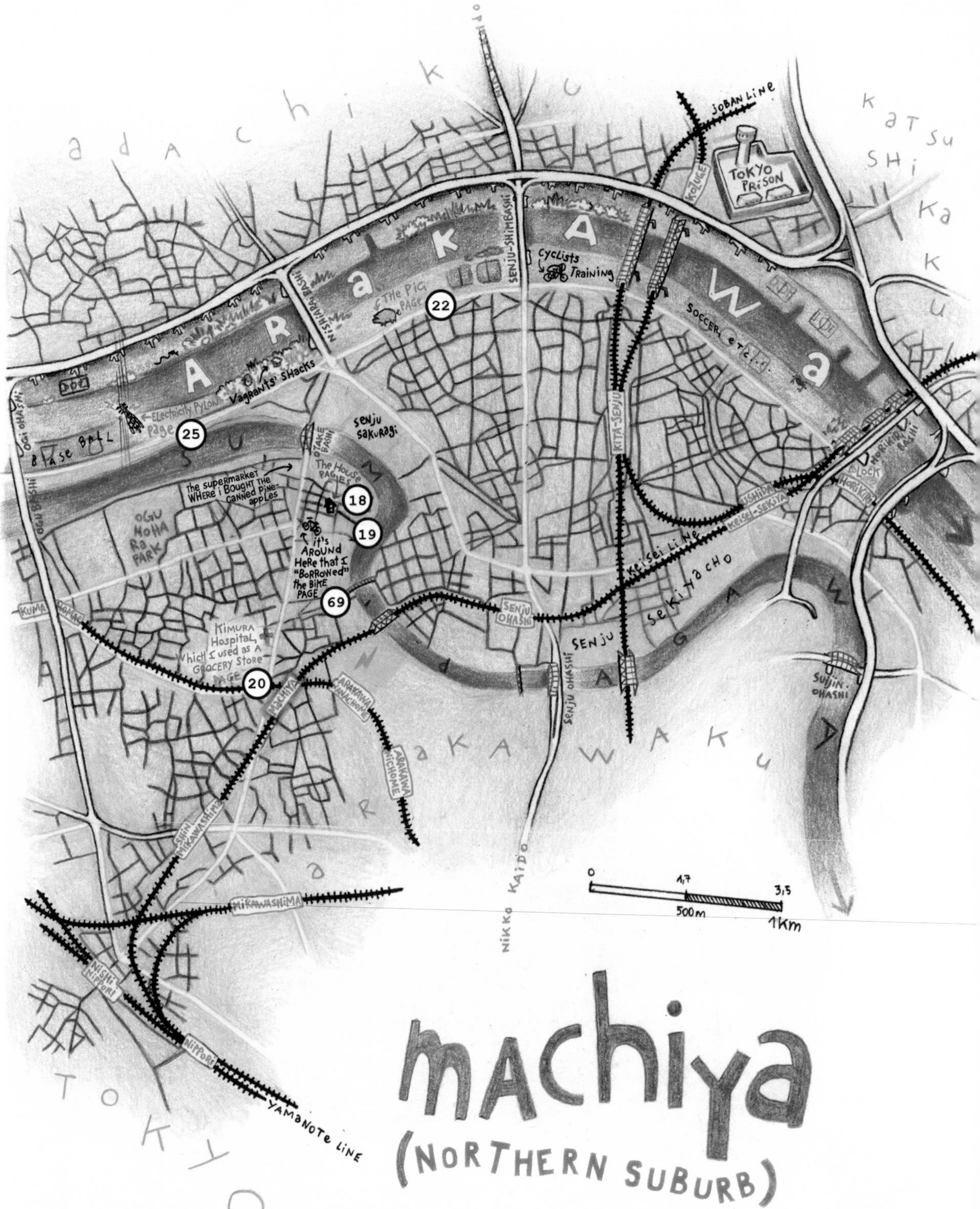
adachi ku
katsushika ku
arakawa ku
TOKYO
ARAKAWA
SUMIDAGAWA
TOKYO PRISON
JOBAN LINE
KOJUKE
SENJU-SHIMBASHI
NISHIARAI BASHI
THE PIG PAGE
22
Cyclists Training
SOCCER, etc.
Vagrants' Shacks
Electricity Pylon page
25
BASE BALL
OGI OHASHI
OGU BASHI
OTAKE BASHI
senju sakuragi
The supermarket WHERE i BOUGHT THE CANNED PINE-APPLES
The House PAGES
18
19
OGU NOHARA PARK
it's AROUND Here that I "BORROWED" the BIKE PAGE
69
KITA-SENJU
USHIDA
KEISEI-SEKIYA
KEISEI LINE
SENJU SEKIYACHO
HORIKIRI BASHI
LOCK
HORIKIRI
SENJU OHASHI
SENJU OHASHI
SUIJIN OHASHI
KUMANOMAE
KIMURA Hospital, Which I used as A GROCERY Store PAGE
20
MACHIYA
ARAKAWA NANACHOME
ARAKAWA NICHOME
NIKKO KAIDO
SHIN MIKAWASHIMA
MIKAWASHIMA
NISHI NIPPORI
NIPPORI
YAMANOTE LINE
0
500m
1Km

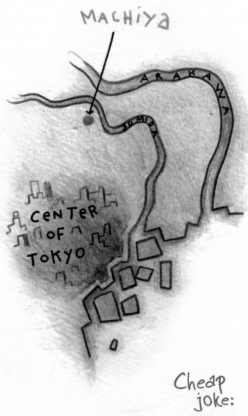

MACHIYA

ARAKAWA

SUMIDA

CENTER OF TOKYO

IN MACHIYA!

CLAIRE got BACK in touch WITH AN Agency THAT DEALS in "GUEST HOUSES," i.e. SHARED HOUSES. We TOOK THE FiRST ONE, Which Was ALSO ONE OF THE CHEAPEST, iN MACHIYA, AN AREA FULL OF MOMS, WAY TO THE NORTH AND PRetty FaR From downtown. We ReNted 2 TATAMi ROOMS. We have A PLACE, AND A roof oveR OUR Heads.

Cheap joke:

Aïe! EEE!

Ai li.

Every MORNING we'RE woken up By the sound of A MiNi-KeyBOARD. I'm tRYing to imagine the FACE of the guy (or ♀) WHO aLWays pLays the same MeLody, At 8 in the MORNING. With FALSE Notes too! ♩!!!...

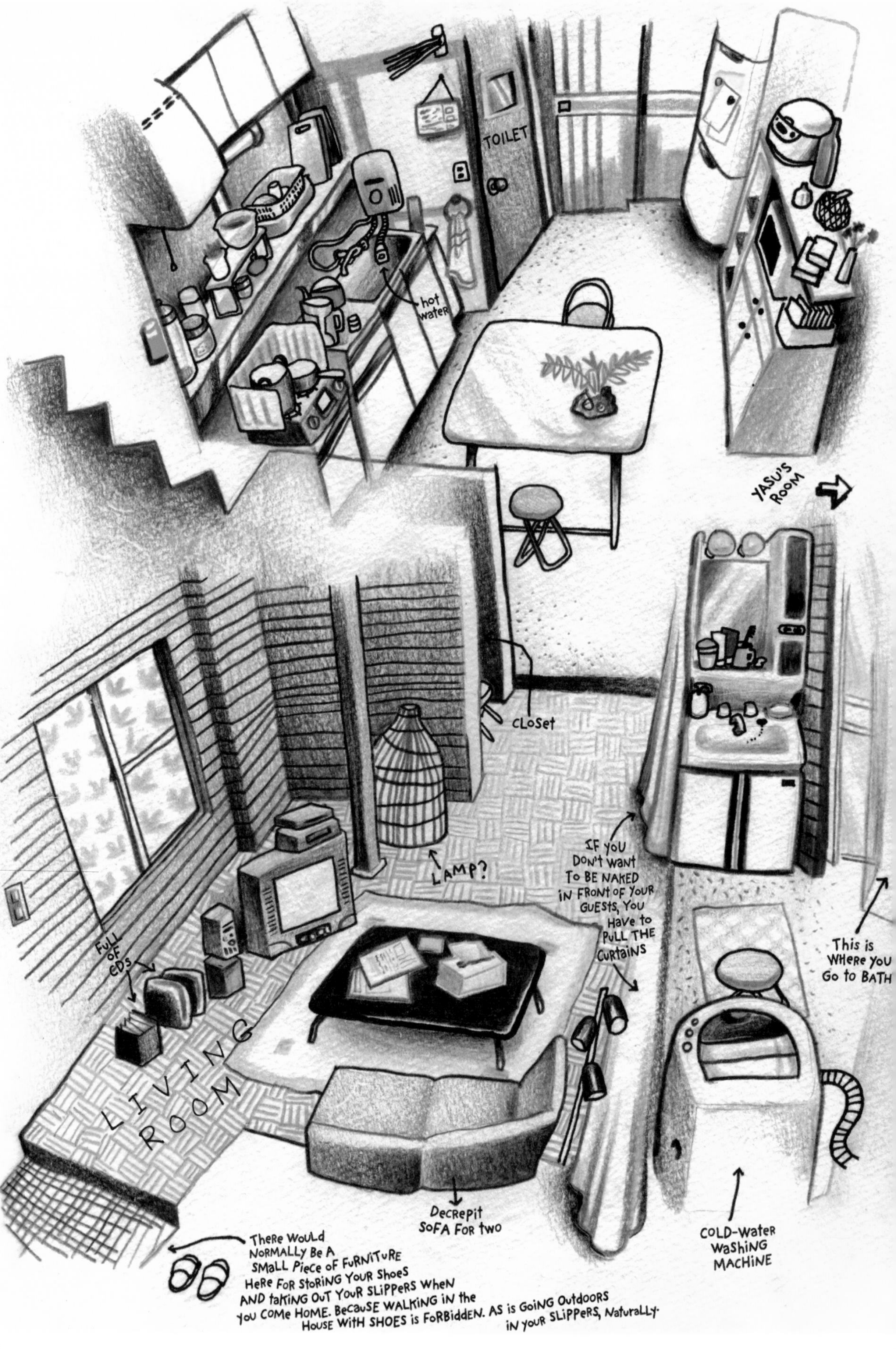
TOILET
hot water
YASU'S ROOM
CLOSET
LAMP?
IF YOU DON'T WANT TO BE NAKED IN FRONT OF YOUR GUESTS, YOU HAVE TO PULL THE CURTAINS
This is WHERE YOU Go to BATH
FULL OF CDs
LIVING ROOM
Decrepit SOFA FOR two
COLD-Water WASHING MACHINE
THERE WOULD NORMALLY BE A SMALL PIECE OF FURNITURE HERE FOR STORING YOUR SHOES AND TAKING OUT YOUR SLIPPERS WHEN YOU COME HOME. BECAUSE WALKING IN the HOUSE WITH SHOES is FORBIDDEN. AS is GOING OUTDOORS IN YOUR SLIPPERS, NATURALLY.

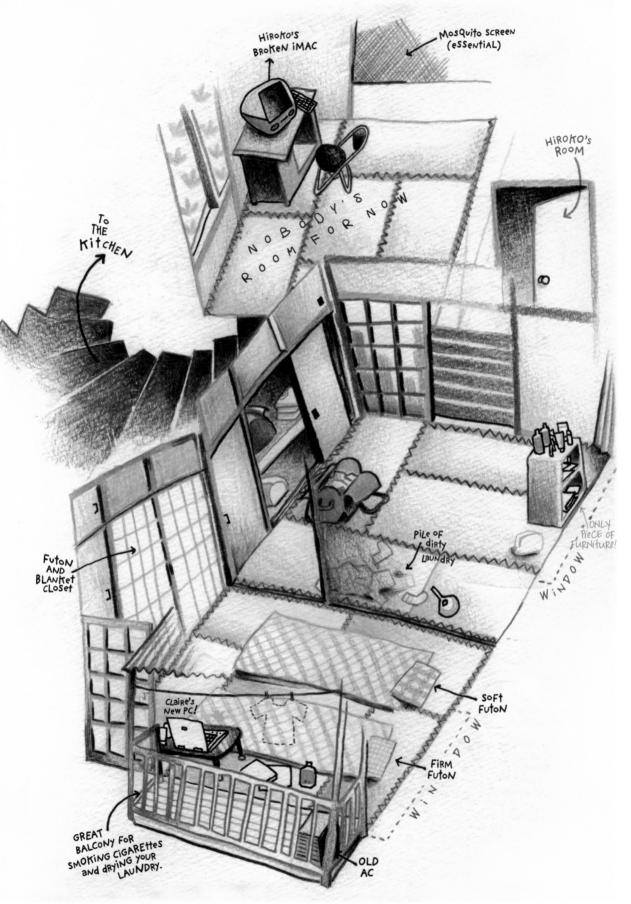

HIROKO'S
BROKEN iMAC

MOSQUITO SCREEN
(ESSENTIAL)

HIROKO'S
ROOM

TO
THE
KITCHEN

NOBODY'S ROOM FOR NOW

FUTON
AND
BLANKET
CLOSET

PILE OF
dirty
LAUNDRY

ONLY
PIECE OF
FURNITURE!

WINDOW

CLAIRE'S
NEW PC!

SOFT
FUTON

FIRM
FUTON

WINDOW

GREAT
BALCONY FOR
SMOKING CIGARETTES
and DRYING YOUR
LAUNDRY.

OLD
AC

19

I GOT SICK WITHIN 3 DAYS OF ARRIVING IN JAPAN. AFTER 2 DAYS OF FEVER AND HEADACHES, I WAS TAKEN TO SEE A DOCTOR AT THE HOSPITAL NEXT DOOR. VERDICT: THE FLU. FIRST I TOOK CAPSULES THEN PILLS, AND FOR DESSERT ANTIBIOTICS.

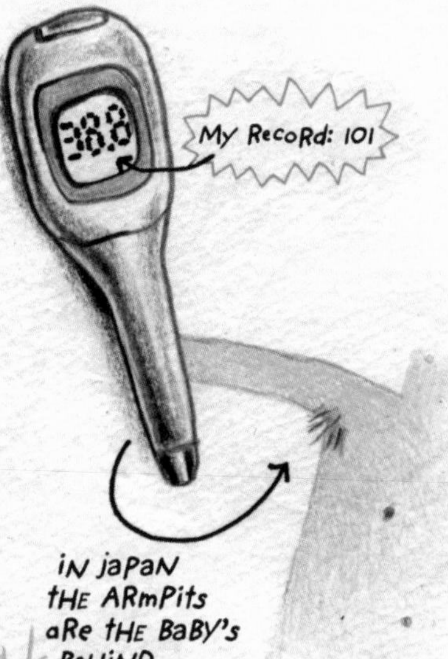

38.8
My Record: 101

IN JAPAN THE ARMPITS ARE THE BABY'S BEHIND.

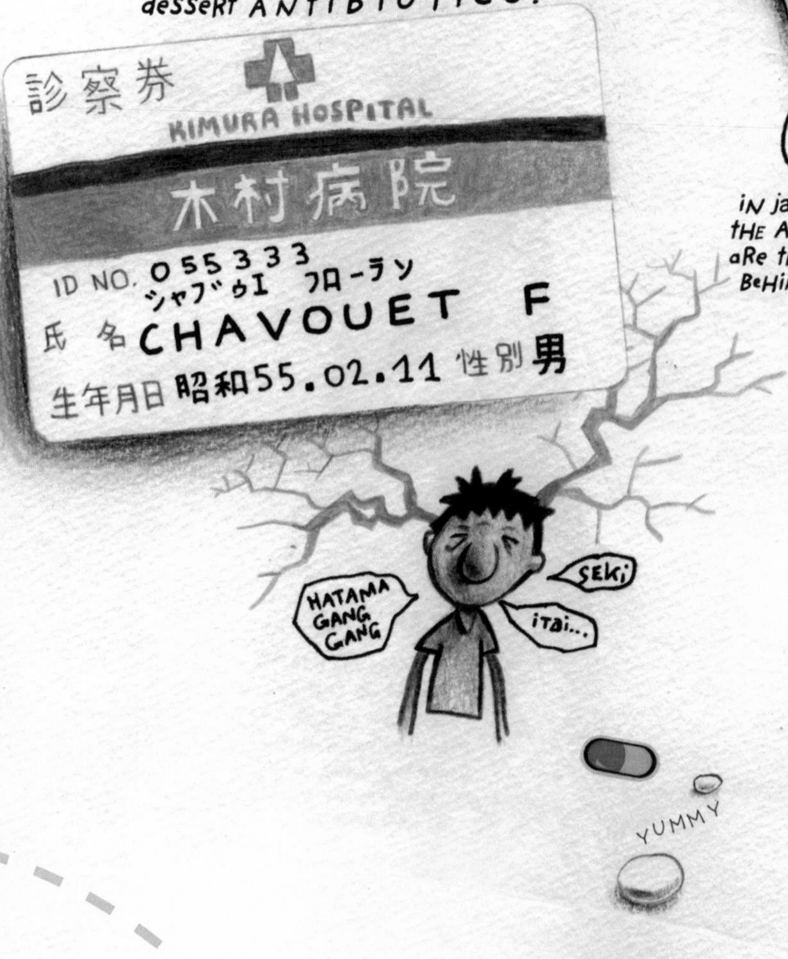

診察券
KIMURA HOSPITAL
木村病院
ID NO. 055333
シャブゥエ フローラン
氏名 CHAVOUET F
生年月日 昭和55.02.11 性別 男
HATAMA GANG GANG
SEKI
itai...
YUMMY

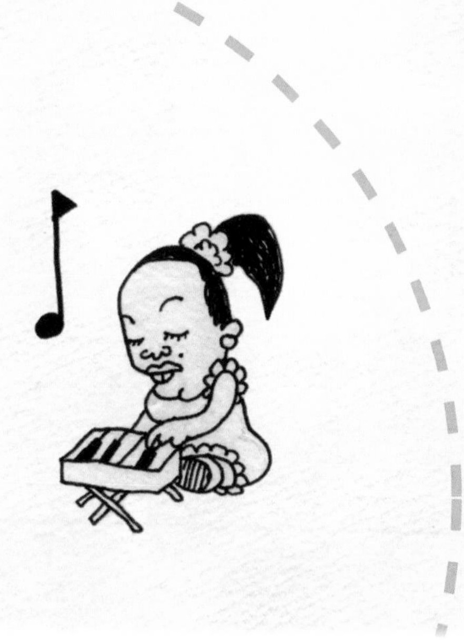

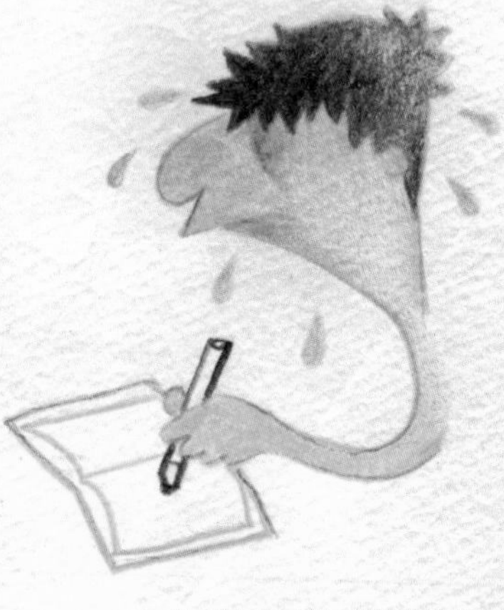

WHICH MEANS I DREW ALL THE PRECEDING PAGES AND SOME OF THE FOLLOWING ONES WITH MY HEALTH DOING A YOYO.

ANECdOTE:

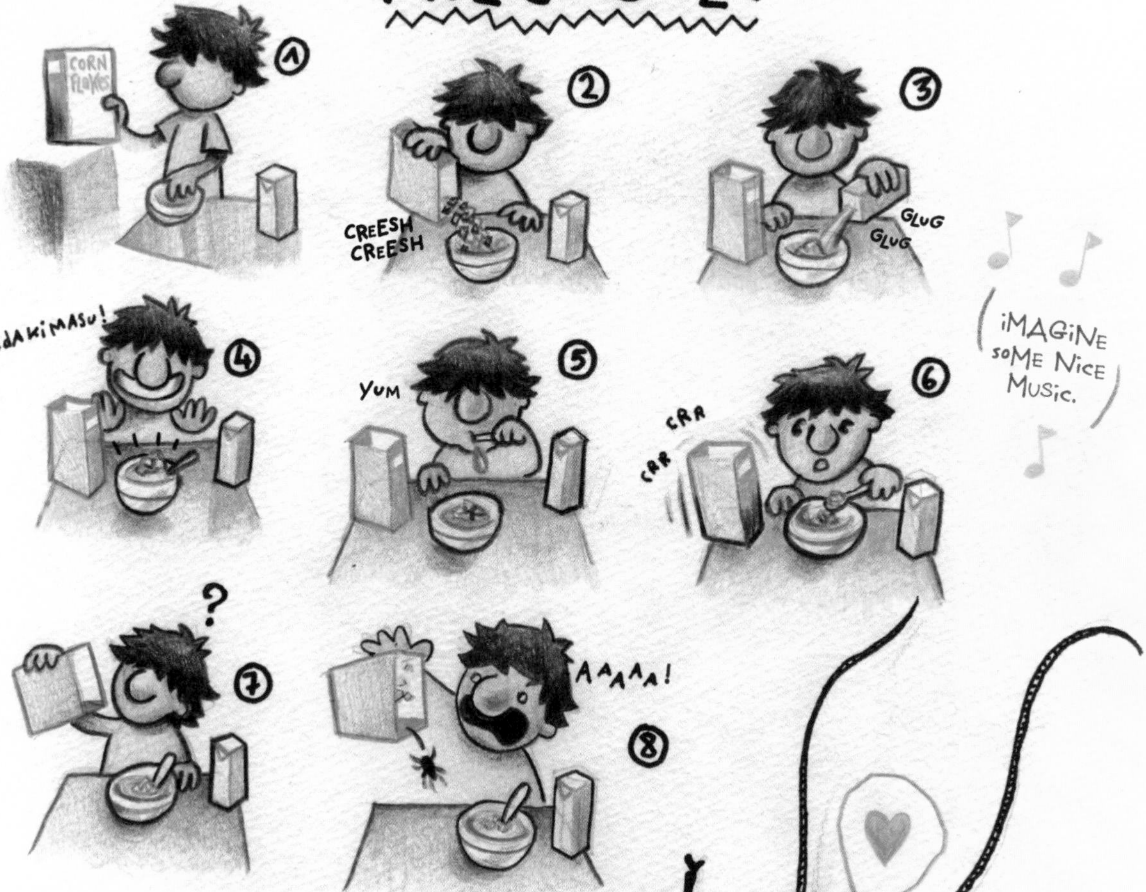

1
CORN FLAKES
2
CREESH CREESH
3
GLUG GLUG
(iMAGiNE SoME NiCE MUSic.)
iTadAKiMASU!
4
YUM
5
CRR CRR
6
?
7
AAAAA!
8

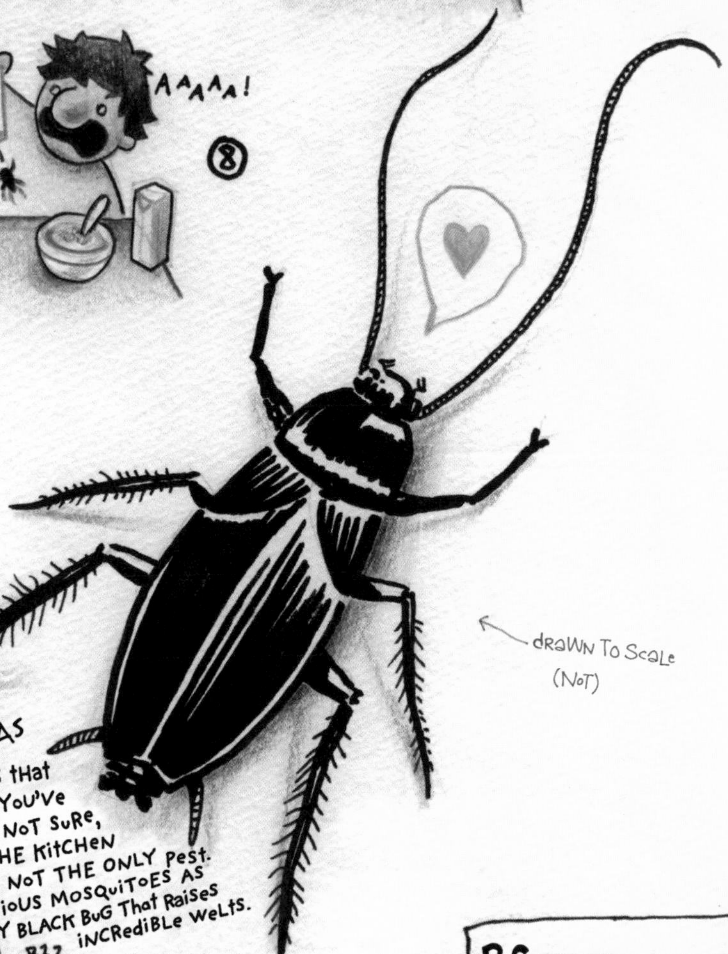

drawN To ScaLe (NoT)

JAPAN is the LANd oF GEiSHAS AND aLSo oF DiSGuSTiNG CocKRoAcHES that SLither iN CoRNeRS WHERE YoU think You've SEEN SoMething MovE But You're NoT SuRe, oR THEY SiMPLY iNVite THEMSeLVES to THE KitCHEN tABLe oR oN the BaTHRooM TiLeS. AND That's NoT THE oNLY Pest. THeRe's ALSo A LaRGe SuPPLY of ReaLLY ViCiouS MoSQuiToES AS WeLL AS A YeT UNidENtiFieD SPeCieS OF VeRY TiNY BLACK BuG That RaiSeS iNCRediBLe WeLts.

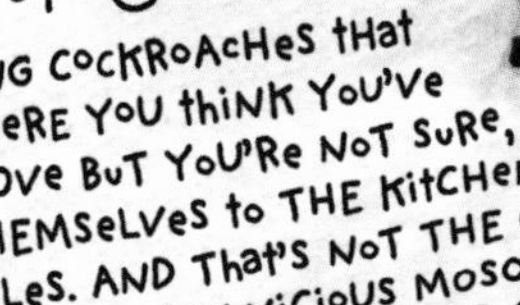

BZZz
It's NoT A fLeA.

AND THAt's Not CouNtiNG CeNtiPeDeS, WhicH i HaveN't ENCouNteRed So FaR (AppoiNtMeNt ScheduLed)

P.S.: The ABove ANecdote didn't ActuaLLy HappeN to me. it was just A way oF eNteRiNg iNto the SuBject.

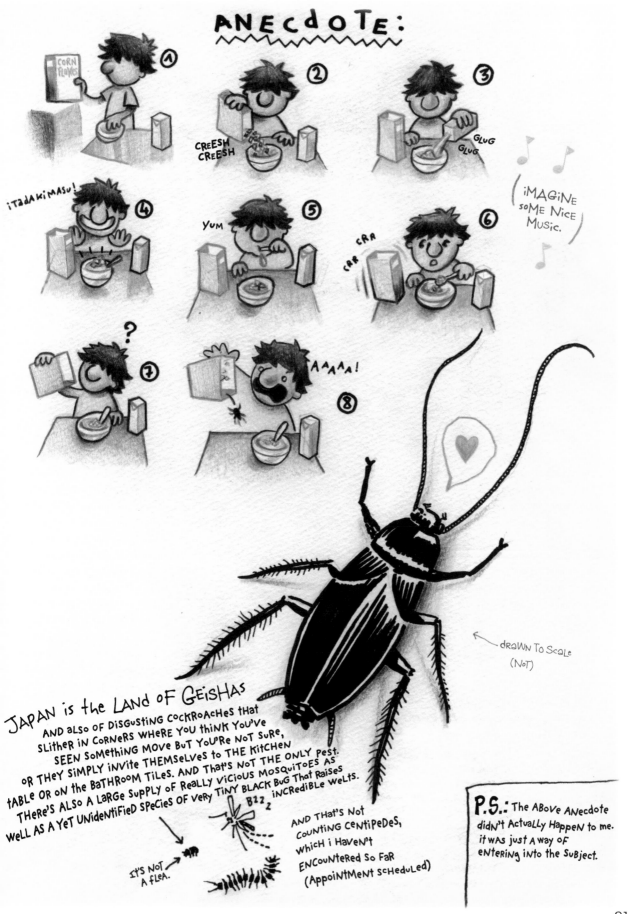

TODAY Little Kim sent 7 firecrackers into the Sea of Japan.

SEEN ON THE banks of the Arakawa: a lady walking her pet pig.

Are you coming, Maxie?

白洋舎
CLEAN LIVING

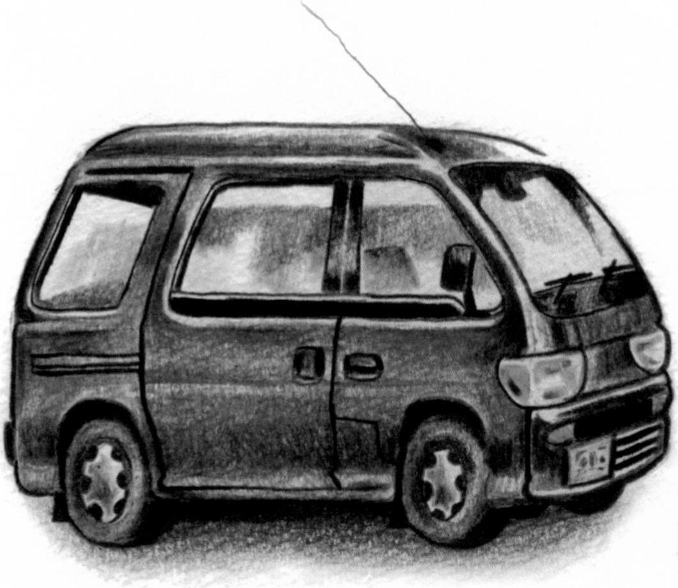

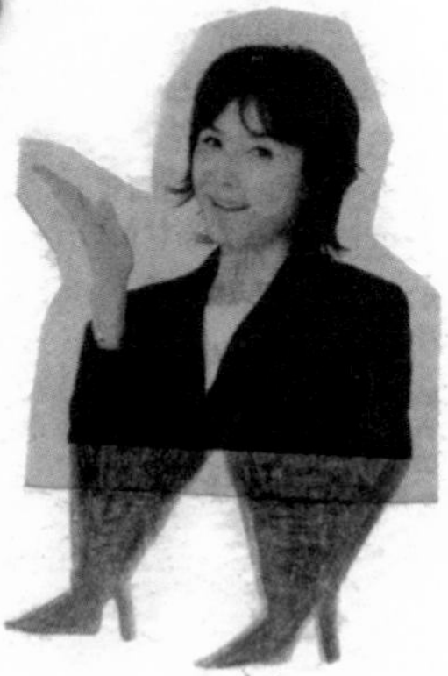

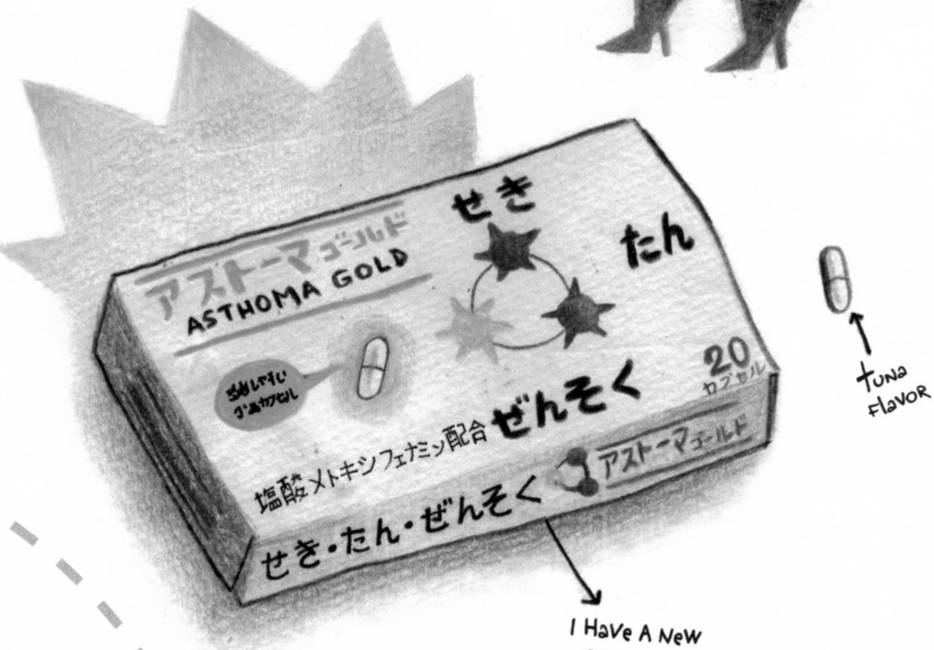
アストーマゴールド
ASTHOMA GOLD
せき
たん
ぜんそく
20 カプセル
塩酸メトキシフェナミン配合
アストーマゴールド
せき・たん・ぜんそく
TUNA FLAVOR

I Have A New
CANdY for
My Cough: ASTHMa GoLd!
A "seKi dOMe"
(LiteRaLLy "Cough STOP").
AND YES,
i'M STiLL
s i c k . . .

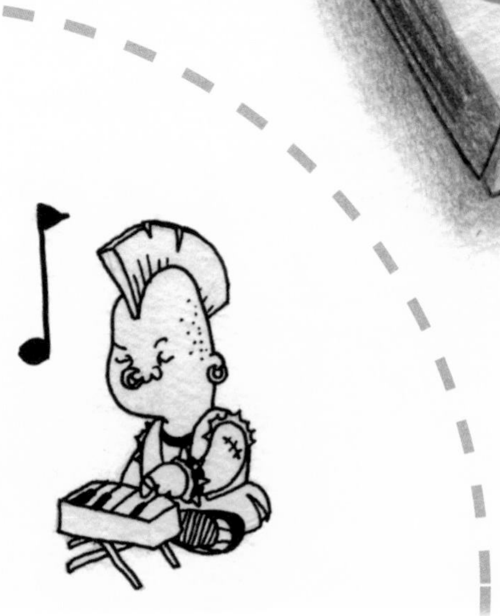

i am Socié.

socié

Movie star Sophie Marceau
is stealing work from movie
star Jean Reno doing ads.

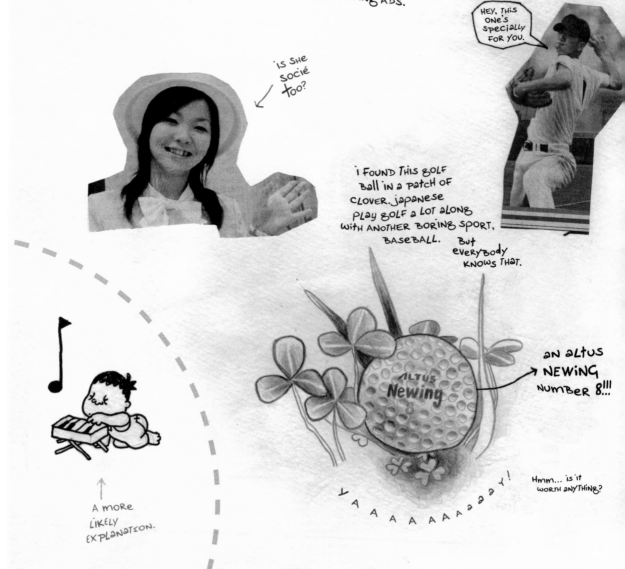

*is she
Socié
too?*

*Hey, this
one's
specially
for you.*

i found this golf
ball in a patch of
clover. japanese
play golf a lot along
with another boring sport,
baseball.

But
everybody
knows that.

an altus
NEWING
number 8!!!

↓ A A A A A A A A a a a Y!

Hmm... is it
worth anything?

↑
A more
likely
explanation.

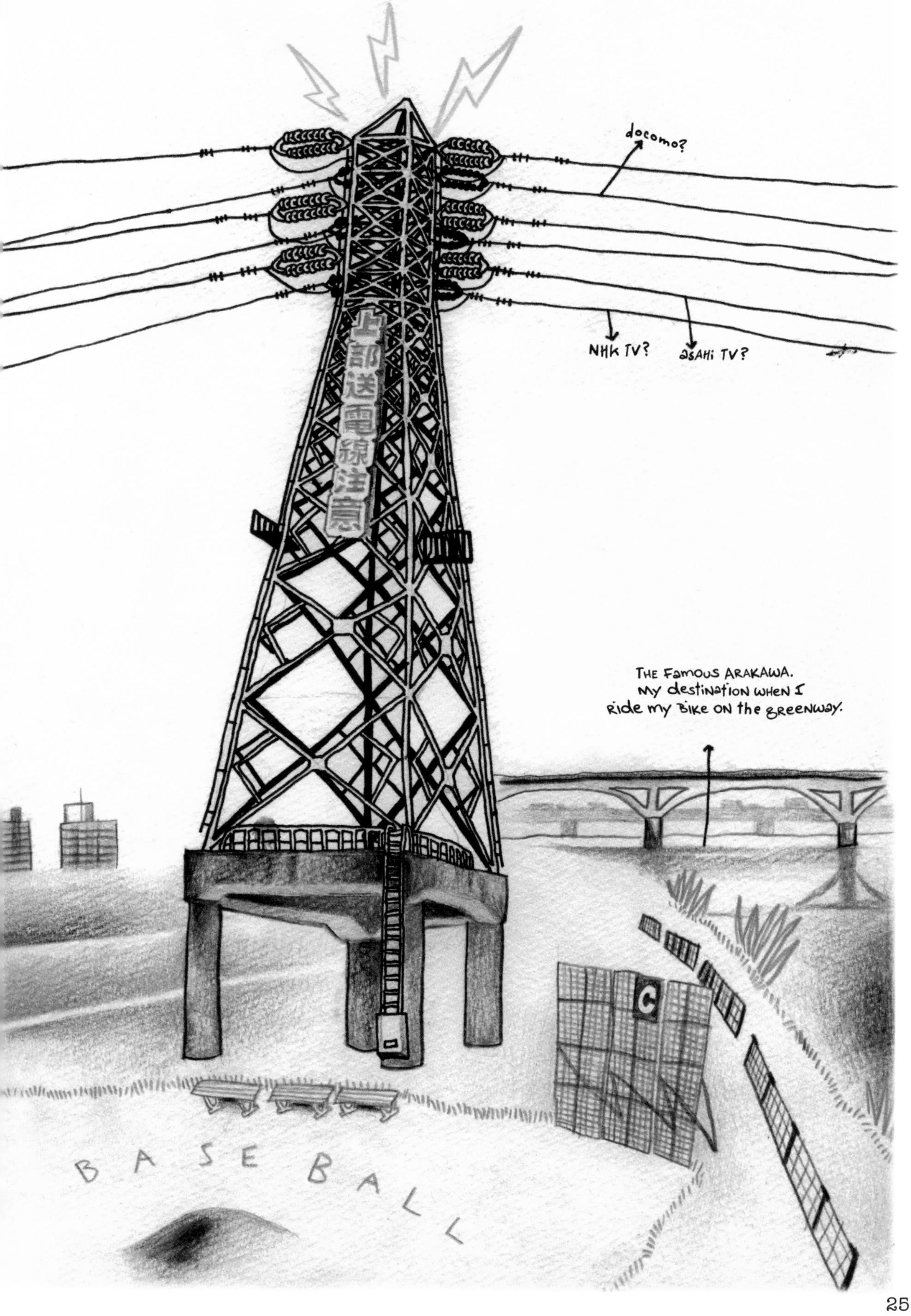
docomo?
上部送電線注意
NHK TV?
asAHi TV?
THE Famous ARAKAWA.
My destination WHEN I
Ride my Bike ON the greenway.
C
BASEBALL

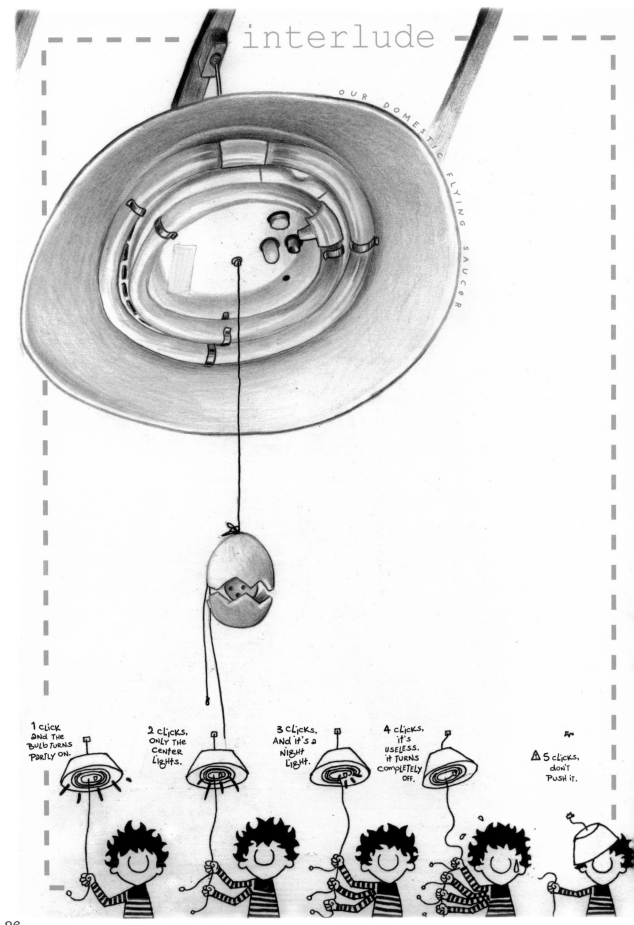

OUR DOMESTIC FLYING SAUCER

1 CLICK
AND THE
BULB TURNS
PARTLY ON.

2 CLICKS,
ONLY THE
CENTER
LIGHTS.

3 CLICKS,
AND IT'S A
NIGHT
LIGHT.

4 CLICKS,
IT'S
USELESS.
IT TURNS
COMPLETELY
OFF.

⚠ 5 CLICKS,
DON'T
PUSH IT.

ikebukuro

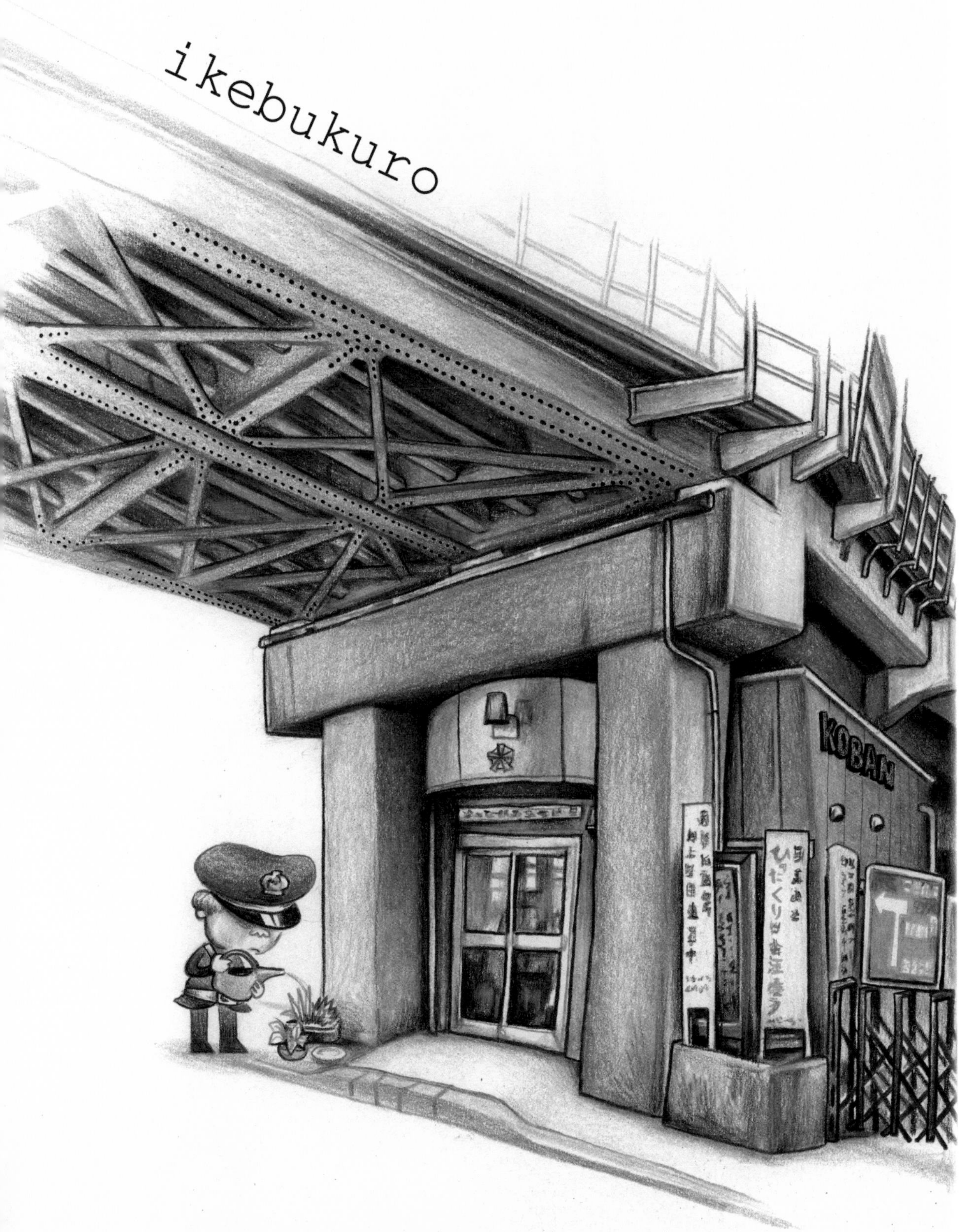
KOBAN

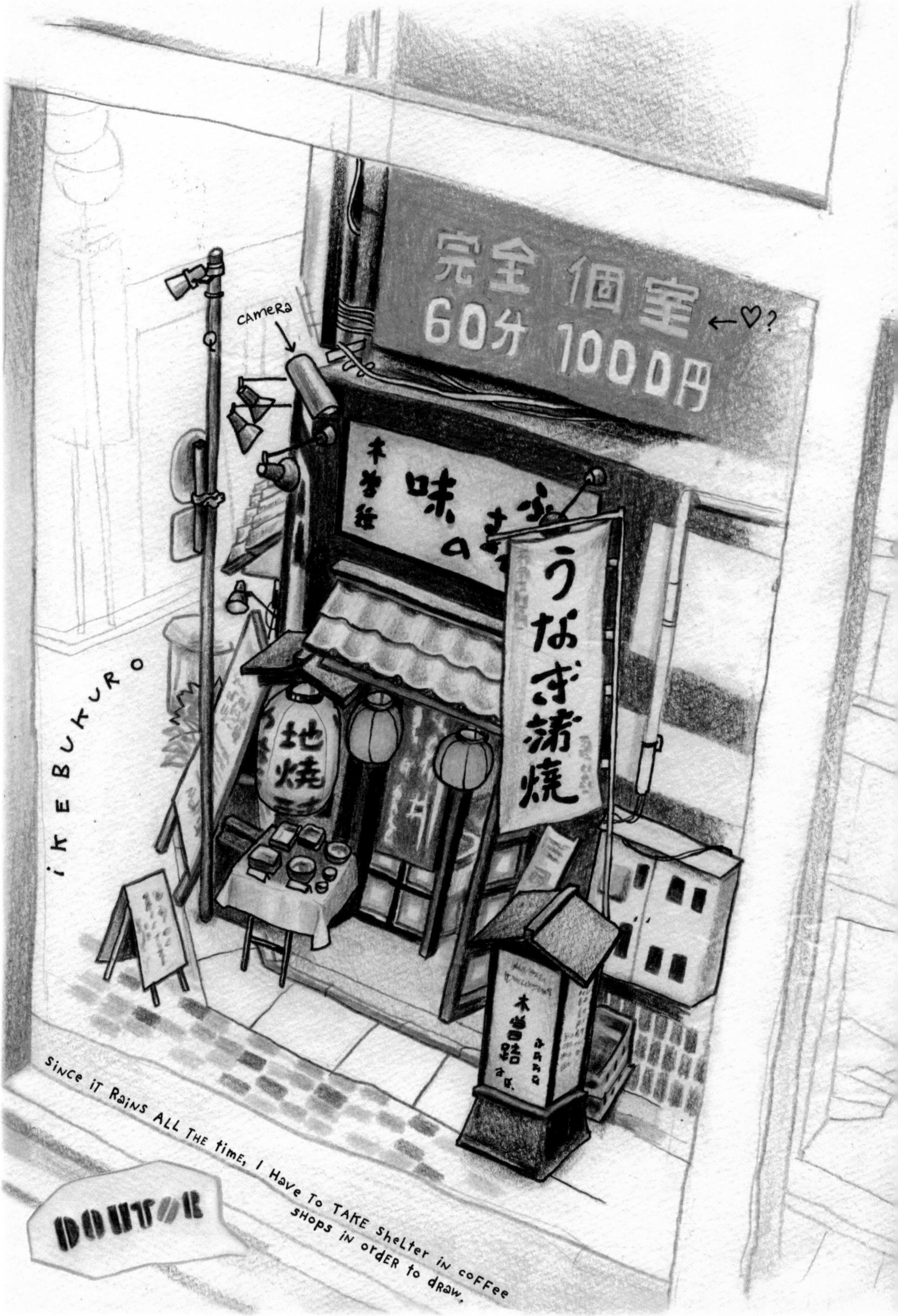
完全 個室
60分 1000円
←♡?
CAMERA
IKEBUKURO
うなぎ蒲焼
地焼
木曽路
Since it Rains ALL The time, I Have To TAKE Shelter in coFFee shops in order to draw.
DOUTOR

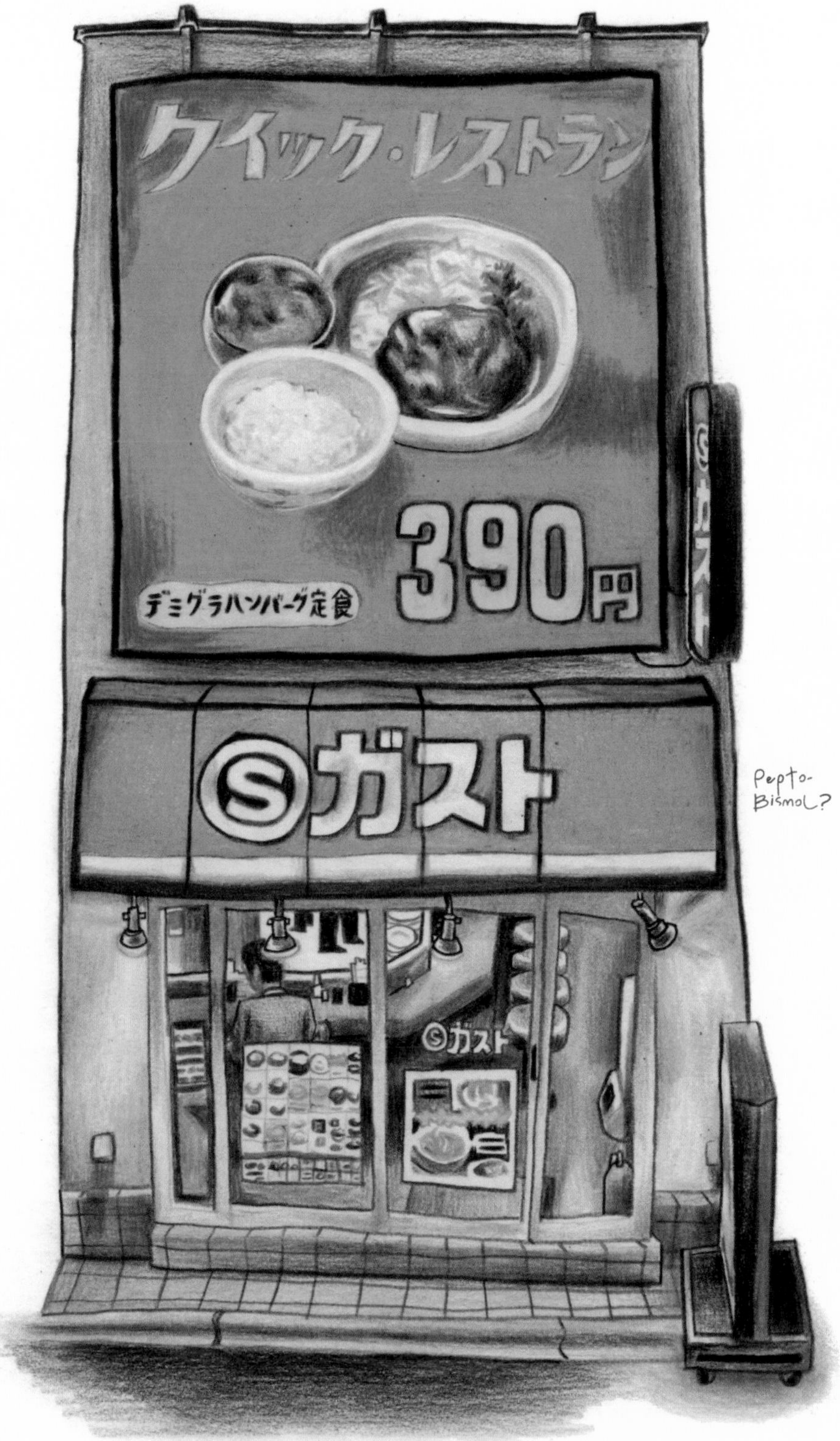
クイック・レストラン
390円
デミグラハンバーグ定食
Ⓢガスト
Pepto-Bismol?

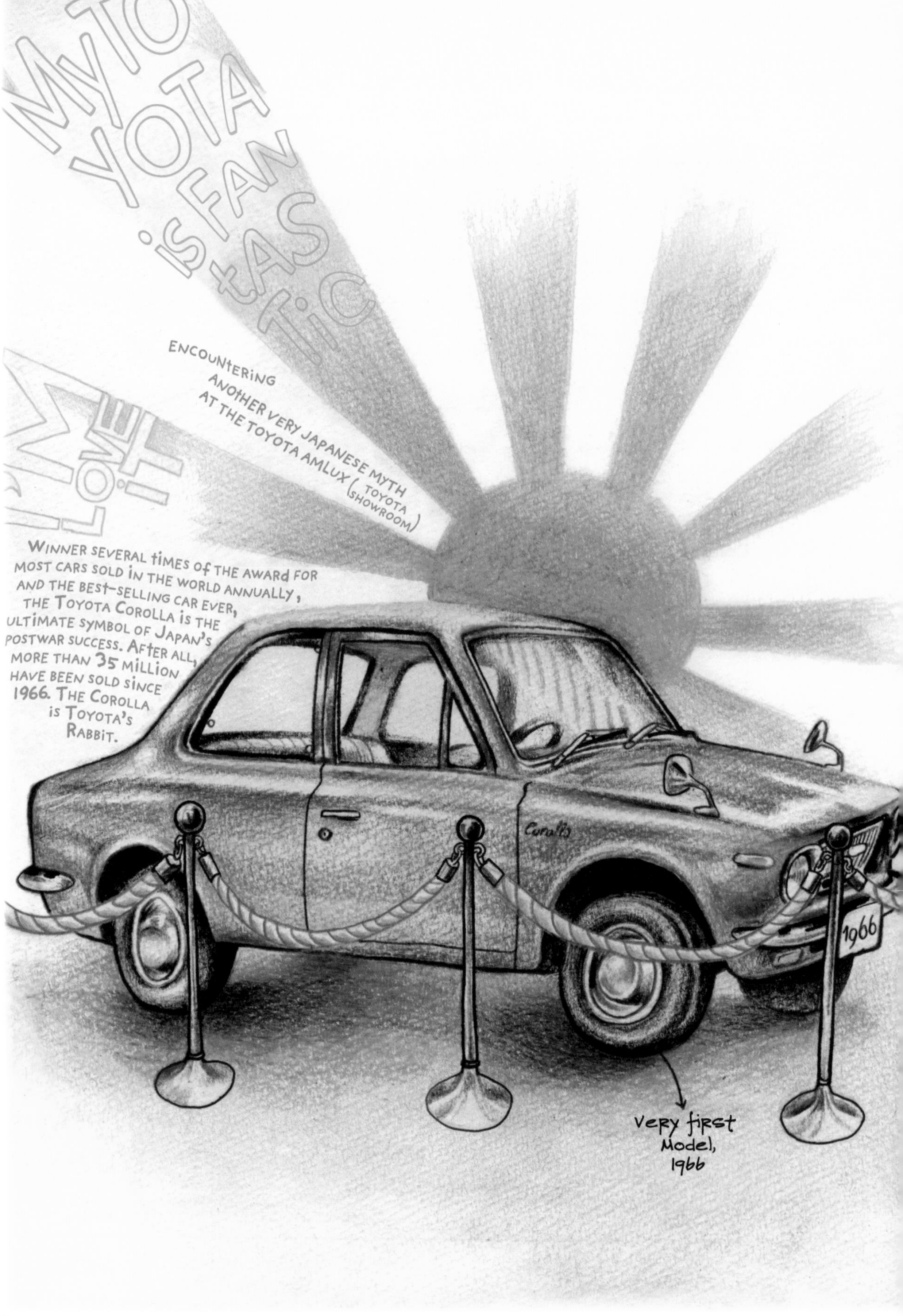
My TOYOTA is FANtAStic
ENCOUNTERING ANOTHER VERY JAPANESE MYTH AT THE TOYOTA AMLUX (TOYOTA SHOWROOM)
WINNER SEVERAL TIMES OF THE AWARD FOR MOST CARS SOLD IN THE WORLD ANNUALLY, AND THE BEST-SELLING CAR EVER, THE TOYOTA COROLLA IS THE ULTIMATE SYMBOL OF JAPAN'S POSTWAR SUCCESS. AFTER ALL, MORE THAN 35 MILLION HAVE BEEN SOLD SINCE 1966. THE COROLLA IS TOYOTA'S RABBIT.
Corolla
1966
Very first Model, 1966

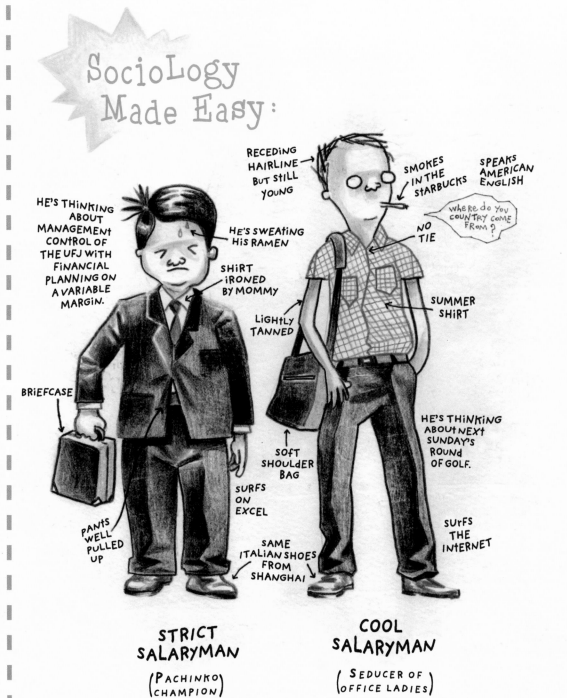

SocioLogy Made Easy:

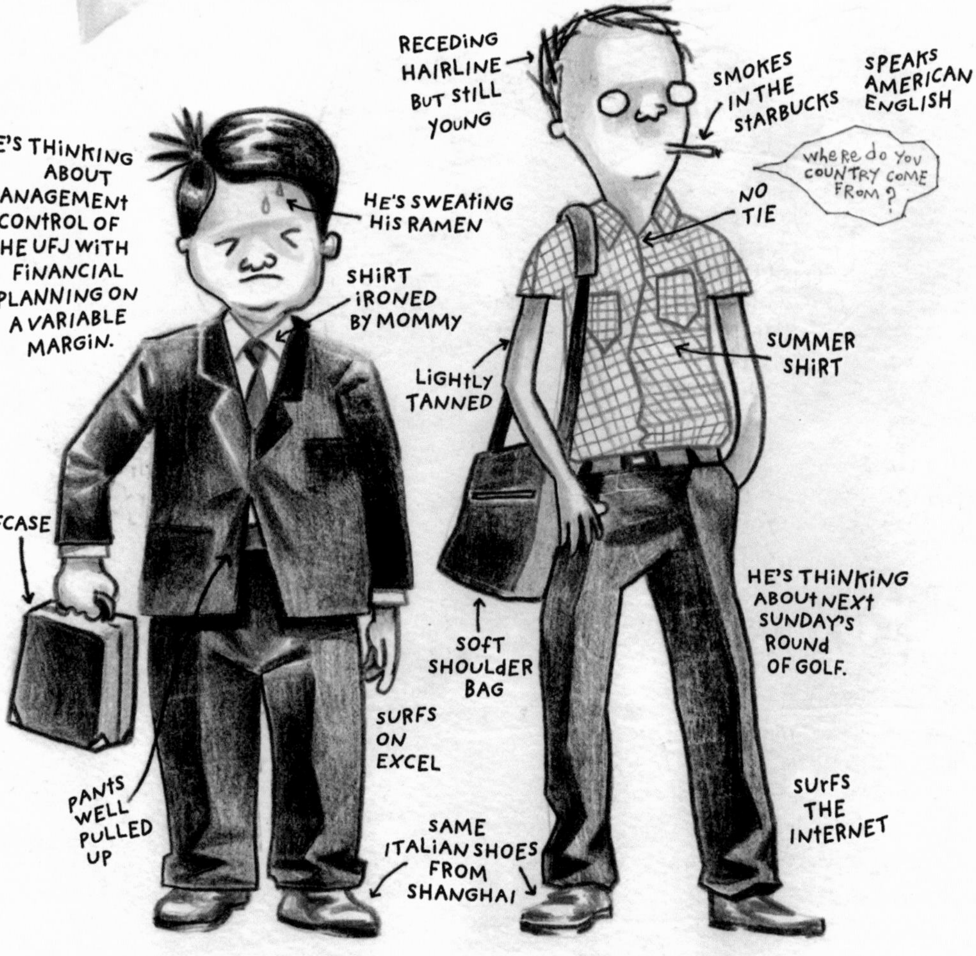
HE'S THINKING ABOUT MANAGEMENT CONTROL OF THE UFJ WITH FINANCIAL PLANNING ON A VARIABLE MARGIN.
HE'S SWEATING HIS RAMEN
SHIRT IRONED BY MOMMY
BRIEFCASE
PANTS WELL PULLED UP
SURFS ON EXCEL
SAME ITALIAN SHOES FROM SHANGHAI
RECEDING HAIRLINE BUT STILL YOUNG
SMOKES IN THE STARBUCKS
SPEAKS AMERICAN ENGLISH
where do you country come from?
NO TIE
LIGHTLY TANNED
SUMMER SHIRT
SOFT SHOULDER BAG
HE'S THINKING ABOUT NEXT SUNDAY'S ROUND OF GOLF.
SURFS THE INTERNET

STRICT SALARYMAN

(PACHINKO CHAMPION)

COOL SALARYMAN

(SEDUCER OF OFFICE LADIES)

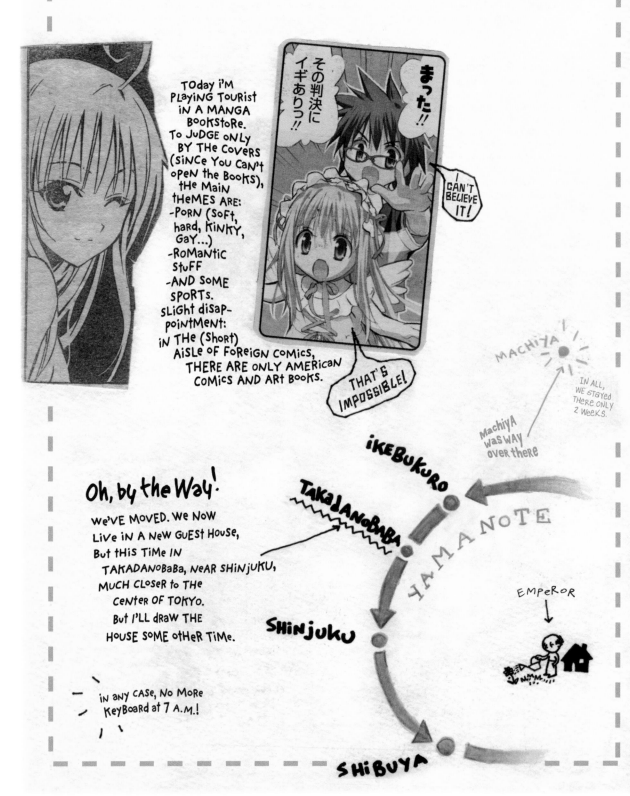

TOday i'M PLAYiNG TOURiST iN A MANGA BOOKSTORe. TO JUDGE ONLY BY THE COVERS (SiNCE YOU CAN'T OPEN the BOOKS), tHE MAiN tHEMES ARE:
- PORN (SOFt, hard, KiNKY, GaY...)
- ROMANtic StuFF
- AND SOME SPORtS.
SLiGHt disappointment: iN THE (Short) AiSLE OF FOReiGN COMiCS, THERE ARE ONLY AMERiCAN COMiCS AND ARt BOOKS.

まった!!

その判決に イギありっ!!

I CAN'T BELIEVE IT!

THAT'S IMPOSSIBLE!

MACHiYA

IN ALL, WE STayed THERE ONLY 2 WEEKS.

MachiYA was WAY over there

iKEBUKURO

TAKADANOBABA

YAMANOTE

Oh, by the WaY!

WE'VE MOVED. WE NOW LiVE iN A NEW GUEST HOUSE, BUT tHiS TiMe iN TAKADANOBABA, NEAR SHiNjUKU, MUCH CLOSeR TO THE CENTER OF TOKYO. BUT I'LL draW THE HOUSE SOME OtHeR TiMe.

iN aNY CASE, NO MORE KeYBoaRD at 7 A.M.!

SHiNjUKU

EMPEROR

SHiBUYA

takadanobaba

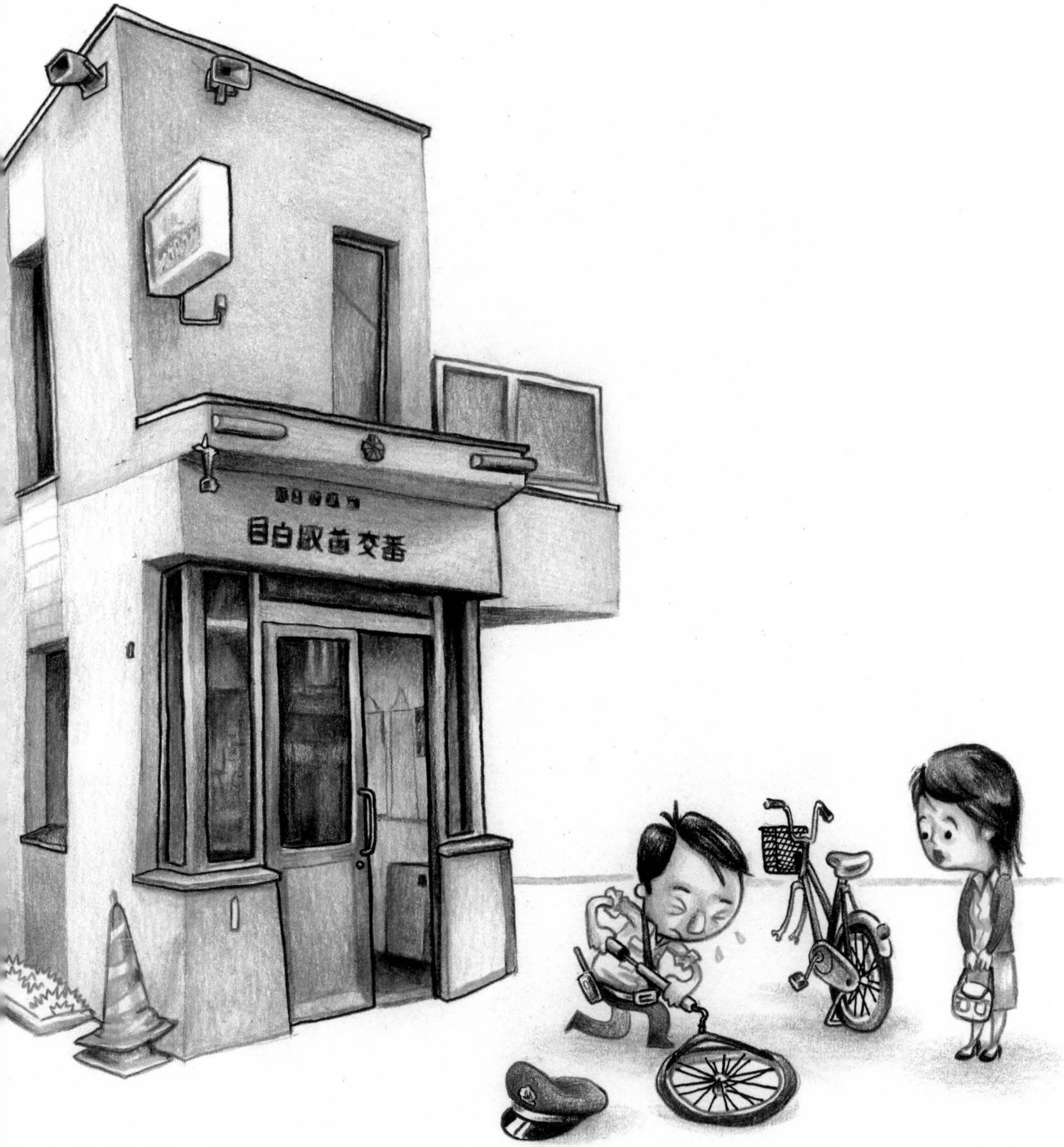
目白駅前交番

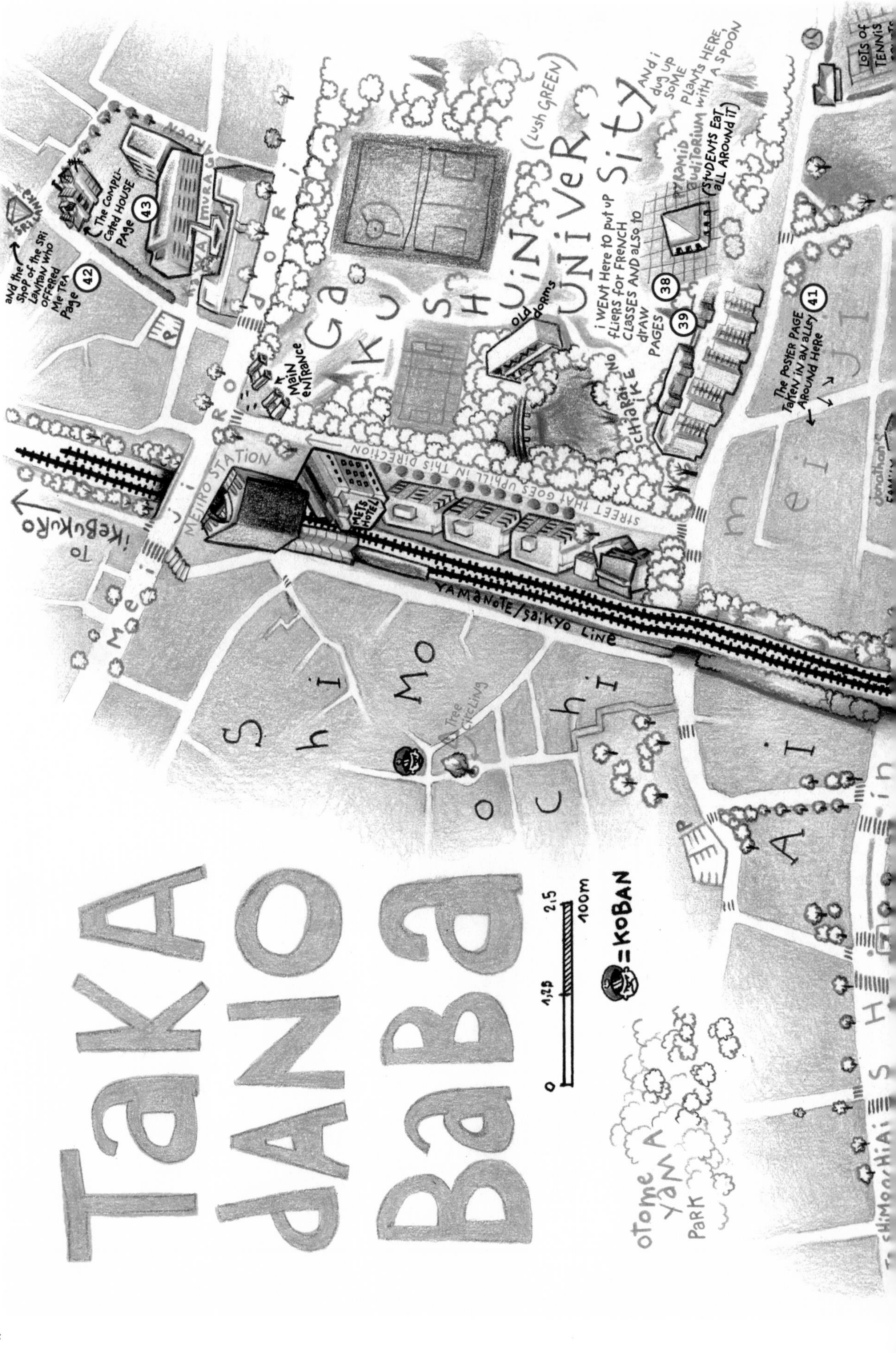
TaKa dANO BaBa
0
1,25
2,5
100m
=KOBAN
otome yaMA PARK
To iKeBuKuRo
MEJiRO STATION
STREET THAT GOES UPHILL IN THIS DIRECTION
METS HOTEL
YAMANOTE/SaiKyo LiNE
Me j i R o d o r i
S h i Mo o c h i A i
m e i J i
Tree CYCLING
Ga K u S H u i N UNiVeRSity
(Lush GREEN)
MAiN eNTRANCE
old dorms
chiaRai iKE NO
i WENT Here to put up fLieRS for FRENCH CLASSES AND also to draw PAGES
38
39
PyRAMiD auditorium
(STUDENTS EAT ALL AROUND IT)
AND i dug up SOME PLANTS HERE, WITH A SPOON
LOTS OF TENNIS
The POSTER PAGE TaKeN iN AN aLLey AROUND HeRe
41
Jonathan's
The COMPLiCated HOUSE PAGE
43
and the Shop of the SRi LANKAN who offered Me TEA Page
42
SRi LANKA
KAWAMURA
P
chiMoochiAi

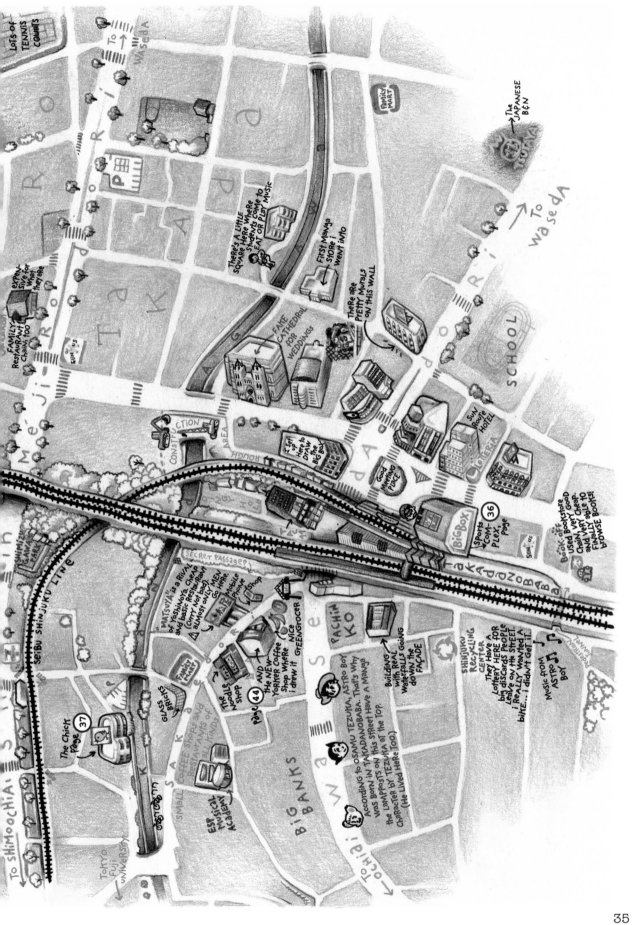

LOTS OF TENNIS COURTS

To → WASEDA

Mejiro-dori Road

EXPEN-sive for what there are

FAMILY RESTAURANT CHAIN, TOO

P

TAKADA-dori Road

SCHOOL

There's a LITTLE SQUARE HERE where students come to EAT or PLAY MUSIC

First Manga STORE I went into

There are PRETTY Murals ON THIS WALL

FAKE CATHEDRAL FOR WEDDINGS

FAMILY MART

To → WASEDA

The JAPANESE BEN

CONSTRUCTION AREA

ROUGH

I set up HERE to DRAW the Big Box!

Good MEETING PLACE

SUN ROUTE HOTEL

OPERA

BigBox

Sports COM-PLEX, page 36

Takadanobaba

Bookstore Used Bookstore CHAIN, very GOOD and VERY CHEAP and VERY ABLE TO FINALLY BROWSE Books!

Shimizu Kawai PARK

SEIBU SHINJUKU LINE

To SHIMOOCHIAI →

Tokyo Fuji UNIVERSITY

Shinjuku Seibu

The Chick page 37

ESP Musical Academy

SMALL COFFEE SHOPS and RESTAURANTS of ALL KINDS

GLASS BRICKS

The Noodle Shop

SECRET PASSAGE?

MATSUYA is a RIVAL of YOSHINOYA & Cheap and basic RESTAURANT (Curry/Not bad!) ▲ almost only 'MEN' GO HERE

Mobile Phone Shop

AND the NEW-YORKER Coffee Shop where i drew it

page 44

Nice GREENGROCER

PACHINKO

According to OSAMU TEZUKA, ASTRO BOY was BORN IN TAKADANOBABA. That's why they Have A Manga CHARACTER by TEZUKA at the Top of the LAMPPOSTS on this street (He LIVED HERE TOO.)

SHINJUKU RECYCLING CENTER They Have A Lottery HERE For big discards People Leave on the street. I REALLY wanted a bike... i didn't get it.

Building with REAL WATERFALLS GOING down the FACADE

Music From ASTRO BOY

PEDESTRIAN TUNNEL

BIG BANKS

Tochiai Road

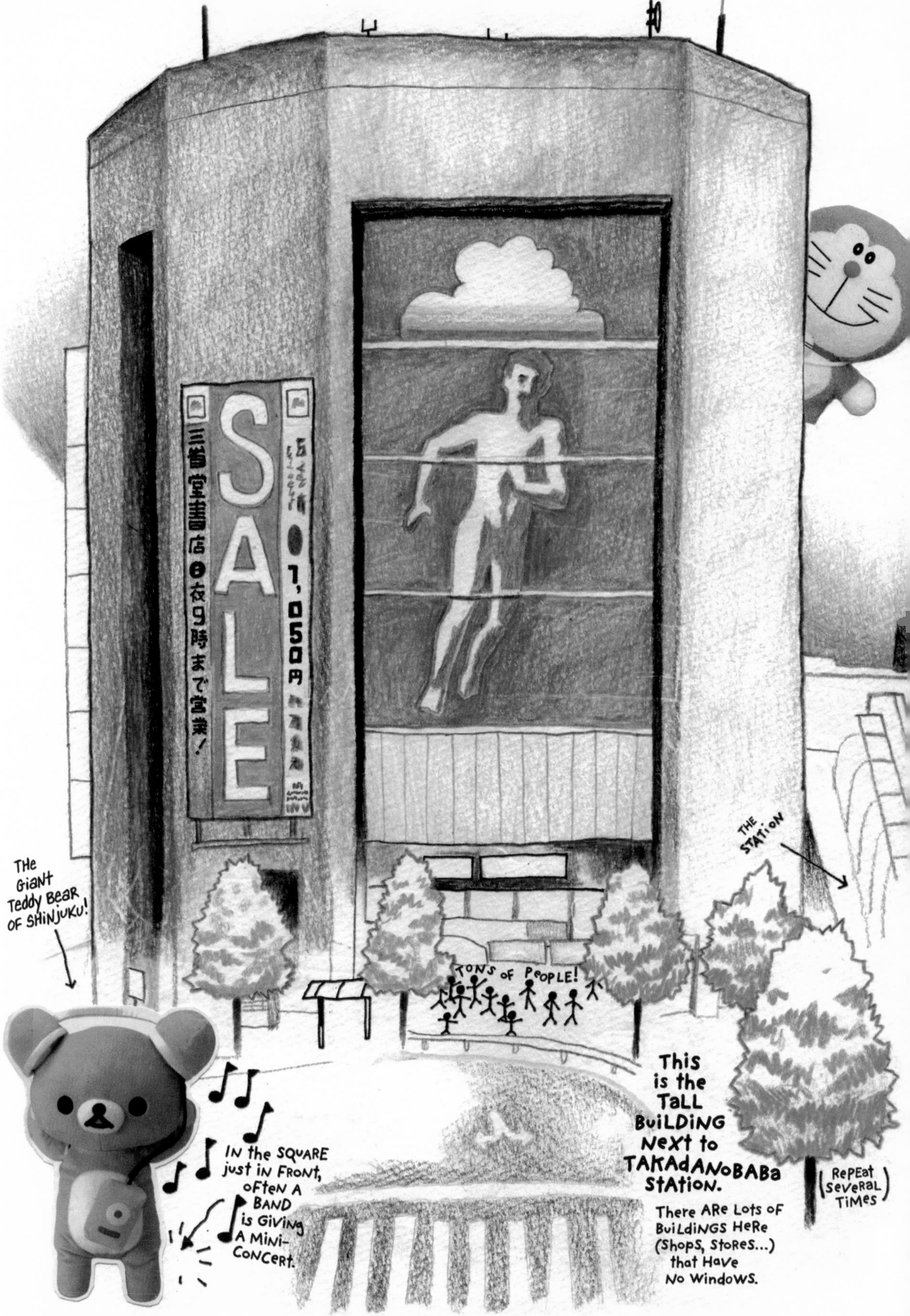
SALE
三省堂書店
日夜9時まで営業!
1,050円
TONS of PeOPLE!
THe Giant Teddy Bear OF SHINJUKU!
THE STATiON
This is the TaLL BuiLDiNG NeXt to TAKAdANOBABa StAtiON.
There ARe Lots of BuiLDiNGS HeRe (ShopS, StoReS...) that Have No WindowS.
IN the SQUARE just in FRONT, oFten A BAND is GiViNG A Mini-CONCeRt.
(RePeat SeVeRAL TiMes)

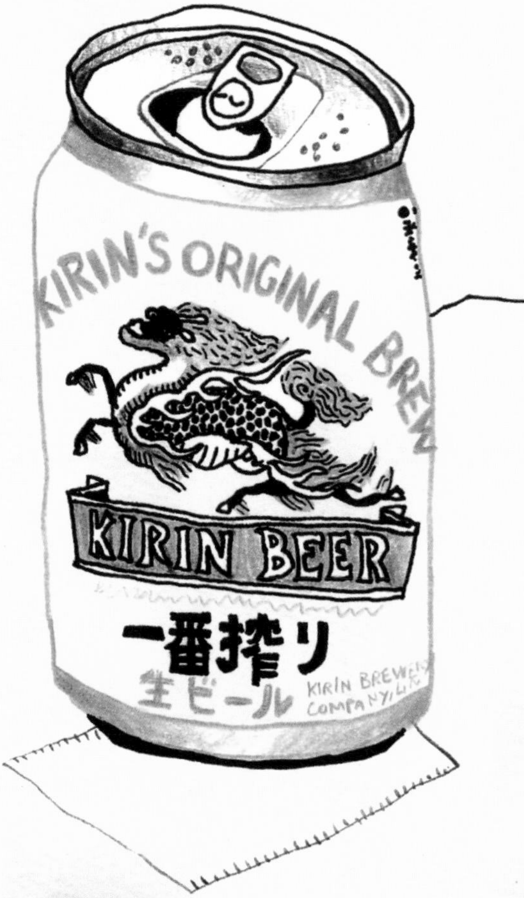
KIRIN'S ORIGINAL BREW
KIRIN BEER
一番搾り
生ビール
¥525!
(DAMN!)

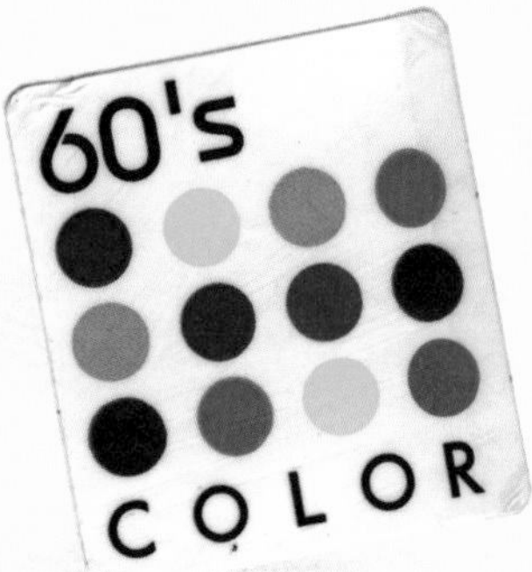
60's
COLOR

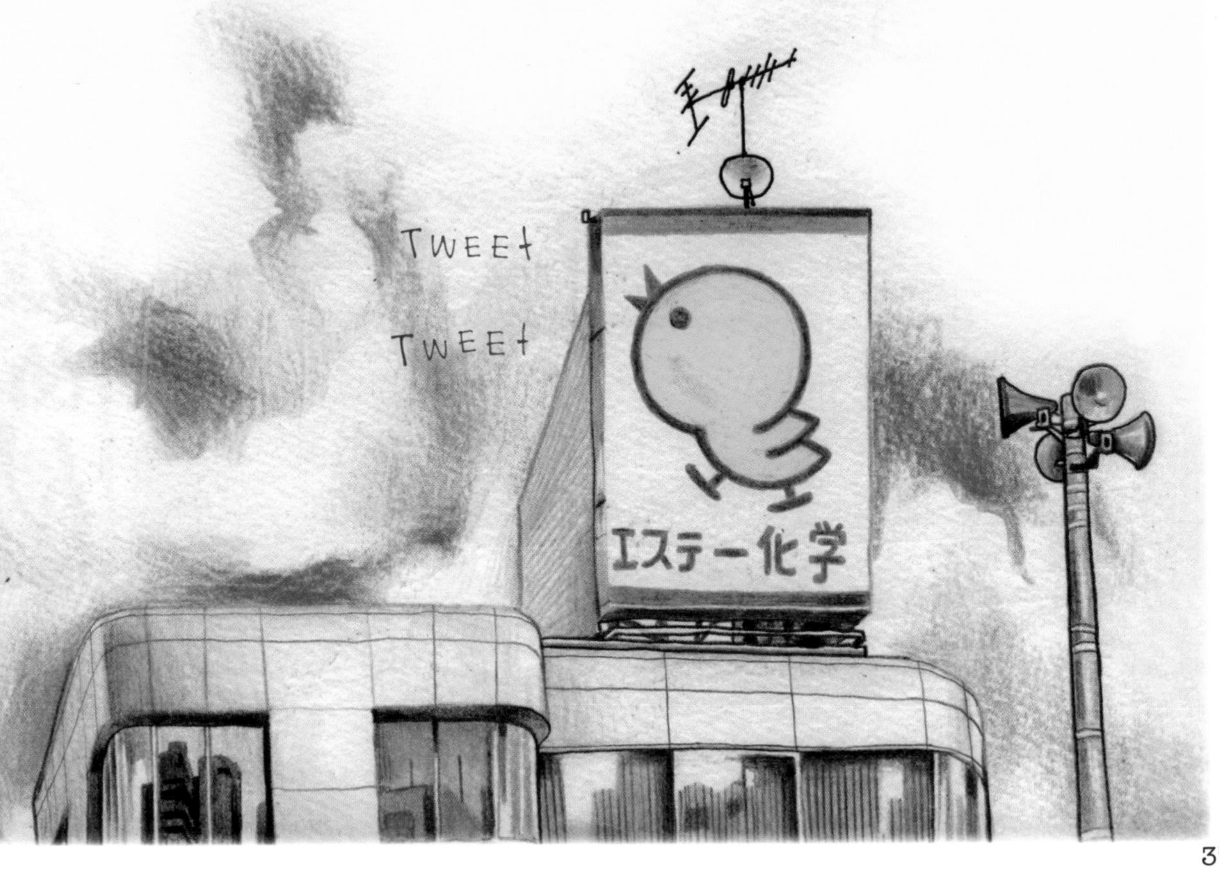
TWEET
TWEET
エステー化学

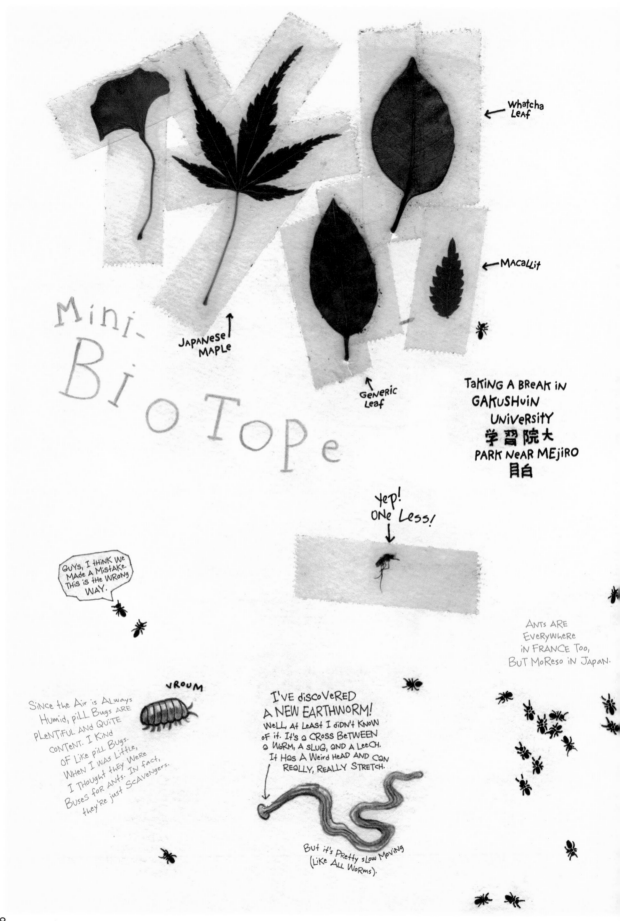

Whatcha Leaf

Macallit

Japanese MAPLe

Mini-BioTope

Generic Leaf

TAKING A BREAK IN
GAKUSHUIN
UNIVERSITY
学習院大
PARK NEAR MEJIRO
目白

Yep!
ONE LESS!

GUYS, I THINK WE MADE A MISTAKE. THIS IS THE WRONG WAY.

ANTS ARE EVERYWHERE IN FRANCE TOO, BUT MORESO IN JAPAN.

VROUM

SINCE THE AIR IS ALWAYS Humid, pILL Bugs ARE PLENTIFUL AND QUITE CONTENT. I KIND OF LIKE PILL BUGS. WHEN I WAS LITTLE, I THOUGHT THEY WERE Buses FOR ANTS. IN FACT, THEY'RE JUST SCAVENGERS.

I'VE DISCOVERED
A NEW EARTHWORM!
WELL AT LEAST I DIDN'T KNOW OF IT. IT'S A CROSS BETWEEN A WORM, A SLUG, AND A LEECH. IT HAS A WEIRD HEAD AND CAN REALLY, REALLY STRETCH.

BUT IT'S PRETTY SLOW MOVING (LIKE ALL WORMS).

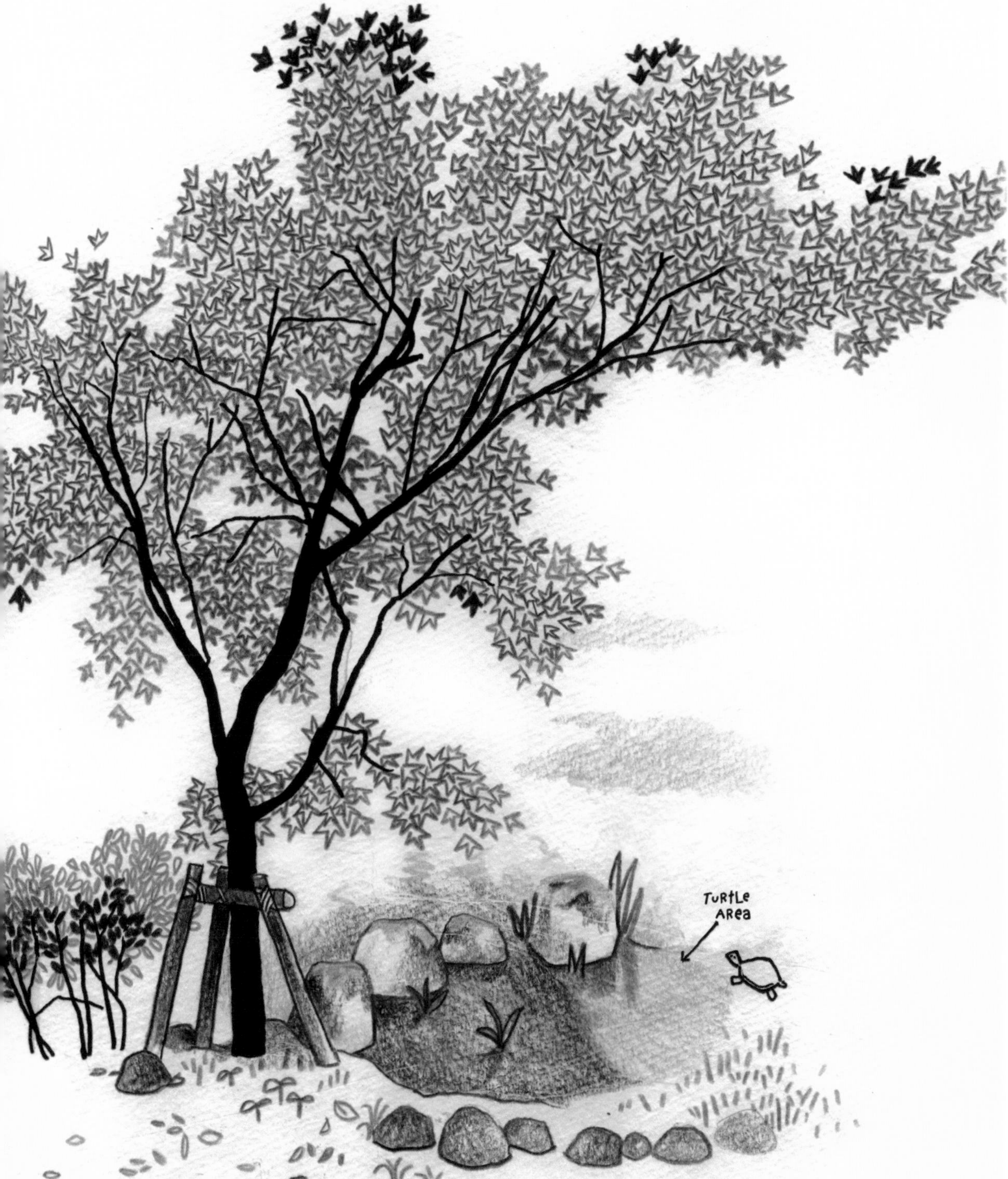
TURTLE AREA

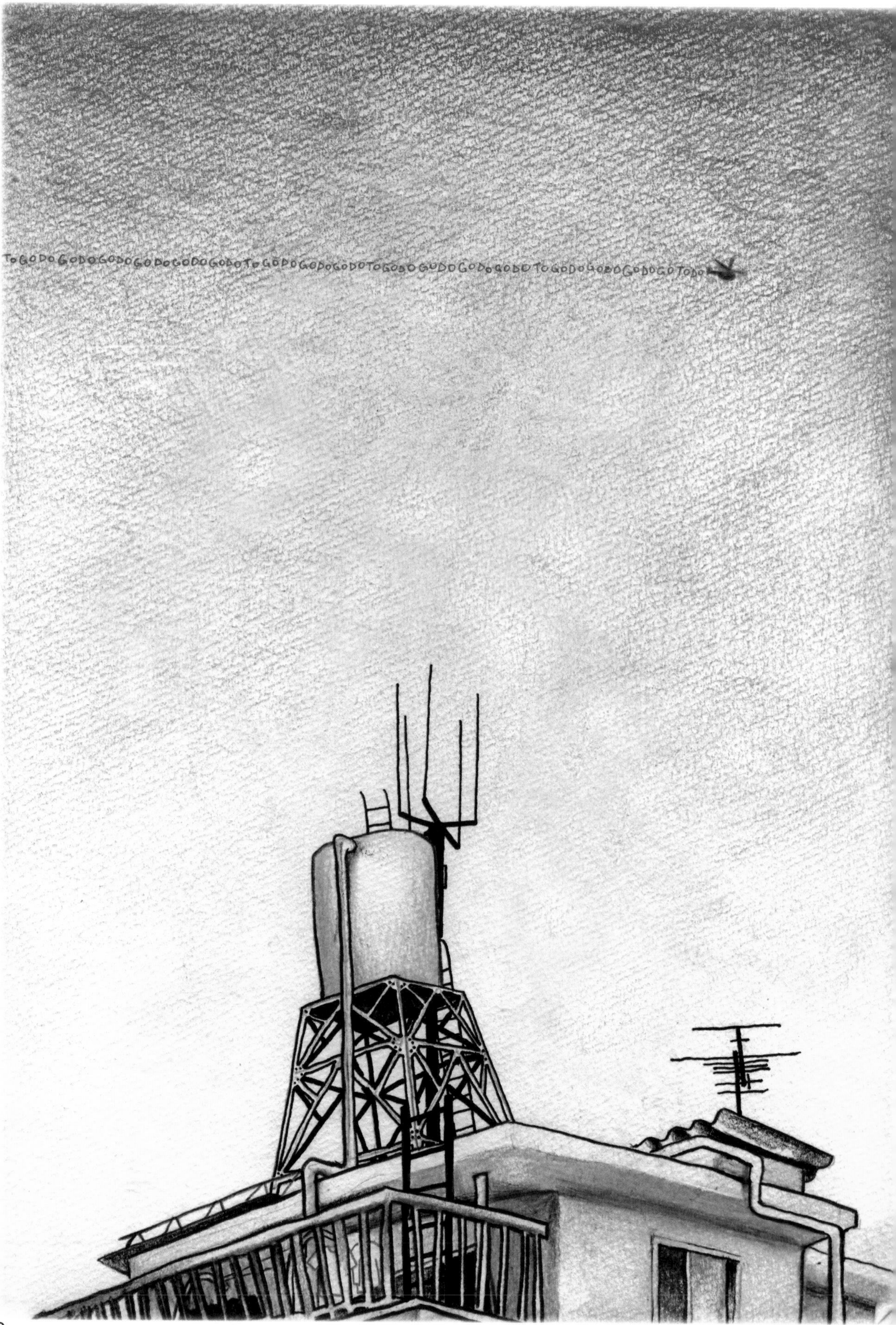
TOGODOGODOGODOGODOGODOGODOTOGODOGODOGODOTOGOSOGUDOGODOGODOTOGODOGODOGODOGOTODO

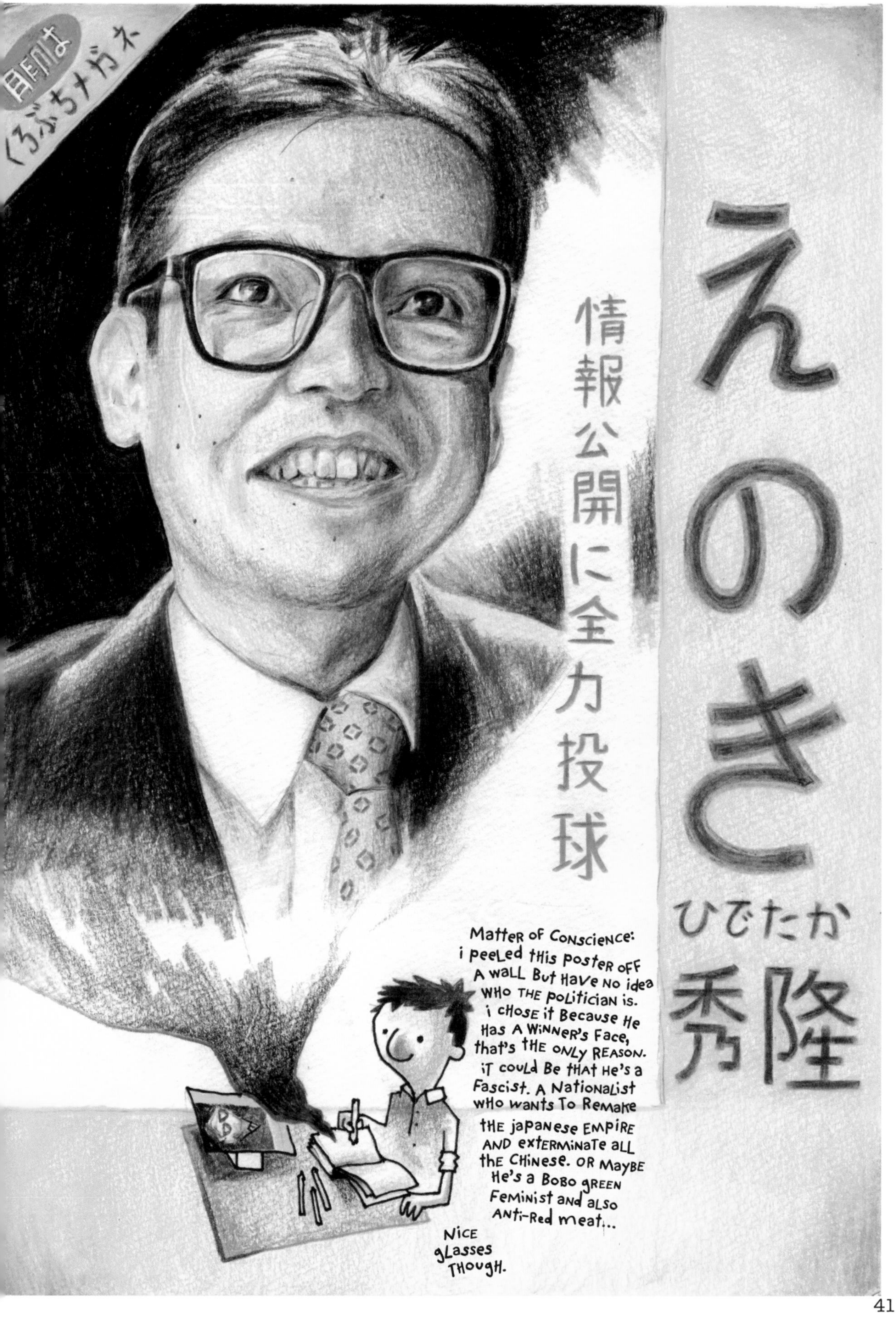
目印は
くろぶちメガネ
えのき
ひでたか
秀隆
情報公開に全力投球
Matter of Conscience: i peeled this poster off a wall but have no idea who the politician is. i chose it because he has a winner's face, that's the only reason. it could be that he's a Fascist. A Nationalist who wants to remake the japanese empire and exterminate all the Chinese. or maybe he's a Bobo green Feminist and also Anti-Red meat...
Nice glasses though.

SRI LANKA GEMS & JEWELRY

He gave Me a Flier (He Wants Me to Find Customers)

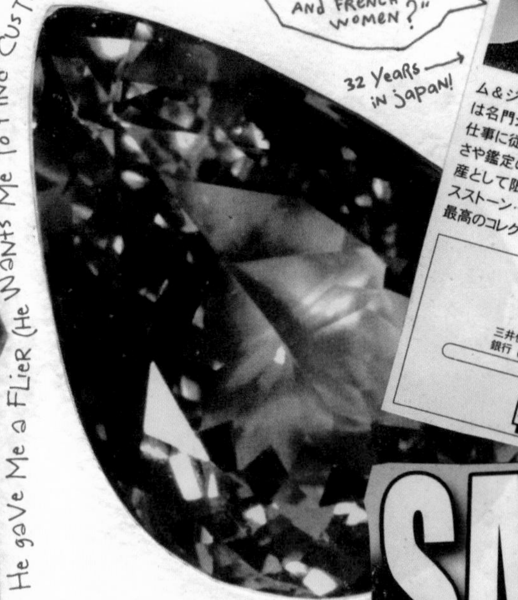

"JAPANESE WOMEN VERY EASY. AND FRENCH WOMEN?"

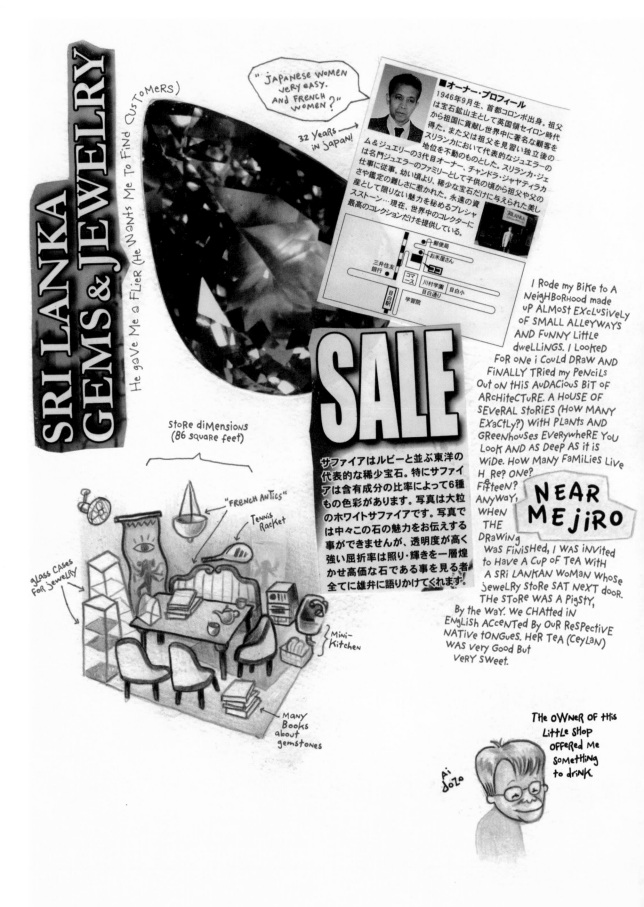

32 YEARS in japan!

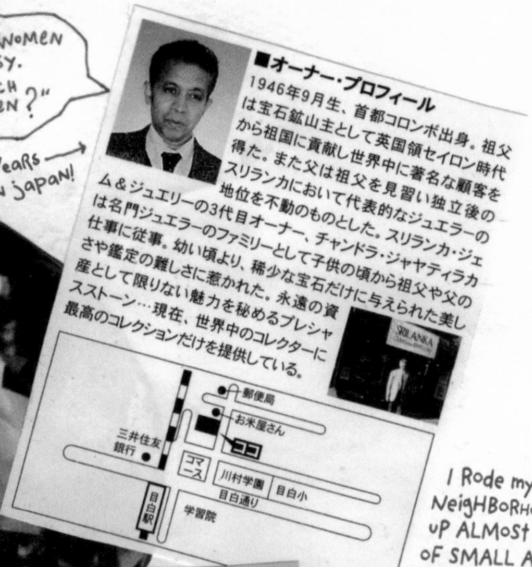

■オーナー・プロフィール
1946年9月生、首都コロンボ出身。祖父は宝石鉱山主として英国領セイロン時代から祖国に貢献し世界中に著名な顧客を得た。また父は祖父を見習い独立後のスリランカにおいて代表的なジュエラーの地位を不動のものとした。スリランカ・ジェム＆ジュエリーの3代目オーナー、チャンドラ・ジャヤティラカは名門ジュエラーのファミリーとして子供の頃から祖父や父の仕事に従事。幼い頃より、稀少な宝石だけに与えられた美しさや鑑定の難しさに惹かれた。永遠の資産として限りない魅力を秘めるプレシャスストーン…現在、世界中のコレクターに最高のコレクションだけを提供している。

郵便局
お米屋さん
ココ
三井住友銀行
コマース
川村学園
目白小
目白通り
目白駅
学習院

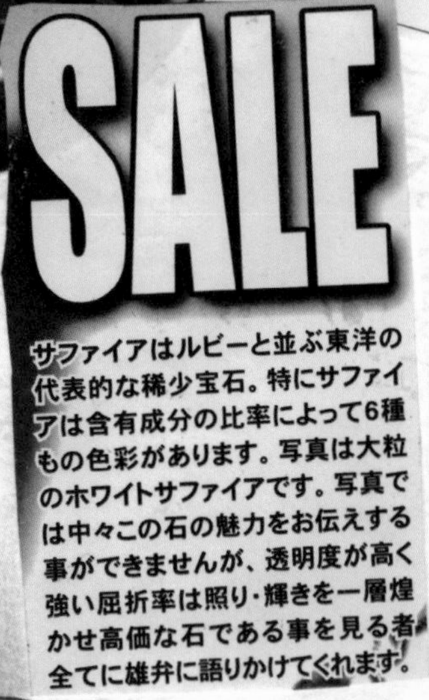

SALE

サファイアはルビーと並ぶ東洋の代表的な稀少宝石。特にサファイアは含有成分の比率によって6種もの色彩があります。写真は大粒のホワイトサファイアです。写真では中々この石の魅力をお伝えする事ができませんが、透明度が高く強い屈折率は照り・輝きを一層煌かせ高価な石である事を見る者全てに雄弁に語りかけてくれます。

I Rode my Bike to A NeighBORhood made up ALMOST EXcLusively OF SMALL ALLeyWAYS AND FUNNY Little dwelLINGS. I Looked FOR ONE i CouLd DRAW AND FINALLY TRied my PeNciLs Out oN tHIS AUDACious BiT OF ARchitecTURE. A HOUSE OF SEveRAL StoRiES (HOW MANY EXactLy?) WitH PLANts AND GReeNhouSES EVERYWHERE YOU LOOK AND AS DEEP AS it is WiDE. HOW MANY FaMiLies Live HeRe? ONE? FifteeN? ANyWaY, WHEN THE DRaWiNg WAS FiNiSHed, I WAS iNVited to HAVe A CuP OF TEA WITH A SRI LANKAN WOMAN WhoSe jewelRy StoRe SAT NEXT dooR. THE STORE WAS A PigSty, By the WaY. We CHAtted iN ENgLiSh ACceNTed By OUR ReSPective NATive tONGues. HER TEA (CEYLAN) WAS Very Good But VeRY SWeet.

NEAR MEjiRO

Store diMensions (86 square feet)

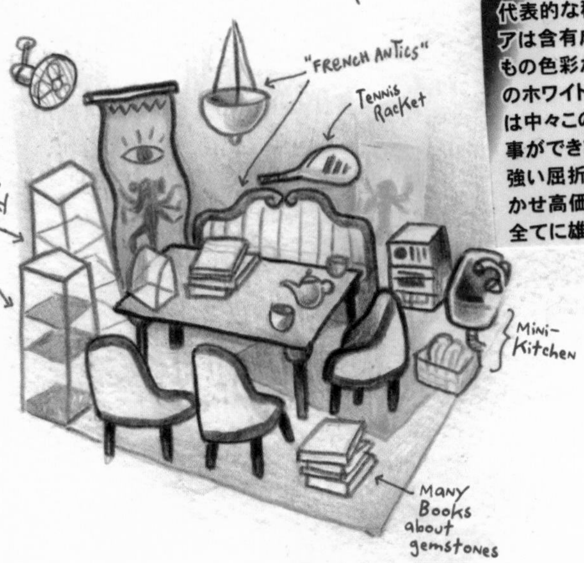
"FRENCH ANTiCS"
Tennis Racket
glass cases for jewelRy
Mini-Kitchen
Many Books about gemstones

THE OWNER OF this Little Shop offered me something to drink.

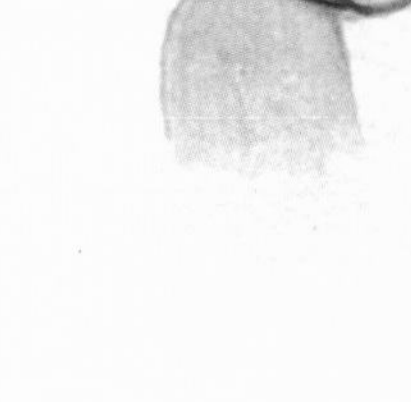
Ai dozo

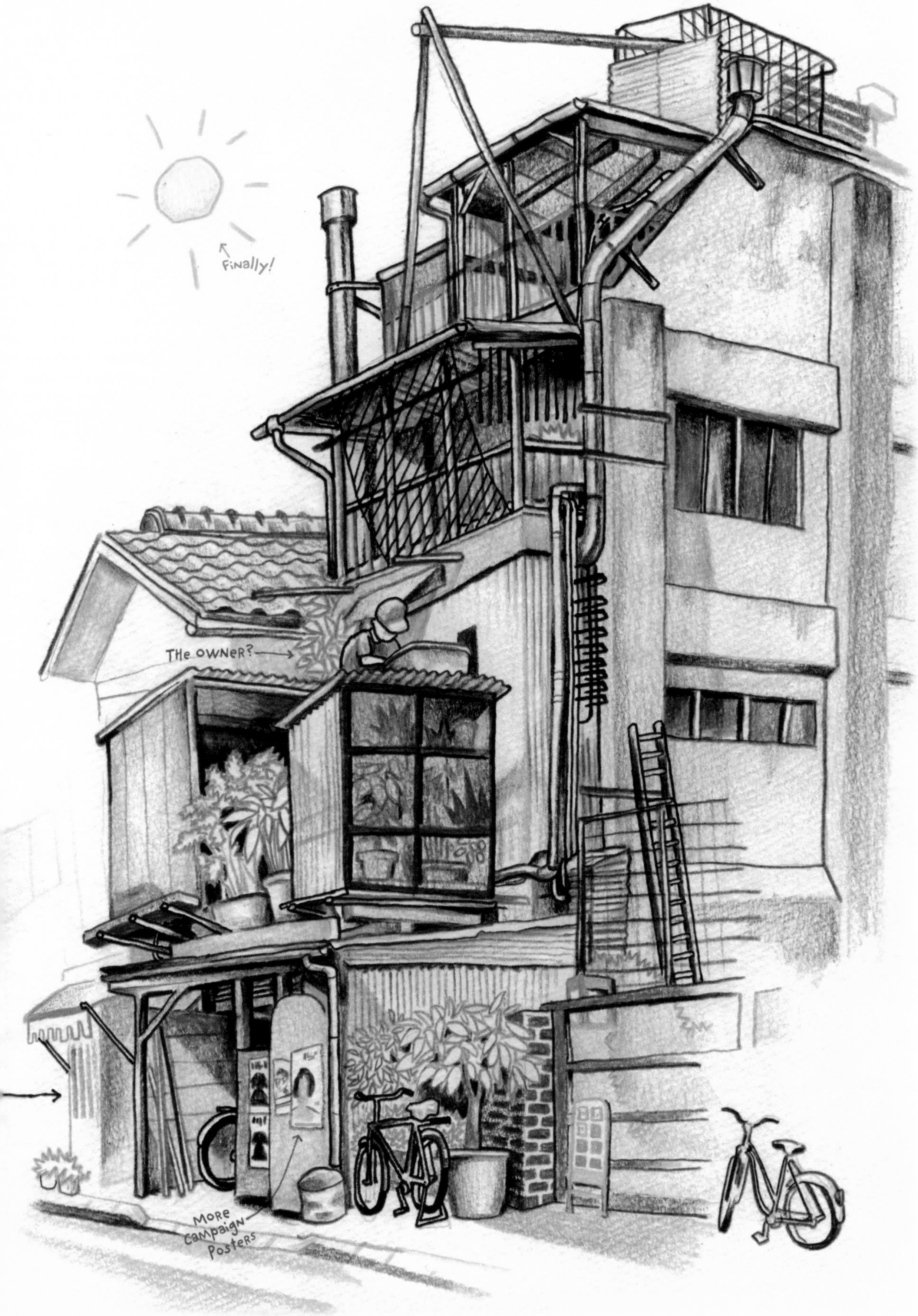
Finally!
THe OWNER?
MORE campaign Posters

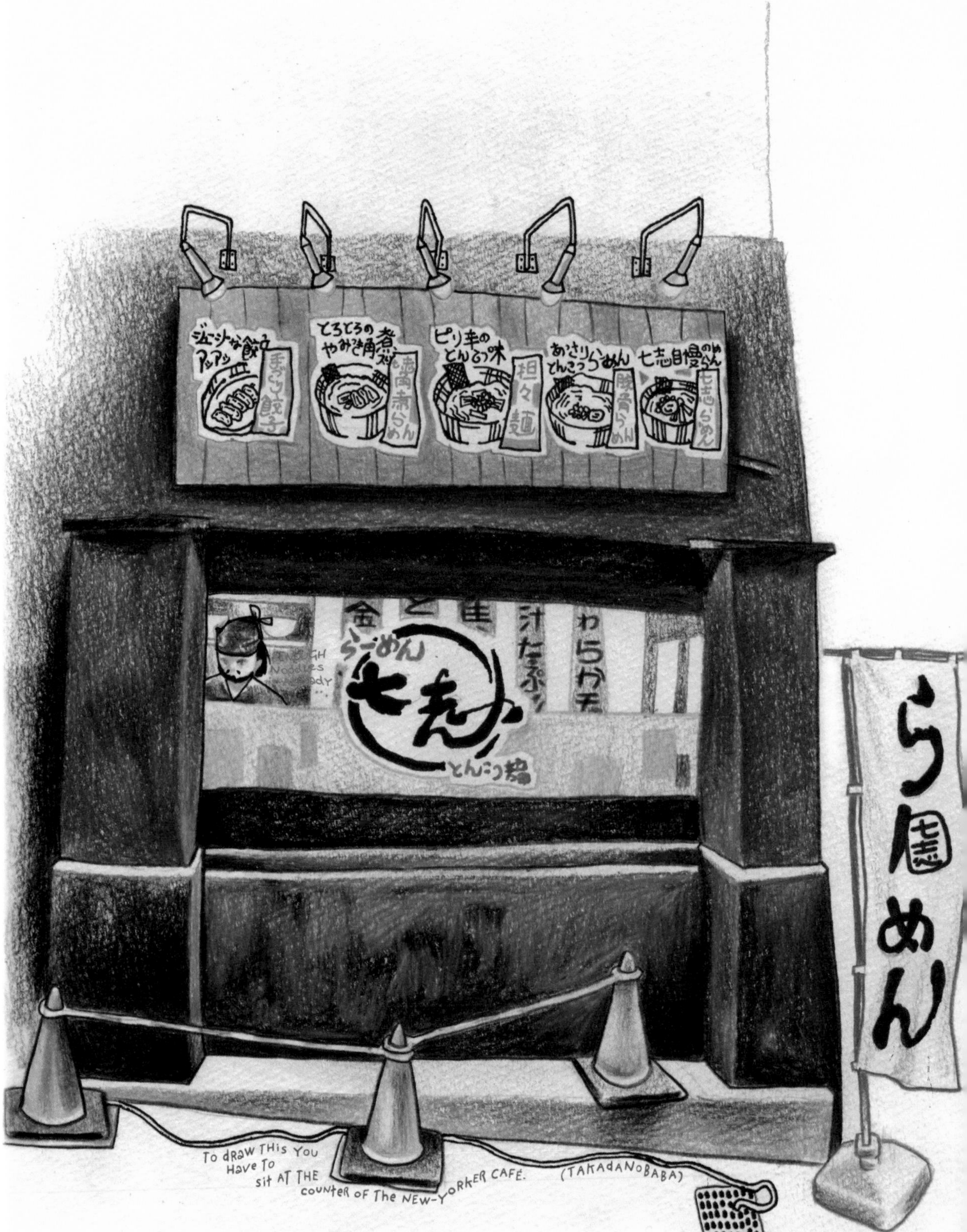
ピリ辛の
とんこつ味
担々麺
七志自慢の
らーめん
ら
めん
To draw THis You Have To sit AT THE counter of The NEW-YORKER CAFÉ.
(TAKAdANOBABA)

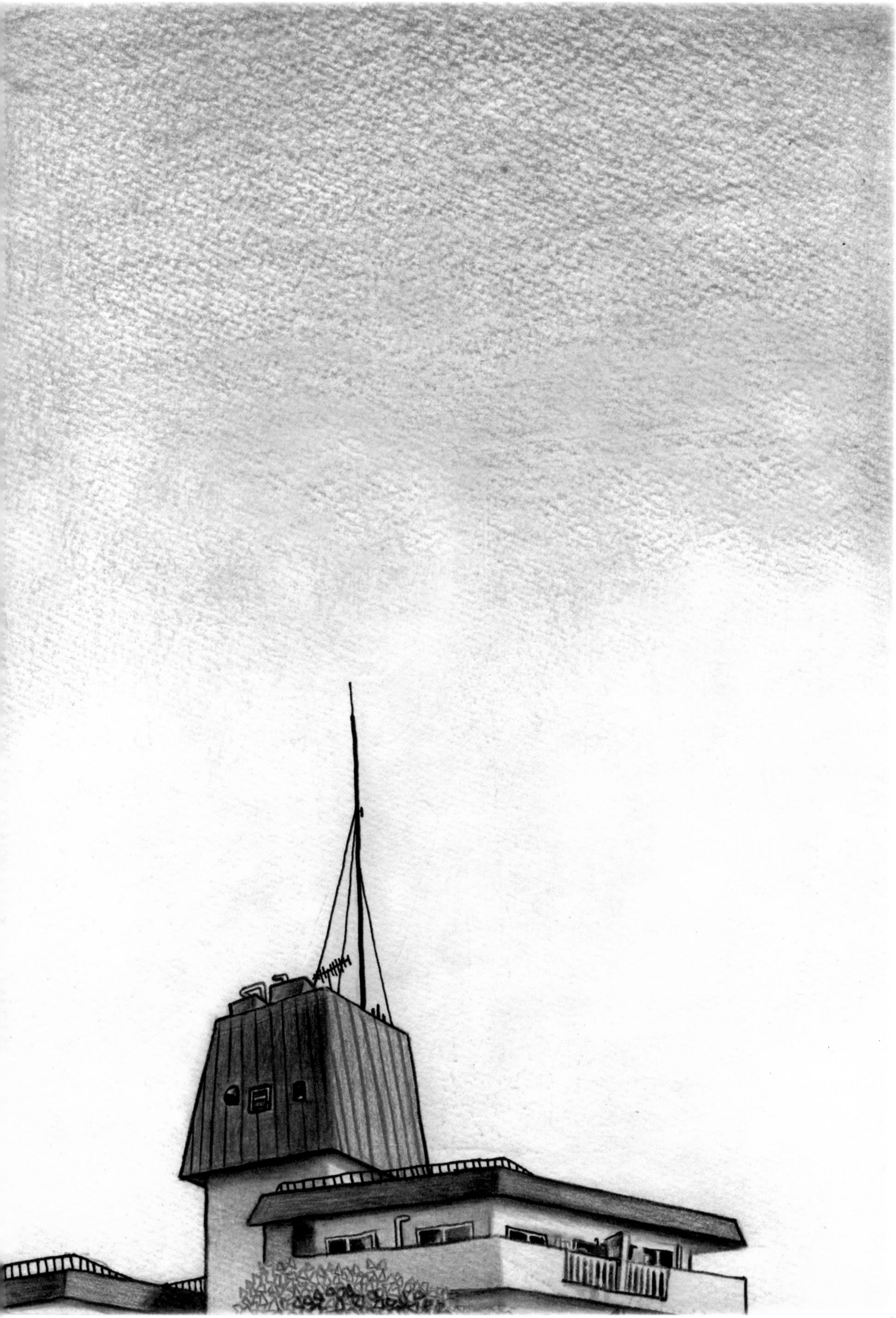

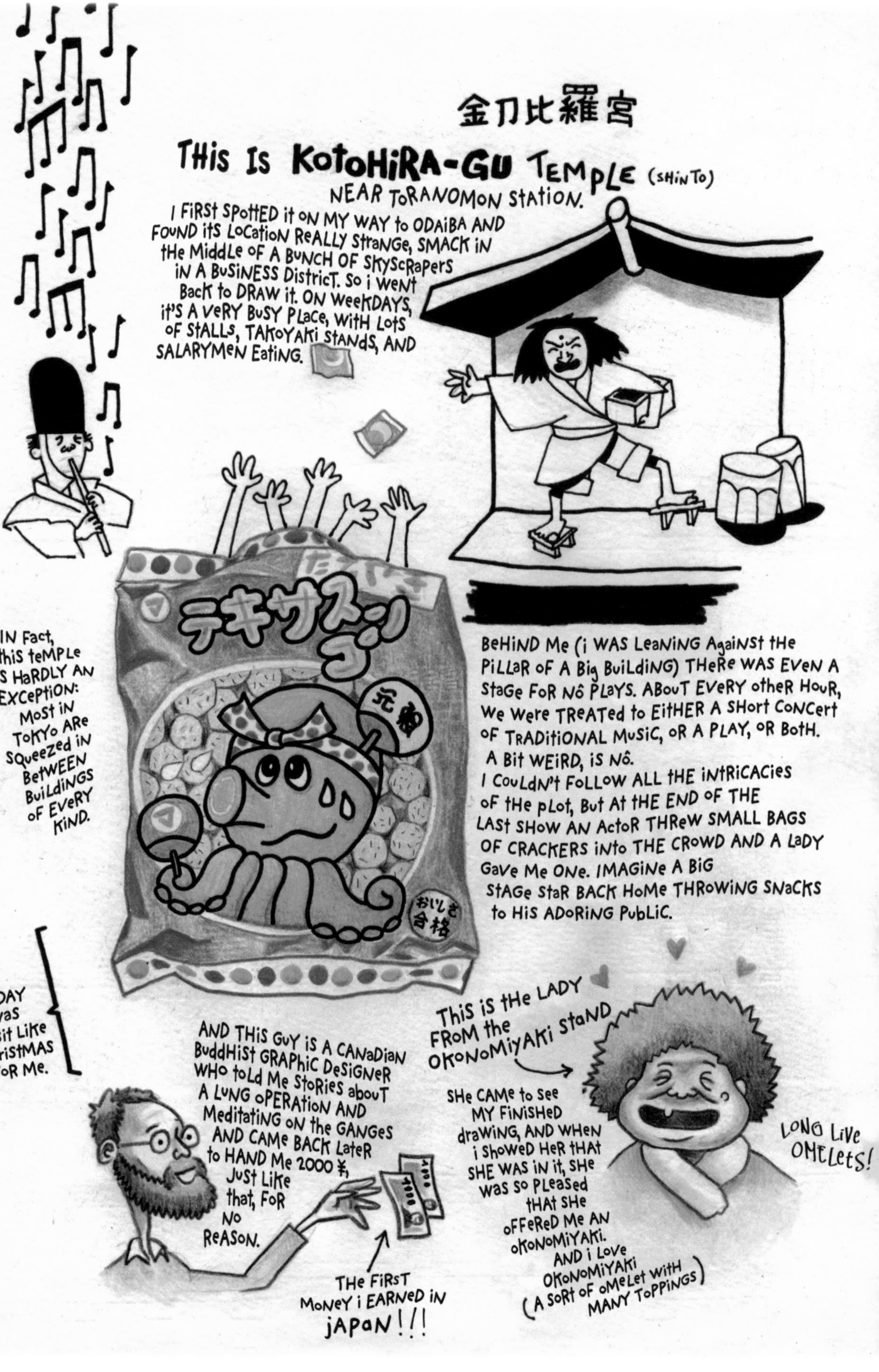
金刀比羅宮
THIS IS KOTOHIRA-GU TEMPLE (SHINTO)
NEAR TORANOMON STATION.
I FIRST SPOTTED IT ON MY WAY TO ODAIBA AND FOUND ITS LOCATION REALLY STRANGE, SMACK IN THE MIDDLE OF A BUNCH OF SKYSCRAPERS IN A BUSINESS DISTRICT. SO I WENT BACK TO DRAW IT. ON WEEKDAYS, IT'S A VERY BUSY PLACE, WITH LOTS OF STALLS, TAKOYAKI STANDS, AND SALARYMEN EATING.
IN FACT, THIS TEMPLE IS HARDLY AN EXCEPTION: MOST IN TOKYO ARE SQUEEZED IN BETWEEN BUILDINGS OF EVERY KIND.
BEHIND ME (I WAS LEANING AGAINST THE PILLAR OF A BIG BUILDING) THERE WAS EVEN A STAGE FOR NÔ PLAYS. ABOUT EVERY OTHER HOUR, WE WERE TREATED TO EITHER A SHORT CONCERT OF TRADITIONAL MUSIC, OR A PLAY, OR BOTH. A BIT WEIRD, IS NÔ. I COULDN'T FOLLOW ALL THE INTRICACIES OF THE PLOT, BUT AT THE END OF THE LAST SHOW AN ACTOR THREW SMALL BAGS OF CRACKERS INTO THE CROWD AND A LADY GAVE ME ONE. IMAGINE A BIG STAGE STAR BACK HOME THROWING SNACKS TO HIS ADORING PUBLIC.
おいしさ合格
TODAY WAS A BIT LIKE CHRISTMAS FOR ME.
AND THIS GUY IS A CANADIAN BUDDHIST GRAPHIC DESIGNER WHO TOLD ME STORIES ABOUT A LUNG OPERATION AND MEDITATING ON THE GANGES AND CAME BACK LATER TO HAND ME 2000 ¥, JUST LIKE THAT, FOR NO REASON.
THE FIRST MONEY I EARNED IN JAPAN!!!
THIS IS THE LADY FROM THE OKONOMIYAKI STAND
SHE CAME TO SEE MY FINISHED DRAWING, AND WHEN I SHOWED HER THAT SHE WAS IN IT, SHE WAS SO PLEASED THAT SHE OFFERED ME AN OKONOMIYAKI. AND I LOVE OKONOMIYAKI (A SORT OF OMELET WITH MANY TOPPINGS)
LONG LIVE OMELETS!

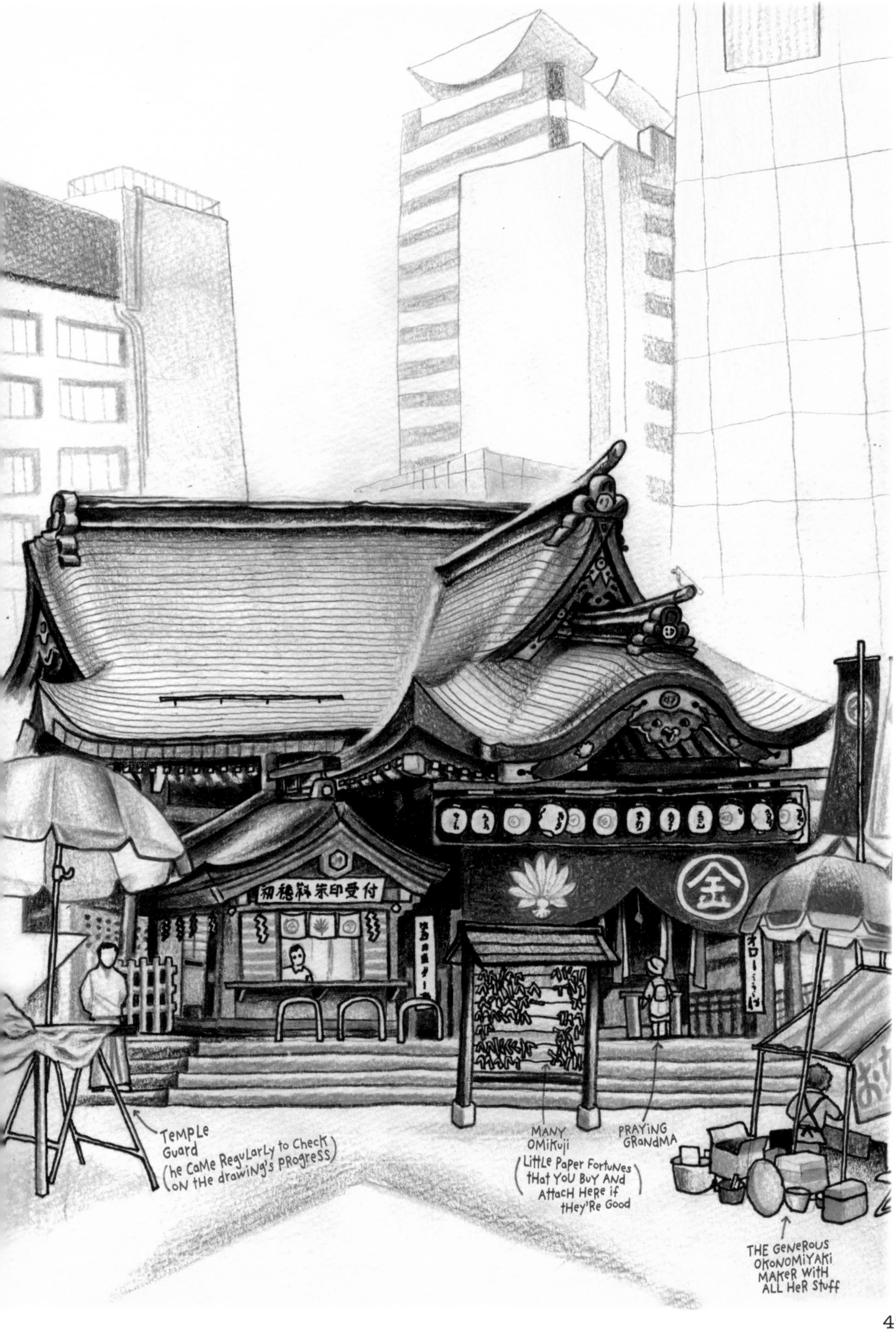
TEMPLE Guard
(he CaMe ReguLarLy to Check oN tHe drawiNg's PRogress)
MANY OMiKuji
(LittLe Paper Fortunes tHat YOU BUY AND AttacH HeRe if tHey'Re Good)
PRAYiNG GRAndMA
THE GeNeROUS OKONOMiYAKi MAKeR WItH ALL HeR Stuff

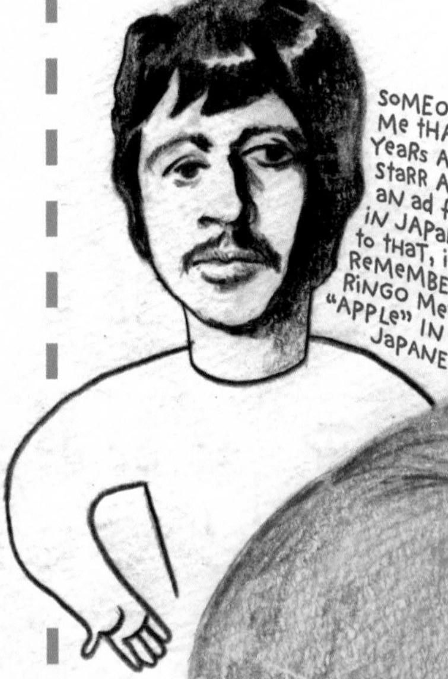

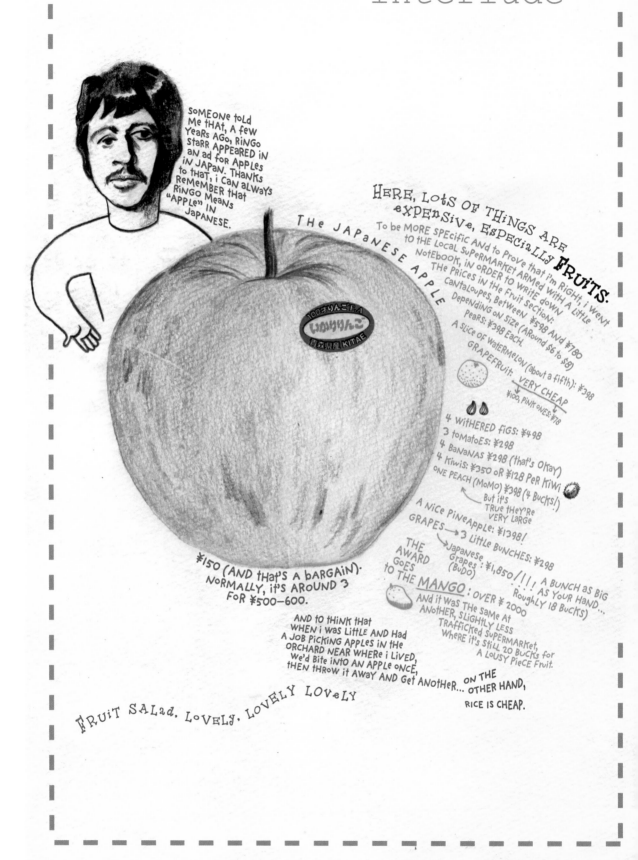

SOMEONE told Me THAT, A few YeaRs AGo, RiNGo StaRR APPEaRED iN an ad for APPLes iN JAPaN. THANKS to THAT, i CAN always ReMeMBER tHat RiNGO MeaNs "APPLe" IN JaPANESE.

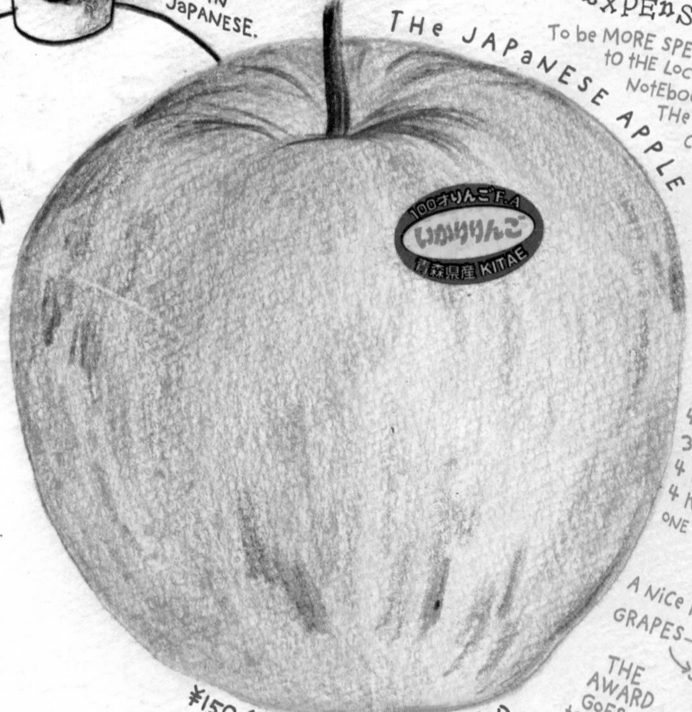

THE JAPaNESE APPLE

¥150 (AND that's A bARGAIN). NoRMALLY, it's AROUND 3 FOR ¥500–600.

HERE, LOTS OF THINGS ARE eXPENSive, EspeciaLLy **FRUITS.**

To be MORE SPECific AND to Prove that i'm RiGHt, i went to THE LocaL SUPERMARKET ARMed WiTH A LittLe NoteBOOK, IN ORDER TO WRITE down THE PRices in tHe Fruit SectioN:

CaNtaLoupes, BetWEEN ¥598 AND ¥780 DepENDiNG ON Size (AROund $6 to $8)

PeaRs: ¥398 EaCH.

A SLice OF WaterMeLON (about a fifth): ¥398

GRAPEFRUiT: VERY CHEAP ¥100, PiNK ONES: ¥78

4 WiTHERED FiGS: ¥498

3 toMatoES: ¥298

4 BaNaNAS ¥298 (that's OKay)

4 Kiwis: ¥350 oR ¥128 PeR Kiwi

ONE PEACH (MoMo) ¥398 (4 Bucks!) But it's TRUE tHey're VERY LarGe

A NiCe PineAppLe: ¥1398!

GRAPES → 3 LittLe BUNCHES: ¥298

→ Japanese Grapes (BuDo): ¥1,850/!!! A BUNCH as Big AS YOUR HAND... RoughLY 18 BUCKS)

THE AWARD GoES to THE MANGO: OVER ¥ 2000

And it Was The same At ANOTHER, SLiGHTLY LESS TRAFFiCKed SuPERMARket, WHERE it's STiLL 20 BUCKs for A LOUSY PieCE Fruit.

AND to THiNK tHat WHEN i was LittLE AND Had A JOB PiCKiNG APPLes iN tHE ORCHARD NEAR WHERE i LiVED, We'd Bite iNTO AN APPLe ONCE, THEN THROW it AWAY AND Get ANOtHeR... ON THE OTHER HAND, RICE IS CHEAP.

FRUiT SALad. LoVELY. LoVELY LOVeLY

around our house (ochiai)

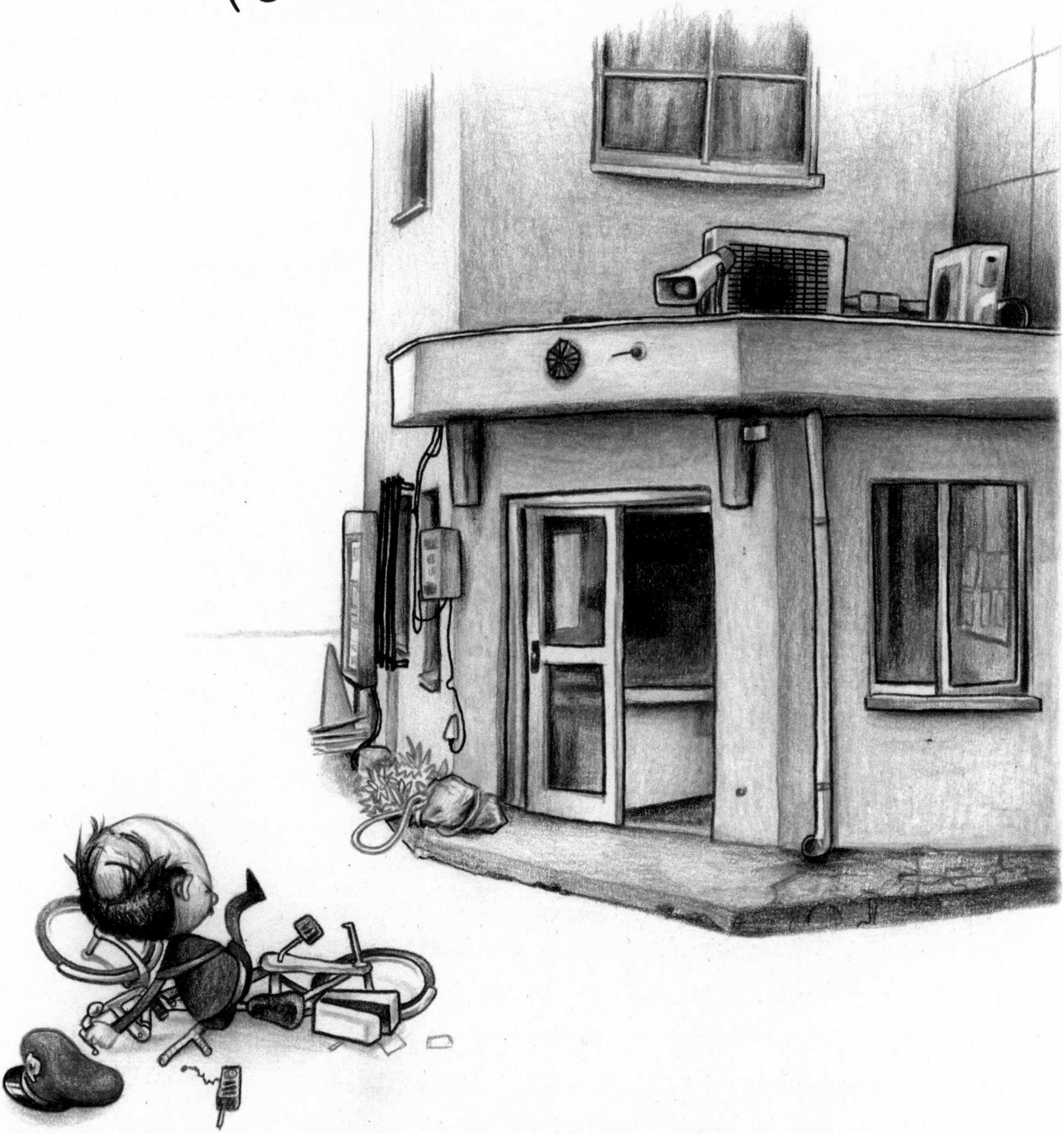

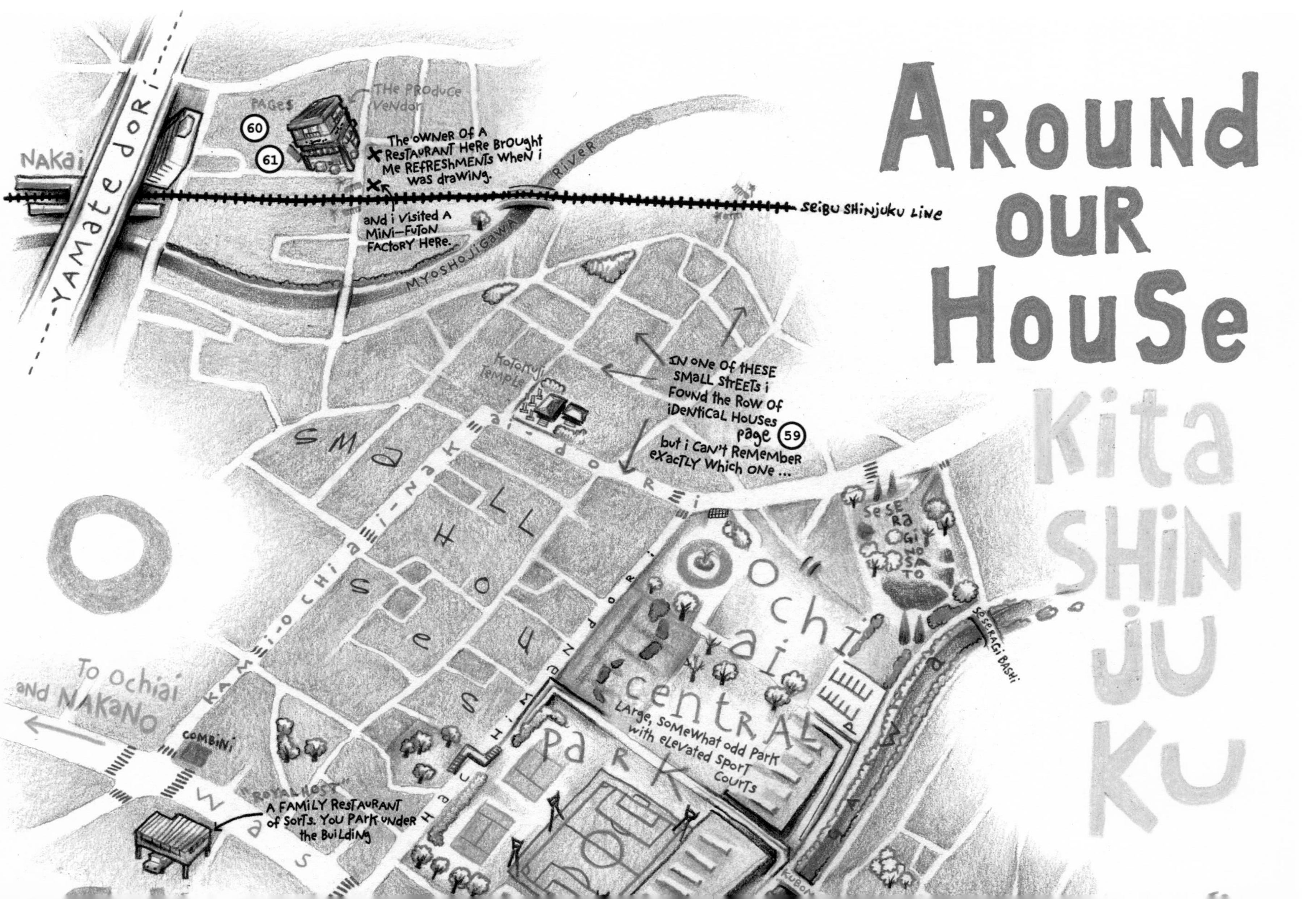

Around our House
Kita Shinjuku
O
Seibu Shinjuku Line
Yamate dori
Nakai
Pages 60 61
The Produce Vendor
The owner of a restaurant here brought me refreshments when i was drawing.
and i visited a mini-futon factory here.
Myoshojigawa River
In one of these small streets i found the row of identical houses page 59
but i can't remember exactly which one ...
Kotokuji Temple
Small houses
Nakai-dori
Kami-ochiai-nakahimondori
Ochiai Central Park
Large, somewhat odd park with elevated sport courts
Seseragi no sato
Seseragi bashi
To Ochiai and Nakano
Combini
"Royal Host" A family restaurant of sorts. You park under the building

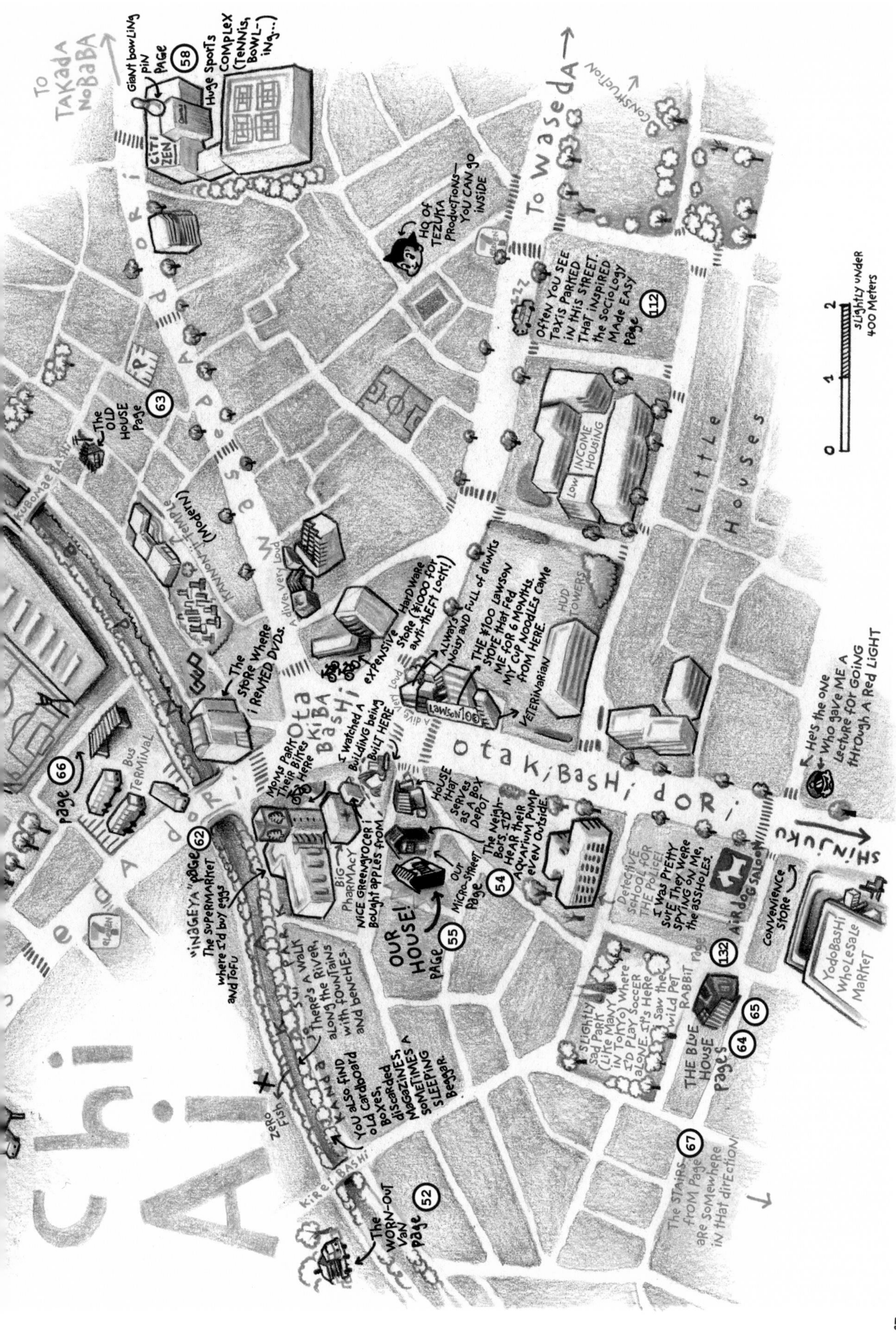

To Takada NoBaBA
Giant bowling pin Page 58
Huge Sports COMPLEX (TENNIS, BOWLing...)
CITIZEN
To Waseda
Construction
HQ of TEZUKA Productions—YOU CAN go INSIDE
Often you see Taxis parked in this street that inspired the Sociology Made Easy Page 112
0 1 2 Slightly under 400 Meters
Little Houses
Low INCOME HOUSING
HUD TOWERS
VETERINARIAN
THE ¥100 LAWSON STORE that fed ME FOR 6 MONTHS. MY CUP NOODLES CAME FROM HERE.
LAWSON 100
Always Noisy and full of drunks
A dive. Very Loud
HardWare Store (¥1000 for anti-theft Lock!)
expensive
A dive. Very Loud
Waseda Dori
The OLD HOUSE Page 63
KUBOMAE BASHI
KANNON Temple (Modern)
The Store where I RENTED DVDs.
Page 66
Bus Terminal
Ota KiBA BaShi
MOMS PARK Their Bikes Here
I watched A Building being Built HERE
HOUSE that serves as a box depot
otakiBaShi dORi
He's the one who gave ME A Lecture for going through A Red LIGHT
SHINJUKU
Big PharMacy
NICE GREENGROCER I Bought apples from
The Neighbors. I'd hear their aquarium pump even outside. 54
OUR MICRO-STREET Page
OUR HOUSE! Page 55
"INAGEYA" Page 62 The Supermarket where I'd buy eggs and Tofu
SUI PARK
There's A WALK along the RIVER with fountains and benches.
Detective School for the Police! I was pretty sure they were spying on me, the assholes.
AIR DOG SALOON
CONVENIENCE STORE
YodoBaShi Wholesale Market
Slightly Sad Park (Like Many in Tokyo) where I'd play soccer alone. It's Here I saw the wild pet Rabbit Page 132
THE BLUE HOUSE Pages 64 65
The Stairs from Page 67 are somewhere in that direction
KANDA
ZERO Fish
You also find old cardboard boxes, discarded magazines, sometimes a sleeping beggar.
KIREI BASHI
The WORN-OUT Van Page 52

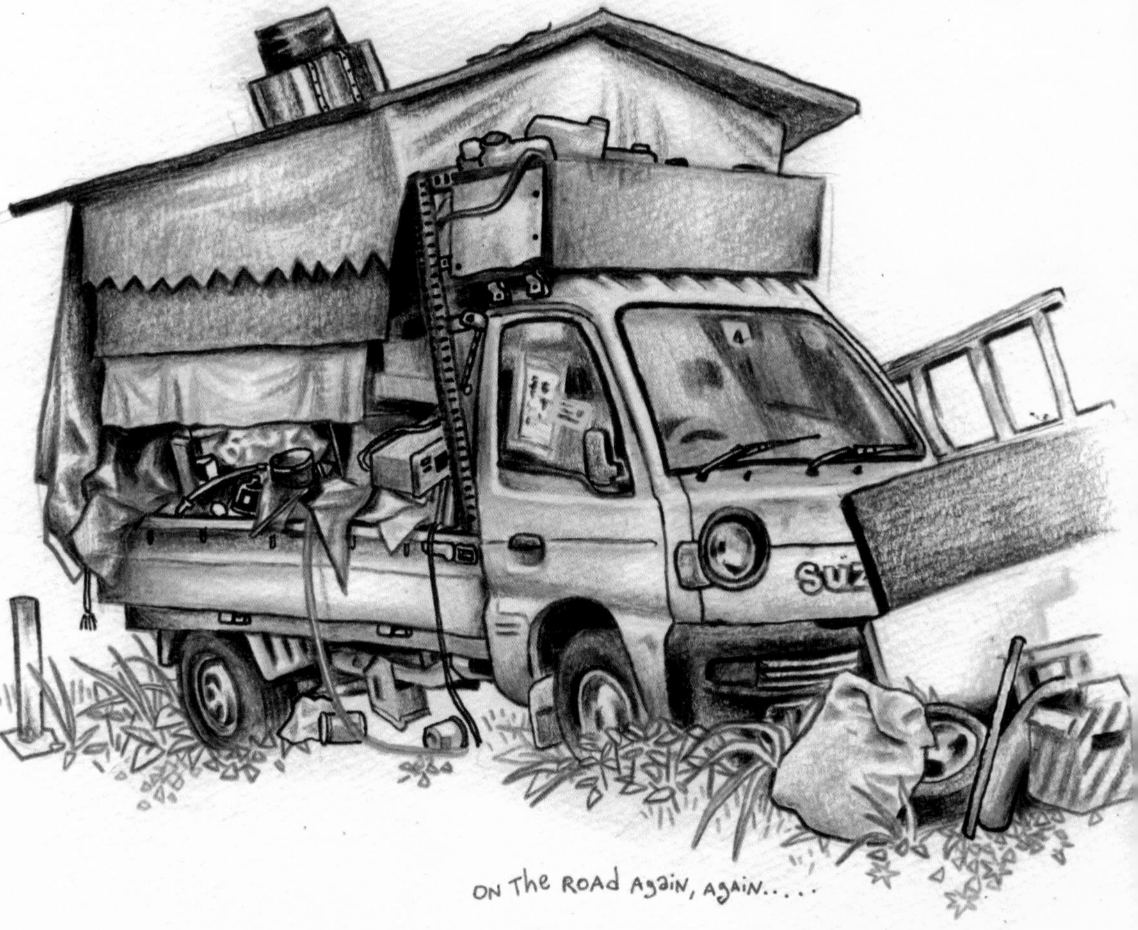
SUZ

ON The ROAD again, again.....

i Lost A Quart of Blood

To draw the Wreck of A Van Next door, i had to sit in A Really UNComFortABLe Position on A Low wall Without Any Room For My Pencils, while a SQuadRoN oF Vicious MosQuitoes did a Number oN Me. Seeing ALL My SuFFeRiNg and SeLF-SacRiFice, A CLub oF MoMs came oVer to compLiMent Me oN My SKetch AND oFFeRed Me A BoTTLe of tea.

GReeN teA

S U G O I !

SHE TOLD Me That This AReA is CALLED HiGASHi NAKANo

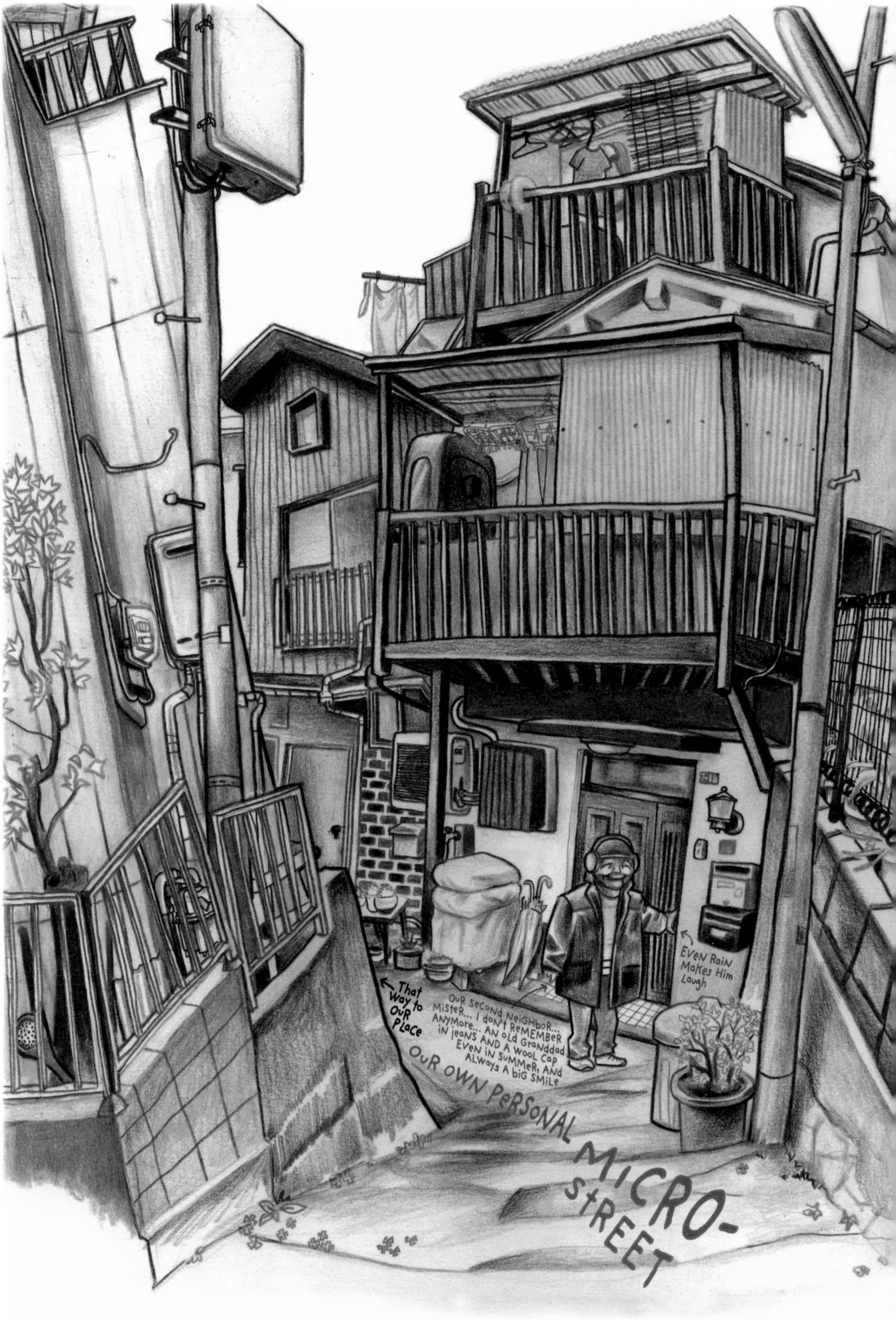
Our Own Personal Micro-Street
Our second neighbor... Mister... I don't remember anymore... An old granddad in jeans and a wool cap even in summer, and always a big smile
Even rain makes him laugh
That way to our place
7-18

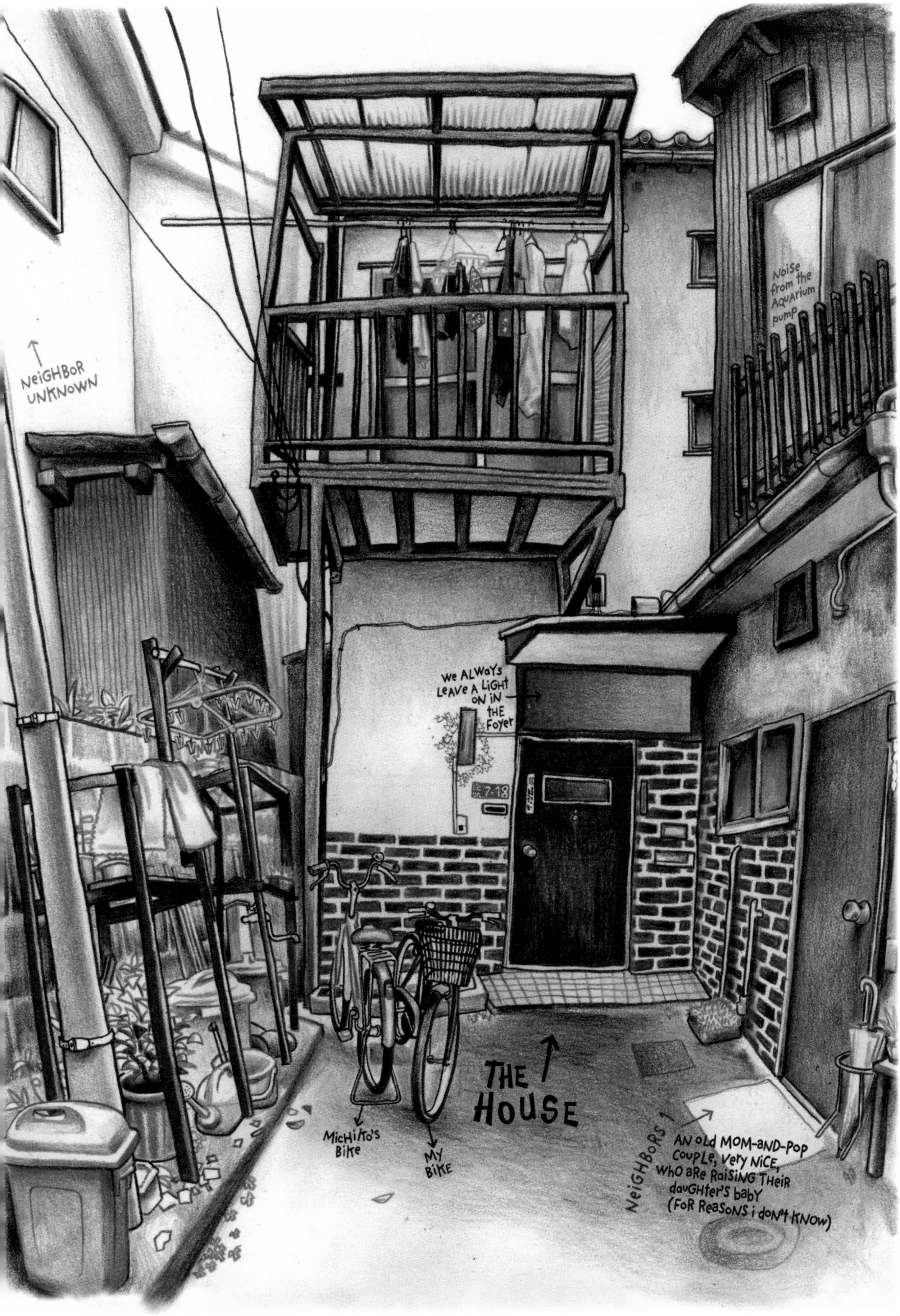
NeiGHBoR UNKNOWN
Noise from the Aquarium pump
We ALWAYS LeAVe A LiGHT ON iN THE Foyer
THE HOUSE
MicHiKo's Bike
My Bike
NeiGHBoRS
AN oLd MOM-aND-Pop CoupLe, Very NiCe, who are RaiSiNG THEiR daugHter's baby (FoR ReaSONS i don't KNoW)

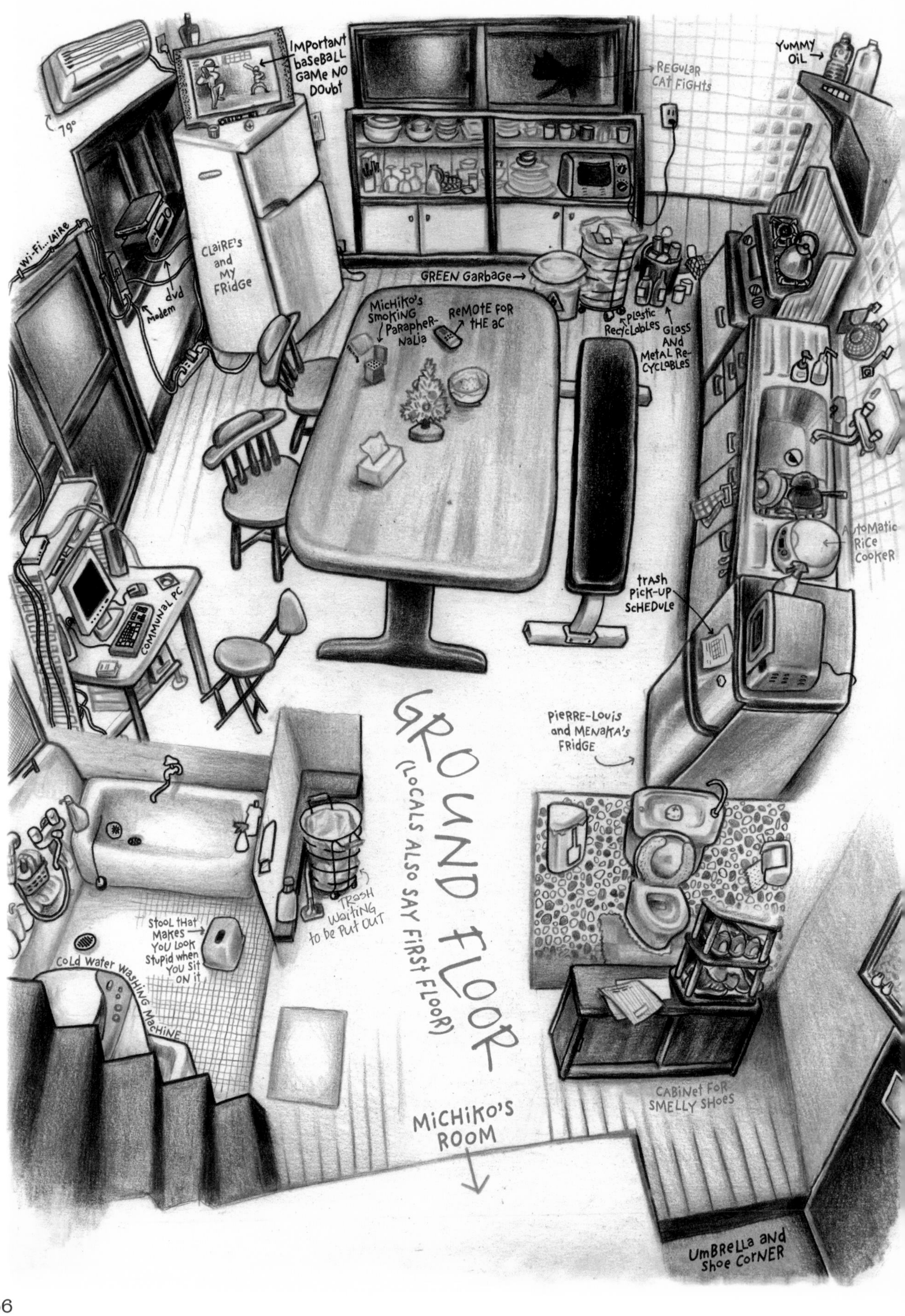

Important baseball game no doubt
79°
Yummy oil
Regular cat fights
Wi-Fi...laire
Claire's and my fridge
dvd
modem
Green garbage
Michiko's smoking parapher-nalia
Remote for the ac
Plastic Recyclables
Glass and Metal Re-cyclables
Automatic Rice Cooker
Communal PC
trash pick-up schedule
Pierre-Louis and Menaka's fridge
GROUND FLOOR
(LOCALS ALSO SAY FIRST FLOOR)
Trash waiting to be put out
Stool that makes you look stupid when you sit on it
Cold water washing machine
Cabinet for smelly shoes
Michiko's room
Umbrella and shoe corner

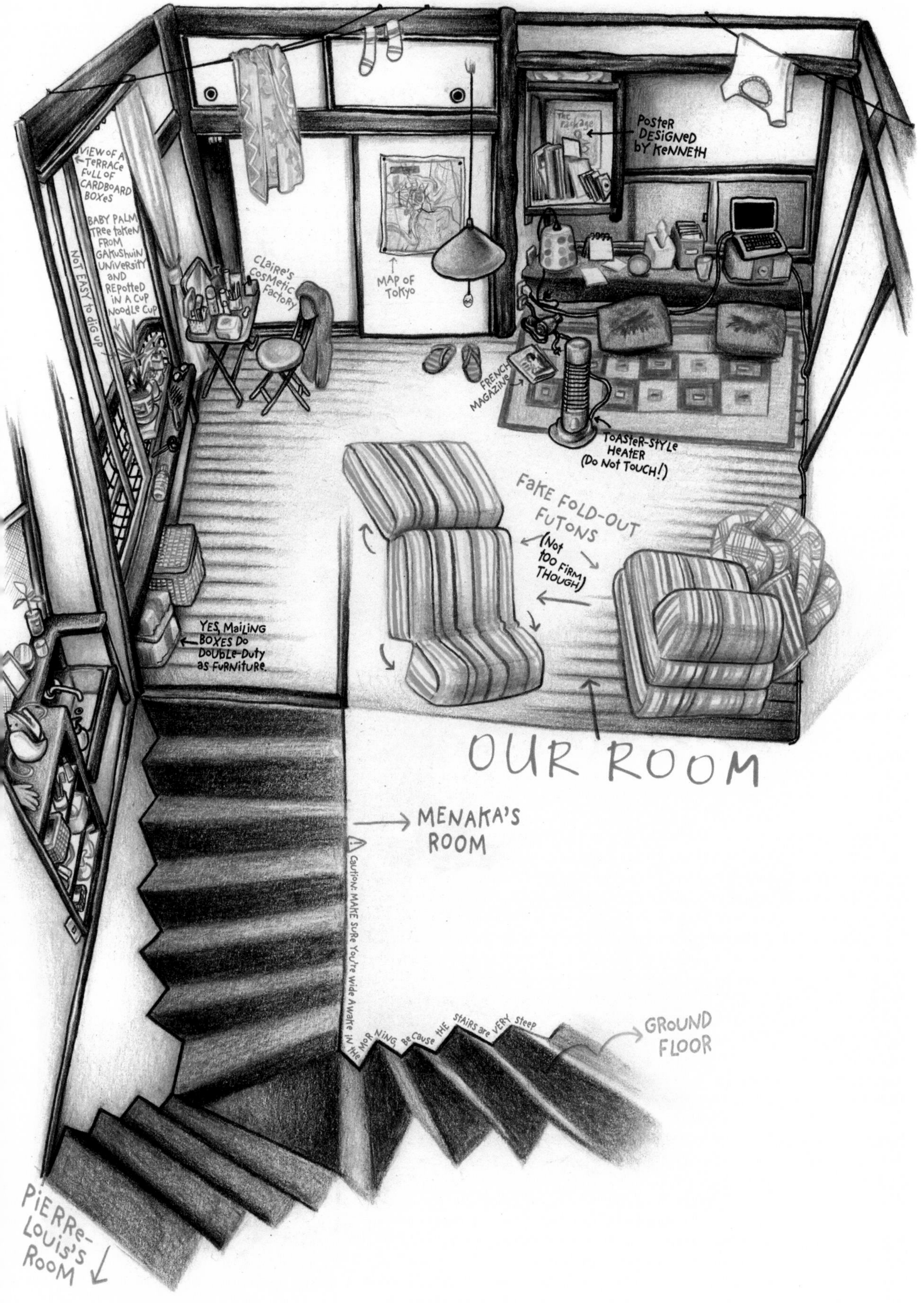
VIEW OF A TERRACE FULL OF CARDBOARD BOXES
BABY PALM TREE taken FROM GAKUSHUIN UNIVERSITY AND REPOTTED IN A CUP NOODLE CUP
NOT EASY to dig up
Claire's Cosmetic Factory
MAP OF TOKYO
Poster DESIGNED by KENNETH
FRENCH MAGAZINE
TOASTER-STYLE HEATER (Do Not TOUCH!)
FAKE FOLD-OUT FUTONS (Not too FIRM THOUGH)
YES, MAILING BOXES Do DOUBLE-DUTY as FURNITURE.
OUR ROOM
MENAKA'S ROOM
Caution: MAKE SURE You're wide Awake in the MORNING, Because THE STAIRS are VERY steep
GROUND FLOOR
PIERRE-Louis's ROOM

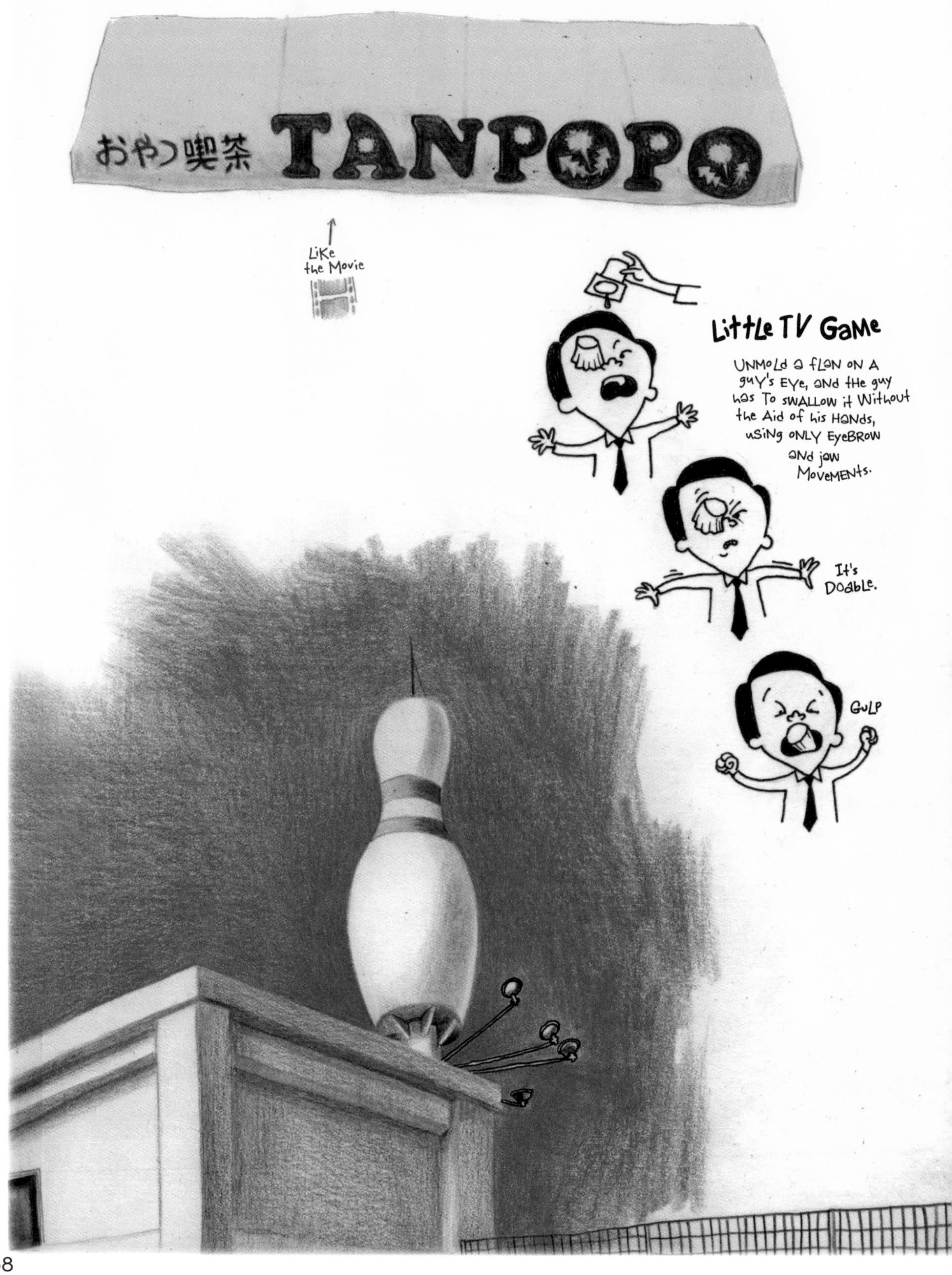
おやつ喫茶 TANPOPO
Like the Movie
Little TV Game
Unmold a flan on a guy's Eye, and the guy has To swallow it Without the Aid of his Hands, using only Eyebrow and jaw Movements.
It's Doable.
Gulp

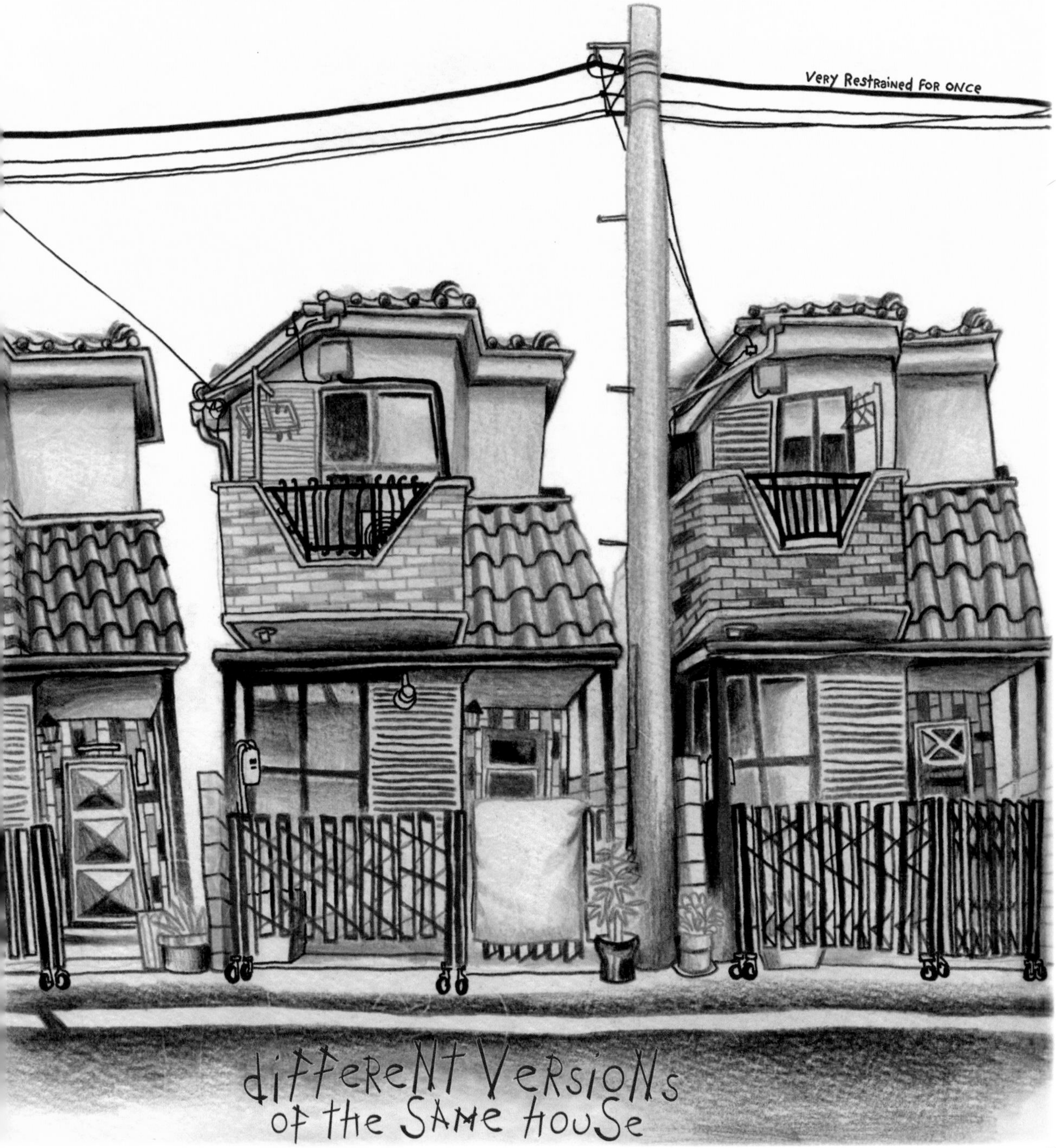
Very Restrained for once
different versions
of the same house

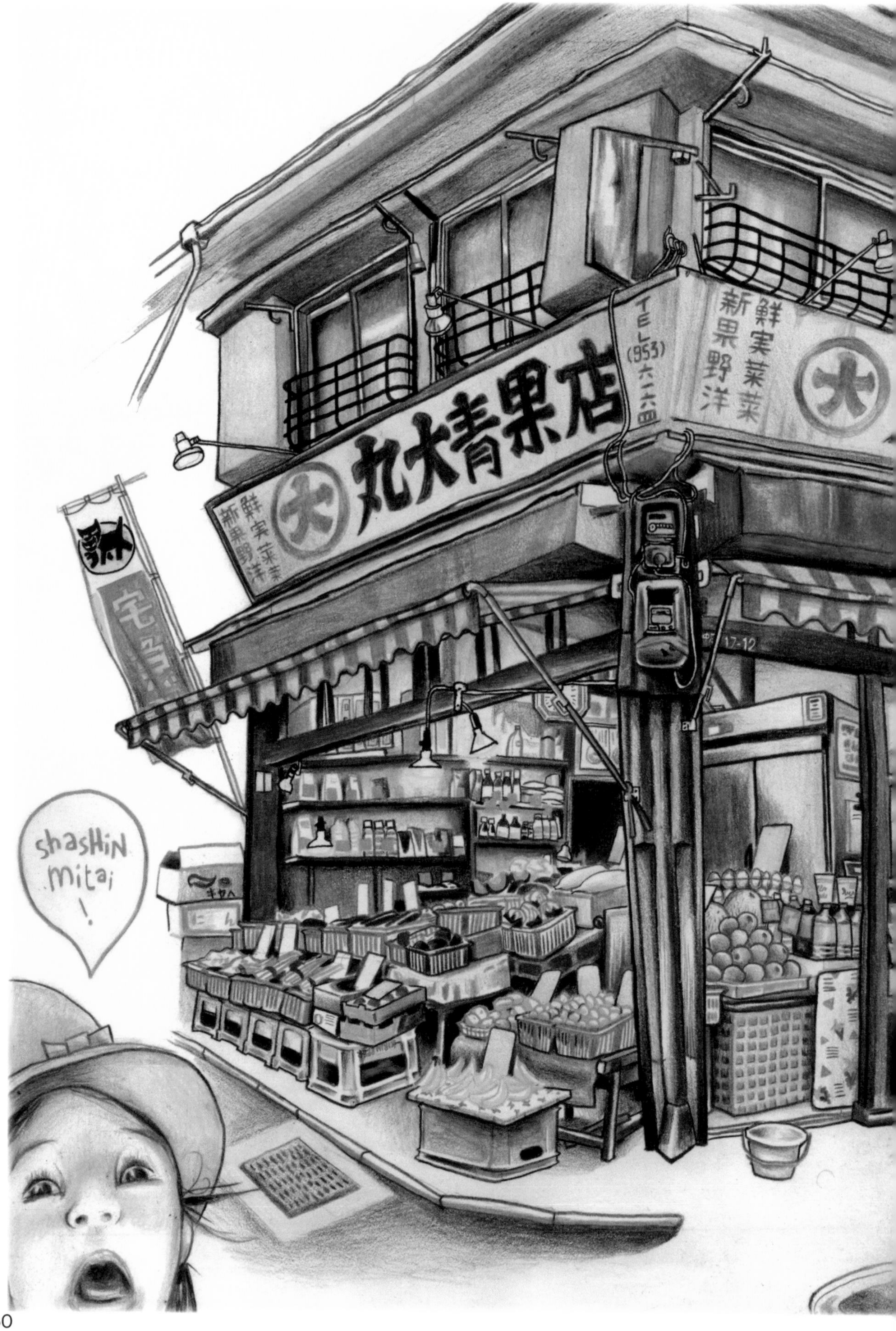
shashin mitai!
丸大青果店
新鮮果実野菜洋菜
TEL (953) 六二六四
17-12

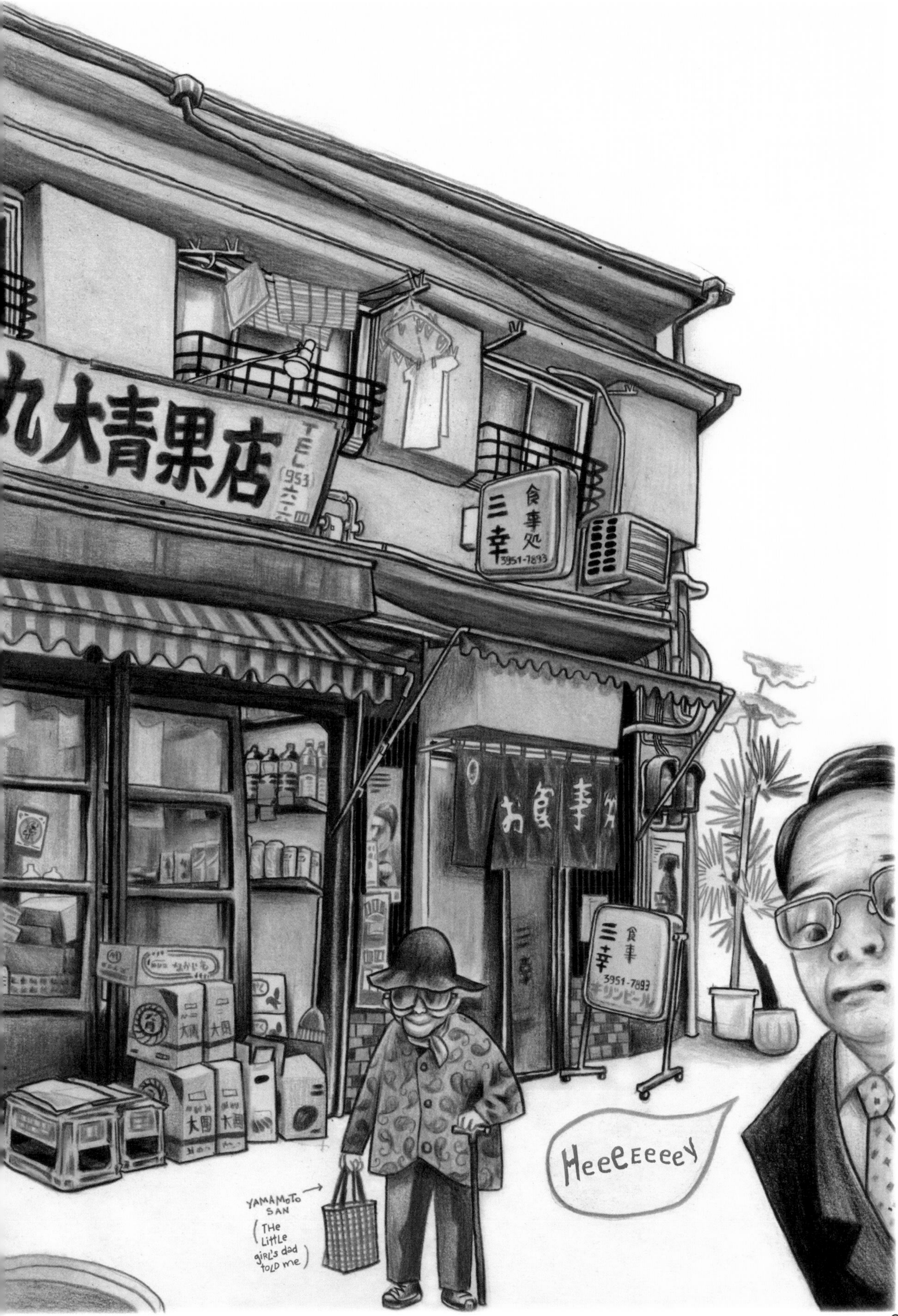
九大青果店
TEL 953
三幸 食事処
3951-7893
お食事処
三幸 食事
3951-7893
キリンビール
Heeeeeeey
YAMAMOTO SAN
(The little girl's dad told me)

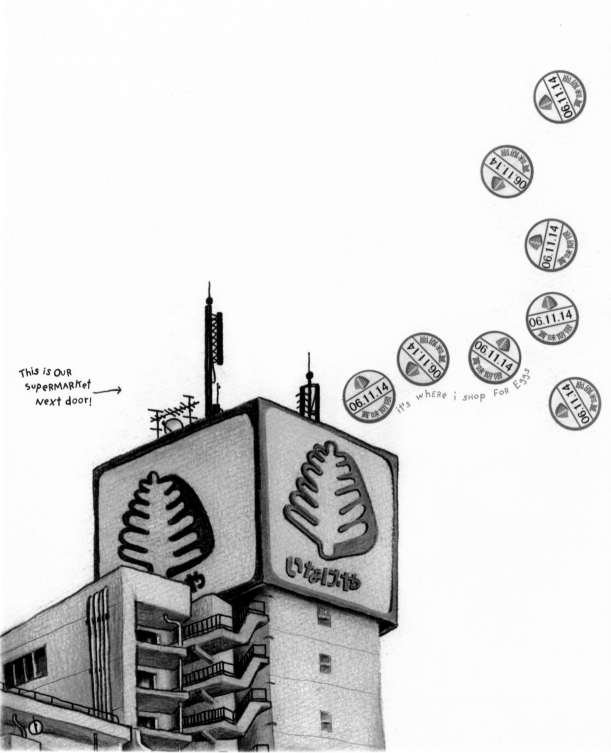

This is OUR
SUPERMARKEt
Next door! →

it's wHeRe i sHoP FoR EggS

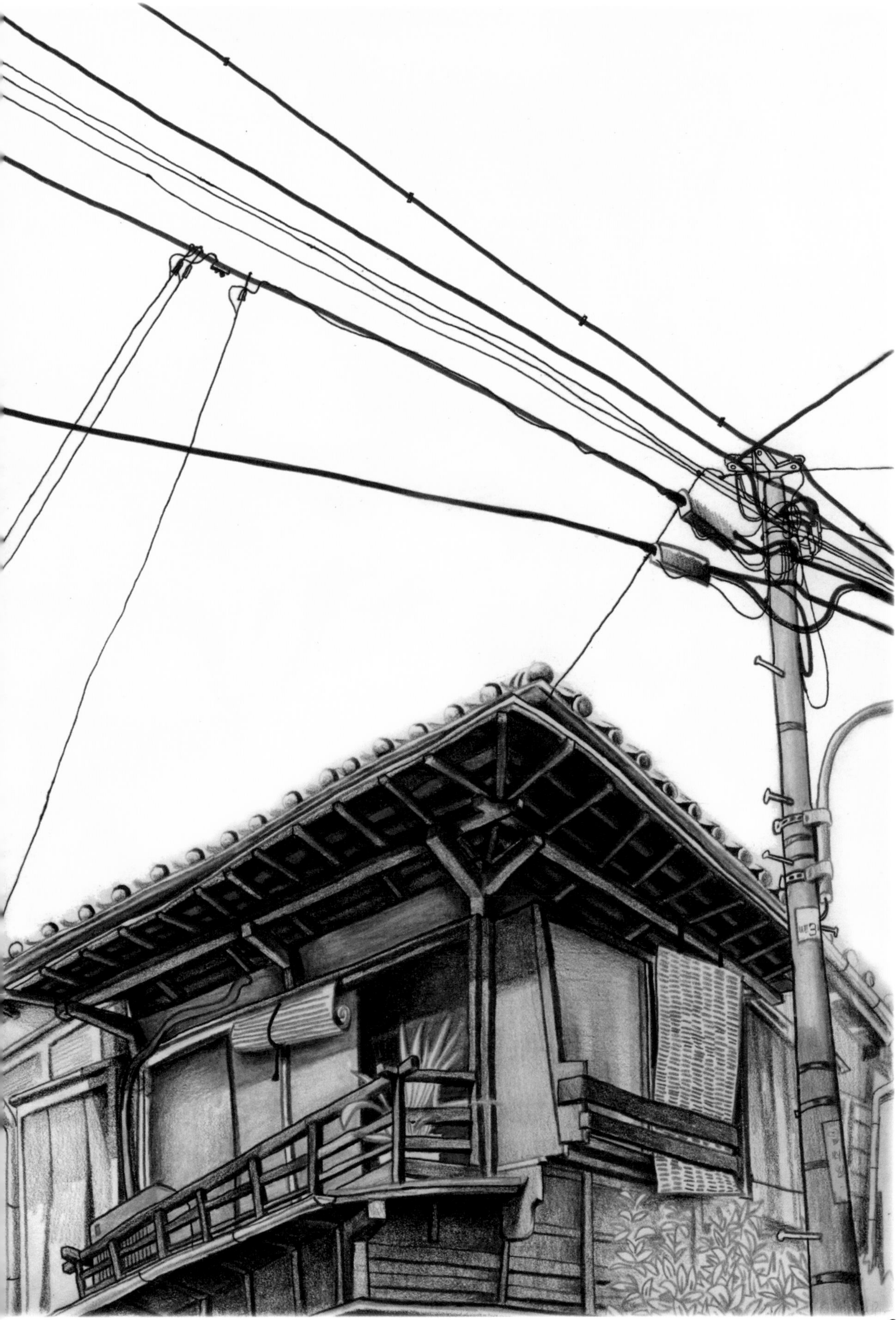

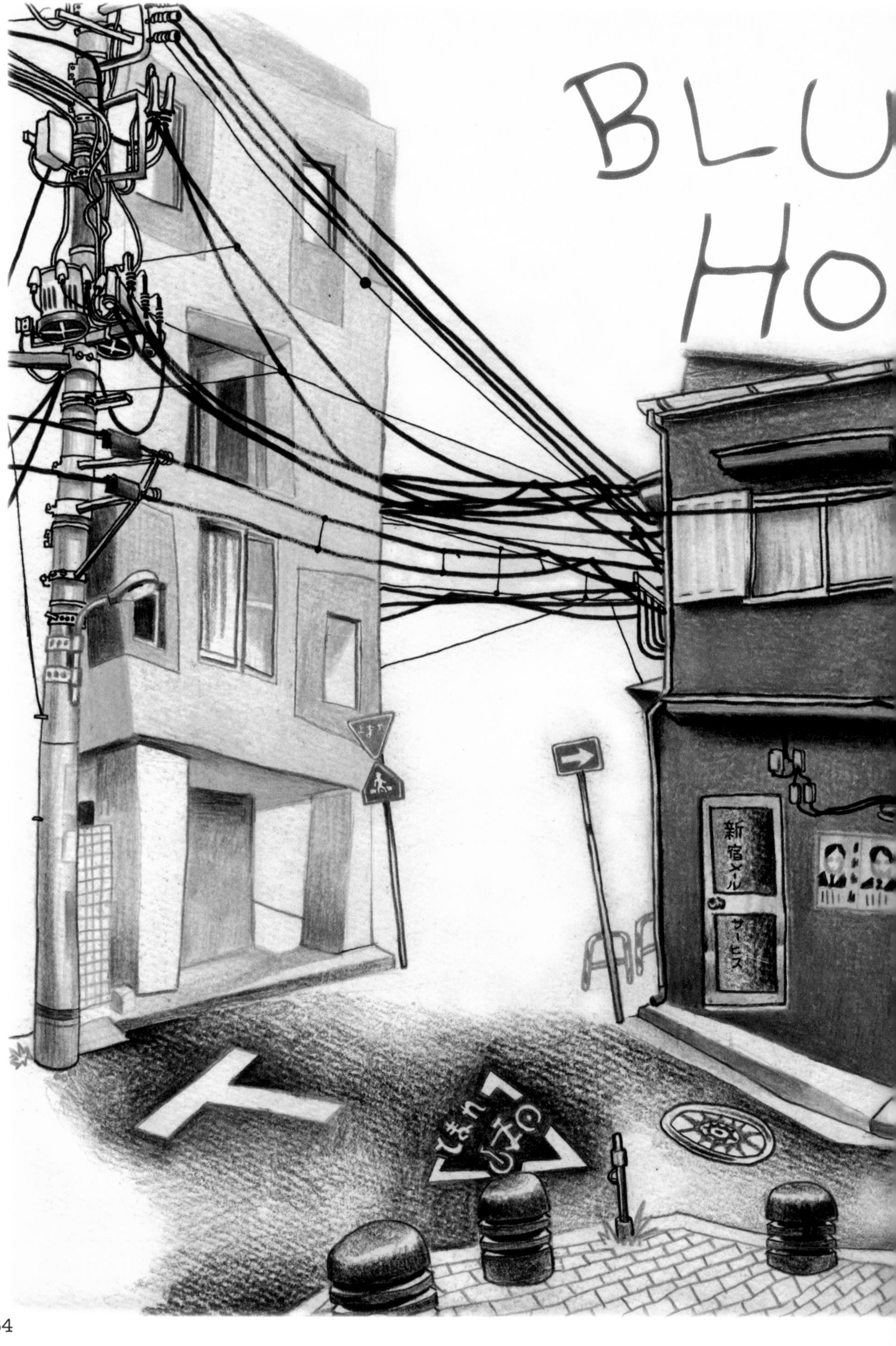
BLU
HO
新宿メール
サービス

e

USe

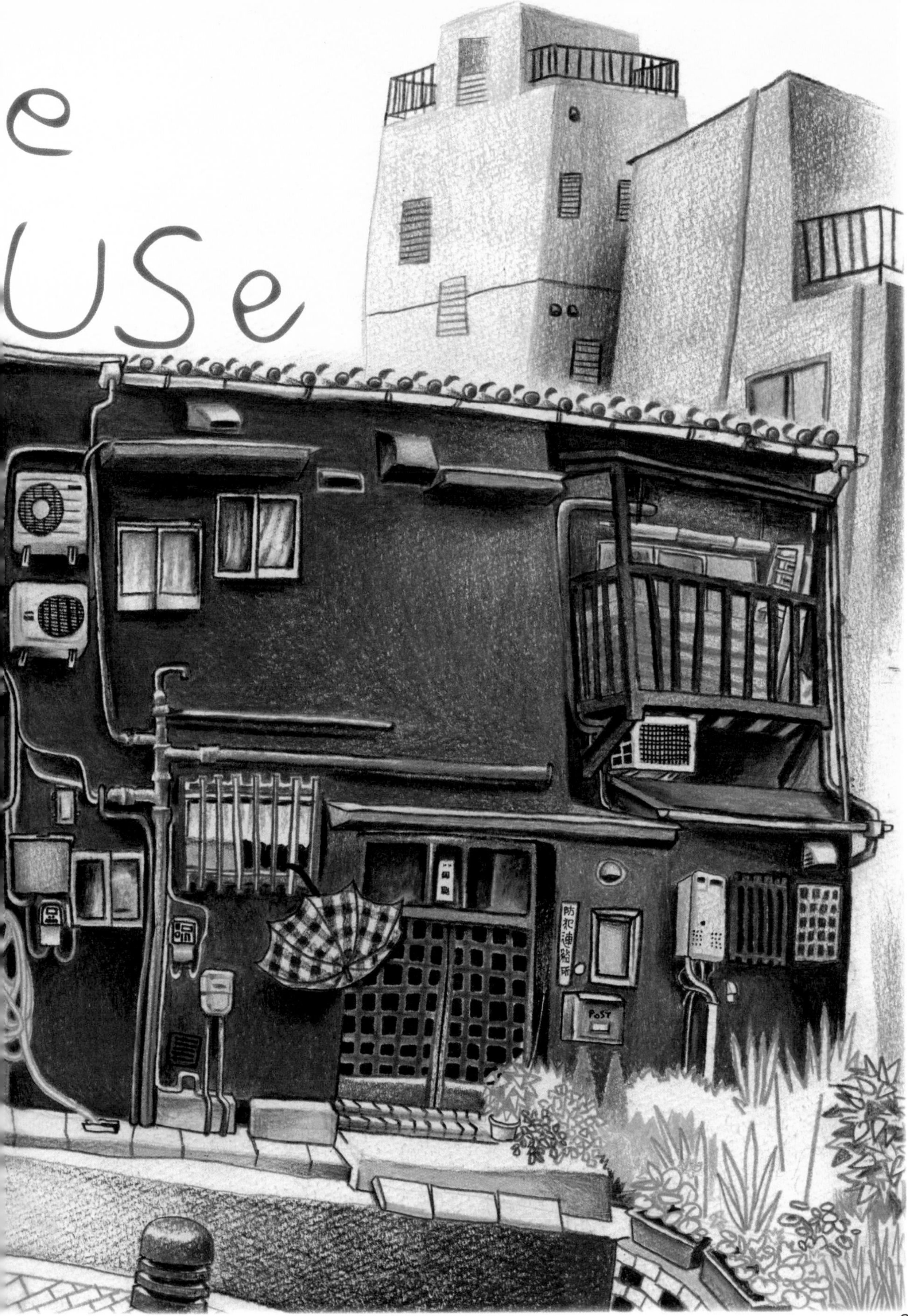
防犯連絡所
POST

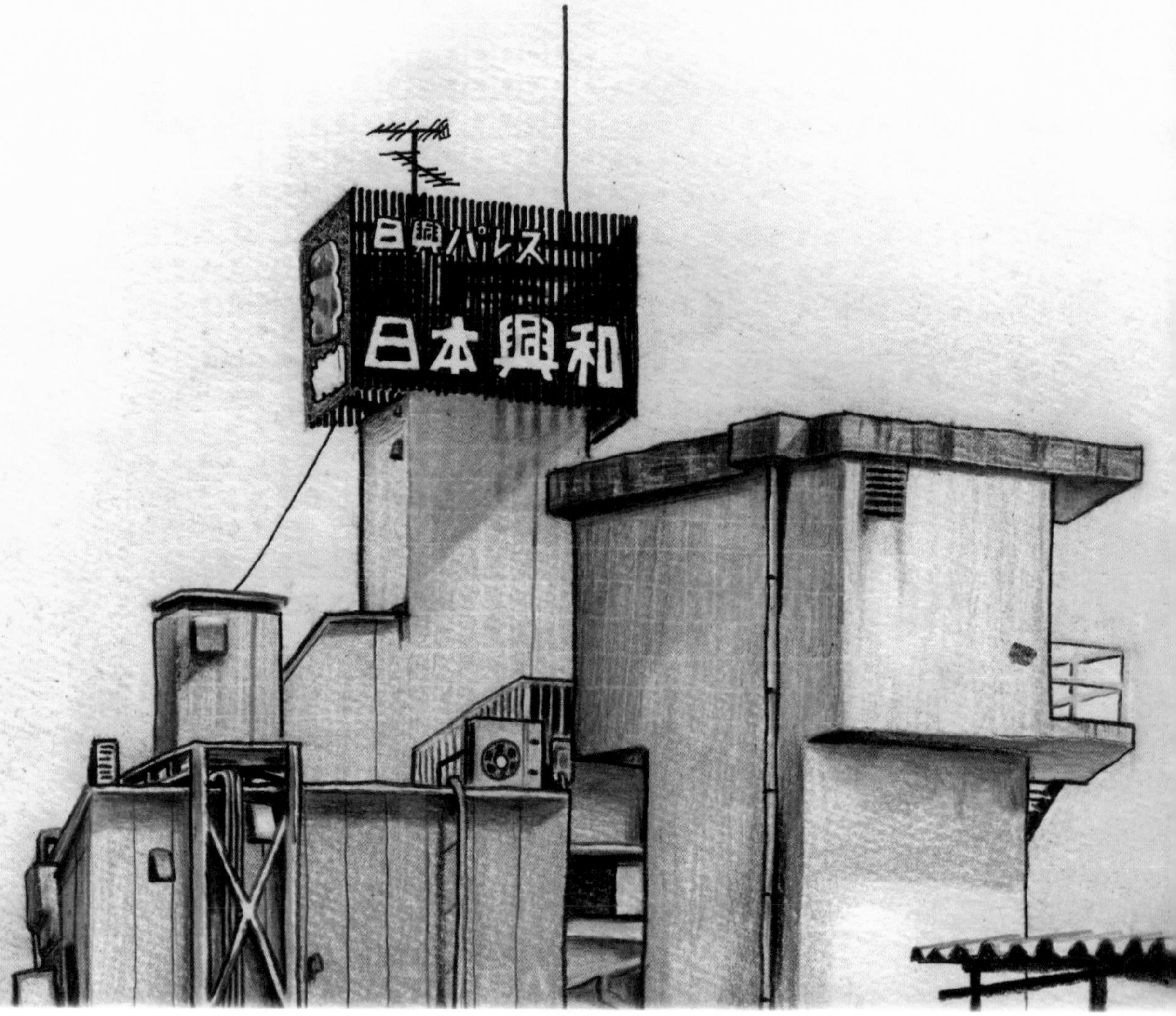
日興パレス
日本興和

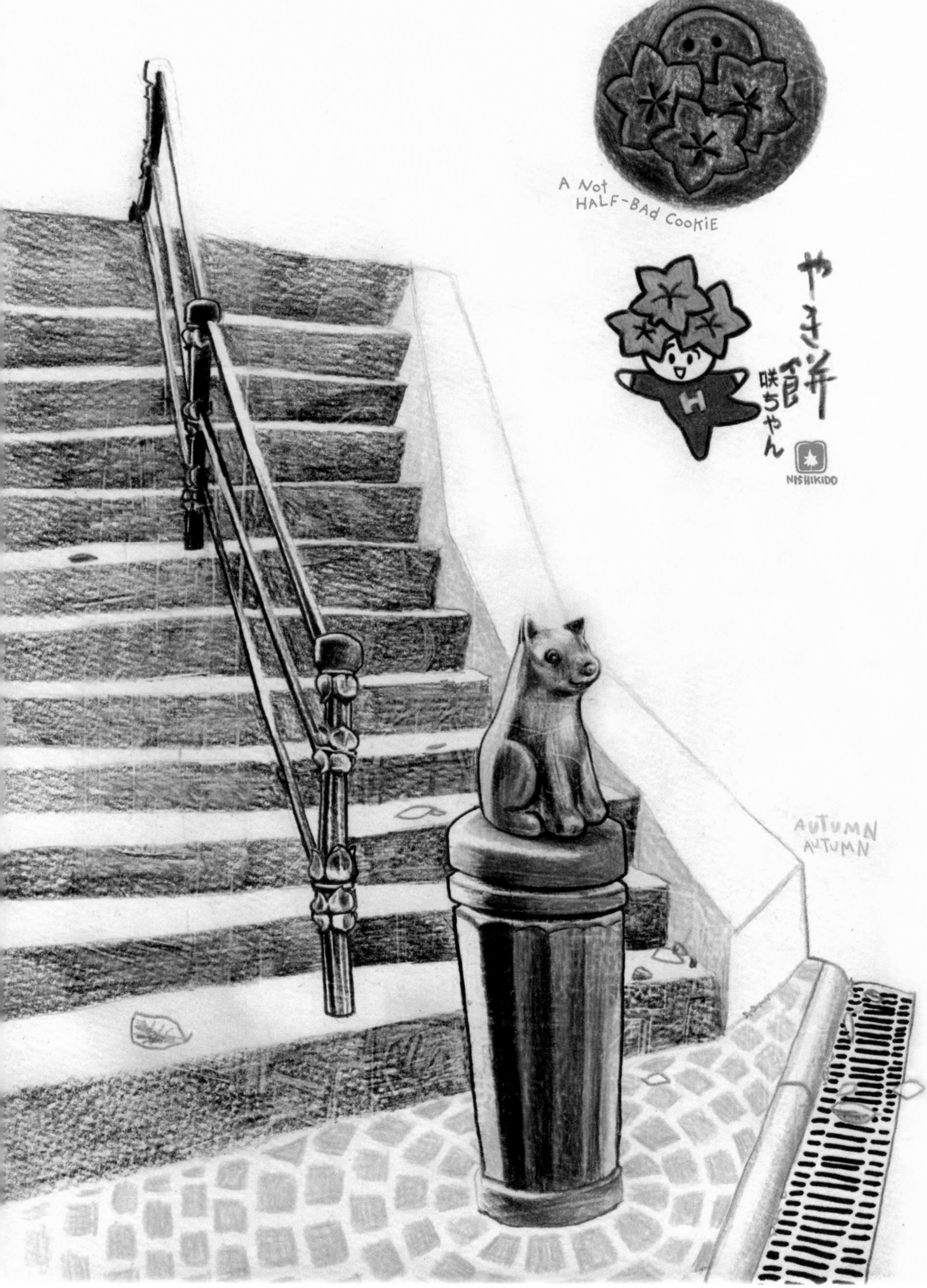
A Not HALF-BAD COOKIE
やき餅館
咲ちゃん
NISHIKIDO
AUTUMN
AUTUMN

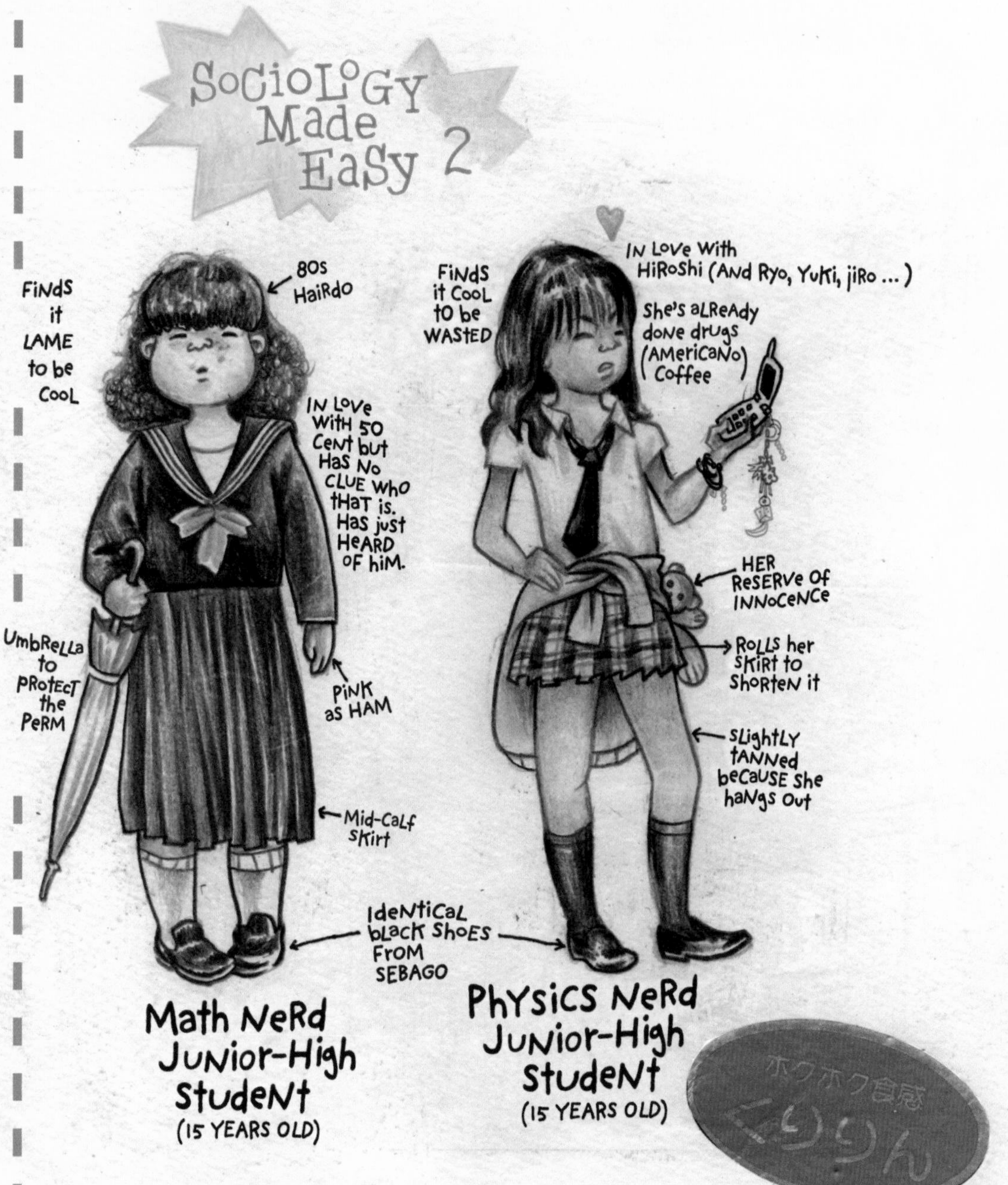
Sociology Made Easy 2
Finds it LAME to be Cool
80s Hairdo
In Love with 50 Cent but Has No Clue who that is. Has just Heard of him.
Umbrella to protect the Perm
Pink as Ham
Mid-Calf Skirt
Identical black Shoes From Sebago
Math Nerd Junior-High Student (15 Years Old)
Finds it Cool to be Wasted
In Love with Hiroshi (And Ryo, Yuki, Jiro ...)
She's already done drugs (Americano) Coffee
Her Reserve of Innocence
Rolls her Skirt to Shorten it
Slightly tanned because She hangs out
Physics Nerd Junior-High Student (15 Years Old)

MY RIdE

MaY i PRESENT ALSUS BRIDGESTONE, MY biKE FOR ALL MY AdVentuRES? i ResCued it FROM A DeSERTed PaRKing Lot WheRe it was aBANDONED, Without FOOD. BeCAUSE of it, there WILL be No drAWings of tHe ToKyo SubWay iN this SKeTchpad.

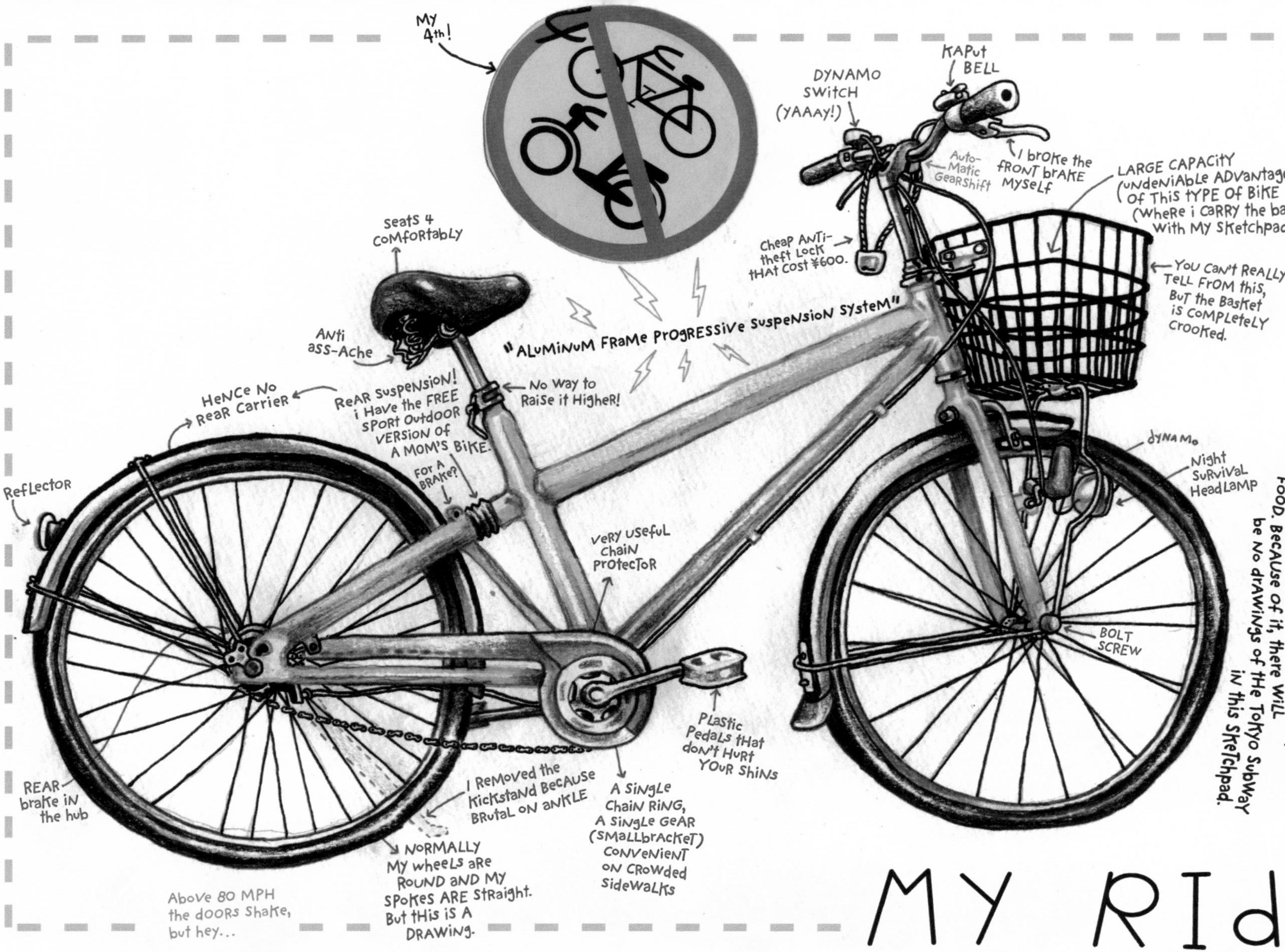
My 4th!
DYNAMO SWitCH (YAAAy!)
KAPut BELL
Auto-Matic GearShift
I broke the FRONT brAKE MYSeLf
LARGE CAPACity (undeniAble ADVANtage OF This tYPE OF BIKE (Where i CARRY the bag With MY SKetchpad)
Cheap ANTI-theft Lock tHAT Cost ¥600.
You Can't ReaLLY TeLL FROM this, But the Basket is COMPLeteLY Crooked.
Seats 4 COMFORTabLY
"ALuMiNuM FRaMe PRoGRESSive SuspeNSioN SysteM"
Anti ass-Ache
HeNCe No ReaR Carrier
ReAR SuspenSioN! i Have the FREE SPoRT OutdOOR VERSioN of A MOM'S BiKE.
No Way to Raise it HigheR!
For A BRAKE?
dyNAMo
Night SuRviVaL HeadLaMP
ReFLector
VeRY uSeFuL ChaiN PRoTecToR
BOLT SCREW
Plastic PedaLs tHat don't HuRT YOUR ShiNs
REAR brake iN the hub
I Removed the KickstaNd BeCAuse BRutaL ON aNKLE
A SiNgLe ChaiN RiNG, A SiNgLe GeAR (SMALLbrackeT) CONVeNieNT ON CRoWded SidewaLks
NORMALLY My wheeLs aRe ROUND aND MY SPoKes ARE Straight. But tHis iS A DRAWiNg.
Above 80 MPH the dOORS Shake, but hey...

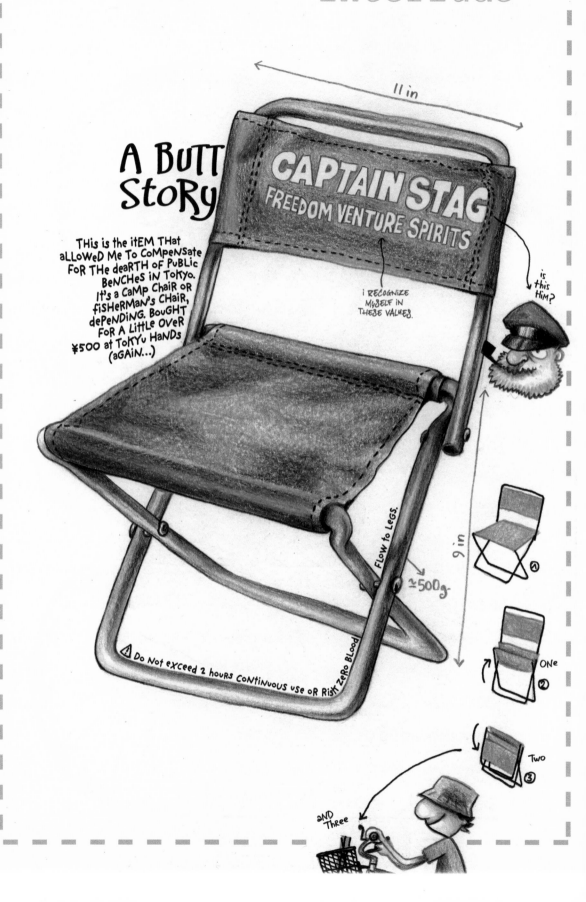

A BUTT
STORy

This is the itEM THat aLLoWeD Me To CoMPeNSate FoR THe deaRTH oF PuBLic BeNCHes iN ToKyo. It's a CaMp CHaiR oR FiSHeRMaN's CHaiR, dePeNDiNG. BoUGHT FoR A LittLe oVeR ¥500 at ToKyu HaNDs (aGaiN...)

CAPTAIN STAG
FREEDOM VENTURE SPIRITS

i RECOGNIZE MySELF iN THESE VaLUES.

is this HiM?

FLow to LeGs.

≈500g

9 in

11 in

⚠ Do Not eXCeeD 2 HouRs CoNTiNuous use oR RisK ZeRo BLooD

A

oNe
②

Two
③

aND Three

70

okubo

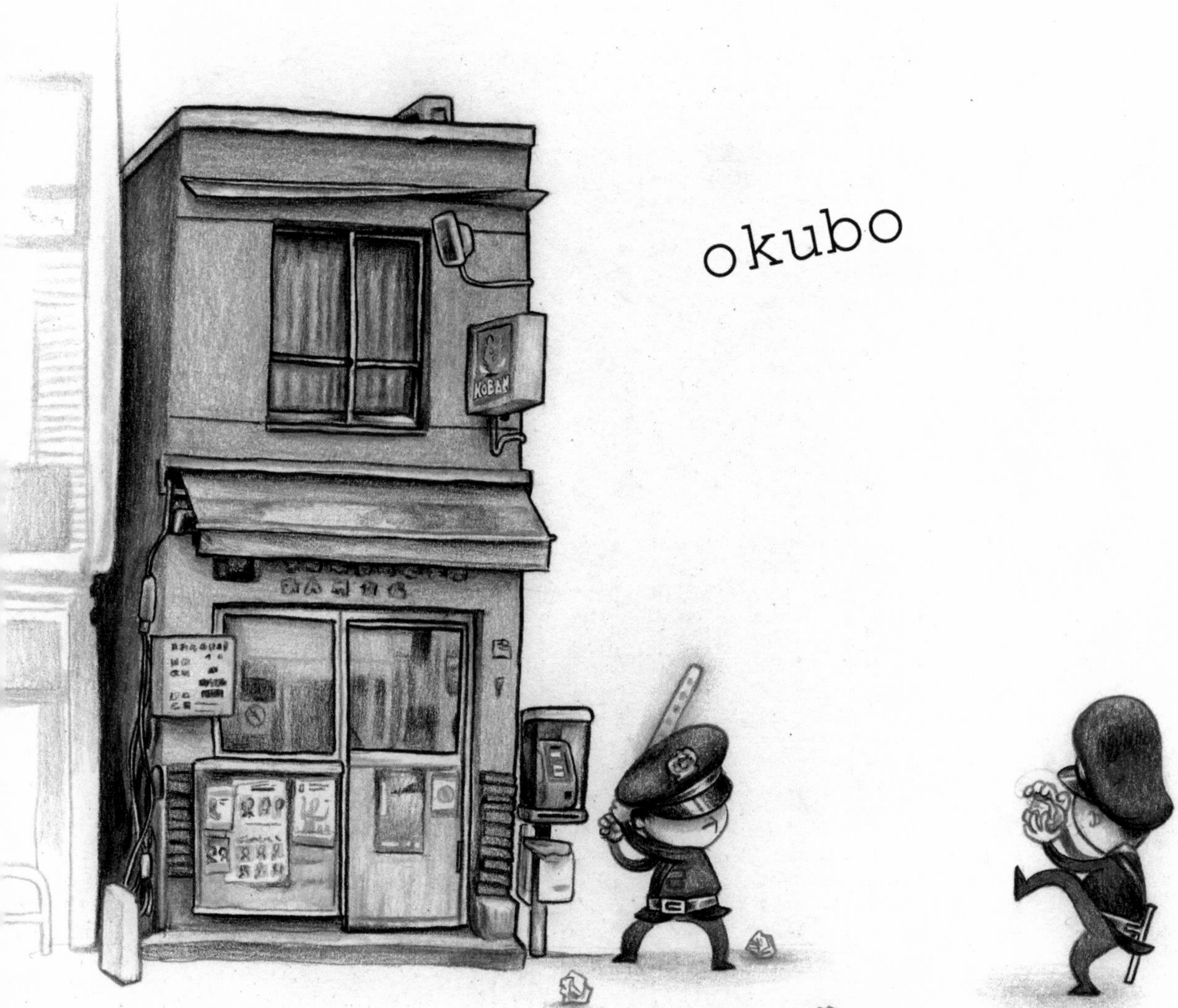
KOBAN

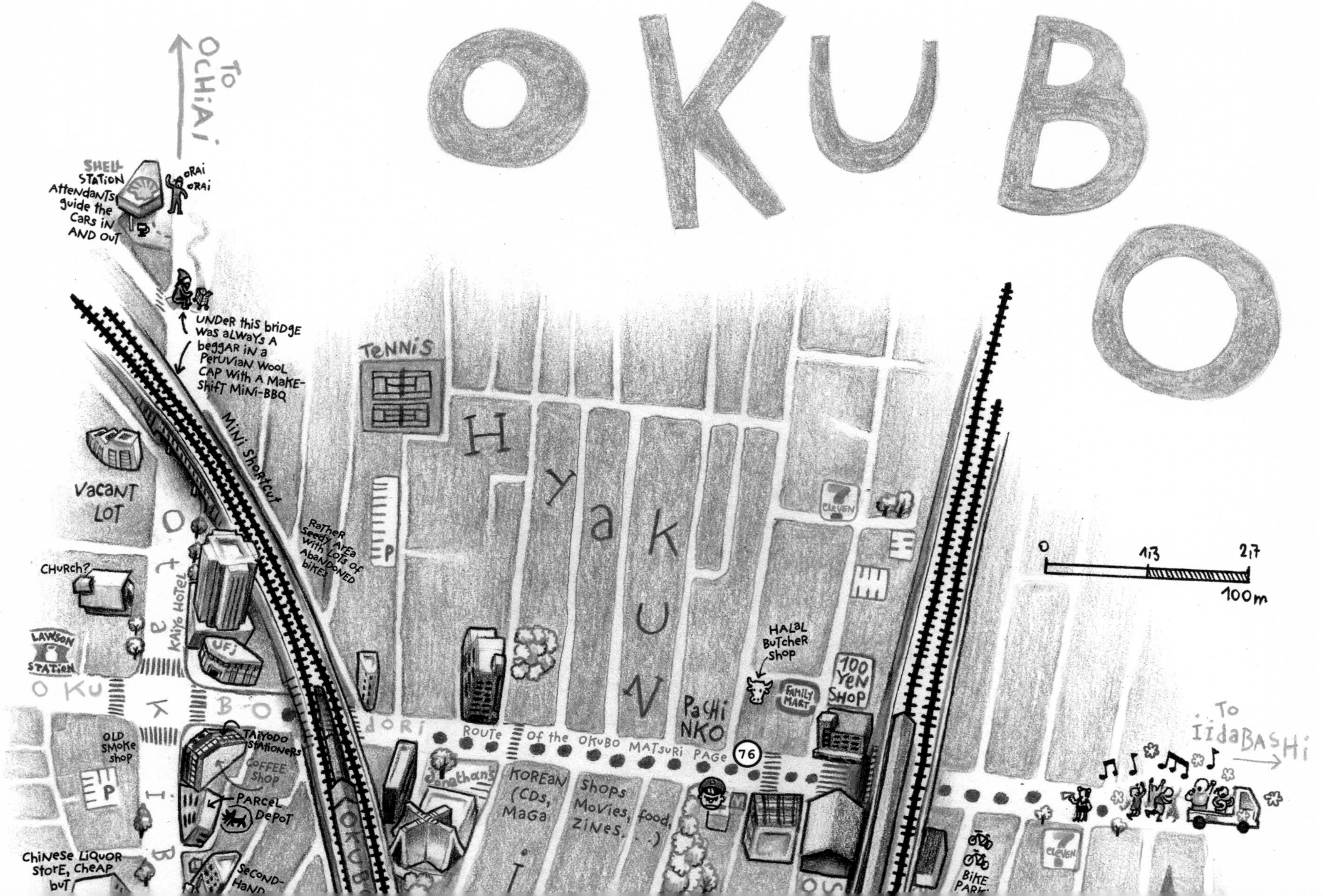
OKUBO
To OCHiAi
SHELL STATION Attendants guide the Cars in AND OUT
oRAi oRAi
UNDER this bridge was always a beggar in a Peruvian wool cap with a make-shift mini-BBQ
Mini Shortcut
Rather seedy area with lots of abandoned bites
TENNIS
Hyakunin
Vacant LOT
CHURCH?
Kaiyo HOTEL
UFJ
LAWSON STATION
OKUBO DORI
OLD SMOKE shop
TAIYODO STATIONERS
COFFEE Shop
PARCEL DEPOT
Chinese Liquor store, cheap but
SECOND-HAND
OKUBO
Route of the OKUBO MATSURI PAGE 76
Jonathan's
KOREAN (CDs, Maga
Shops Movies, food, ZINES...)
PaChiNKO
HALAL BUTCHER Shop
FAMILY MART
100 YEN SHOP
7 ELEVEN
0
1/3
2/3
100m
To IidaBASHi
BIKE PARK

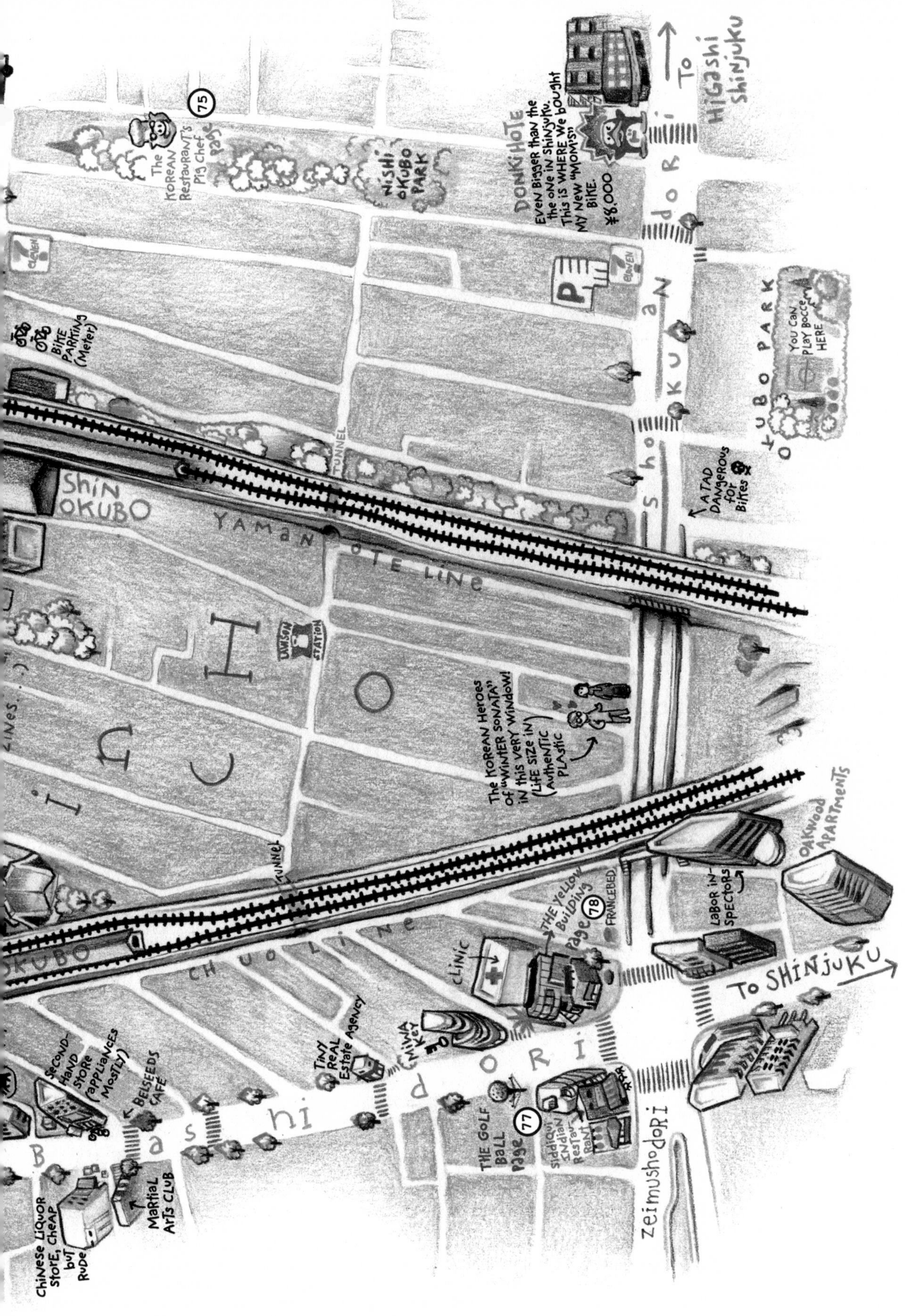
The KOREAN Restaurant's Pig Chef Page 75
NISHI OKUBO PARK
DONKIHOTE Even Bigger than the one in Shinjuku. This is WHERE we bought MY New "MOM'S" BIKE. ¥8,000
To HIGASHI SHINJUKU
7 ELEVEN
7 ELEVEN
P
BIKE PARKING (Meter)
Shokuan dori
OKUBO PARK
YOU CAN PLAY BOCCE HERE
A TAD DANGEROUS for BIKES
TUNNEL
Shin OKUBO
YAMANOTE LINE
LAWSON STATION
The KOREAN Heroes of "WINTER SONATA" in this very window! (LIFE SIZE IN AUTHENTIC PLASTIC)
TUNNEL
CHUO LINE
CLINIC
THE YELLOW BUILDING Page 78
FRANCEBED
LABOR IN-SPECTORS
OAKWOOD APARTMENTS
To SHINJUKU
MIWA KEY
TINY REAL Estate Agency
SECOND-HAND STORE (APPLIANCES MOSTLY)
BELSEEDS CAFE
MARTIAL ARTS CLUB
CHINESE LIQUOR STORE, CHEAP but RUDE
THE GOLF BALL Page 77
SIDDIQUI INDIAN RESTAURANT
Zeimusho dori

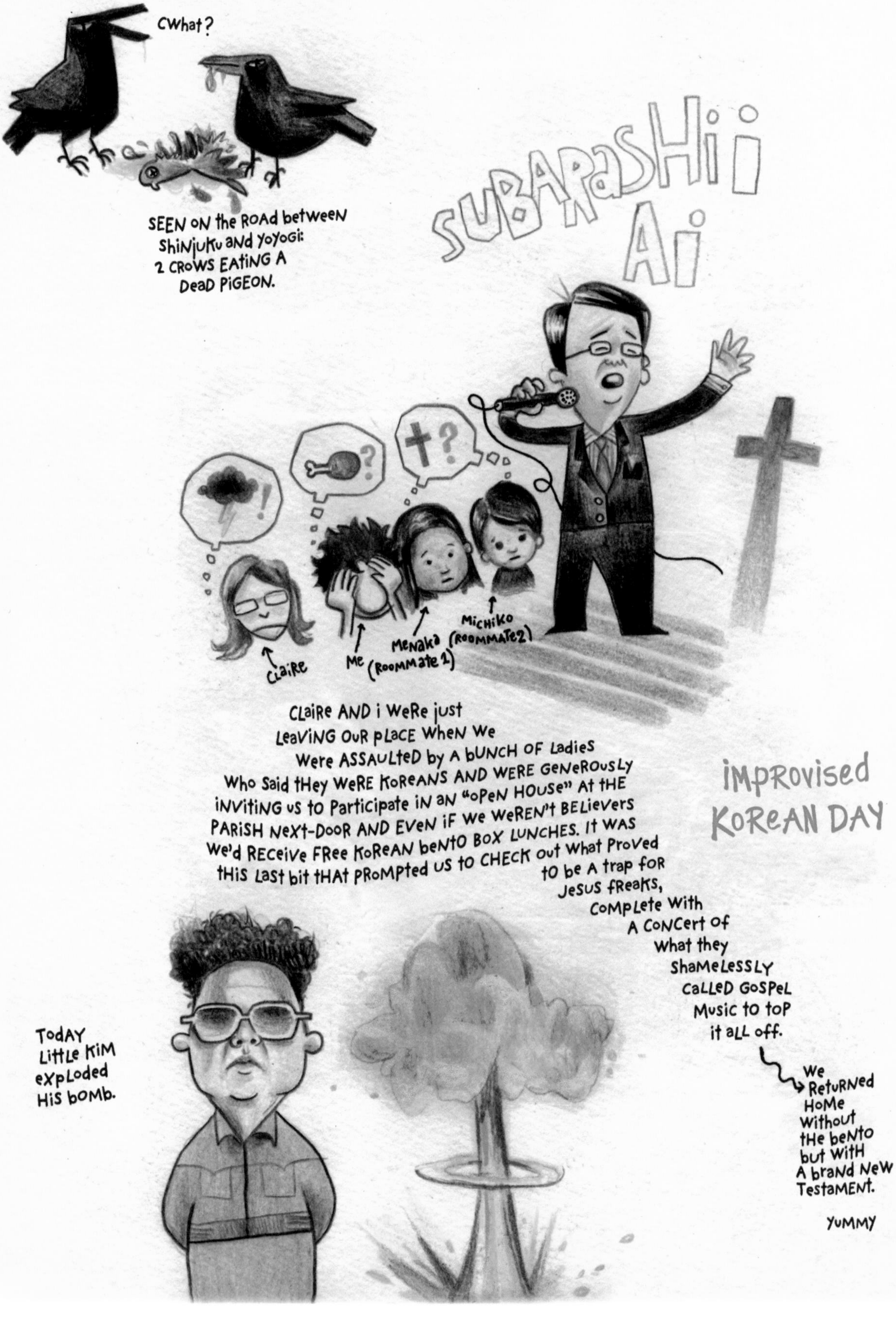
CWhat?
SEEN ON the ROAD between Shinjuku and yoyogi: 2 CROWS EATING A DEAD PIGEON.
SUBARASHIi Ai
Claire
Me
Menaka (Roommate 1)
Michiko (Roommate 2)
Claire AND i WeRe just leaving OUR place when we were ASSAULTED by A bUNCH OF Ladies who said they were KOREANS AND WERE GENEROUSLY INVITING US to Participate iN an "OPEN HOUSE" AT THE PARISH NEXT-DOOR AND EVEN iF we WEREN'T BELIEVERS we'd RECEIVE FREE KOREAN bento BOX LUNCHES. It WAS THIS LAST bit THAT PROMPTED US TO CHECK out What Proved to be A trap for Jesus freaks, complete with A Concert of what they shamelessly called gospel music to top it all off.
improvised KOREAN DAY
TODAY Little Kim exploded His bomb.
We Returned Home without the bento but with A brand New Testament.
YUMMY

SoMe CaR NaMES WORTH NoTinG:

THE MAJESTA
THE ARiSTo
THE SUPER DELuXe CEDRIC (Nissan)
THE SUPER CuSToM CEDRIC (Nissan)
THE EVERY (Suzuki)
THE MiRA (Fake Micra)
THE DuTRo (Light Truck)
THE ELgRANd (Nissan)
THE EDiX
THE CERVO
THE LAFESTa
THE PREsage

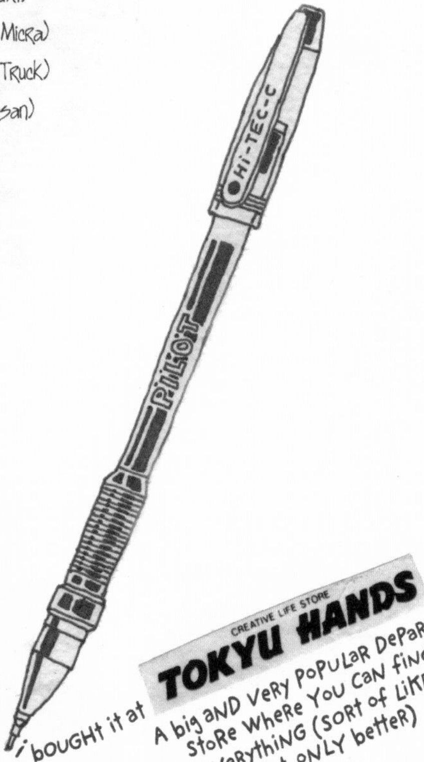

HI-TEC-C
PILOT
CREATIVE LIFE STORE
TOKYU HANDS

i bOUGHt it at

A big AND VeRy PoPULaR DePaRtMeNt StoRe WheRe You CaN find eveRythiNG (SoRt of LiKE target, oNLY betteR)

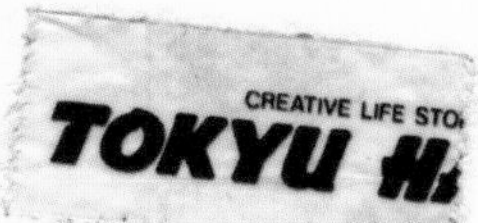

TOKYU

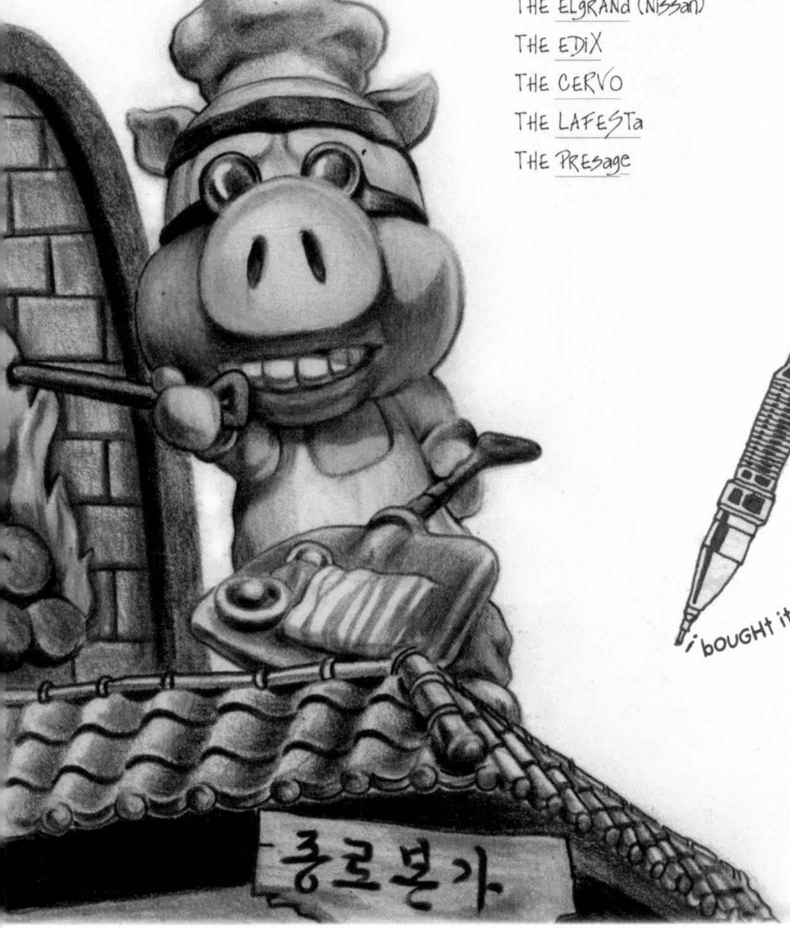

종로본가

THE OLd DRUNKARd's DANCE

PERFORMED DURING THE ASia FESTIVAL OF OKUBO MATSURI

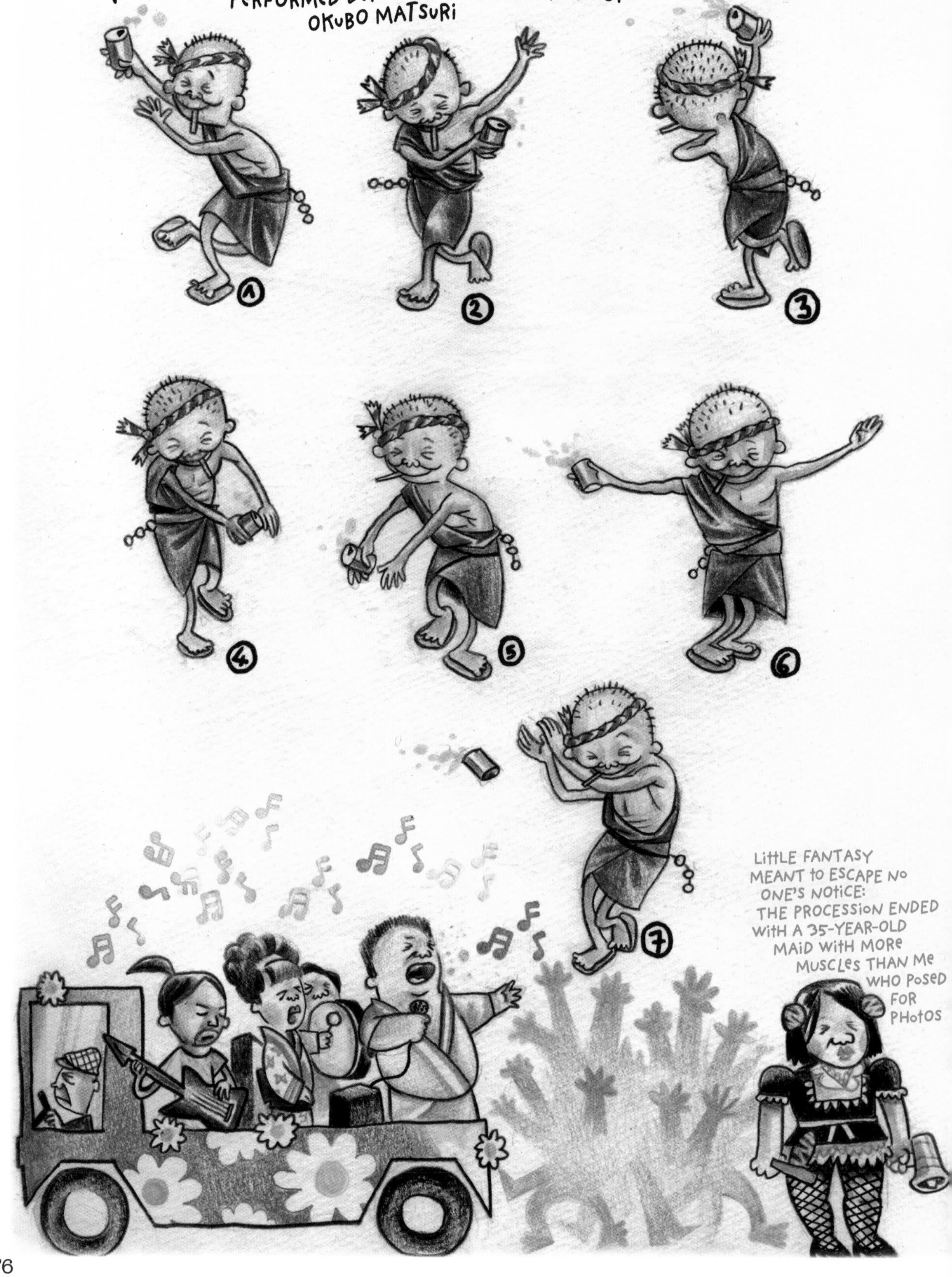
1
2
3
4
5
6
7
LittLE FANTASY MEANT to ESCAPE NO ONE'S NOTICE: THE PROCESSION ENDED WITH A 35-YEAR-OLD MAID WITH MORE MUSCLES THAN ME WHO POSED FOR PHOTOS

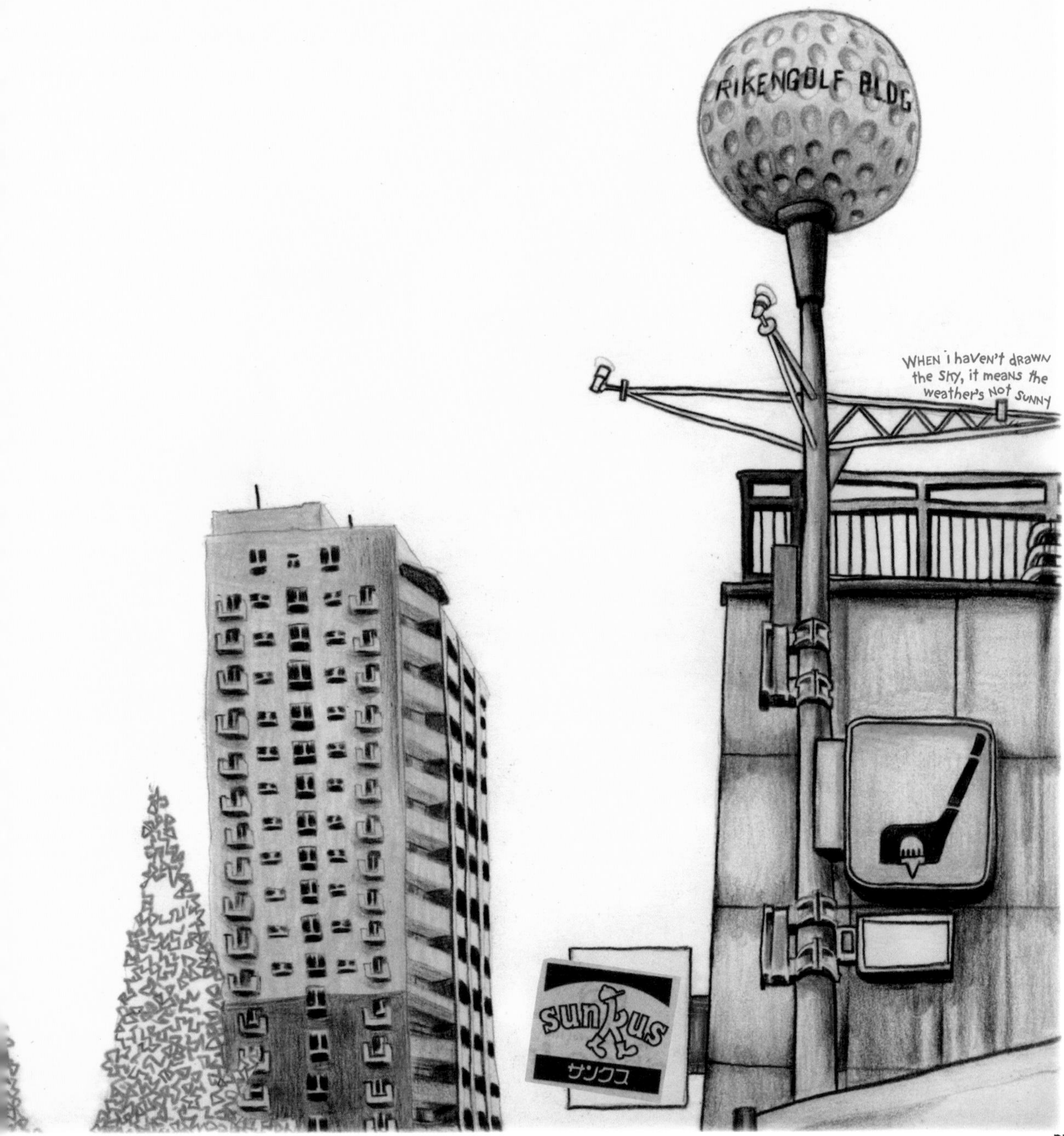
RIKENGOLF BLDG
WHEN i haven't drawn the sky, it means the weather's Not sunny
sunkus
サンクス

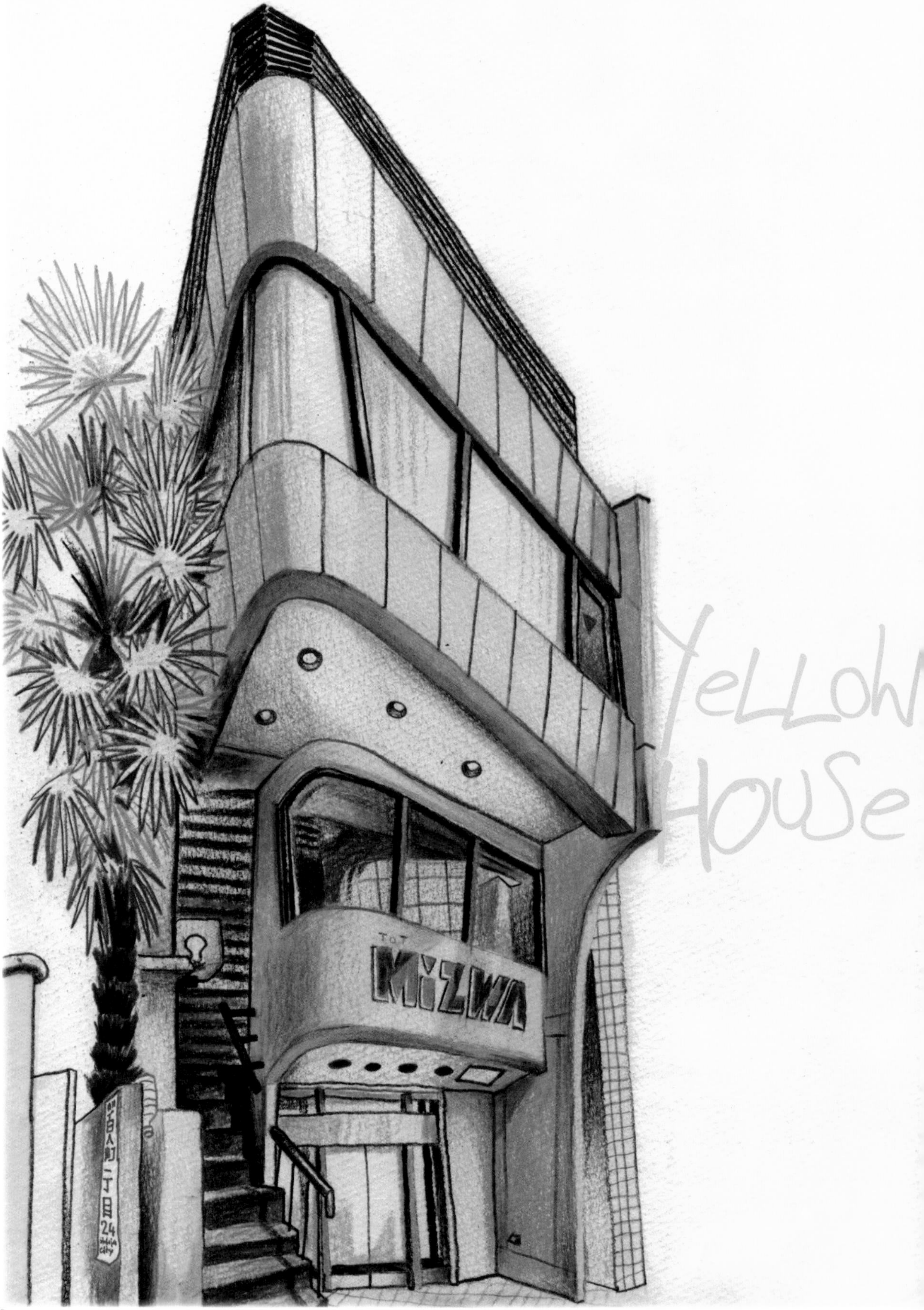
YeLLOW
HOUSe
MiZWA
白人町
二丁目
24

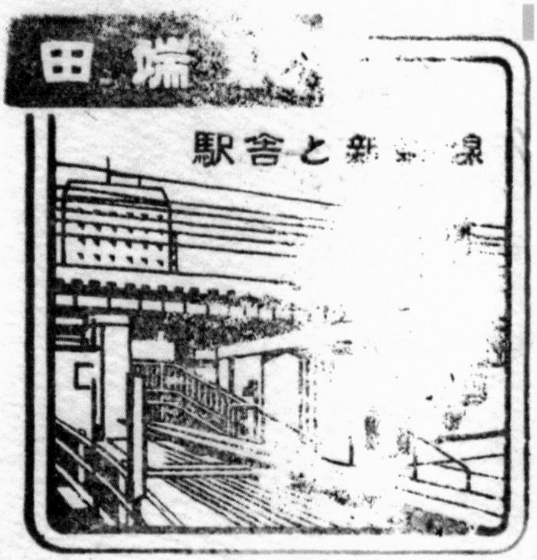
田端
駅舎と新

TABATA Station

It's self-colored (it's its true color on the sketch)

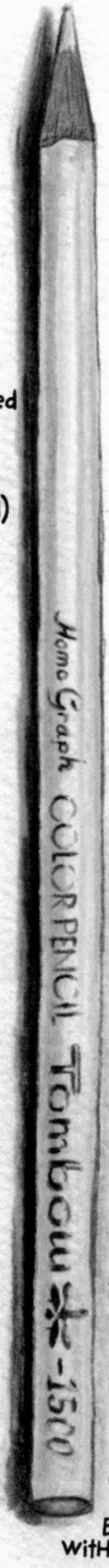
Homo Graph COLOR PENCIL Tombow -1500

MY NEW BRAND of PenciL: TomBow. It's supposed to be well known. A very old company that makes markers too. In any case, and as opposed to the Mitsubishi ones i bought, I'm really happy with it. The lead is solid, and the price is the lowest on the shelf (¥82, i think). i only have 2 for the moment, 2 colors i don't use much, which is dumb, but at least I'm contributing to the local economy. Down with German pencils!

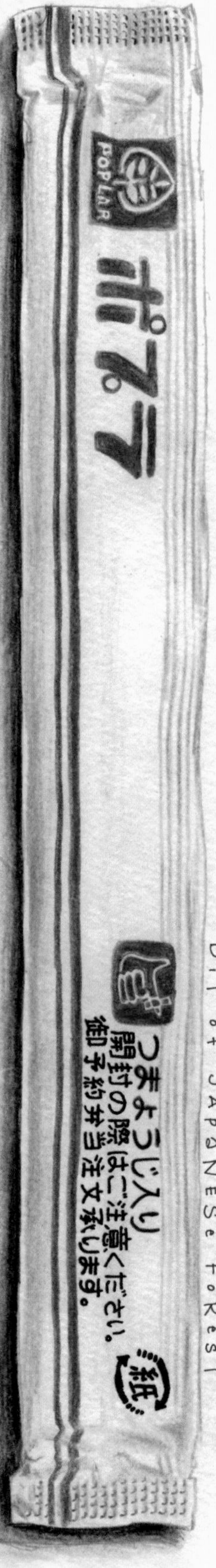
POPLAR
ポプラ
つまようじ入り
開封の際はご注意ください。
御予約弁当注文承ります。
紙

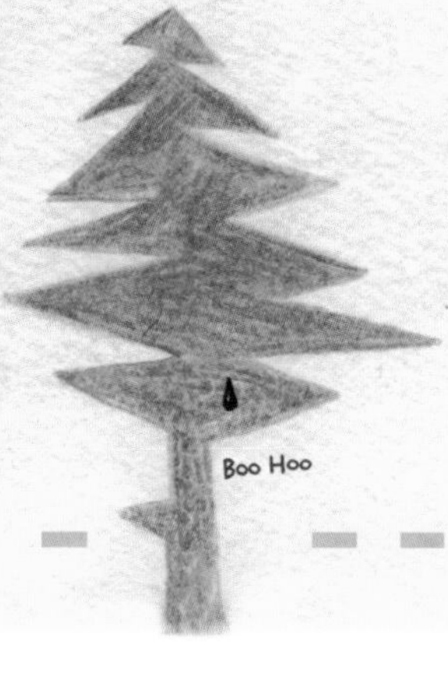
Boo Hoo

BiT of JAPaNESe FoReST

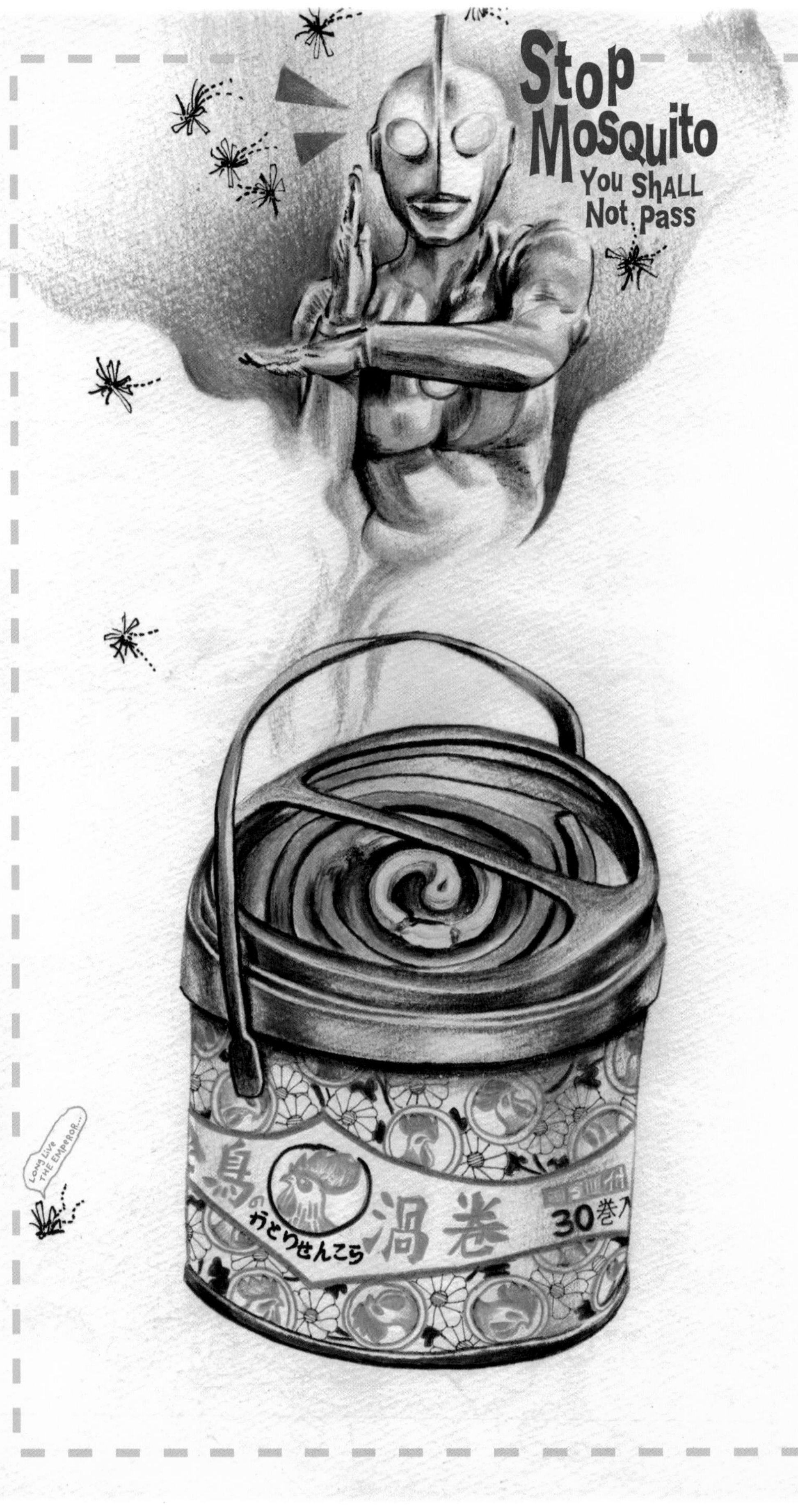
Stop Mosquito
You ShALL Not Pass
Long Live THE EMPEROR...
鳥の
かとりせんこら
渦巻
30巻入

ueno

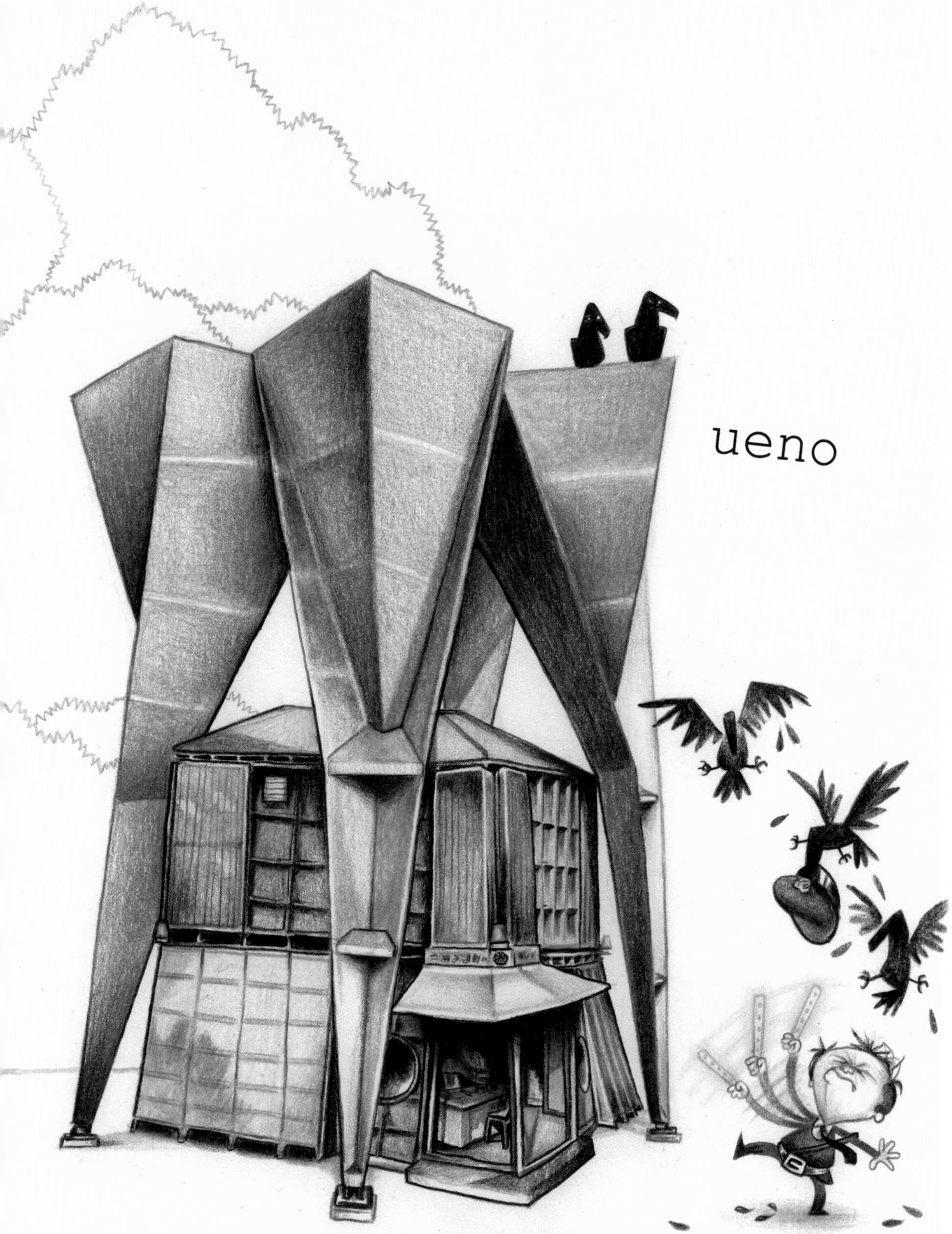

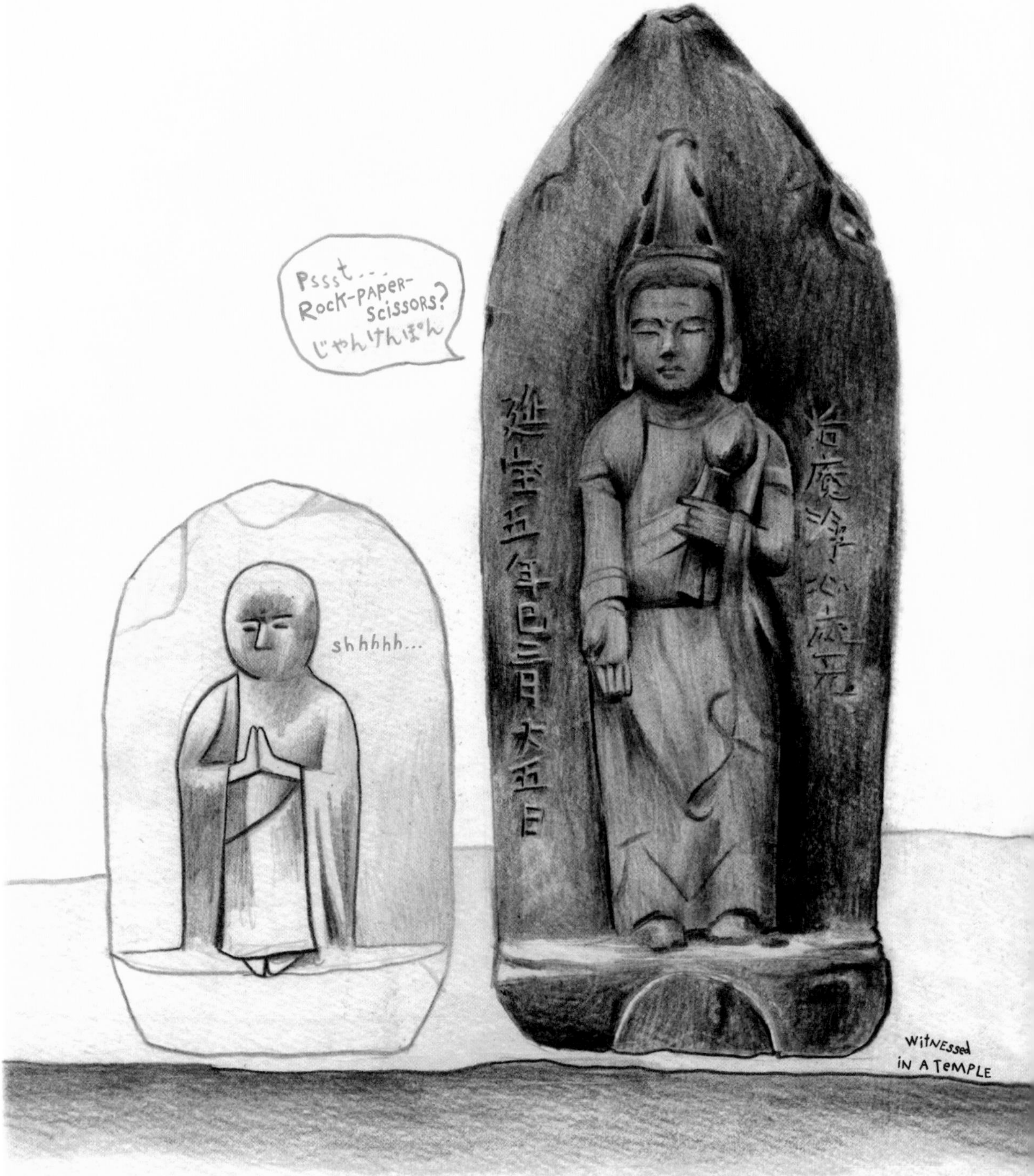
Pssst...
Rock-paper-scissors?
じゃんけんぽん
shhhhh...
Witnessed in a temple

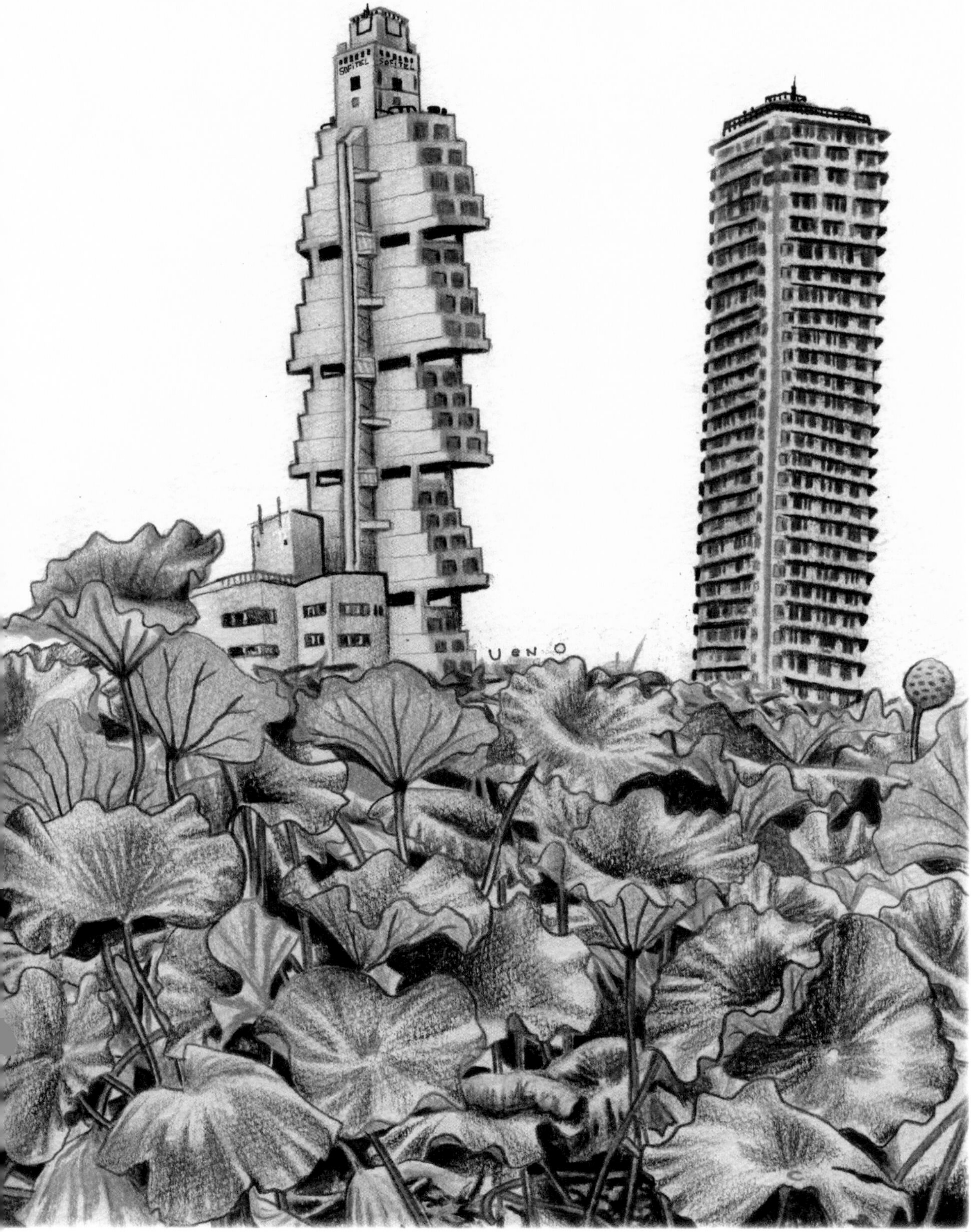
SOFITEL
SOFITEL
UeNO

VIGNETTE FROM UENO

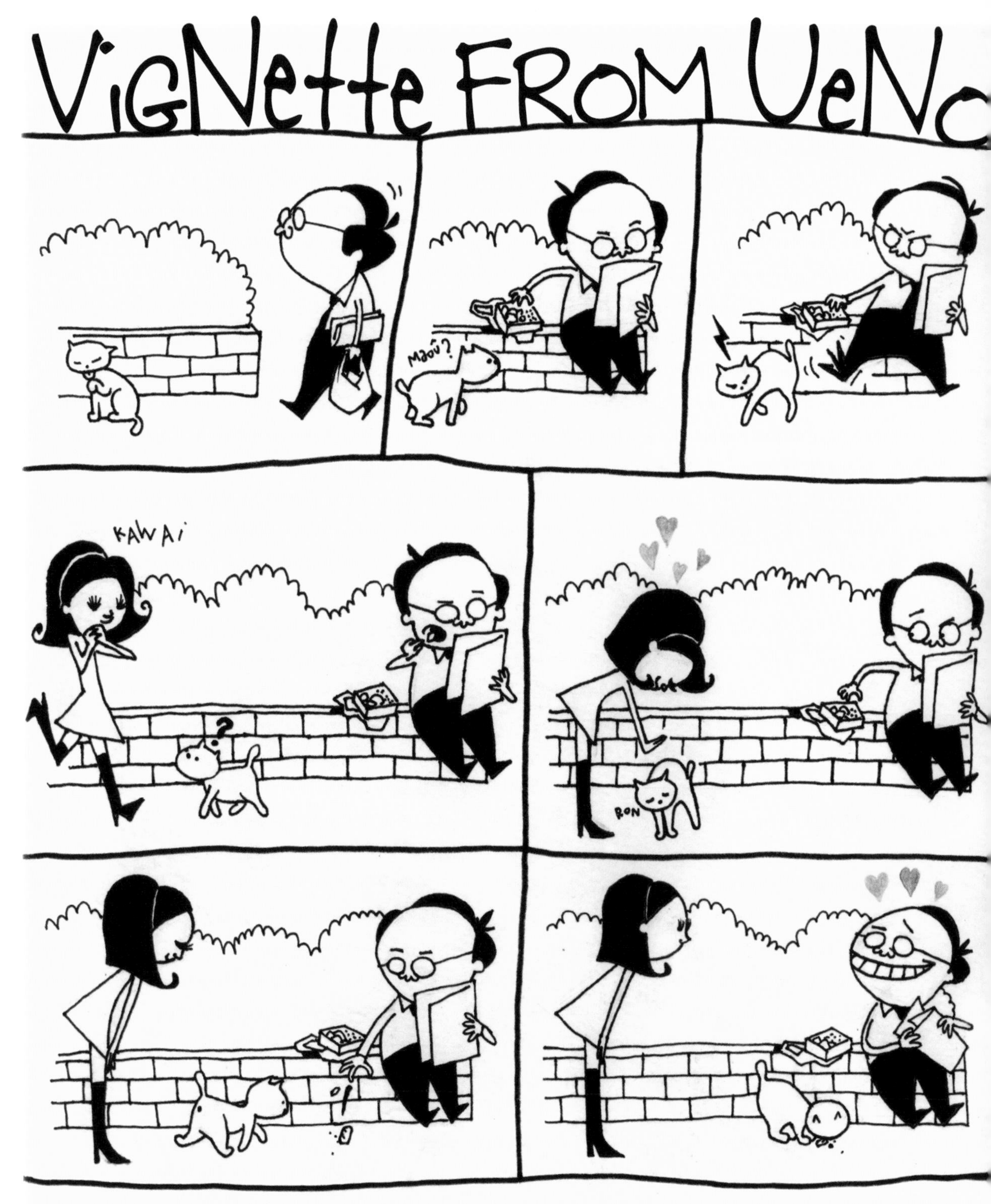
MAOU?
KAWAI
?
BON

interlude

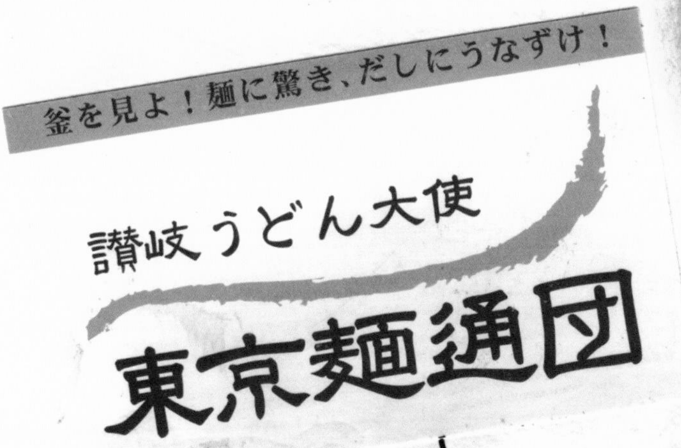

釜を見よ！麺に驚き、だしにうなずけ！
讃岐うどん大使
東京麺通団

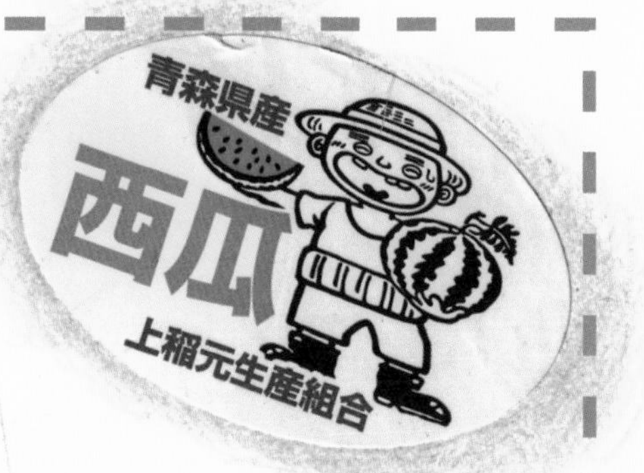

青森県産
西瓜
上稲元生産組合

This is a really good udon restaurant. First you choose the type of udon you want (cold, hot, thick...), the cook gives you the bowl when you come in, and then it's like a a cafeteria with your little tray, where you choose toppings (tempura, etc.) to complement your choice. You pay at the end and then you sit

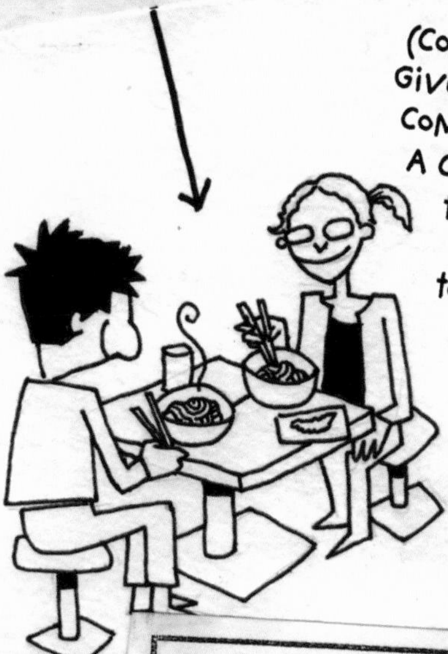

(in an all-wood interior with a decor that subtly evokes Shikoku, the birthplace of the udon noodle).

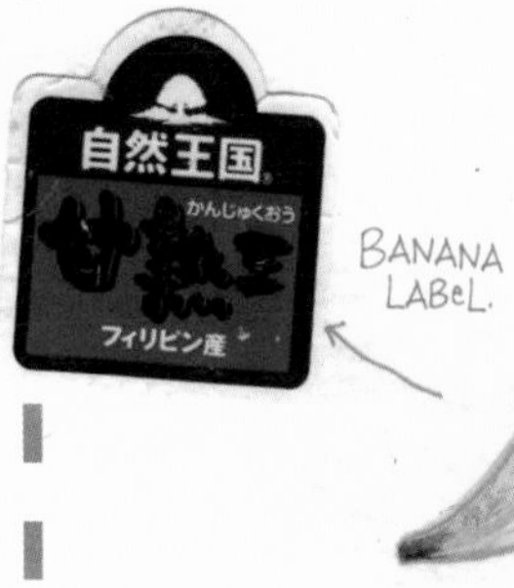

自然王国
甘熟王
かんじゅくおう
フィリピン産

Banana label.

And this is not so good. It's a parking violation sticker that someone is paid to slap onto bikes parked where they shouldn't be (meaning everywhere).

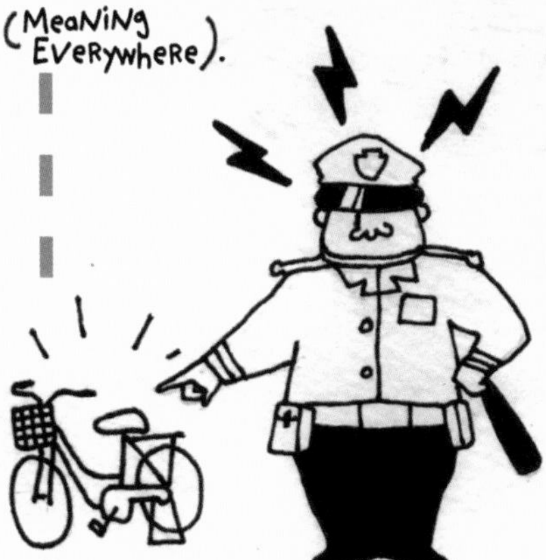

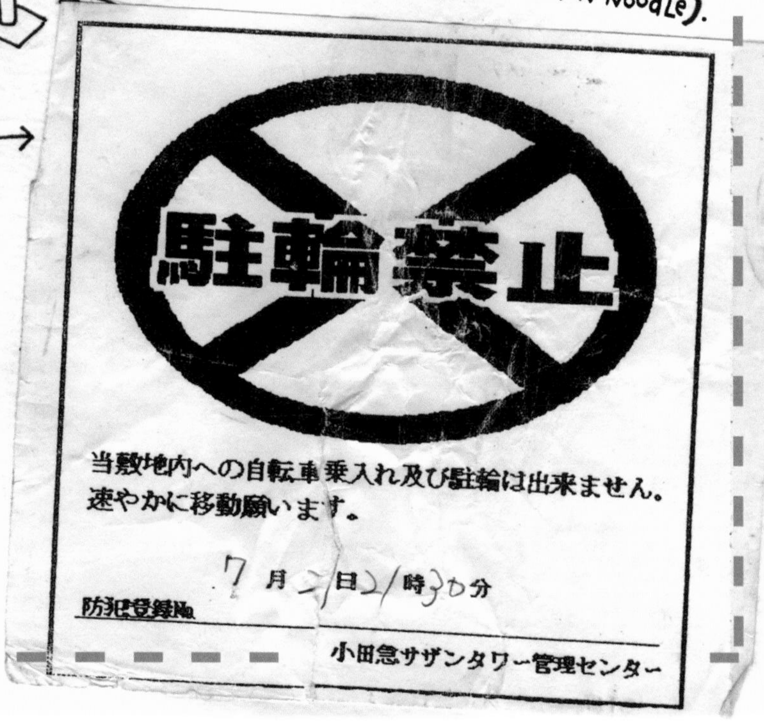
駐輪禁止

当敷地内への自転車乗入れ及び駐輪は出来ません。
速やかに移動願います。

7 月 2 日 21 時 30 分

防犯登録No.

小田急サザンタワー管理センター

The Little
Pleasures:
Jogging in
A K-WAY
Tracksuit
When it's
95 iN
the shade

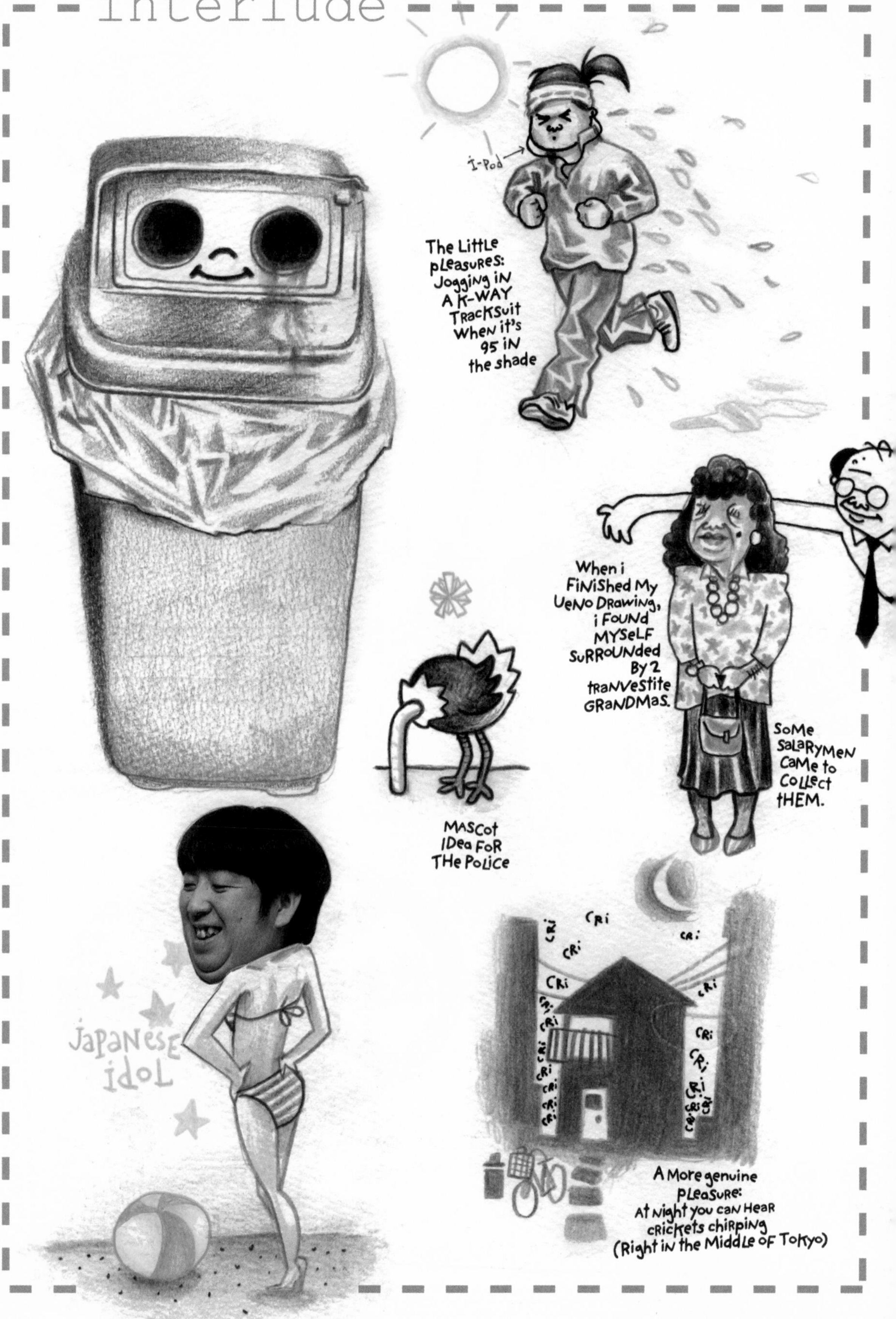

i-Pod →

When i
FINiSHed My
UeNo DRawiNg,
i FOUND
MYSeLF
SuRRouNDed
By 2
tranvestite
GRaNDMas.

SOMe
SaLaRyMeN
CaMe to
COLLect
tHEM.

MASCot
IDea FoR
THe PoLice

JAPANESE
idoL

CRi
CRi
CRi
CRi
CRi
CRi
CRi
CRi
CRi
CRi
CRi
CRi
CRi
CRi
CRi
CRi
CRi
RiG

A More genuine
PLeasuRe:
At night you caN Hear
cRickets chirping
(Right iN the Middle of Tokyo)

ochanomizu

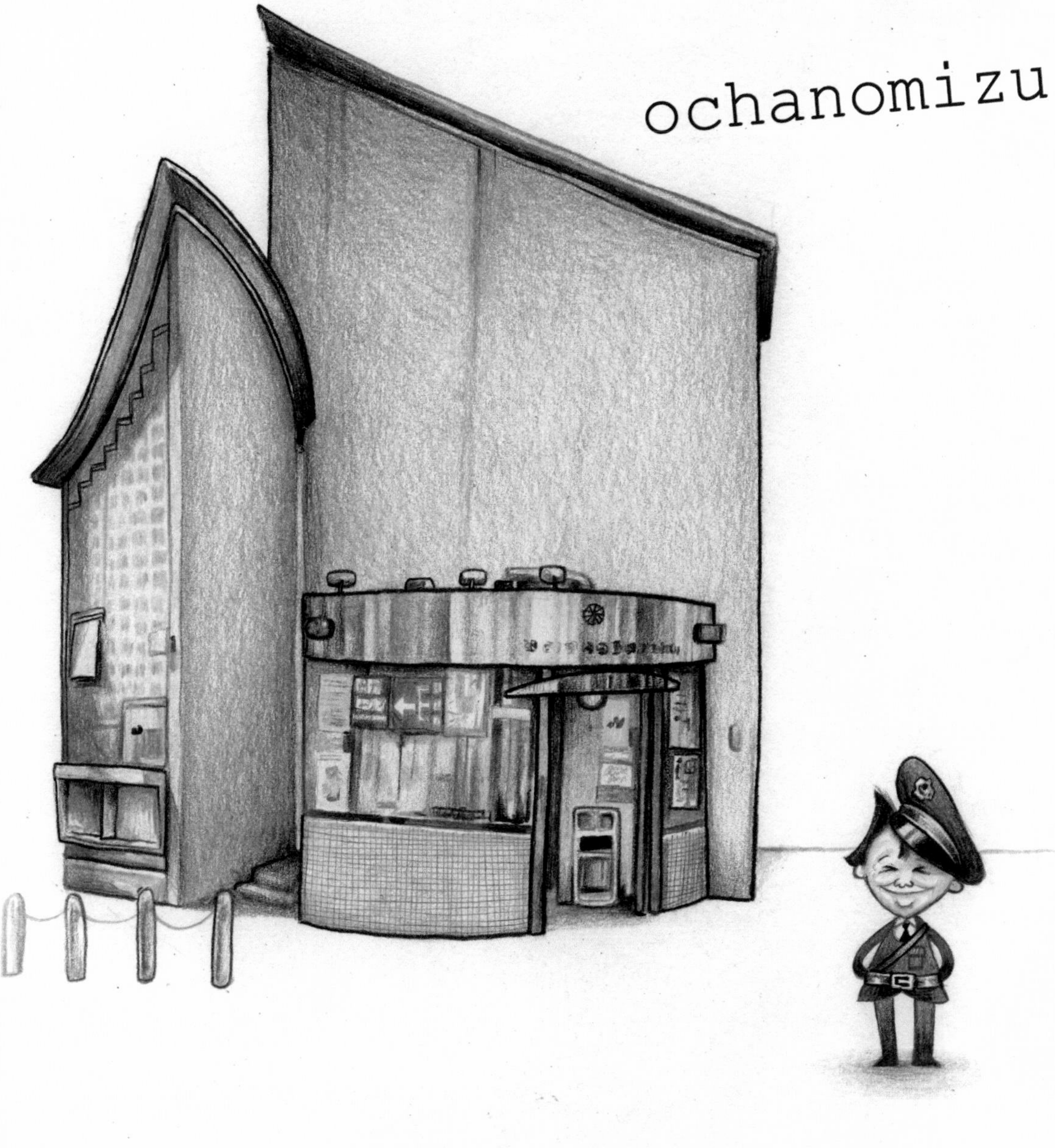

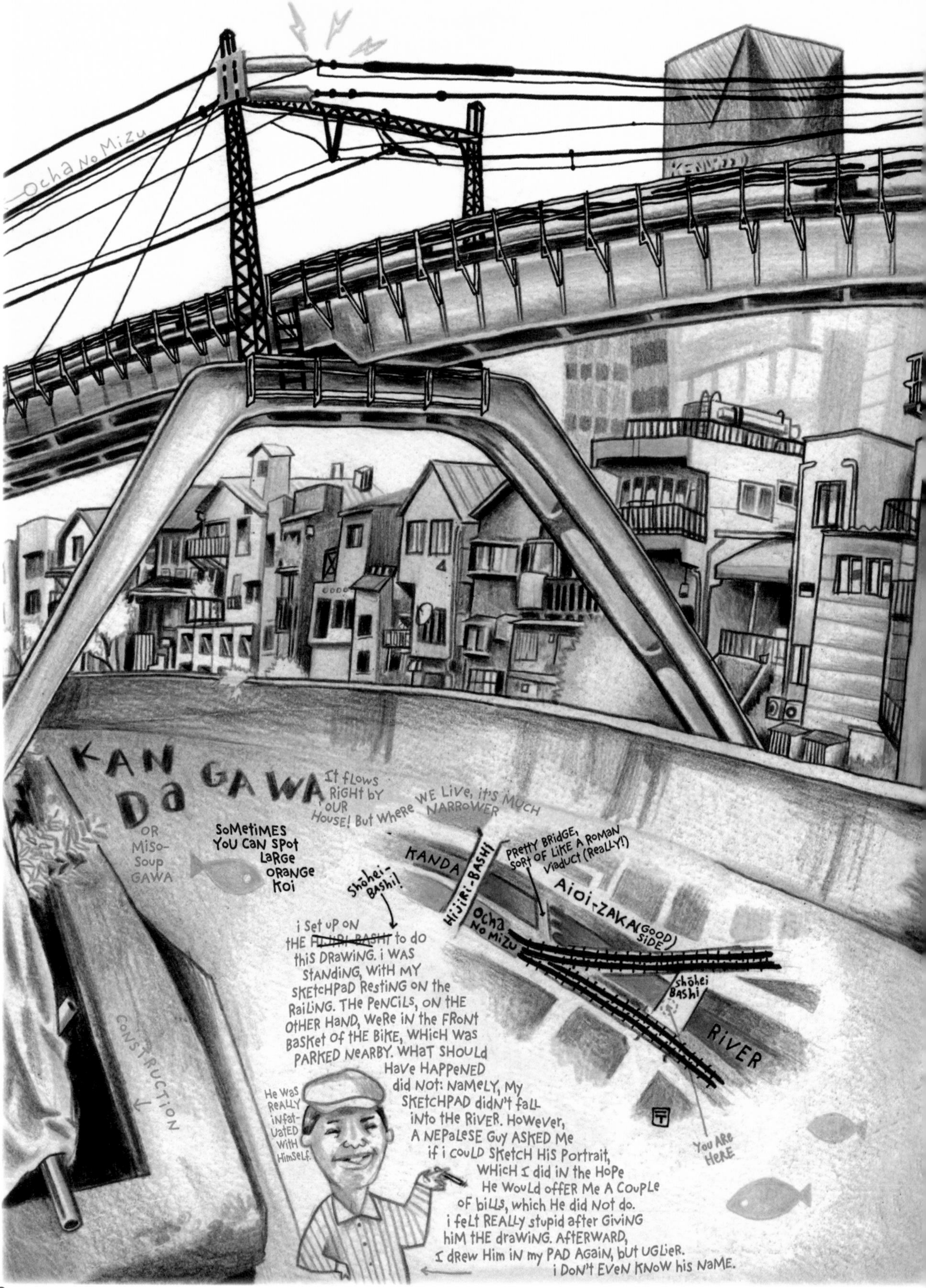

Ocha No Mizu
KENWOOD
KAN Da GAWA
OR Miso-Soup GAWA
It flows RIGHT by OUR HOUSE! But where WE Live, it's MUCH NARROWER
SoMetIMES YOU CAN Spot LaRge ORANGE Koi
KANDA
HiJiRi-BASHi
PRetty BRIDGE, SORT OF LIKE A ROMAN Viaduct (ReaLLY!)
Aioi-ZAKA (GOOD SIDE)
Shōhei-BASHi!
Ocha NO MiZU
Shōhei BASHi
RiVER
CoNSTRUCTION
You ARE HERE
i Set up on the ~~HIJIRI-BASHI~~ to do this DRAWiNG. i WAS STANDiNG, WiTH MY SKETCHPAD ResTiNG ON THE RaiLiNG. THE PENCiLS, ON THE OTHER HAND, WERE iN THE FRONT BASKET OF THE BIKE, WHICH WAS PARKED NEARBY. WHAT SHOULD HAVE HAPPENED did NOT: NAMELY, MY SKETCHPAD didN'T FALL INTO THE RiVER. HOWEVER, A NEPALESE GUY ASKED ME if i COULD SKETCH HIS PORTRAiT, WHICH I did IN THE HOPE HE WOULD OFFER ME A COUPLE OF BiLLS, WHiCH HE did NOT do. i FELT REALLY STUPiD AFTER GiVING HiM THE DRAWiNG. AFTERWARD, I DREW HIM IN MY PAD AGAIN, BUT UGLIER. i DON'T EVEN KNOW HIS NaME.
He WAS REALLY iNFAT-UATED WITH HiMSELF.

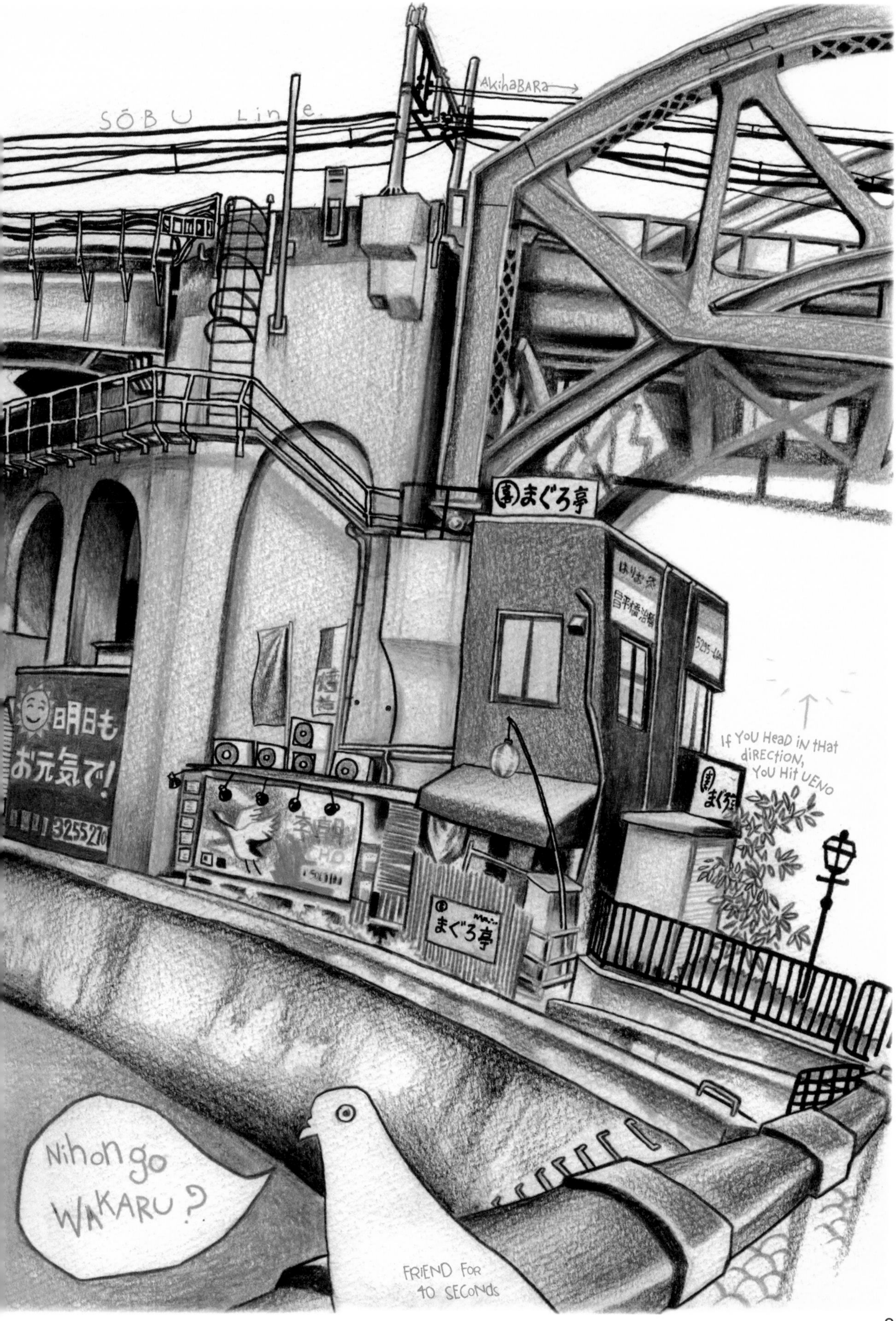
SŌBU Line
AKihaBARA →
まぐろ亭
明日も
お元気で!
まぐろ亭
↑ If YOU HeaD iN tHat diRECtioN, YOU Hit UENO
Nihongo WAKARU?
FRIEND FOR 40 SECONDS

FREEZE-DriEd Veggies ↑

Cup Noodles ARE LiKe PARty-FAVoR bags. So MaNy GOODiES iNSide.

oil

キューピー
からし
マヨネーズ

かやく ス

液1体ソース

3 POUCHES!

CABBAGE, GrEENS, sTUff

MAYoNNaise (SURPRISINGLY POPULAR iN JAPAN)

THIS ENTIRE FEAST FOR ONLY ¥705

JaPANESE "BBQ" SaUCE FOR A YAKi-SoBA ATMOSPHERE iN +HE HOME

P.S: ToDay I WaS detaiNed BECauSe I Crossed (a stREEt, oN fooT) oN A RED Light (for Pedestrians).

90

interlude

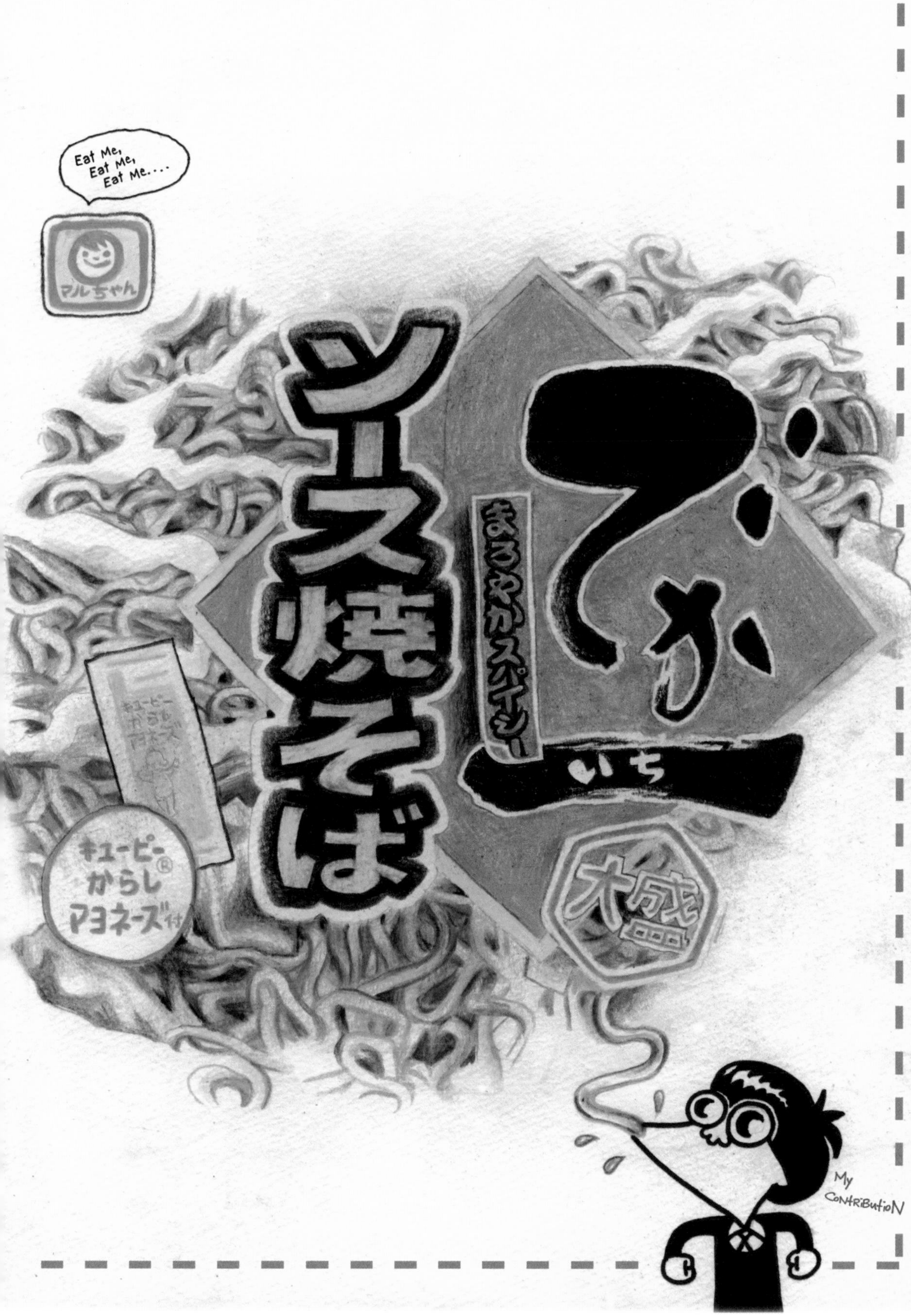
Eat Me,
Eat Me,
Eat Me....
マルちゃん
でか一
いち
まろやかスパイシー
ソース焼そば
大盛
キユーピー®
からし
マヨネーズ付
My
ContRiButioN

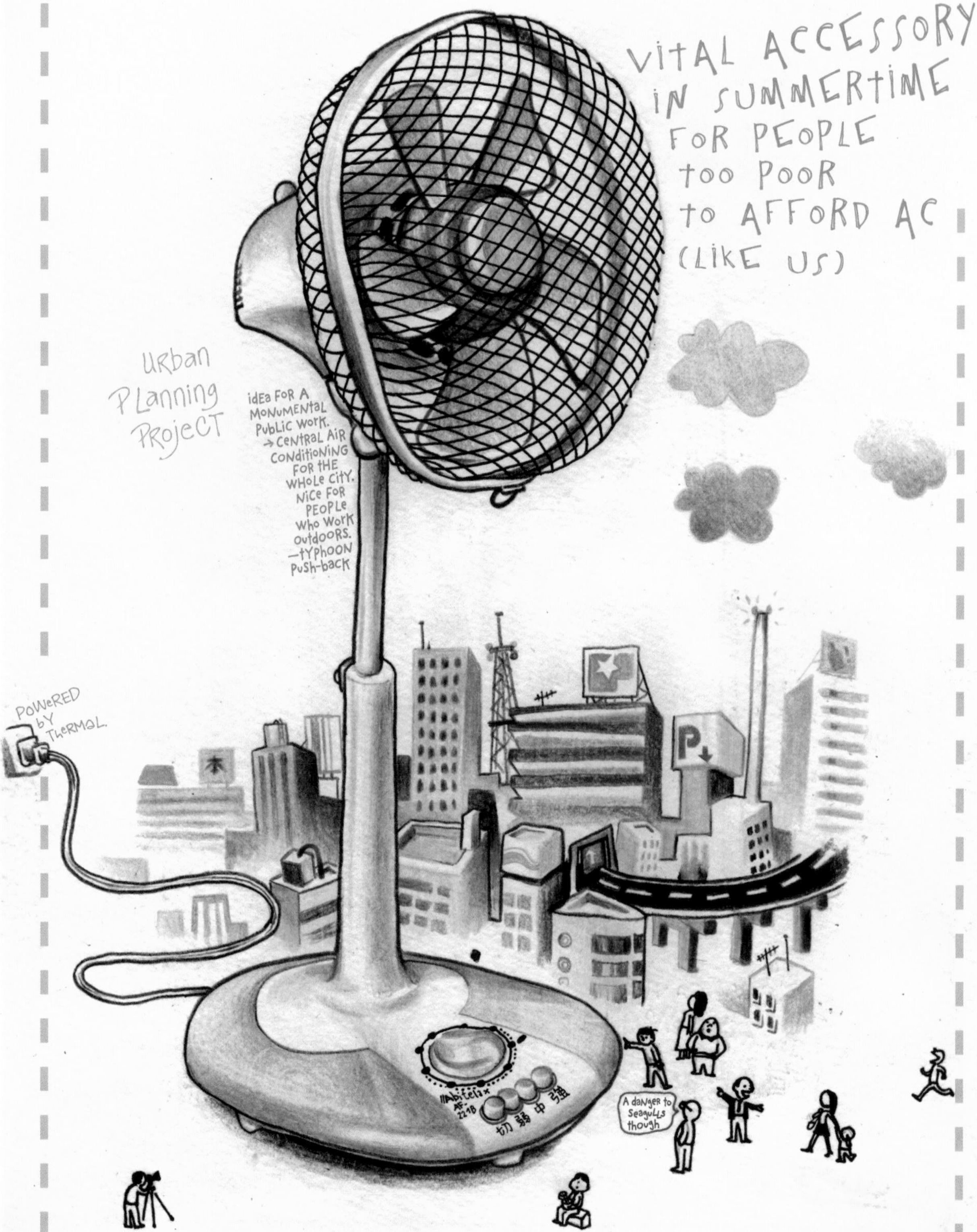
VITAL ACCESSORY
IN SUMMERTIME
FOR PEOPLE
too POOR
to AFFORD AC
(LIKE US)
URban
PLanning
ProjecT
idEa FOR A
MONuMENtaL
PubLic work.
→ CeNtRaL AiR
CONditioNiNG
FOR tHE
WHOLe CitY.
NiCe FOR
PEOPLe
Who Work
outdoORS.
—tYPhoON
PuSh-back
POWeRED
bY
TheRMaL.
Abitelax
AF-
221B
切 弱 中 強
A danger to
Seagulls
though

ichigaya

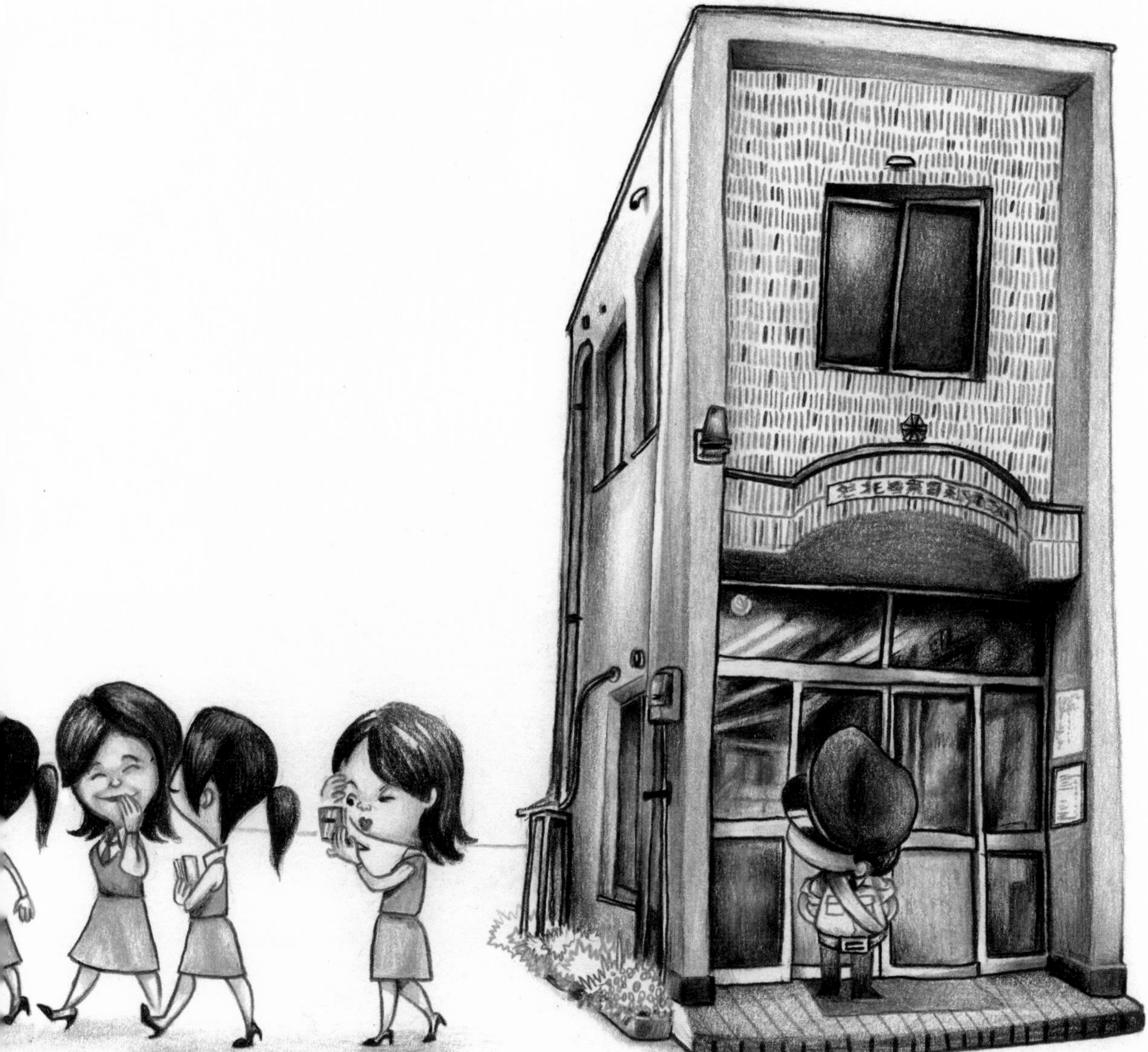

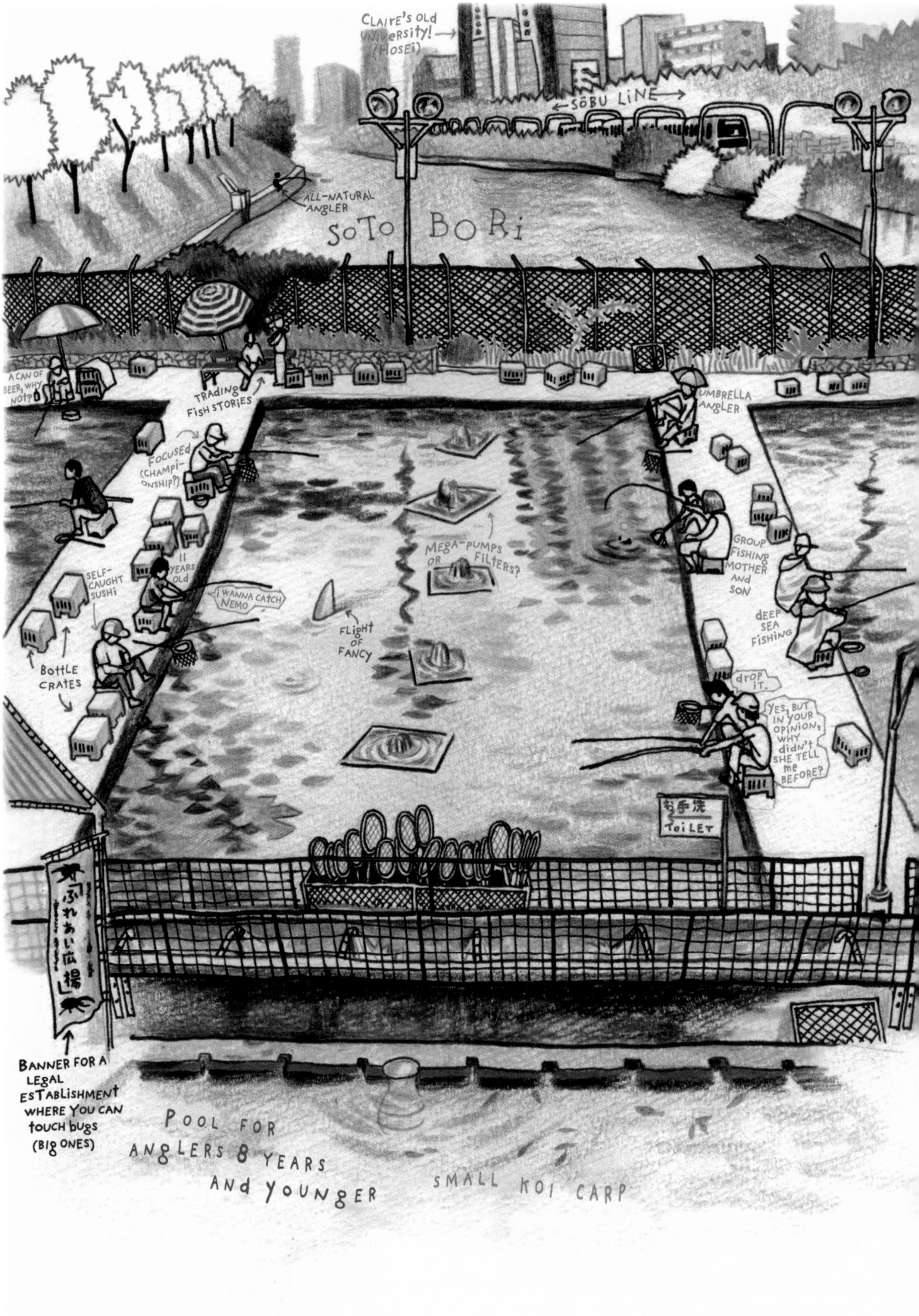

CLAIRE'S OLD UNIVERSITY! (HOSEI)
SŌBU LINE
ALL-NATURAL ANGLER
SOTO BORI
A CAN OF BEER, WHY NOT?
TRADING FISH STORIES
UMBRELLA ANGLER
FOCUSED (CHAMPIONSHIP?)
11 YEARS OLD
SELF-CAUGHT SUSHI
I WANNA CATCH NEMO
MEGA-PUMPS OR FILTERS?
FLIGHT OF FANCY
GROUP FISHING MOTHER AND SON
DEEP SEA FISHING
BOTTLE CRATES
DROP IT.
YES, BUT IN YOUR OPINION, WHY DIDN'T SHE TELL ME BEFORE?
お手洗
TOILET
ふれあい広場
BANNER FOR A LEGAL ESTABLISHMENT WHERE YOU CAN TOUCH BUGS (BIG ONES)
POOL FOR ANGLERS 8 YEARS AND YOUNGER
SMALL KOI CARP

FISHING TRIP

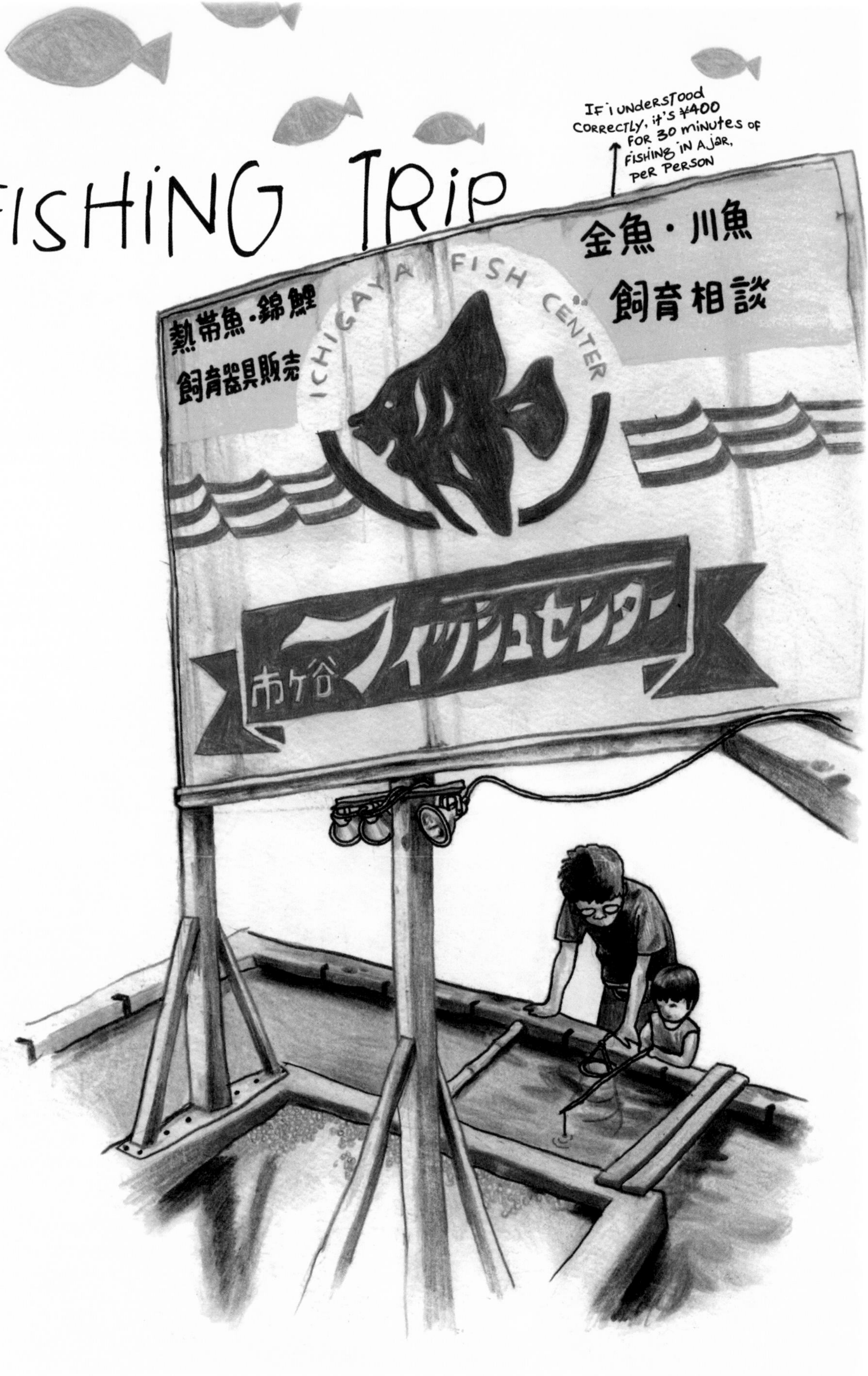

If i understood correctly, it's ¥400 for 30 minutes of fishing in a jar, per person
熱帯魚・錦鯉
飼育器具販売
ICHIGAYA FISH CENTER
金魚・川魚
飼育相談
市ヶ谷 フィッシュセンター

ANOTHER TICKET! WHAT, YOU DON'T LIKE MY BIKE?

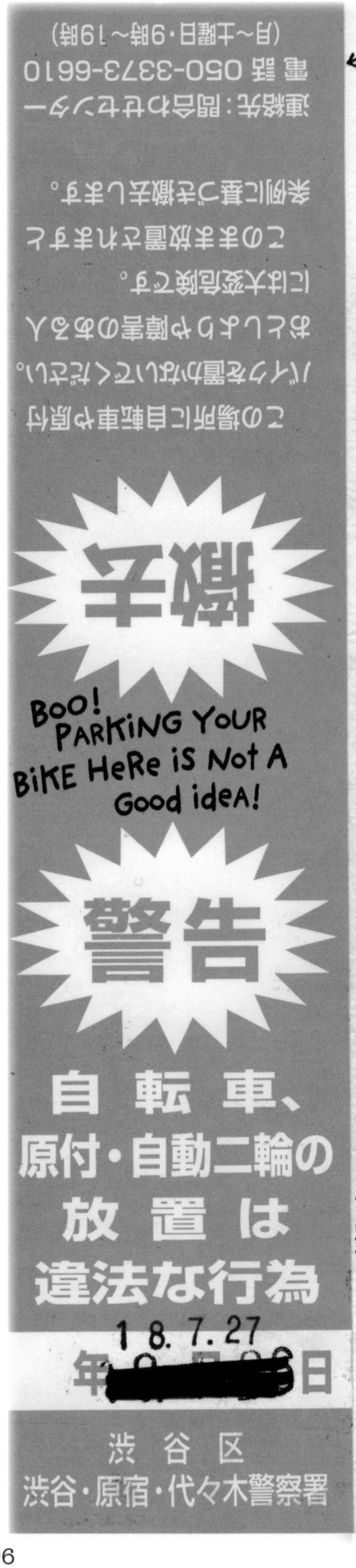
(月～土曜日・9時～19時)
電話 050-3373-6610
連絡先：問合わせセンター
条例に基づき撤去します。
このまま放置されますと
には大変危険です。
お年寄りや障害のある人
バイクを置かないでください。
この場所に自転車や原付
撤去
BOO! PARKING YOUR BIKE HERE IS NOT A GOOD IDEA!
警告
自転車、
原付・自動二輪の
放置は
違法な行為
18.7.27
年[redacted]日
渋谷区
渋谷・原宿・代々木警察署

- interlude - -

LET'S TALK MONEY

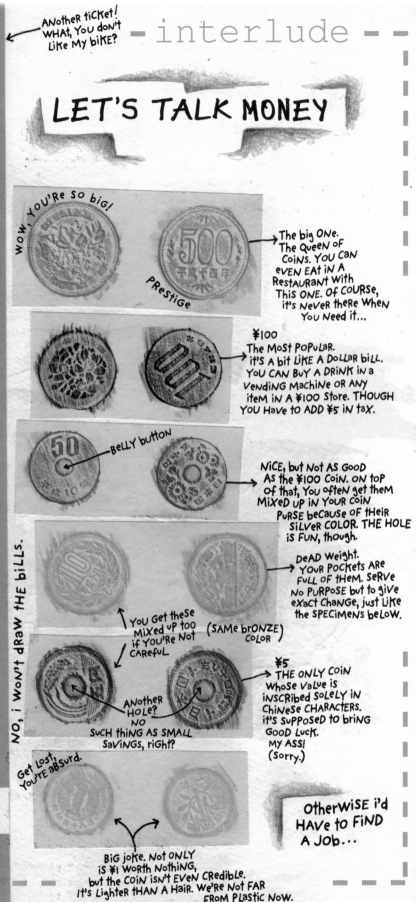

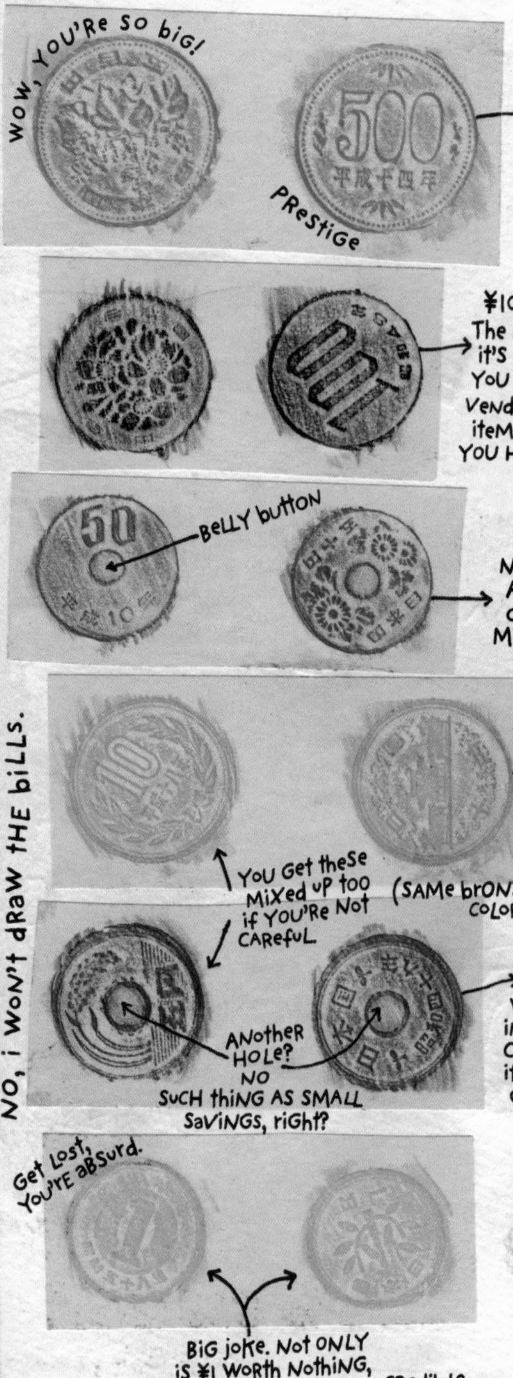
WOW, YOU'RE SO BIG!
PRESTIGE
BELLY BUTTON
NO, I WON'T DRAW THE BILLS.
YOU GET THESE MIXED UP TOO IF YOU'RE NOT CAREFUL.
(SAME BRONZE COLOR)
ANOTHER HOLE? NO SUCH THING AS SMALL SAVINGS, RIGHT?
GET LOST, YOU'RE ABSURD.

The big ONE. The QUEEN OF COINS. YOU CAN EVEN EAT IN A RESTAURANT WITH THIS ONE. OF COURSE, IT'S NEVER THERE WHEN YOU NEED IT...

¥100
The MOST POPULAR. IT'S A BIT LIKE A DOLLAR BILL. YOU CAN BUY A DRINK IN A VENDING MACHINE OR ANY ITEM IN A ¥100 STORE. THOUGH YOU HAVE TO ADD ¥5 IN TAX.

NICE, BUT NOT AS GOOD AS THE ¥100 COIN. ON TOP OF THAT, YOU OFTEN GET THEM MIXED UP IN YOUR COIN PURSE BECAUSE OF THEIR SILVER COLOR. THE HOLE IS FUN, THOUGH.

DEAD WEIGHT. YOUR POCKETS ARE FULL OF THEM. SERVE NO PURPOSE BUT TO GIVE EXACT CHANGE, JUST LIKE THE SPECIMENS BELOW.

¥5
THE ONLY COIN WHOSE VALUE IS INSCRIBED SOLELY IN CHINESE CHARACTERS. IT'S SUPPOSED TO BRING GOOD LUCK. MY ASS! (SORRY.)

BIG JOKE. NOT ONLY IS ¥1 WORTH NOTHING, BUT THE COIN ISN'T EVEN CREDIBLE. IT'S LIGHTER THAN A HAIR. WE'RE NOT FAR FROM PLASTIC NOW.

OTHERWISE I'D HAVE TO FIND A JOB...

west shinjuku

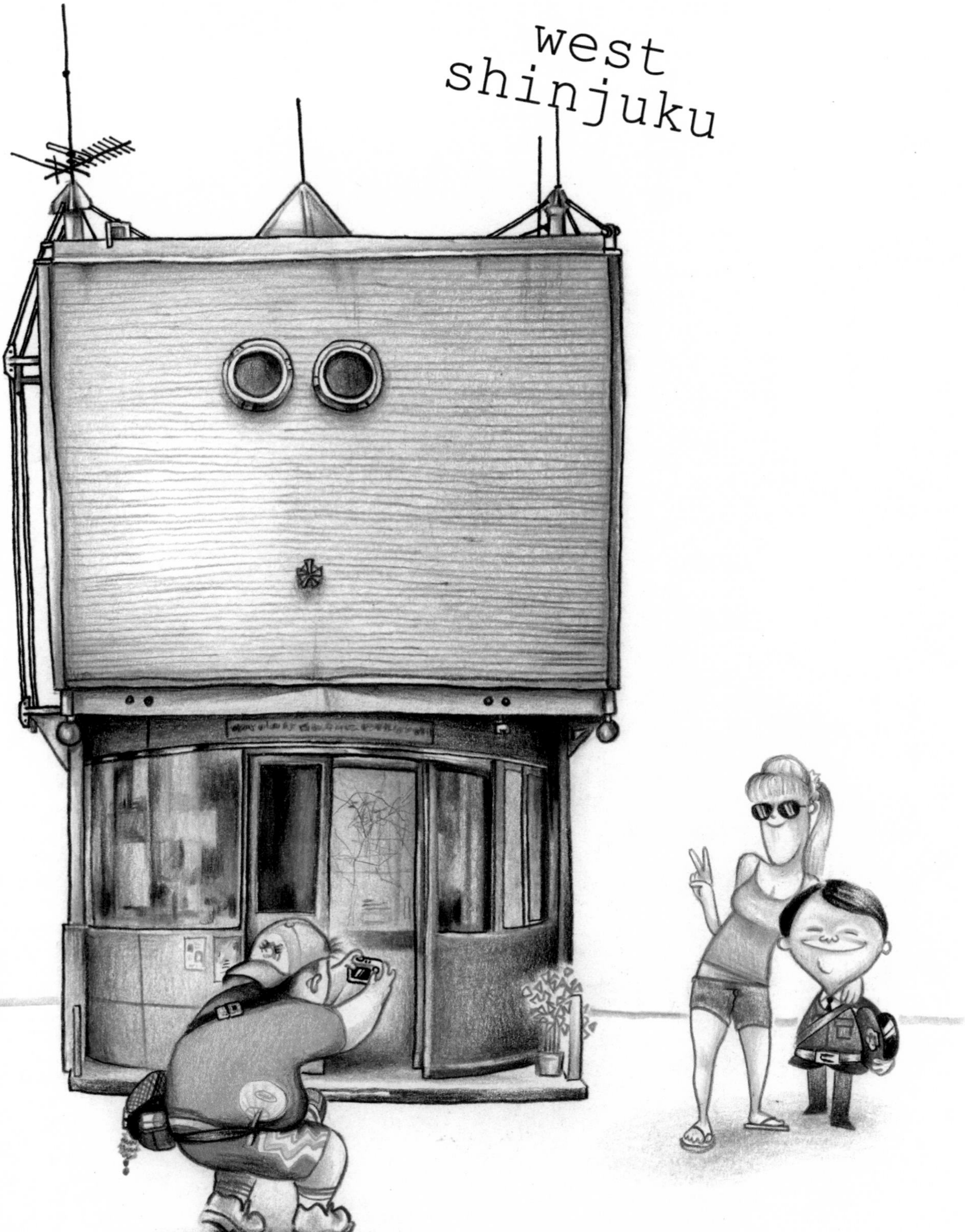

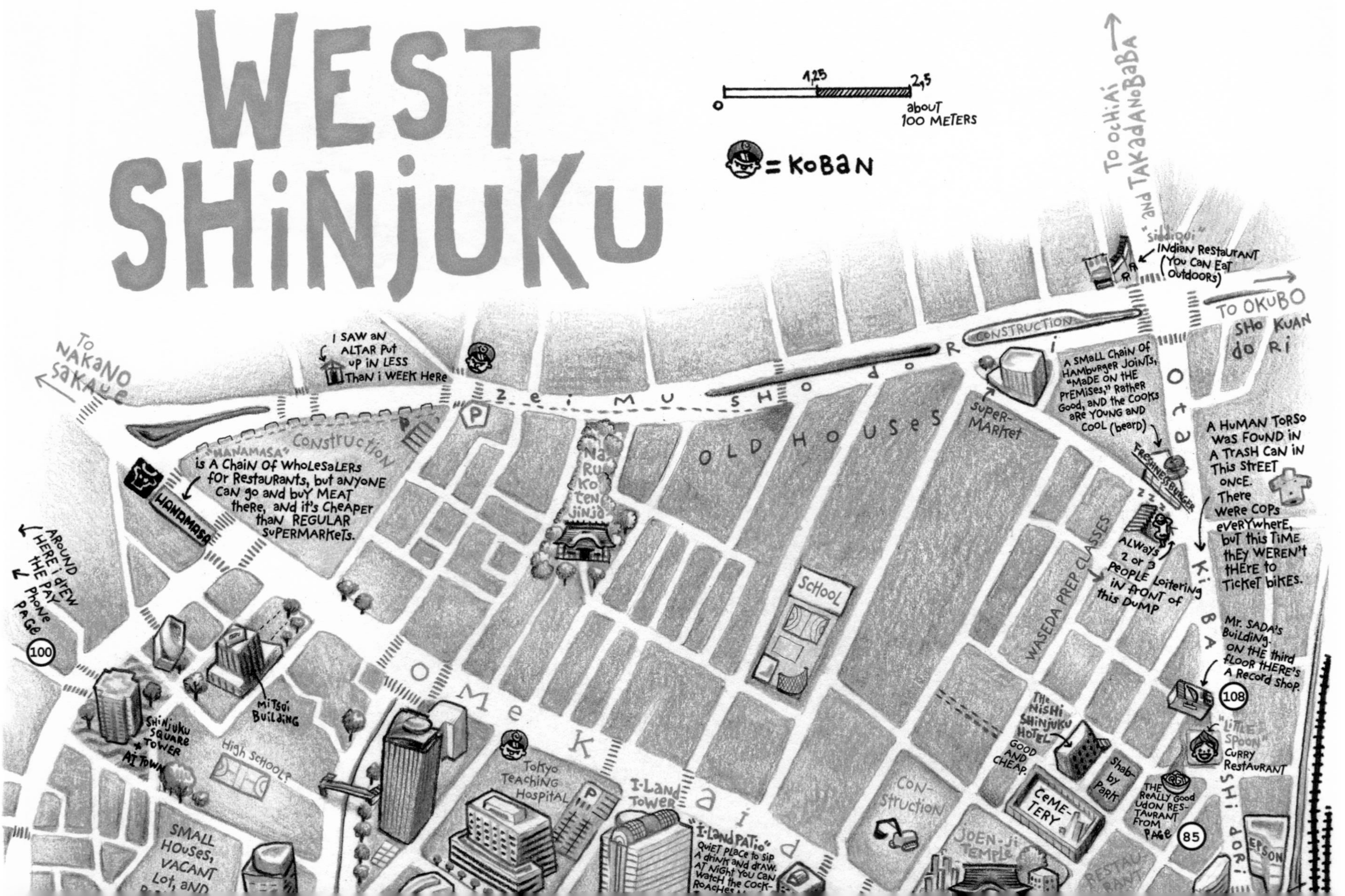
WEST SHiNjuKu
0
1,25
2,5
about 100 METERS
= KoBaN
To ocHiAi and TAKadaNoBaBA
"siddiqui" INdian Restaurant (You Can Eat outdoors)
TO OKUBO
SHo KUAN do Ri
TO NAKaNO SaKaue
I SAW aN ALTAR Put up iN LESS Than i WEEK Here
CONSTRUCTION
ZeiMU SHO doRi
A SMall Chain of Hamburger Joints, "MaDE ON THE PREMISES," Rather Good, aND the Cooks aRe YOUNG aND COOL (beard)
FRESHNESS BURGER
OTa
A HuMAN TORSO Was FOUND iN A TRASH CaN iN This STREET ONCE. There were COPs everywhere, buT this TiME they WEREN'T tHEre to TicKeT biKES.
SUPER-MARKet
OLD HOUSES
"NANAMASA" is A Chain Of Wholesalers for Restaurants, but anyone can go and buy MEAT there, and it's Cheaper than REGULAR SUPERMARKETS.
Construction
NANAMASA
NaRuKo tenjinja
SCHOOL
WASEDA PREP CLASSES
ALways 2 or 3 PEOPLE Loitering iN fRONT of this DUMP
KiBA
Mr. SADA's Building. ON THE third FLOOR THERE's A Record Shop.
108
AROUND HERE i drew THE PAY Phone PaGe
100
MiTsui Building
SHiNjuku SQUARE TOWER + AI TOWN
High School?
OMEKaido
Tokyo Teaching Hospital
I-Land Tower
"I-LandPATio" QUIET PLACE to sip A drink and draw. AT NIGHT YOU CAN WatcH the COCK-ROACHES.
CON-Struction
THE NISHi SHiNjuku HOTEL GOOD AND CHEAP.
Shab-by Park
CeMe-TERY
JOEN-JI TEMPLE
"LITTLE SPOON" CURRY RESTAURANT
THE REALLY Good UDON RES-TAURANT FROM PAGE 85
SMALL HOUSES, VACANT Lot, aND
SHi dORi

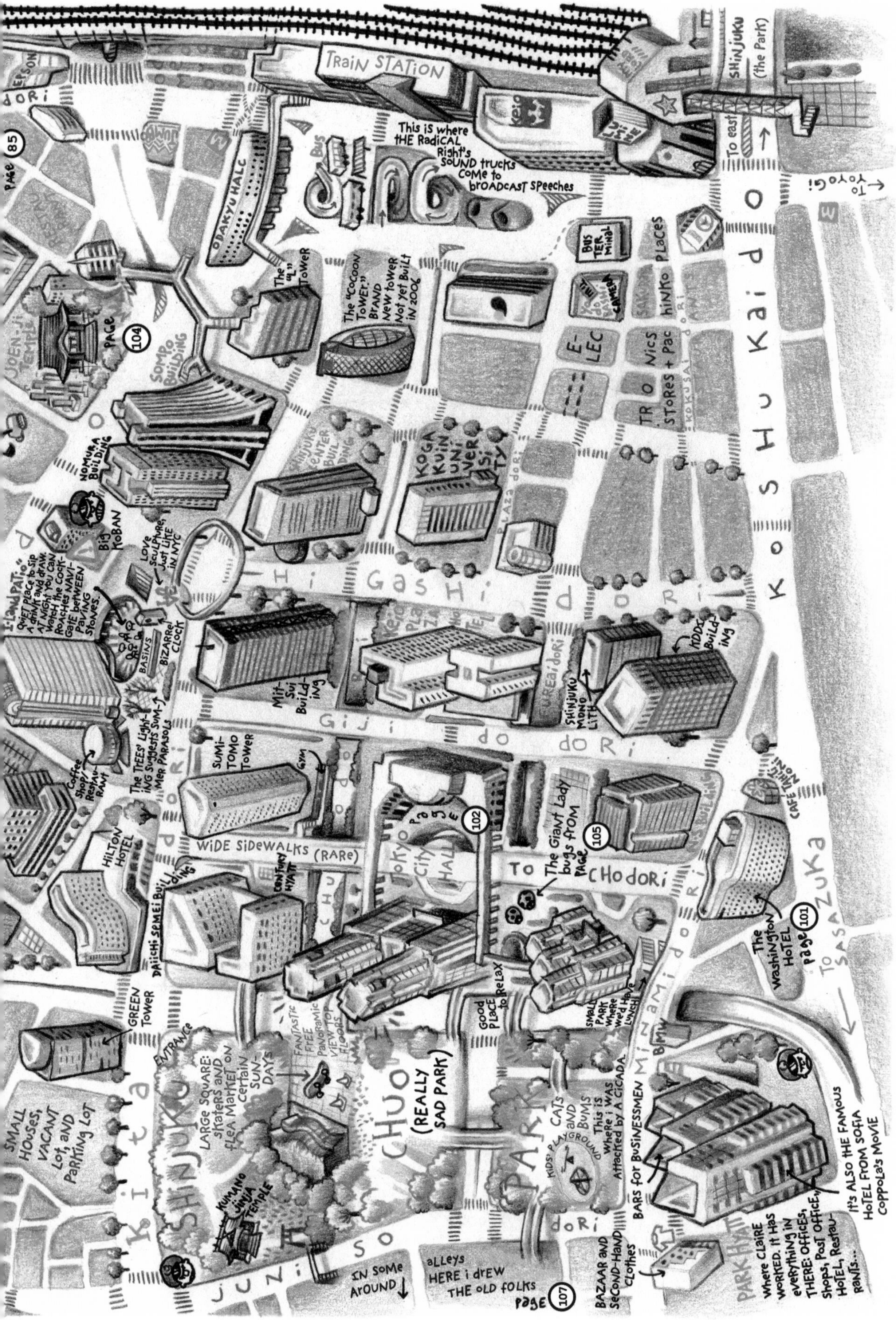
TRAIN STATION
This is where tHE RadiCAL Right's SOUND trucks COME to broadcast Speeches
Bus
ODAKYU HALC
keio
SHINJUKU (the Park)
To east
TO YOYOGI
PAGE 85
dORi
BUS TER MINAL
CAMERA
ELEC TRO NICS STORES + Pachinko PLACES
KOKUSAI dORI
KOSHU KAIDO
The "L" TOWER
The "COCOON TOWER" BRAND NEW TOWER NOT YET BUILT IN 2006
SOMPO BUILDING
PAGE 104
JOEN-JI TEMPLE
NOMURA BUILDING
SHINJUKU CENTER BUILDING
KOGA KUIN UNI VER SI TY
PLAZA dORi
Big KOBAN
Love sculpture, just like in NYC
I-LAND PATIO "quiet place to sip a drink and draw. At night you can watch the cockroaches navigate between paving stones."
BASINS
BIZARRE CLOCK
HiGaSHi dORi
Keio Plaza Hotel
Mitsui Building
CHUO dORi
SHINJUKU MONOLITH
KDDI Building
The TREES' Lighting Suggests Summer Parasols
Coffee Shop/Restaurant
GiJidO dORi
SUMITOMO TOWER
GYM
HILTON HOTEL
WIDE SIDEWALKS (RARE)
Tokyo City HALL page 102
The Giant Lady bugs FROM page 105
NS Building
CAFE NONI
TO CHODORi
DAI-ICHI SEIMEI BUILDING
CENTURY HYATT
The Washington HOTEL page 101
TO SASAZUKA
GREEN TOWER
ENTRANCE
FANTASTIC FREE PANORAMIC VIEW TOP FLOORS
Good PLACE to ReLax
SMALL PARK WHERE we'd have LUNCH
MINAMI DORI
BMW
SMALL HOUSES, VACANT Lot, AND PARKING LOT
KITA
SHINJUKU CHUO PARK (REALLY SAD PARK)
LARGE SQUARE: SKATERS AND FLEA MARKET ON CERTAIN SUNDAYS
CATS AND BUMS
KIDS' PLAYGROUND
This is where i was attacked by A CICADA.
KUMANO JINJA TEMPLE
JUNISO dORi
BARS FOR BUSINESSMEN
IN SOME alleys AROUND HERE i drew THE OLD folks page 107
BAZAAR AND SECOND-HAND clothes
PARK HYATT Where CLAIRE WORKED. It has everything in there: offices, shops, post office, hotel, restaurants...
It's ALSO THE FAMOUS HOTEL FROM SOFIA COPPOLA's MOVIE

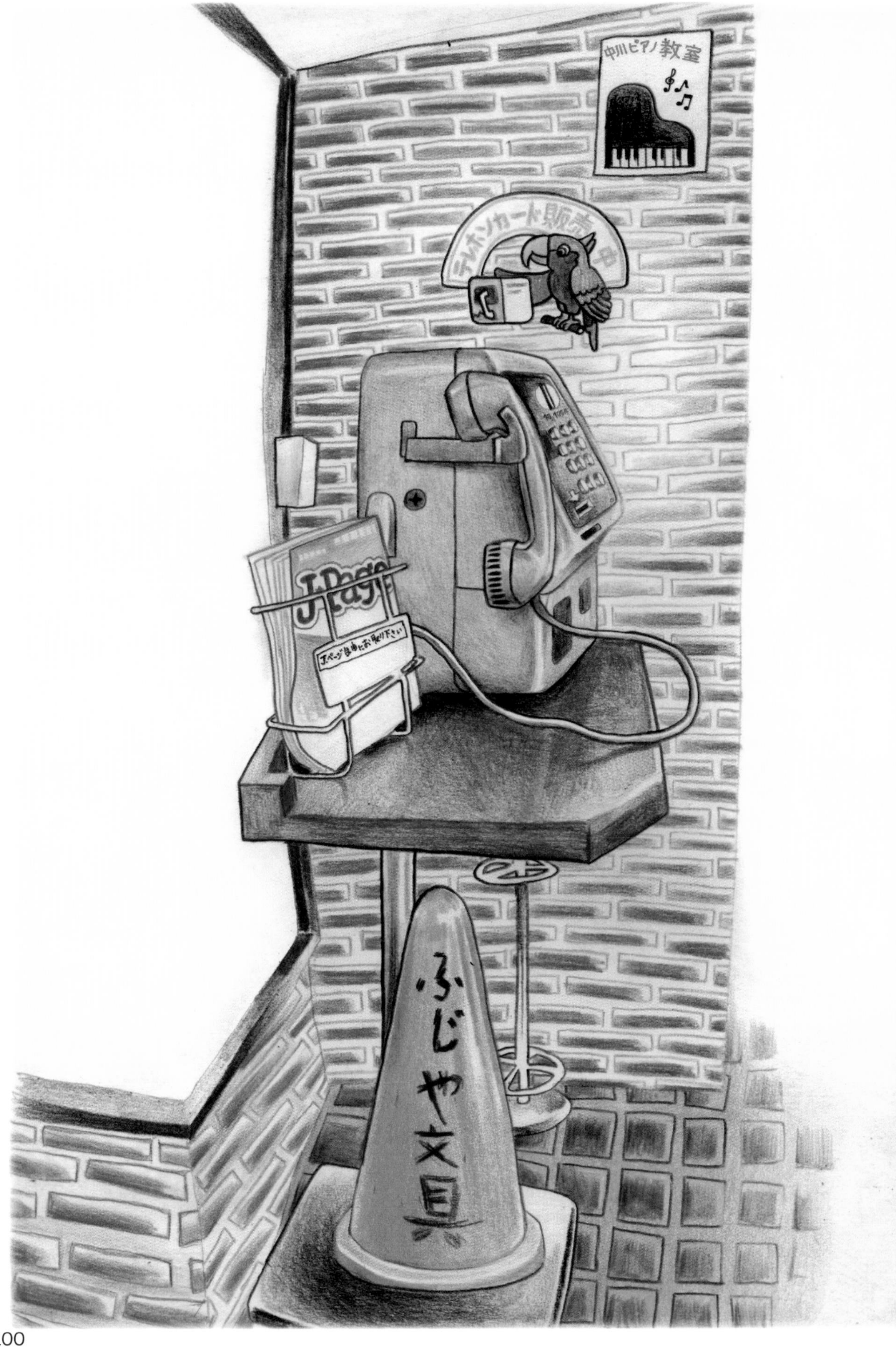
中川ピアノ教室
テレホンカード販売中
J-Page
Jページ自由にお取り下さい
ふじや文具

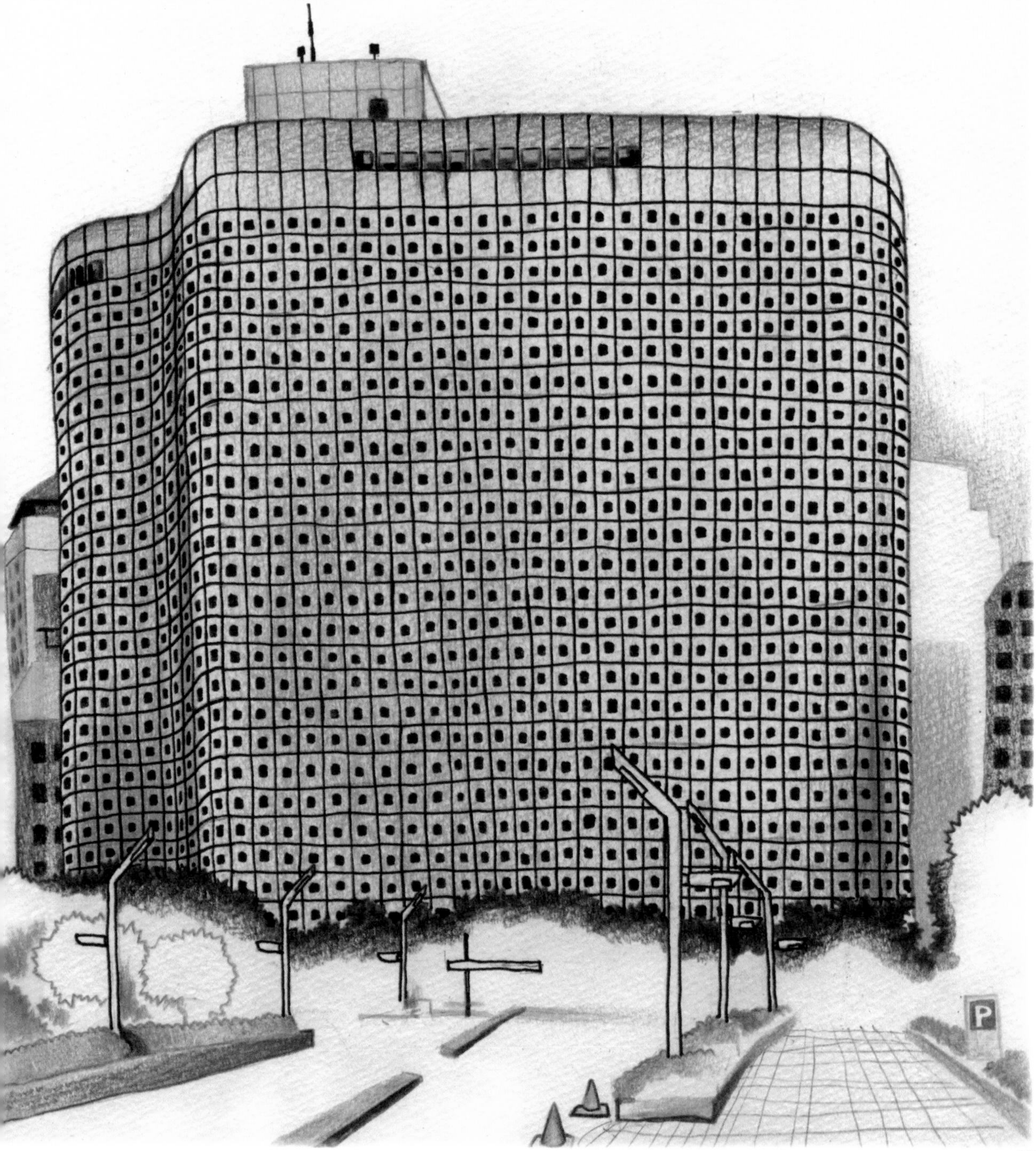
P

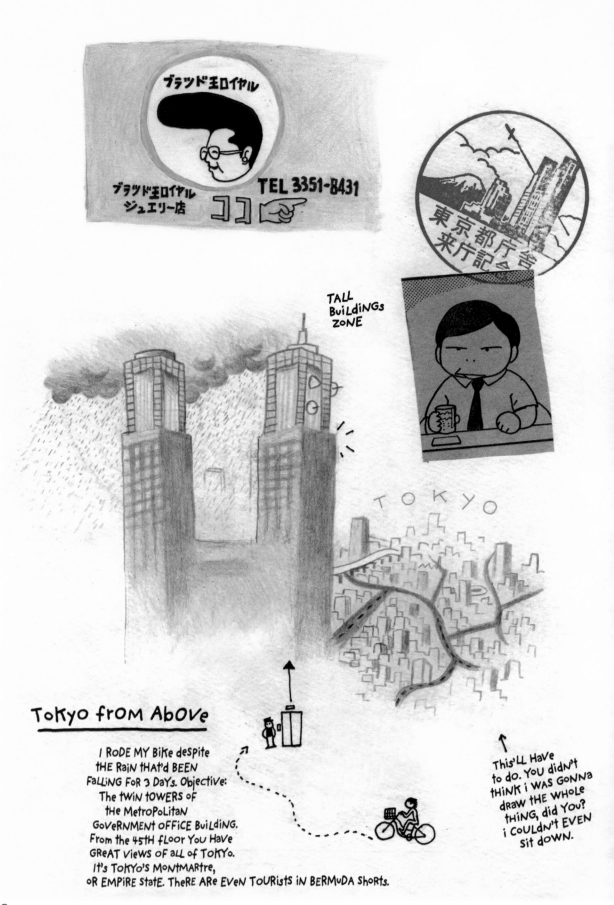

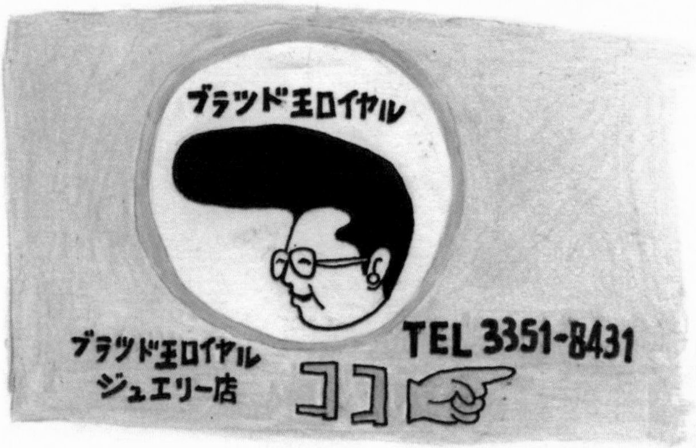
ブラッド王ロイヤル
ブラッド王ロイヤル
ジュエリー店
ココ
TEL 3351-8431

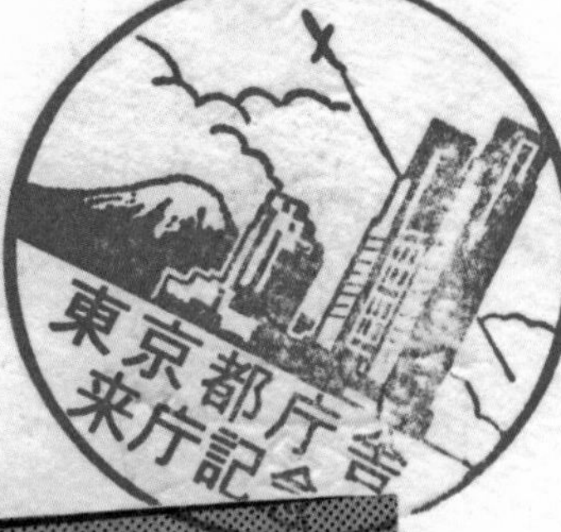
東京都庁
来庁記念

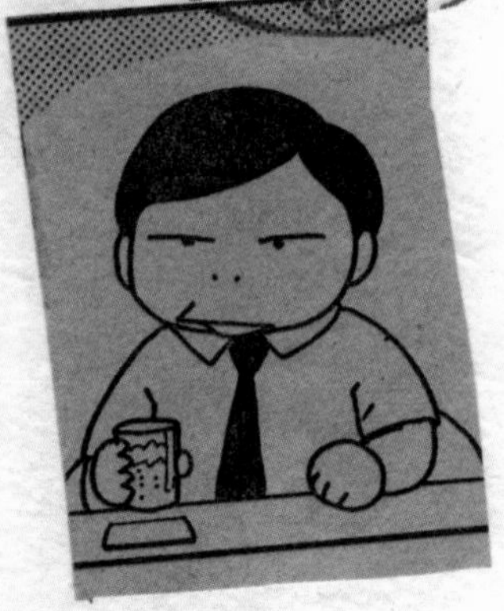

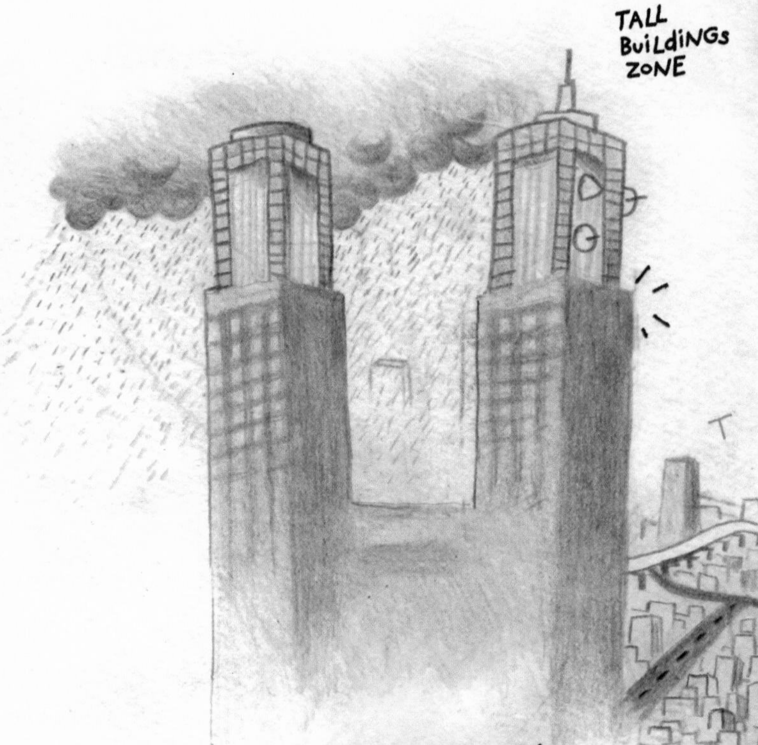
TALL BUILDINGS ZONE

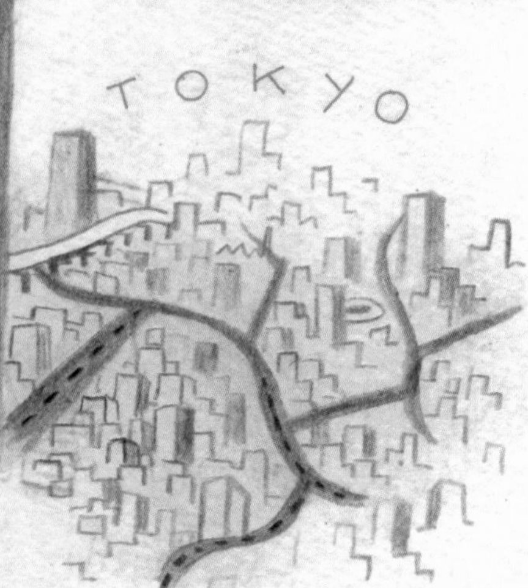
TOKYO
This'll Have to do. You didn't think i was gonna draw the whole thing, did you? i couldn't even sit down.

Tokyo from Above

I rode my bike despite the rain that'd been falling for 3 days. Objective: The twin towers of the Metropolitan Government Office Building. From the 45th floor you have great views of all of Tokyo. It's Tokyo's Montmartre, or Empire State. There are even tourists in Bermuda shorts.

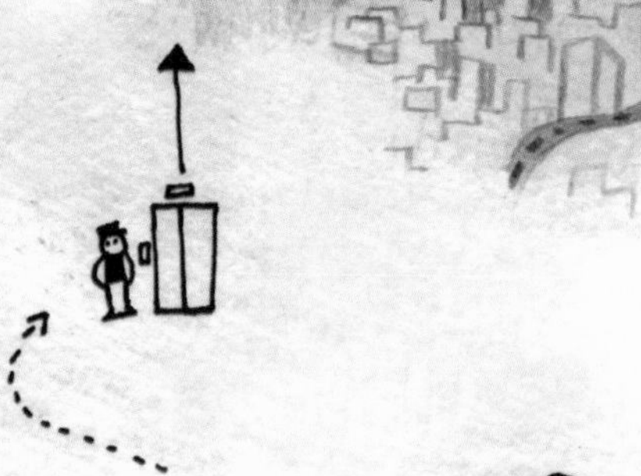

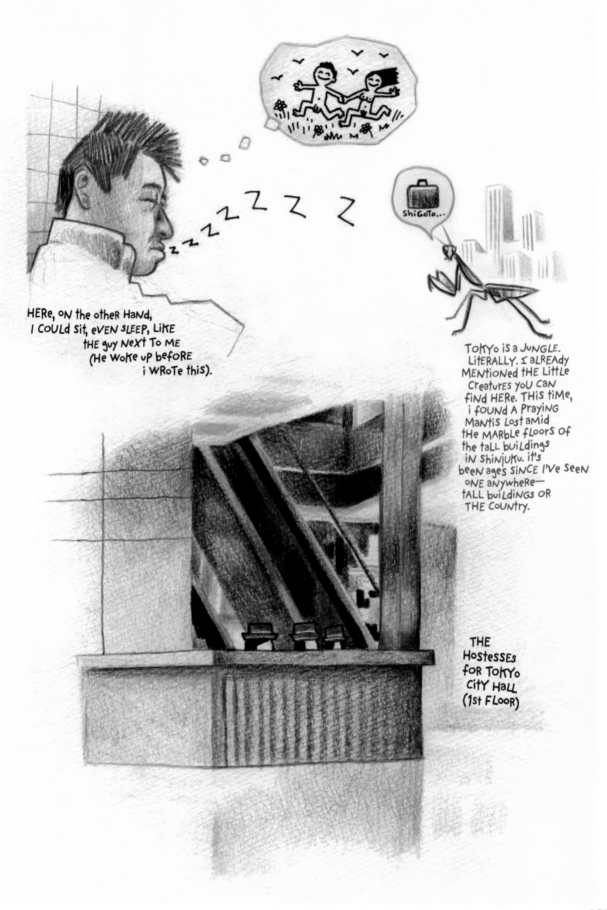

ShiGoTo...

HERe, ON the other HaNd, I COULd Sit, eVEN SLEEP, LiKe tHE guy NeXt To Me (He woke uP befORE i wRoTe this).

TOKYo iS a JUNGLE. LiteRALLY. I aLReAdy MeNTioNed tHE LiTtLe Creatures you caN fiNd HERe. THis time, i fOUNd A Praying MaNtis Lost amid tHe MARble flOoRs Of the taLL buildiNgs iN SHiNjuKu. it's beeN ages SiNCE I've SeeN ONE aNyWHeRe— taLL buildiNgs OR THE COUNTRy.

THE HostesSes fOR TOKYo CiTy HaLL (1st FLoOR)

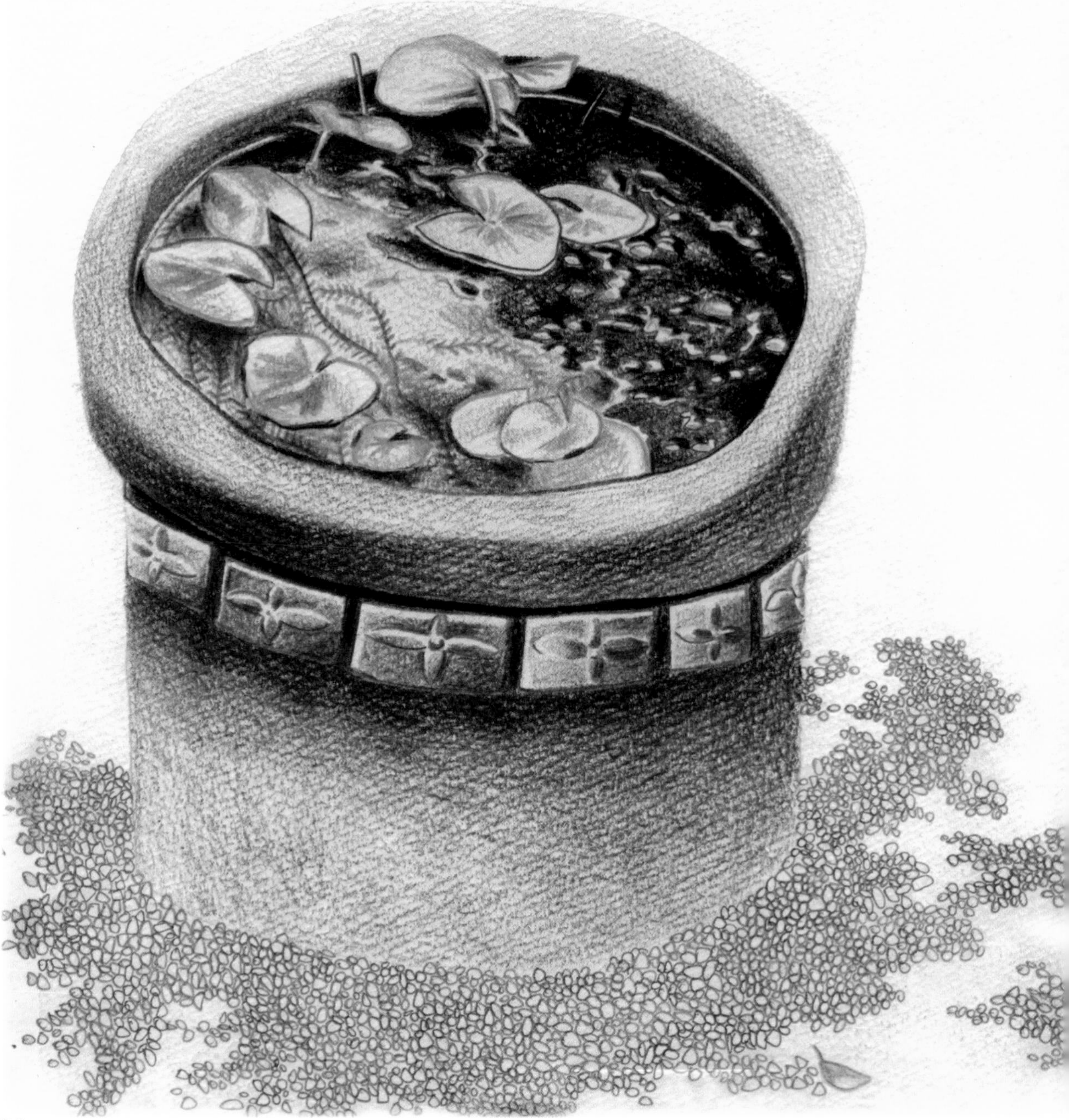

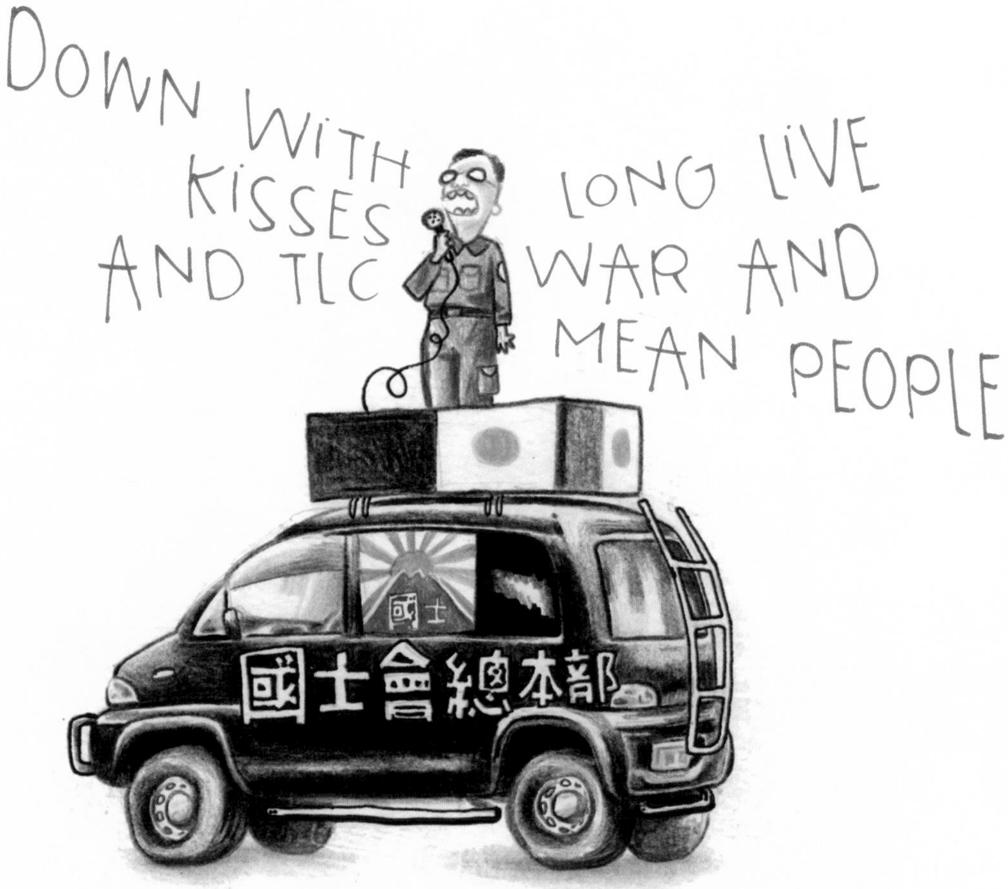
DOWN WITH KISSES AND TLC
LONG LIVE WAR AND MEAN PEOPLE
國士
國士會總本部

Giant LADYBUGS at THE base of THE MetROPOLITAN GOV't office TOWERS. i WAITED HERE to go eat WITH CLAIRE, SINCE Her office is NEARBY.

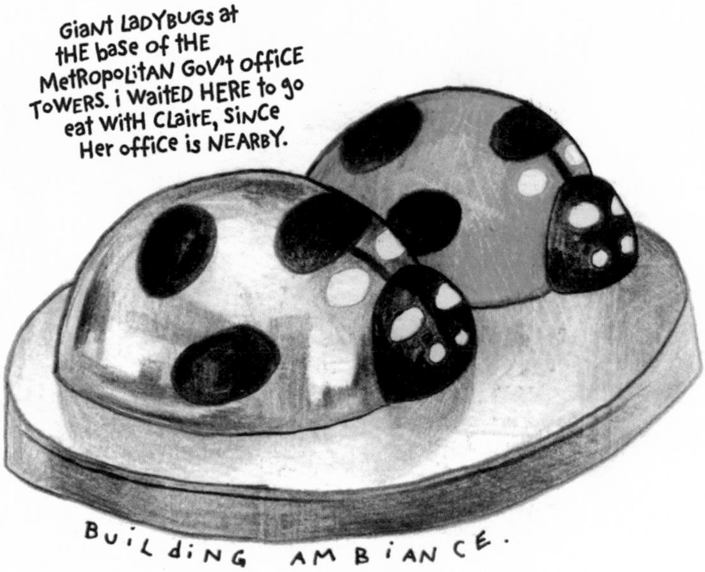

BUILDING AMBIANCE.

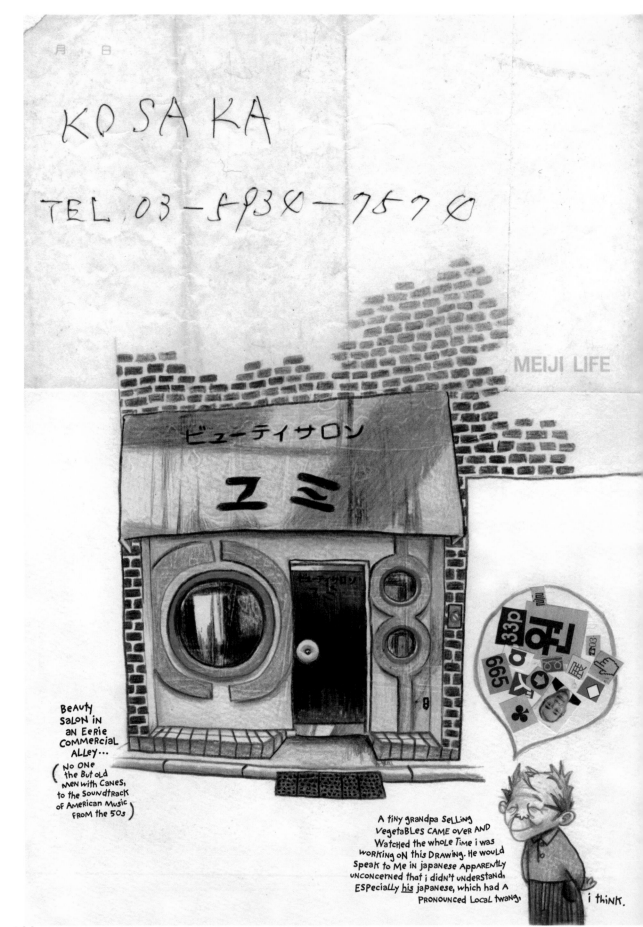

KOSAKA

TEL 03-593X-7570

MEIJI LIFE

ビューティサロン

ユミ

BEAUTY
SALON IN
AN EERIE
COMMERCIAL
ALLEY...

(No ONE
the But old
MEN with CANES,
to the SoundtrAck
of AMERICAN MUSIC
FROM the 50s)

A tiny grAndpa SeLLing
VegetaBLes CAME oVER AND
WatcheD the whoLE Time i was
WoRKiNg oN this DRAWiNg. He would
SpeAk to ME in japanese APPARENtLY
unconceRneD that i didN't unDERStAnD,
ESPeciaLLy his japanese, which had A
PRoNounced LocAL twang,

i thiNk.

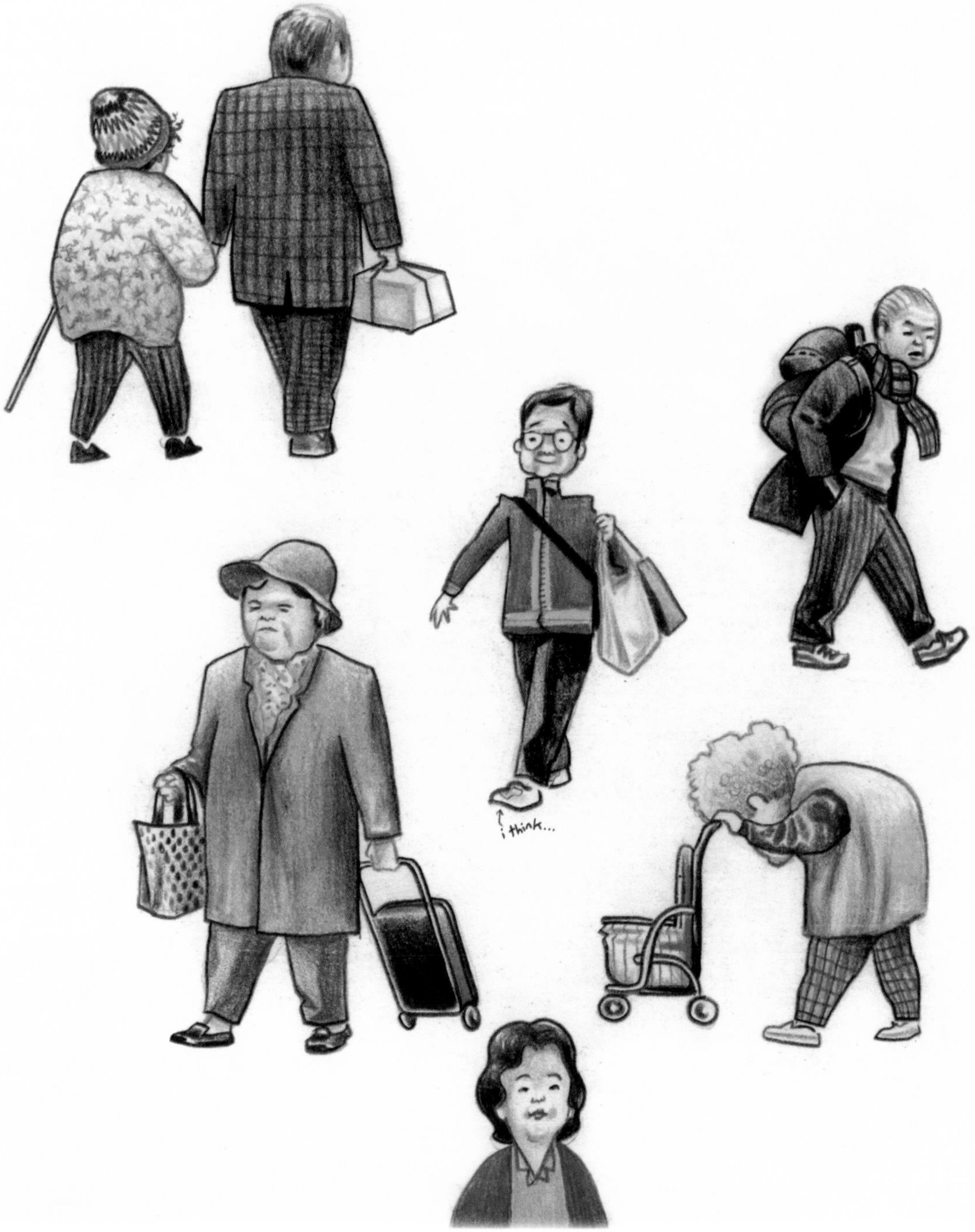
i think...

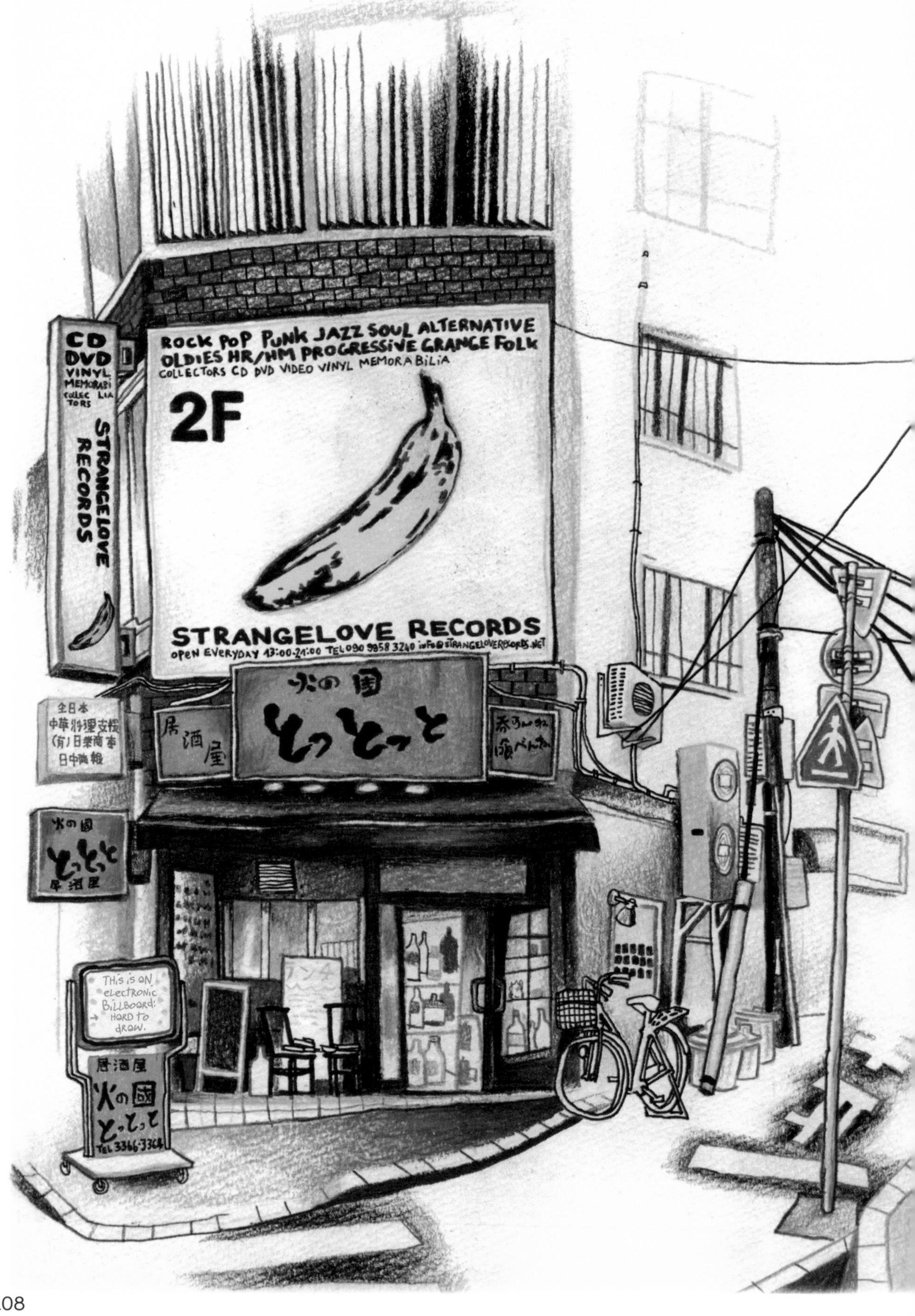
ROCK POP PUNK JAZZ SOUL ALTERNATIVE
OLDIES HR/HM PROGRESSIVE GRANGE FOLK
COLLECTORS CD DVD VIDEO VINYL MEMORABILIA
2F
STRANGELOVE RECORDS
OPEN EVERYDAY 13:00-21:00 TEL 090 9858 3240 info@STRANGELOVERECORDS.NET
CD
DVD
VINYL
STRANGELOVE RECORDS
火の國
とっとっと
居酒屋
THIS IS AN ELECTRONIC BILLBOARD: HARD TO DRAW.
居酒屋
火の國
とっとっと
TEL 3366-3364

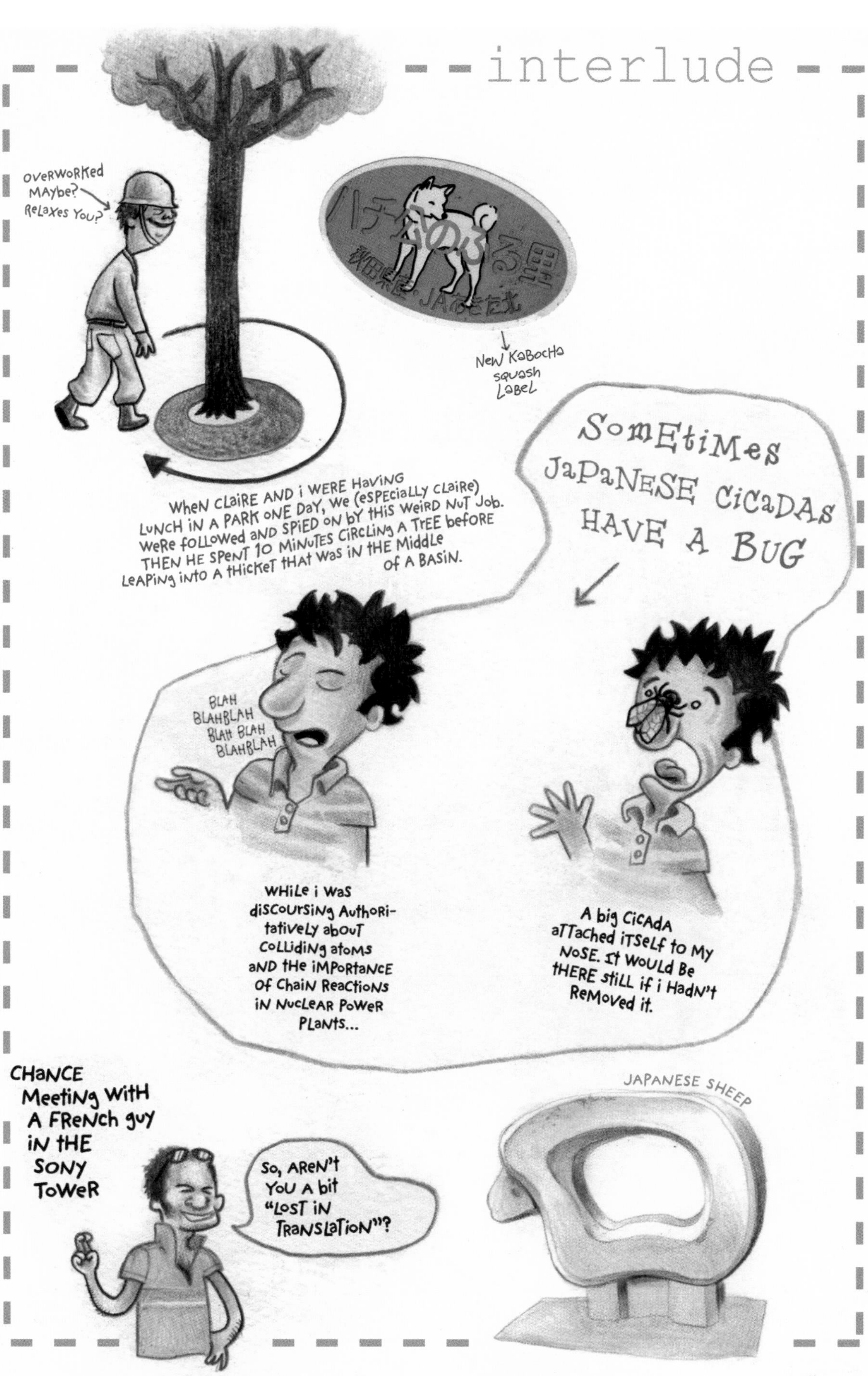
OVERWORKED
MAYbe?
ReLaxes You?
New KaBocHa squash Label
WheN CLAiRE AND i WERE HaviNG LuNCH iN A PARK ONE DaY, We (esPECiaLLY CLaiRe) WeRe foLLOWed aND SPiED ON bY tHiS WeiRD NuT Job. THEN HE SPeNT 10 MiNuTES CiRCLiNg A TrEE before LeAPiNg iNTo A tHicKeT tHAT Was iN tHE MiddLe of A BASiN.
SoMEtiMes JaPaNESE CiCaDAs HAVE A BUG
BLAH BLAHBLAH BLAH BLAH BLAHBLAH
WHiLe i Was disCOURsiNg AuthoRi-tativeLy abouT CoLLidiNg atoMs aND tHe iMPoRtaNCE of Chain ReactioNs iN NucLEAR PoWeR PLaNts...
A big CiCaDA aTTached iTSeLf to My NoSE. It WouLd Be tHERE stiLL if i HadN't ReMoved it.
CHaNCE Meeting WitH A FReNch guy iN tHE SONY ToWeR
So, AReN't YoU A bit "LoST iN TRaNSLaTioN"?
JAPANESE SHEEP

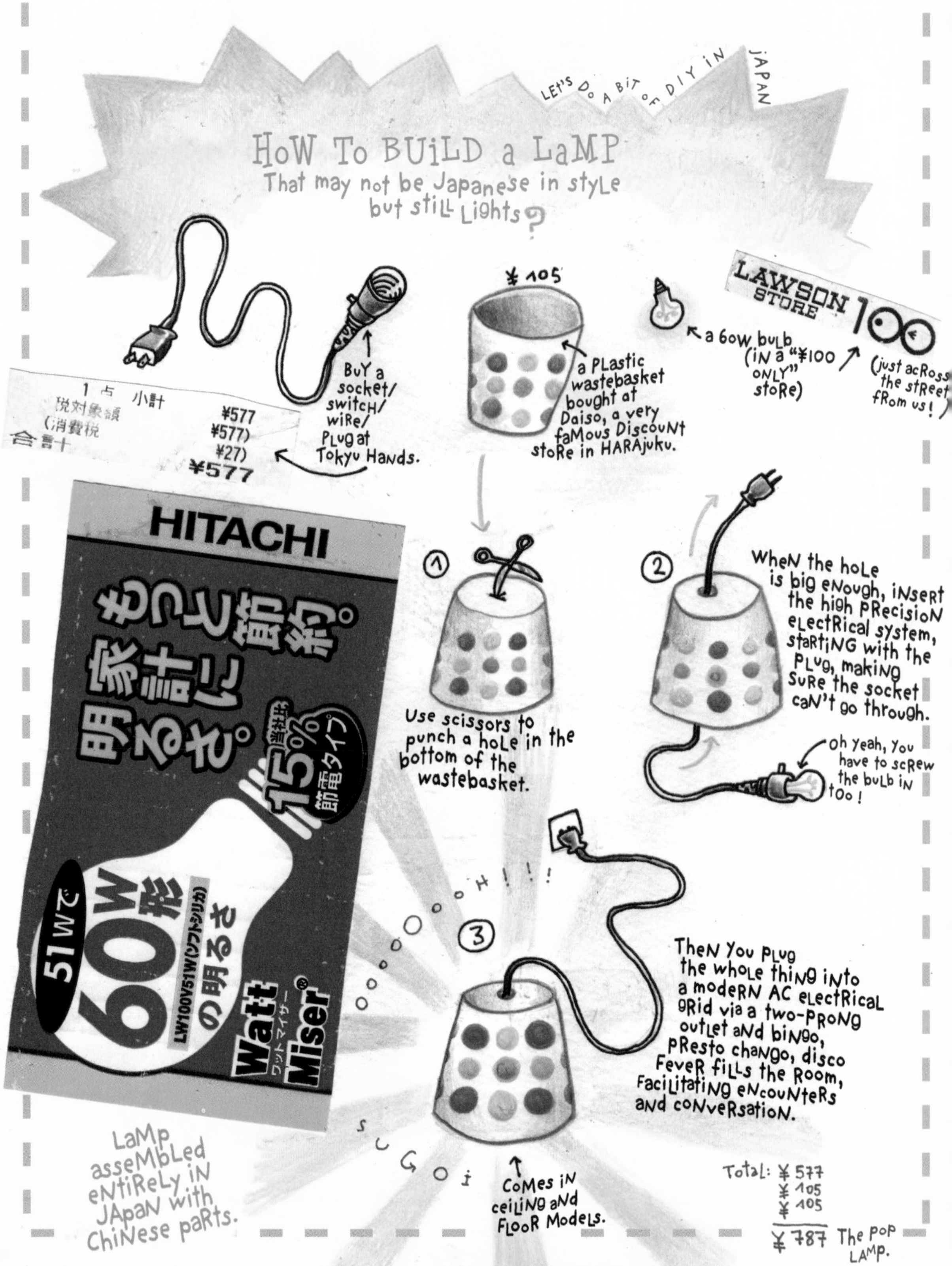
LET'S DO A BIT OF DIY IN JAPAN
HOW TO BUILD a LaMP
That may not be Japanese in style but still Lights?
BuY a socket/switcH/wiRe/PLug at Tokyu Hands.
1点 小計
税対象額
(消費税
合計
¥577
¥577)
¥27)
¥577
¥105
a PLastic wastebasket bought at Daiso, a very faMous DiscouNt stoRe in HARAjuku.
a 60W bulb (IN a "¥100 ONLY" stoRe)
LAWSON STORE 100
(just acRoss the stReet fRom us!)
HITACHI
もっと節約。家計に明るさ。
当社比 15% 節電タイプ
51Wで 60W形の明るさ
LW100V51W(ソフトシリカ)
Watt ワットマイザー Miser®
1
Use scissors to punch a hoLe in the bottom of the wastebasket.
2
When the hoLe is big eNough, iNsert the high pRecisioN eLectRical system, staRtiNG with the PLug, making sure the socket can't go through.
oh yeah, You have to scRew the buLb iN too!
3
Oooooo H!!!
Then You pLug the whoLe thing iNto a modeRN AC eLectRicaL gRid via a two-pRONG outLet aNd bingo, pResto chaNgo, disco FeveR fiLLs the Room, FaciLitating eNcouNteRs and coNveRsatioN.
SUGOi
Comes iN ceiLiNg aNd FLooR ModeLs.
LaMp asseMbLed eNtiReLy iN JApaN with ChiNese paRts.
Total: ¥577
¥105
¥105
¥787 The pop LAMP.

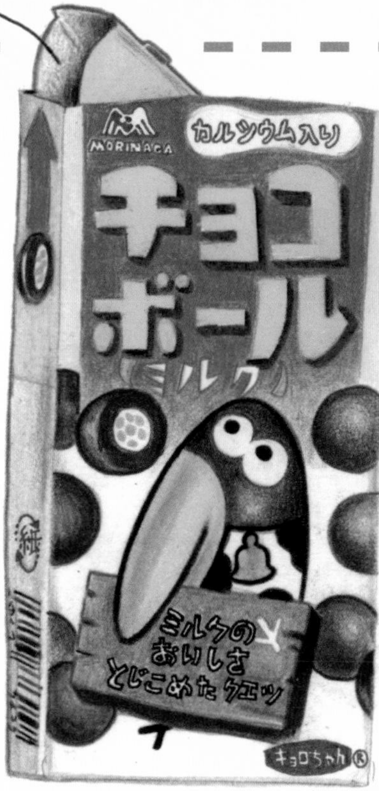
MORINAGA
カルシウム入り
チョコボール
(ミルク)
ミルクの
おいしさ
とじこめた クエッ
キョロちゃん®

ONE SMALL QUESTION ABOUT JAPAN

WHAT DOES AN INDUSTRIAL ONIGIRI MACHINE LOOK LIKE?

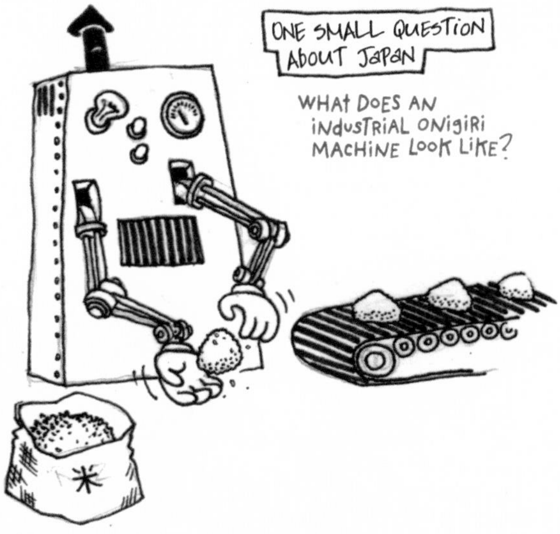

THAT'S A WRAP

WHETHER IT'S THE MULTIPLE POUCHES IN CUP NOODLES, OR THE POCKYS INDIVIDUALLY WRAPPED IN POUCHES INSIDE FRESHNESS PACKS FOR SINGLE PORTIONS TO GO, PACKAGING AND A CONCERN FOR PRESENTATION SOMETIMES JUSTIFY HEFTY PRICES FOR CERTAIN ITEMS (GRAPES?).

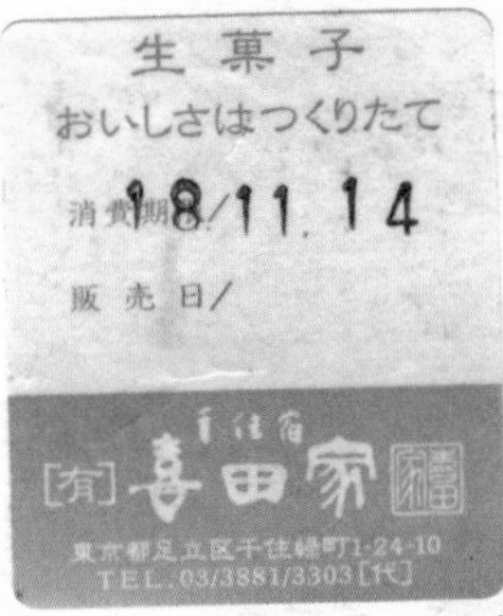
生菓子
おいしさはつくりたて
18.11.14
販売日/
[有] 喜田家
東京都足立区千住緑町1-24-10
TEL.03/3881/3303[代]

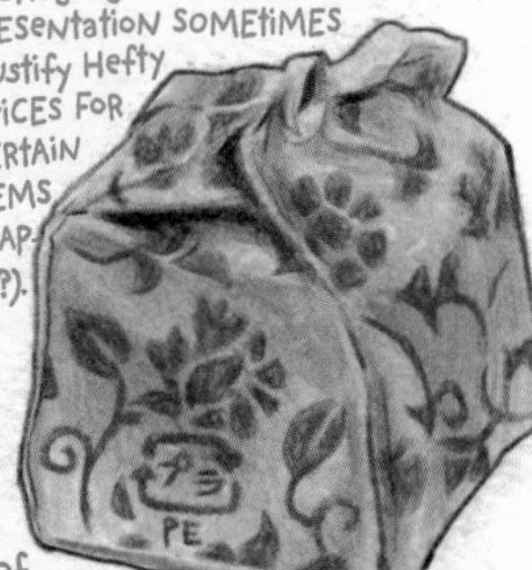
PE

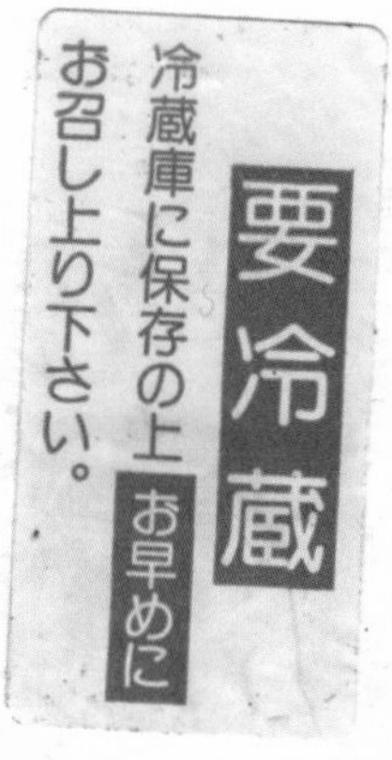
要冷蔵
冷蔵庫に保存の上
お早めに
お召し上り下さい。

HERE IS A BEAUTIFUL EXAMPLE OF THE ELABORATE WRAPPING OF SOMETHING VERY SIMPLE THAT, WHERE I LIVE, WE'D HAVE STUCK IN A CARDBOARD BOX. (EXAMPLE GENEROUSLY DONATED BY A LADY WHO LIKED MY SKETCHES QUITE A BIT!)

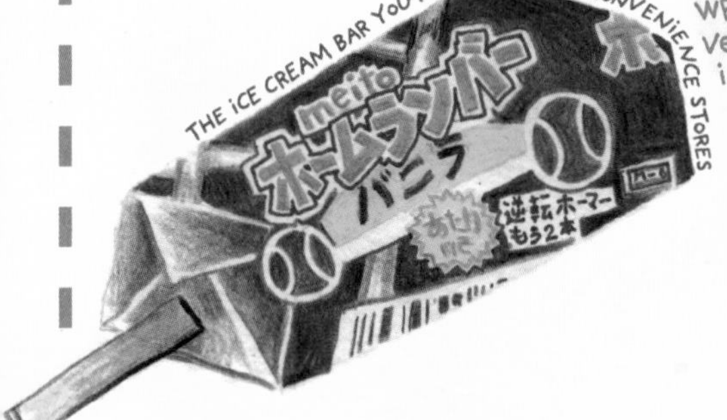
meito
ホームランバー
バニラ
逆転ホーマー
もう2本

THE ICE CREAM BAR YOU FIND IN ALL THE CONVENIENCE STORES

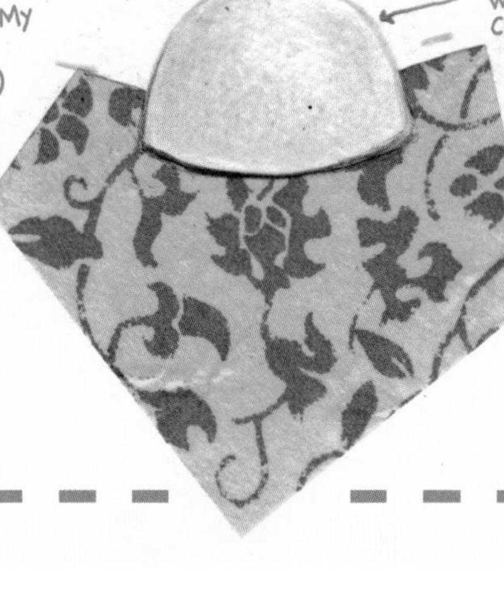

VERY SOFT WHITE CHOCOLATE (WHITE CHOCOLATE CENTER)

NAH, ACTUALLY, IT'S WHITE BEAN PASTE INSIDE.

Biiiiku ♪ ♫ Biku Biku Biku CAMERA.

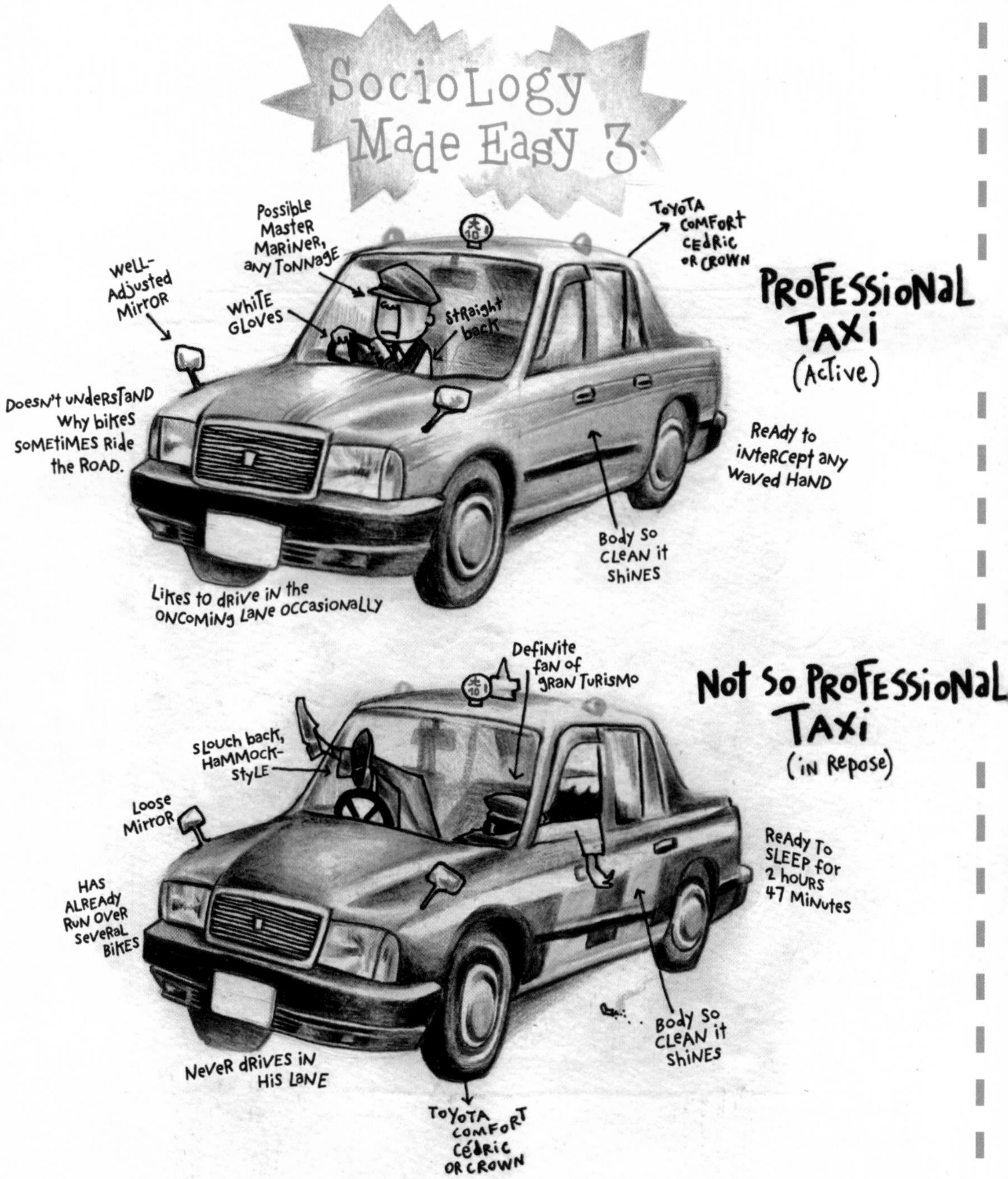
SocioLogy Made Easy 3:
Possible Master Mariner, any Tonnage
TOYOTA COMFORT CEDRIC OR CROWN
PROFESSIONAL TAXI
(Active)
WELL-Adjusted Mirror
White Gloves
Straight back
Doesn't understand why bikes sometimes ride the road.
Ready to intercept any waved hand
Body so clean it shines
Likes to drive in the oncoming lane occasionally
Definite fan of Gran Turismo
Not So PROFESSIONAL TAXI
(in Repose)
Slouch back, hammock-style
Loose Mirror
Ready to sleep for 2 hours 47 Minutes
Has already run over several bikes
Body so clean it shines
Never drives in his lane
TOYOTA COMFORT CÉDRIC OR CROWN

east shinjuku

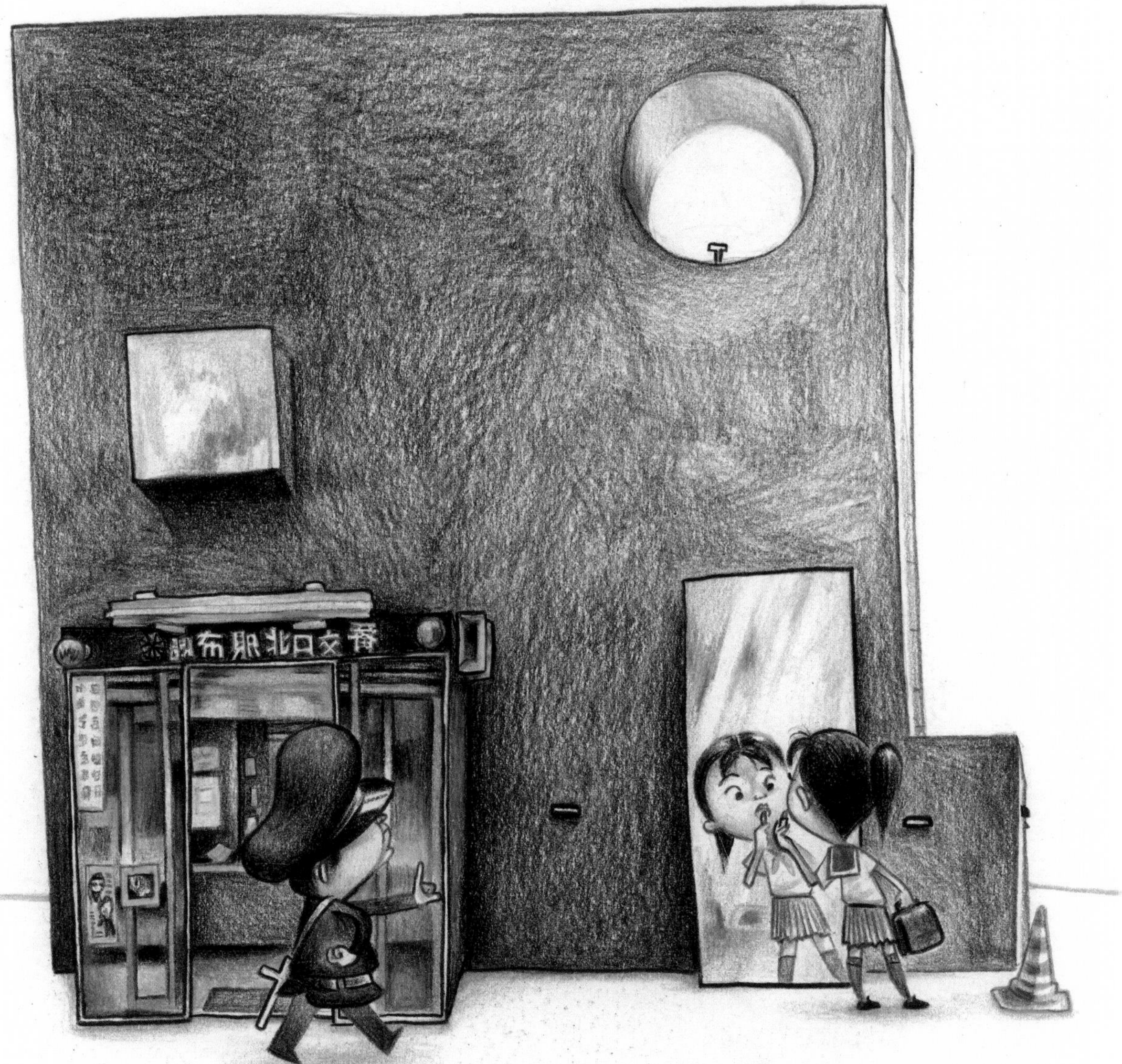
調布駅北口交番

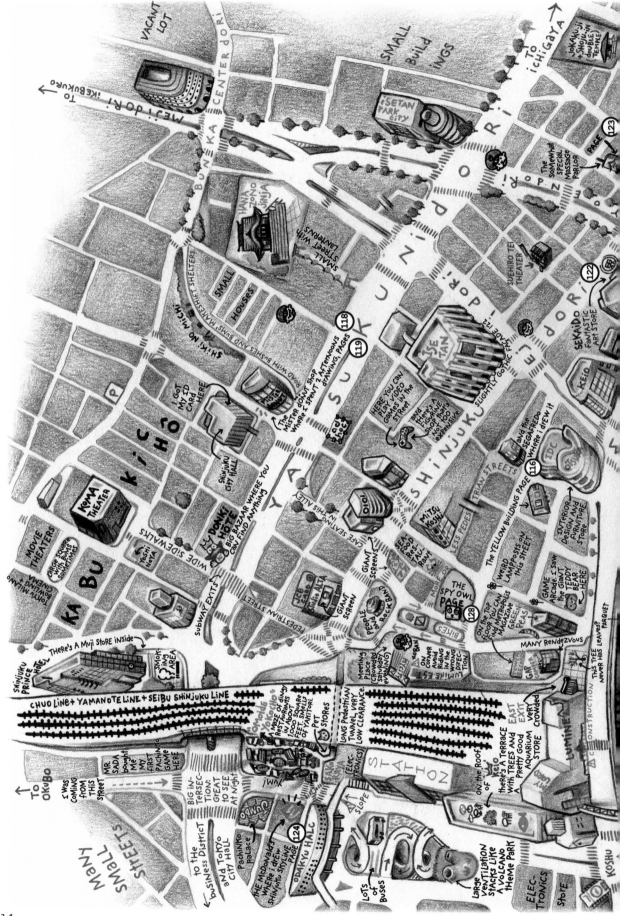

114

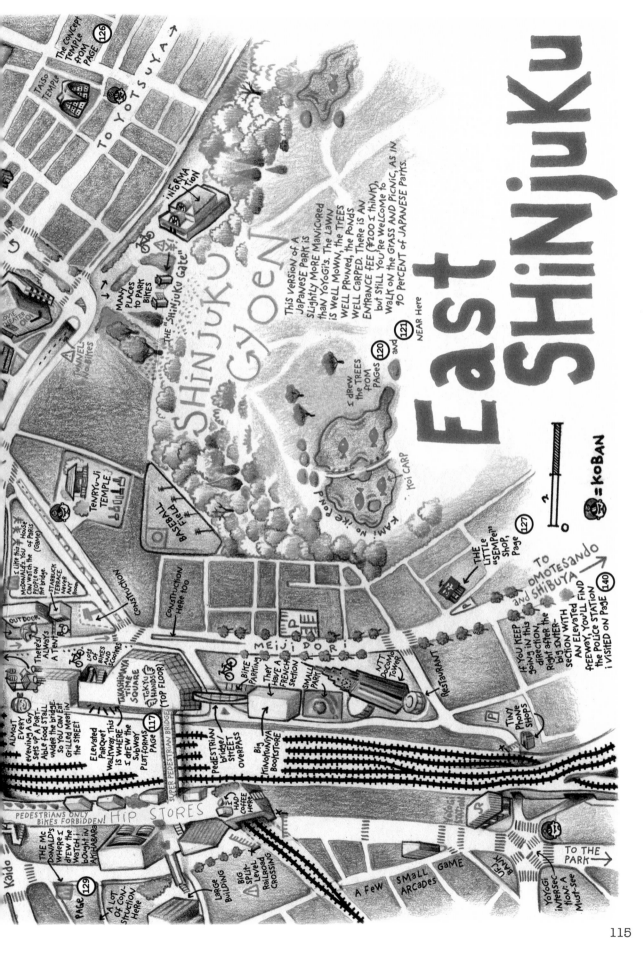

East SHINjuKu

The Concept TEMPLE FROM PAGE 126

TAISO TEMPLE

TO YOTSUYA →

Information

MANY PLACES TO PARK BIKES

The "SHiNjuKu Gate"

SHINjuKu GYOEN

This version of a Japanese park is slightly more manicured than YoYogi's. The lawn is well mown, the TreES well pruned, the Ponds well carped. There is an entrance fee (¥200 I think), but still you're welcome to walk on the grass and picnic, as in 90 percent of Japanese parks.

NEAR HERE

120 and 121

I drew the trees from pages 120

Koi CARP

KAMI No ike Pond

MOVIE THEATER

TUNNEL No Bikes

TENRYU-Ji TEMPLE

I like this House of Paris (Game) I can watch the People on the bridge. McDONALD'S You can watch People on the bridge. STARBUCK TERRACE Never any Room

BASEBALL FIELD

CONSTRUCTION

CONSTRUCTION HERE Too

There's Always a Tent

OUTDOOR

Lots of Bikes and Scooters

MEIJI DORI

Bike PARKING

THE LITTLE "SEMPE" SHOP, Page 127

TO OMOTESANDO and SHIBUYA 140

If you keep going in this direction, Right after the big intersection with an elevated freeway, you'll find the Police STATION i visited on Page 140

= KOBaN

TAKASHIMAYA TIME SQUARE

TOKYU HANDS (TOP FLOOR)

SUPER PEDESTRIAN BRIDGE

Elevated ParQUET WalkWay, This is where I drew the SubWay Platforms Page 117

PEDESTRIAN bridge / STREET OVERPASS

Big KINOKUNiYA BookSTORE

They have a FRENCH Section

SMALL PARK

NTT DOCOMO Tower

RESTAURANT

Tiny Phone SHOPS

ALMOST EVERY EVENING A Guy Sets up A Portable food stall under the bridge, So You Can Eat GRILLED Meat in the STREET

PEDESTRIANS ONLY BIKES FORBIDDEN! HIP STORES

THE McDONALD's where I drew the watch I bought in Akihabara

Kaido

A LOT OF Construction Here

Page 129

LARGE BUILDING

BIG SPLIT-LEVEL RailRoad CROSSING

I HAD COFFEE HERE

A Few SMALL ARCades

GAME

UFJ BANK

TO THE PARK →

YoYogi intersection: A Must-see

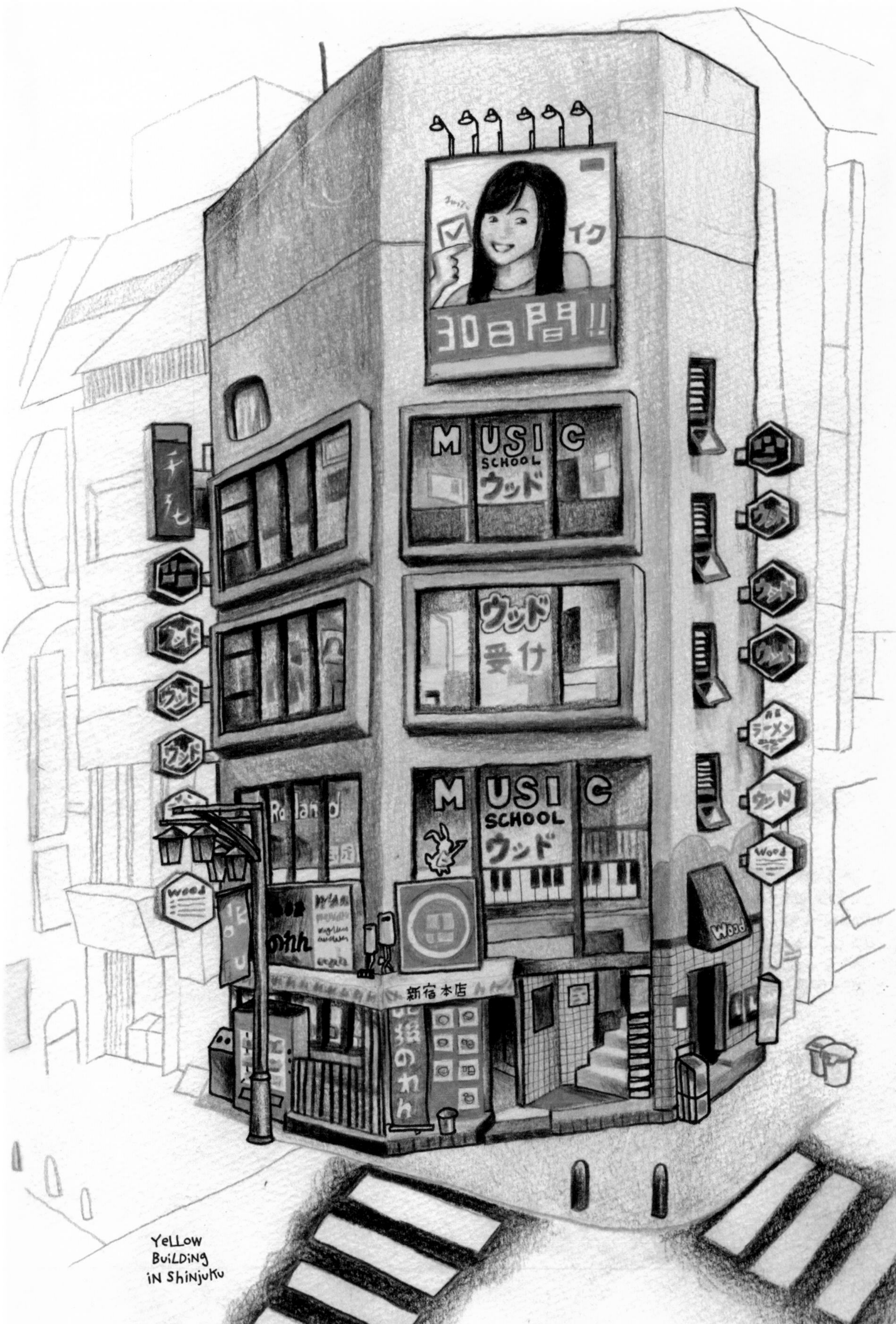
イク
30日間!!
MUSIC
SCHOOL
ウッド
ウッド
受付
MUSIC
SCHOOL
ウッド
Roland
新宿本店
Wood
YELLOW BUILDING IN SHINJUKU

WELL, Yes, i did END UP doiNG A SKetcH Of the SubwaY. OR traiN. They're aLMost tHE SaMe thiNG iN ToKYO.
ON the SECONd fLOOR OF THE TAKASHiYaMa DEPARtMENt STORE, THERE'S A SMaLL WaLKWaY fROM WHiCH YOU CAN SPY DOWN ON tHE StatioN PLatfoRMs.

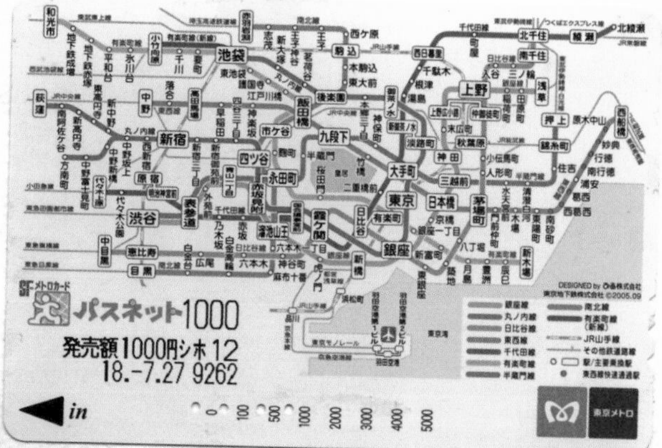
パスネット1000
発売額1000円シホ12
18.-7.27 9262
in

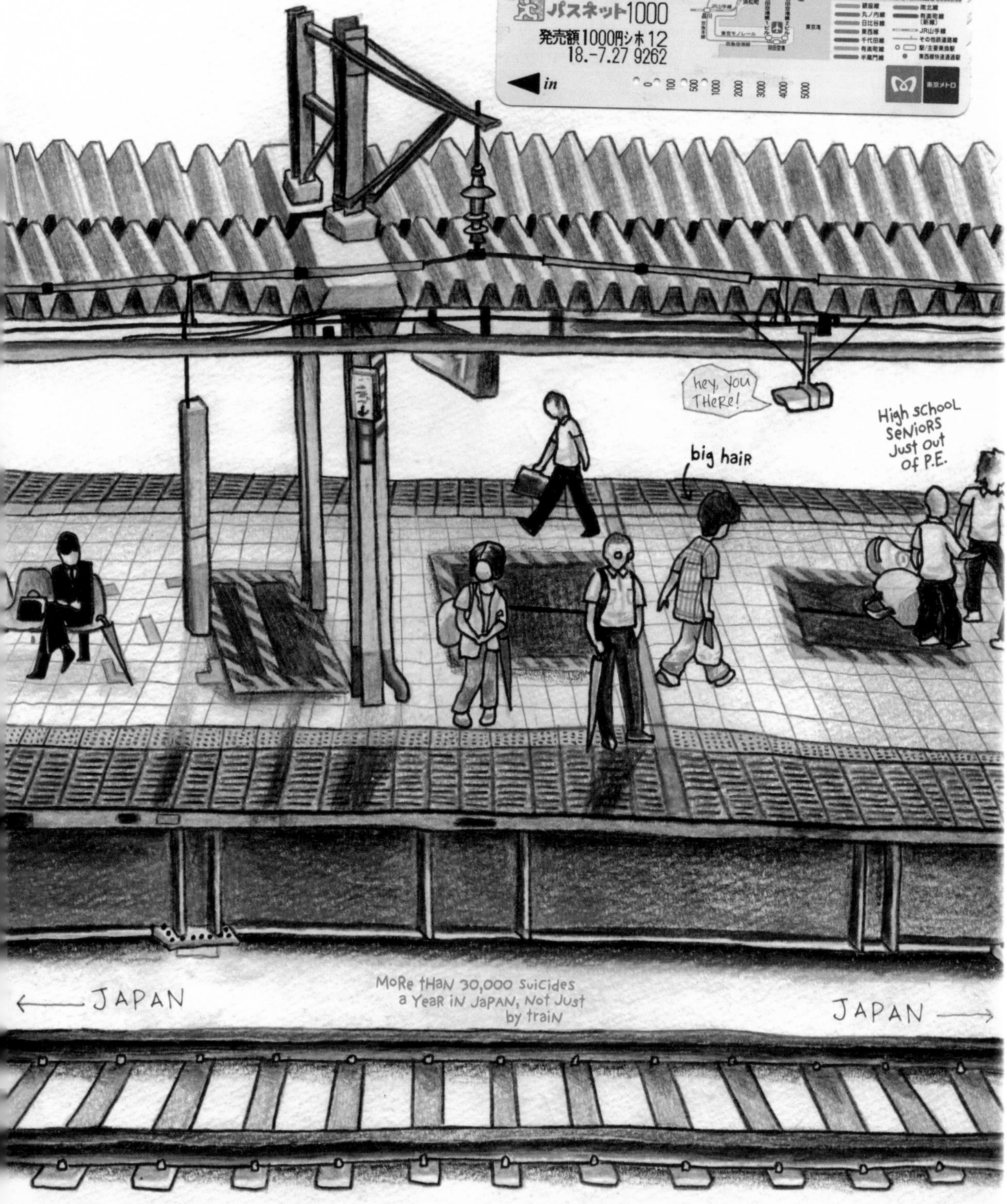
hey, you THere!
big haiR
High school seNioRS Just out of P.E.
JAPAN
MoRe tHAN 30,000 suicides a YeaR iN JAPAN, Not Just by traiN
JAPAN

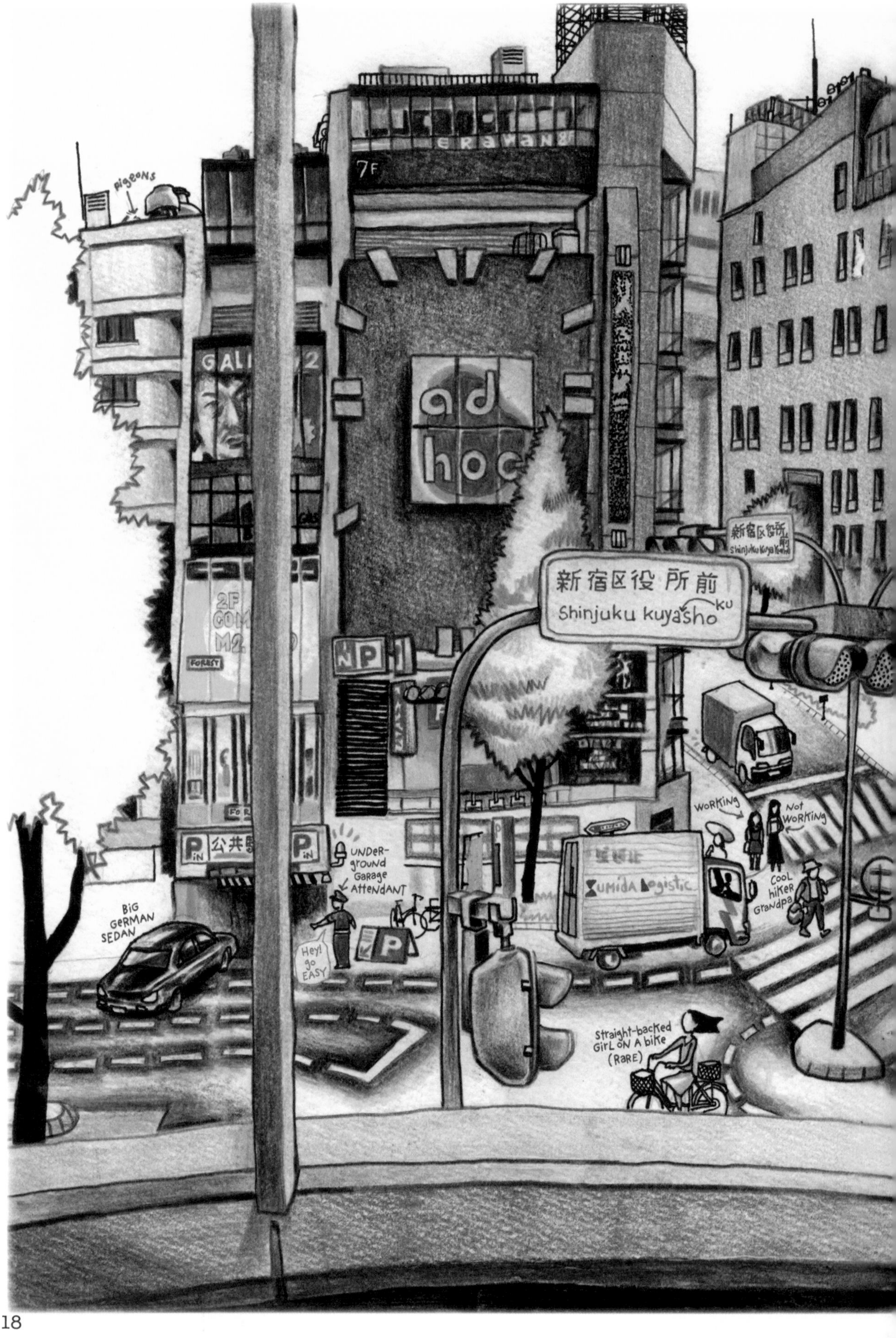

Pigeons
ERAWAN
7F
ad hoc
新宿区役所前
Shinjuku kuyasho ku
新宿区役所前
Shinjuku Kuyakusho
NP
UNDERground Garage Attendant
Big German Sedan
Hey! go EASY
Zumida Logistic
WORKING
Not WORKING
Cool hiker Grandpa
Straight-backed girl on a bike (RARE)

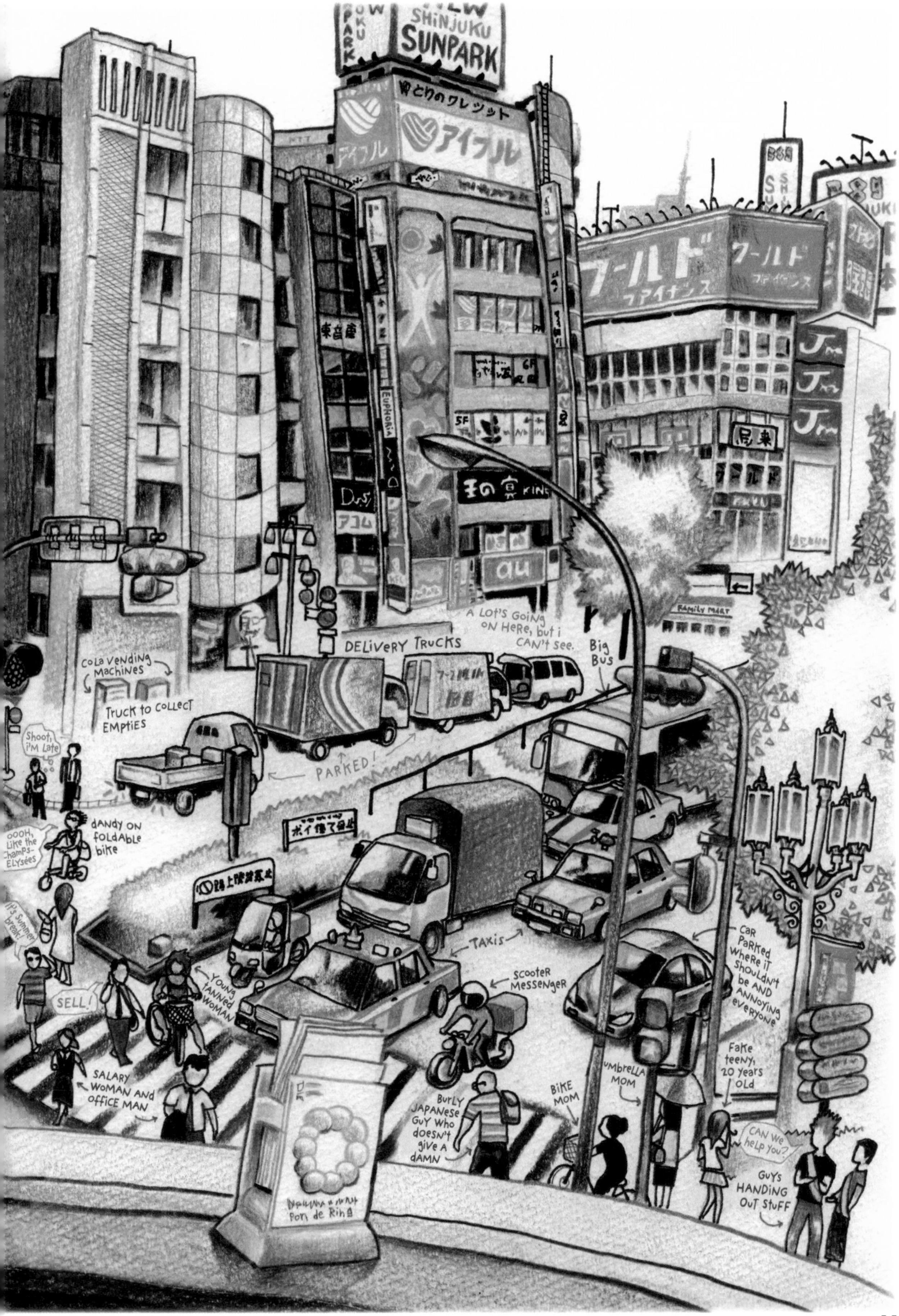
SHINJUKU
SUNPARK
アイフル
ワールド
ファイナンス
EUPHORIA
5F
6F
au
FAMILY MART
A LOT'S GOING ON HERE, but i CAN'T see.
DELIVERY TRUCKS
Big Bus
CoLa vending Machines
Truck to collect EMPties
Shoot, i'M Late
PARKED!
dandy on foldable bike
OOOH, Like the Champs-Elysées
It's Summer break!
SELL!
Young Tanned WOMAN
TAXIS
Scooter Messenger
Car Parked where it shouldn't be AND annoying everyone
Fake teeny, 20 years old
SALARY WOMAN AND office MAN
Burly JAPANESE Guy who doesn't give a dAMN
Bike MOM
Umbrella MOM
CAN we help you?
Guys HANDING OUT STUFF
Pon de Ring

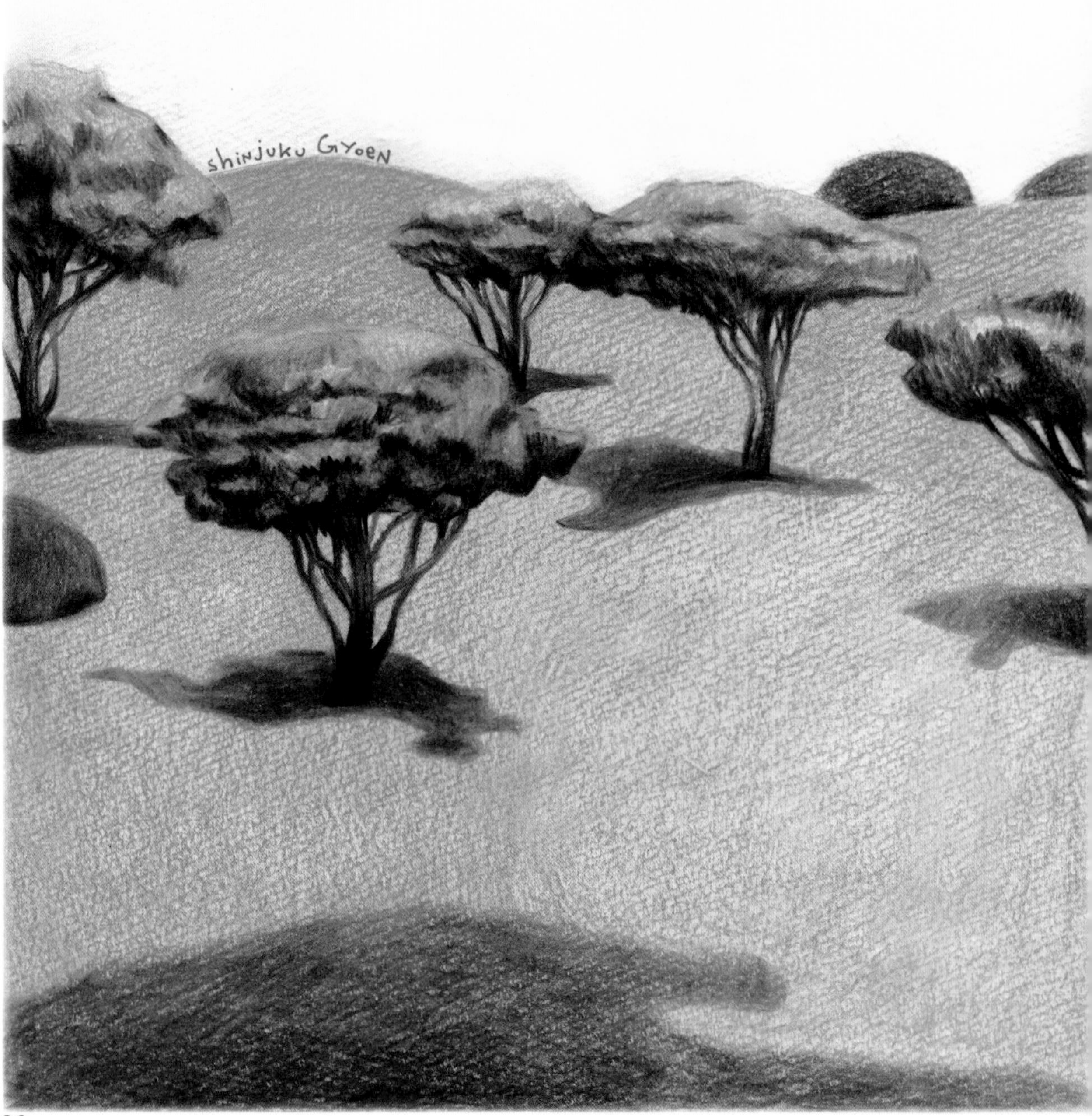
shinjuku GYoeN

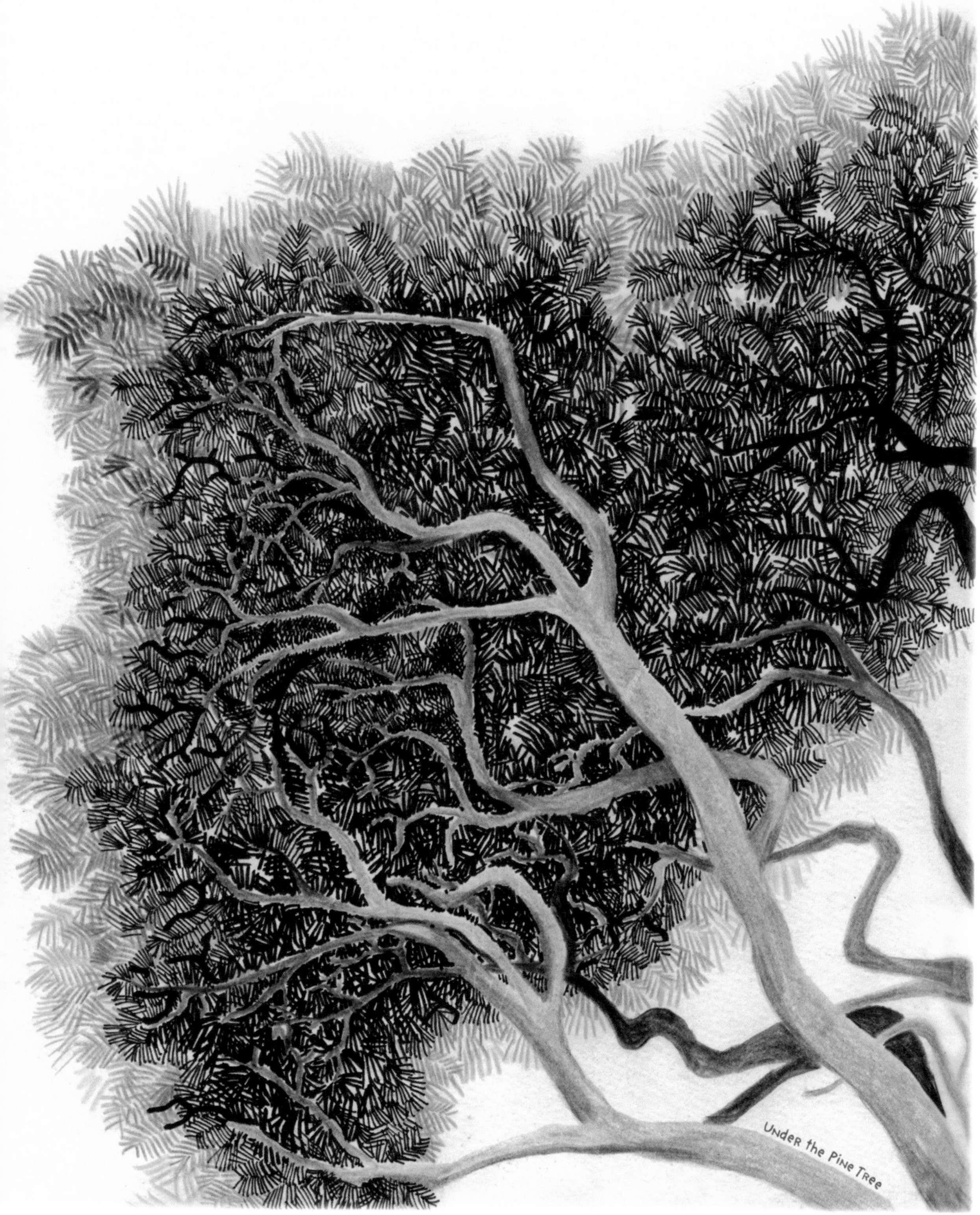
Under the Pine Tree

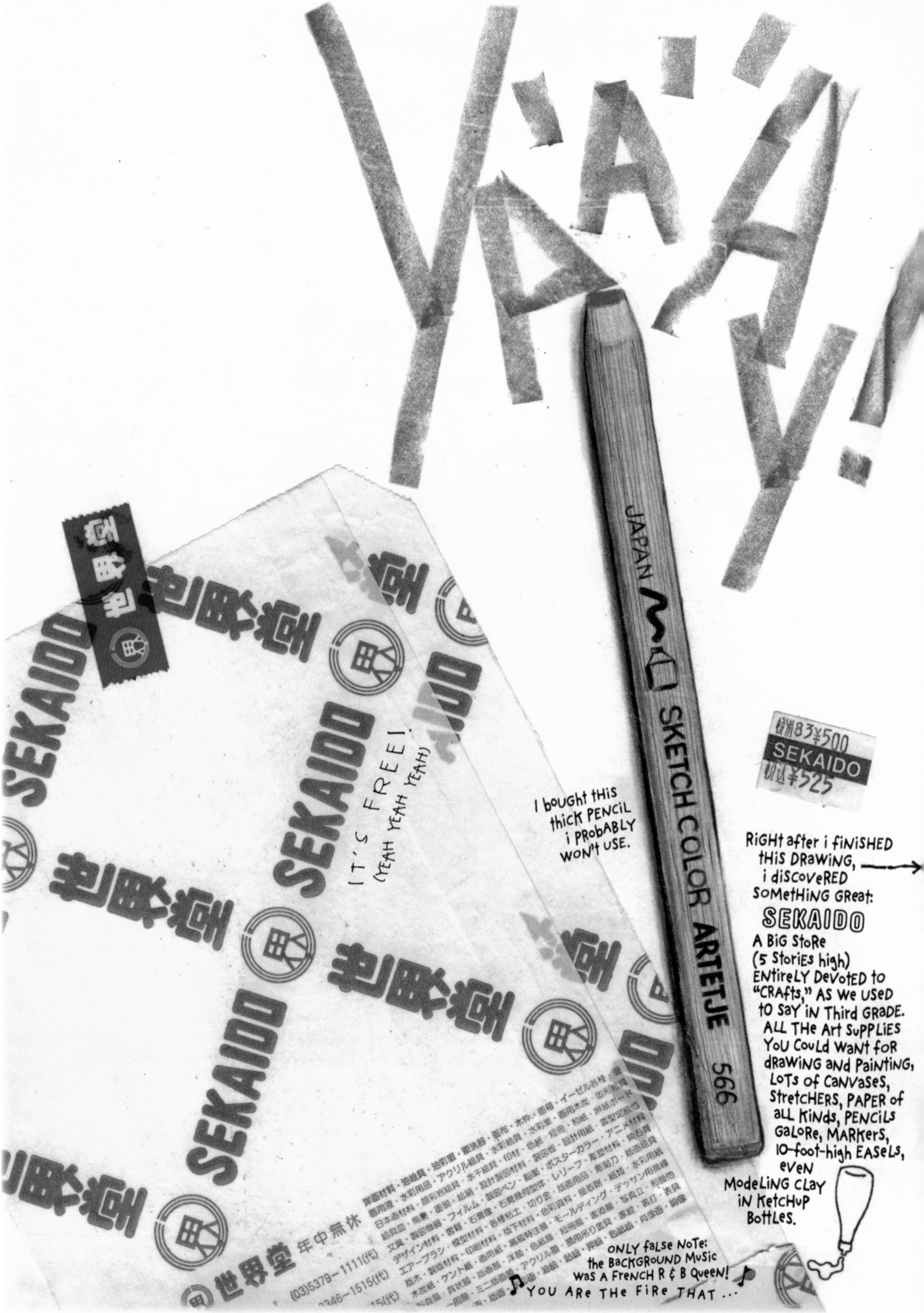
YA'A'A'Y!
JAPAN
SKETCH COLOR ARTETJE
566
SEKAIDO
世界堂
世界堂 年中無休
(03)5379-1111(代)
SEKAIDO
¥500
税込¥525
IT'S FREE!
(YEAH YEAH YEAH)

I bought this thick pencil i probably won't use.

Right after i finished this drawing, i discovered something great: →

SEKAIDO

A big store (5 stories high) entirely devoted to "crafts," as we used to say in third grade. All the art supplies you could want for drawing and painting, lots of canvases, stretchers, paper of all kinds, pencils galore, markers, 10-foot-high easels, even modeling clay in ketchup bottles.

Only false note: the background music was a French R & B queen! ♪ You are the fire that ... ♪

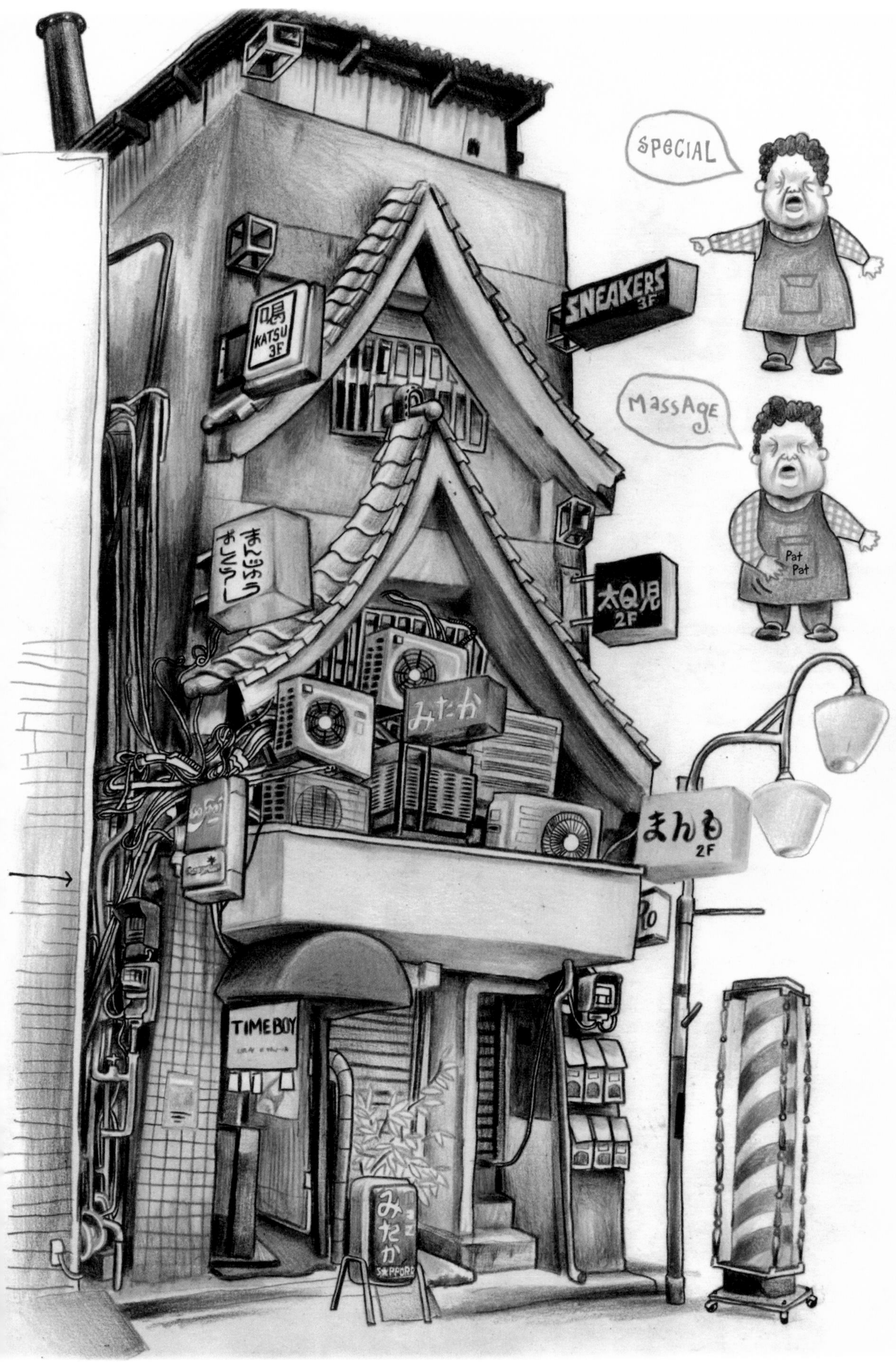
SPECIAL
MASSAGE
Pat Pat
SNEAKERS 3F
KATSU 3F
まんじゅう
太Q児 2F
みたか
まんも 2F
TIMEBOY
みたか
SAPPORO

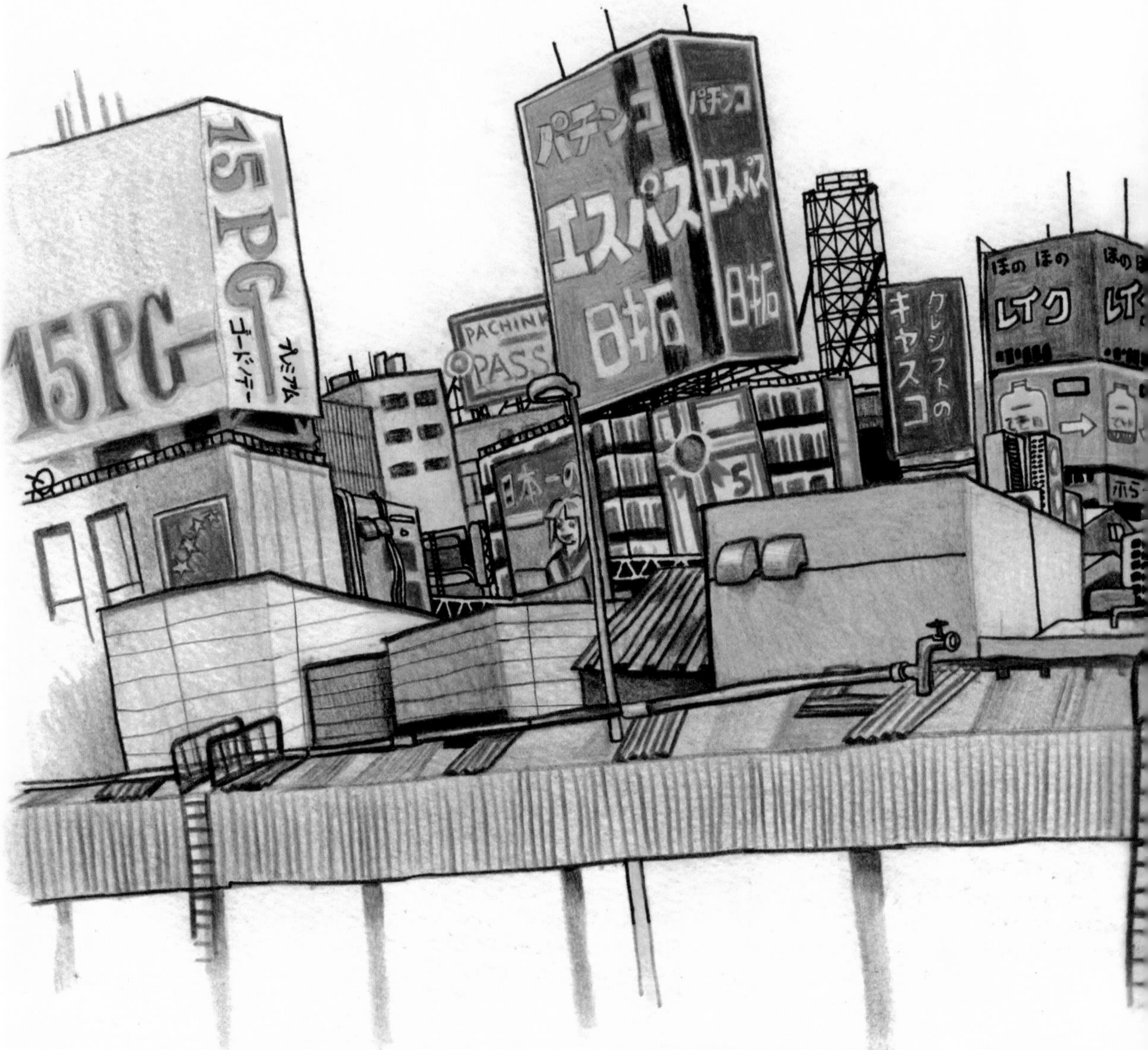
15PG
15PG
パチンコ
エスパス
日拓
パチンコ
エスパス
日拓
PASS
キャスコ
レイク
日本一の

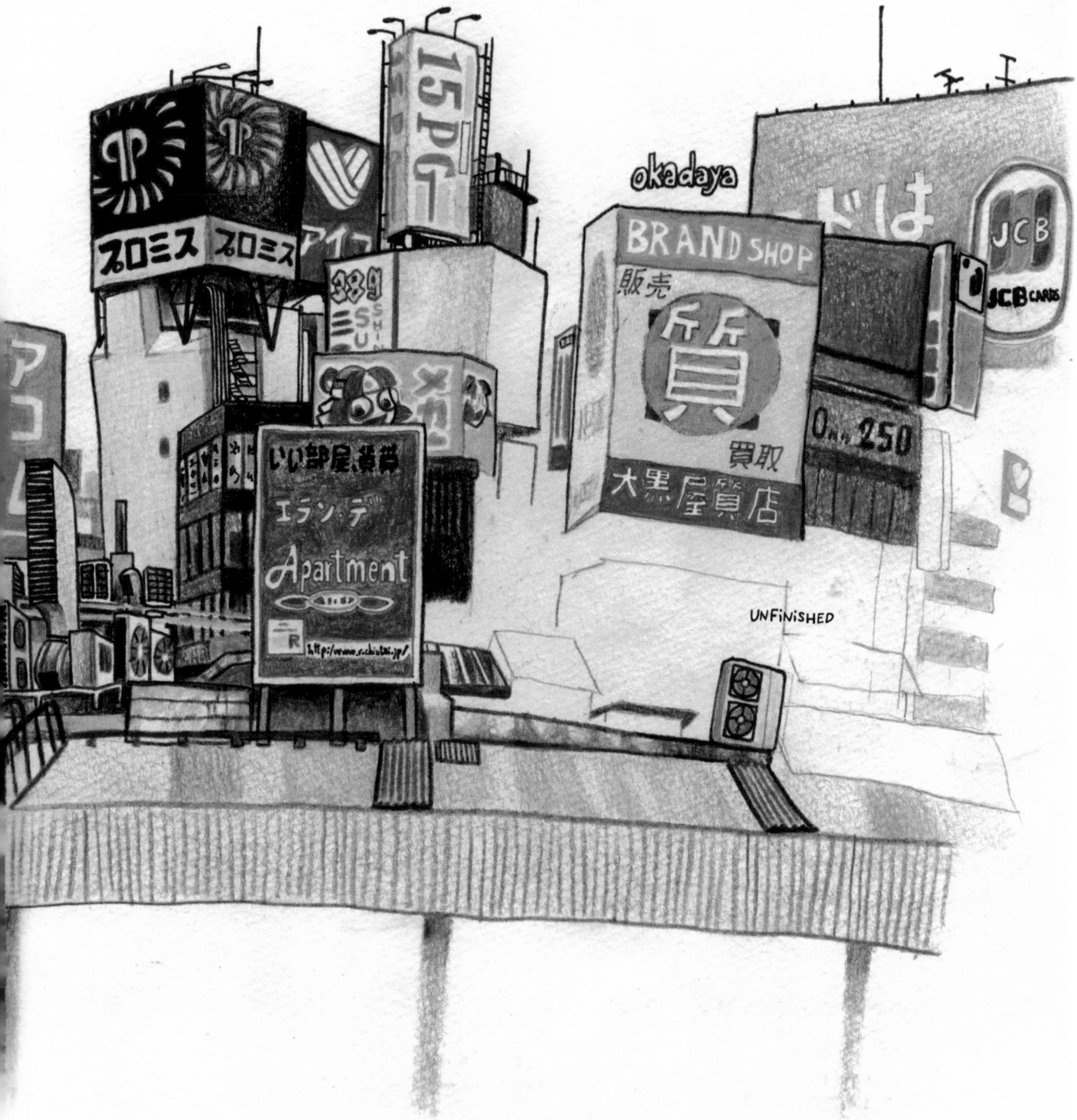
プロミス
プロミス
okadaya
BRAND SHOP
販売
質
買取
大黒屋質店
JCB
JCB CARDS
Apartment
UNFINISHED

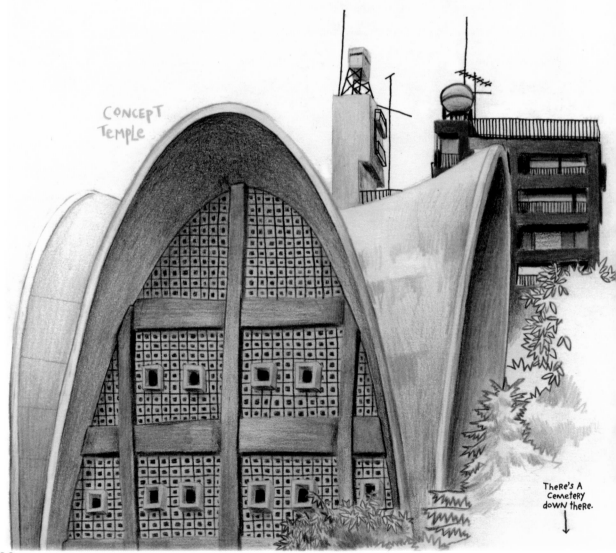

CONCEPT
TEMPLE

THERE'S A
CEMETERY
DOWN THERE.
↓

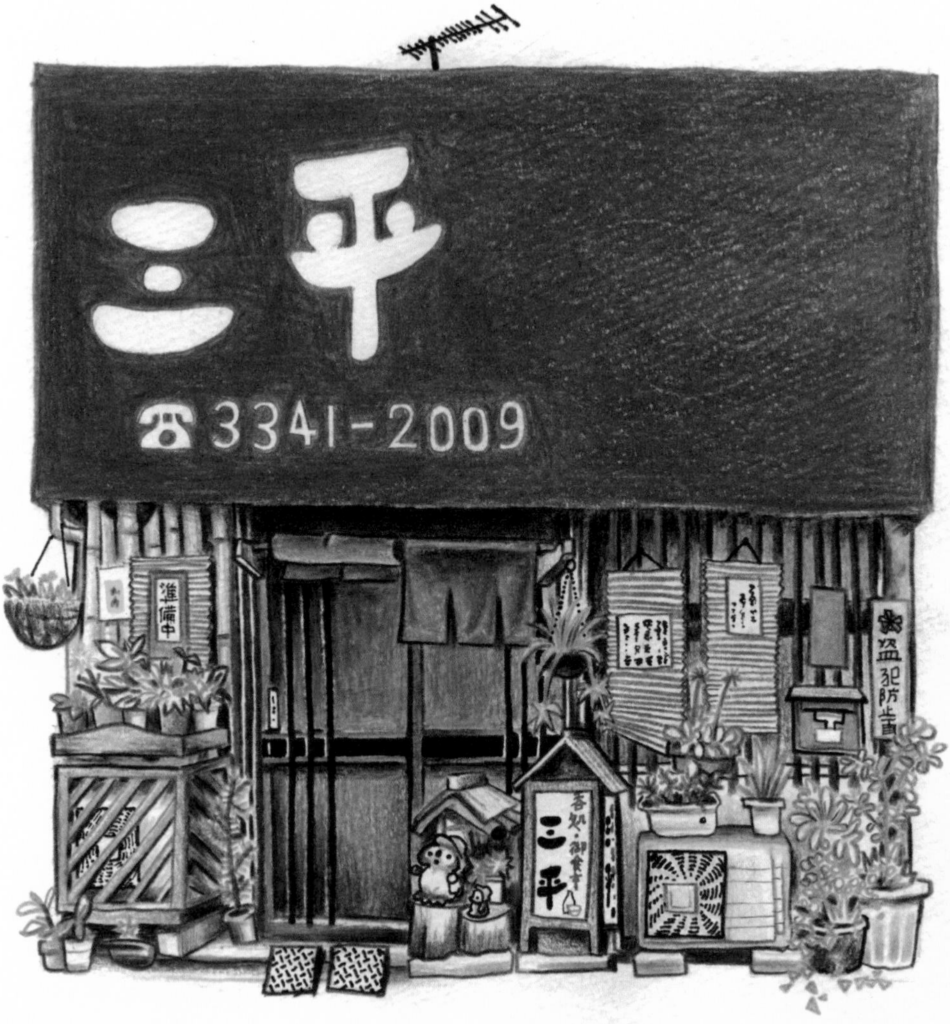
三平
☎3341-2009
準備中
盗犯防止
三平

FROM a Muji store:

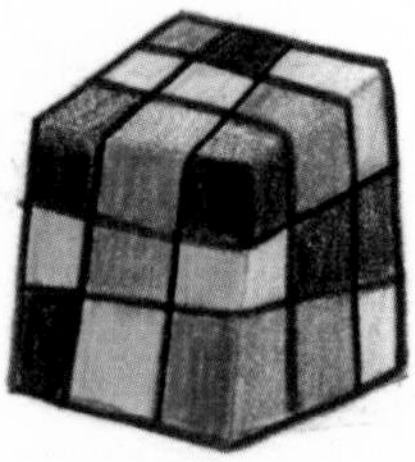

the Muji RuBix Cube

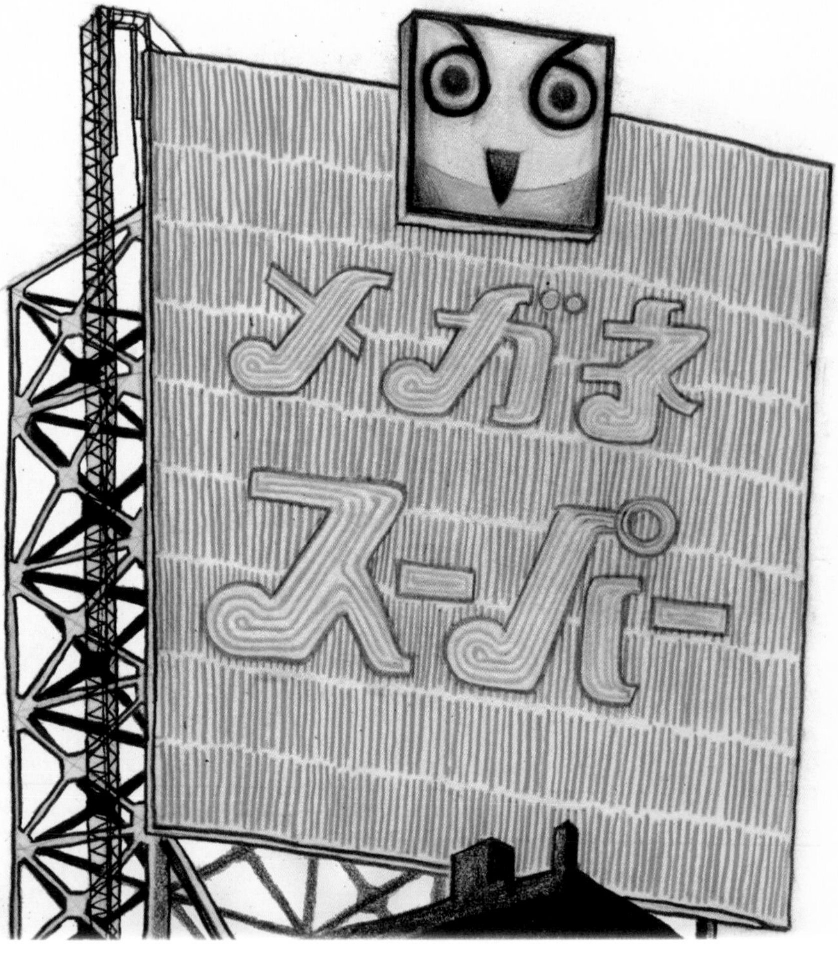
メガネ
スーパー

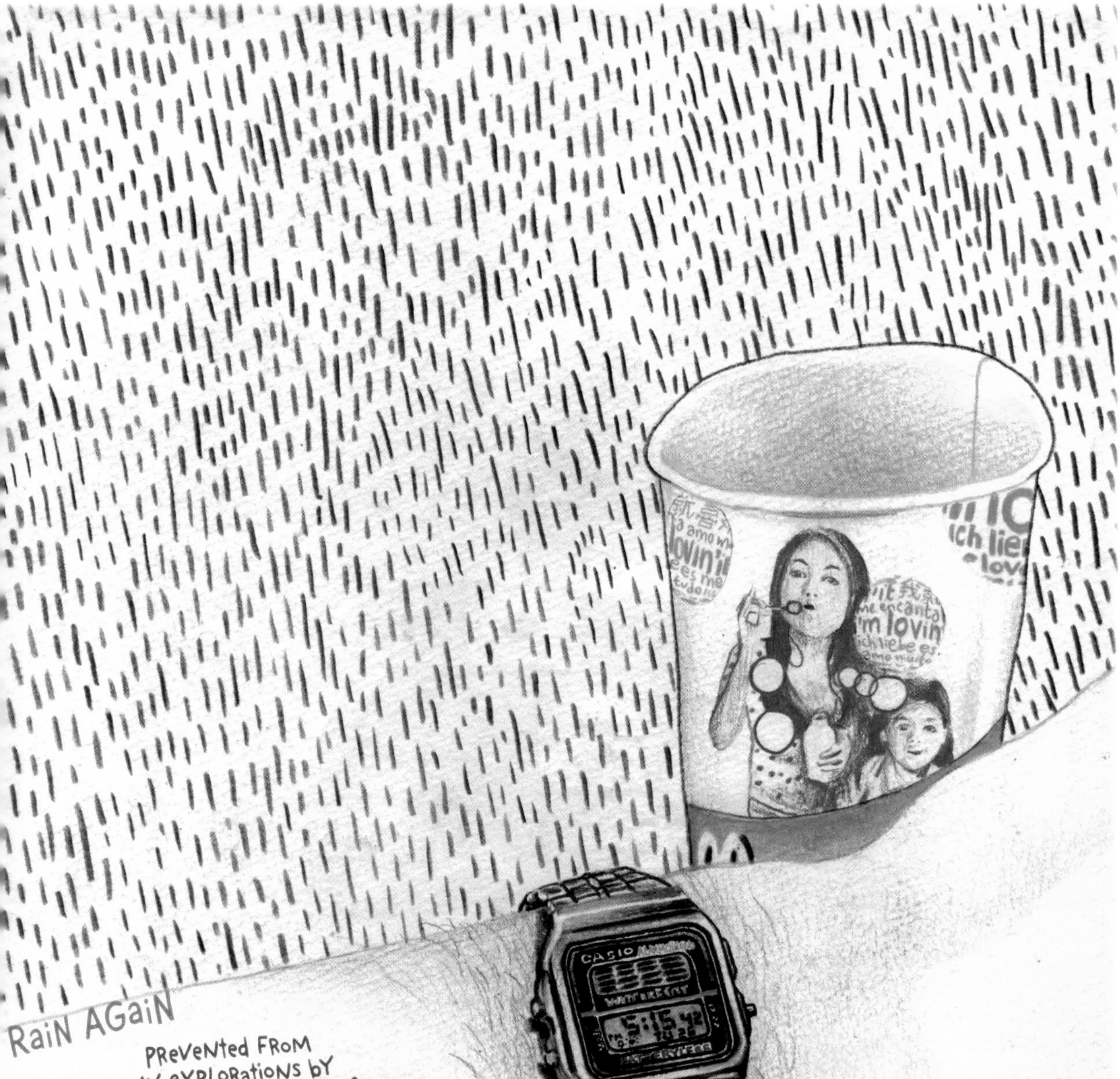

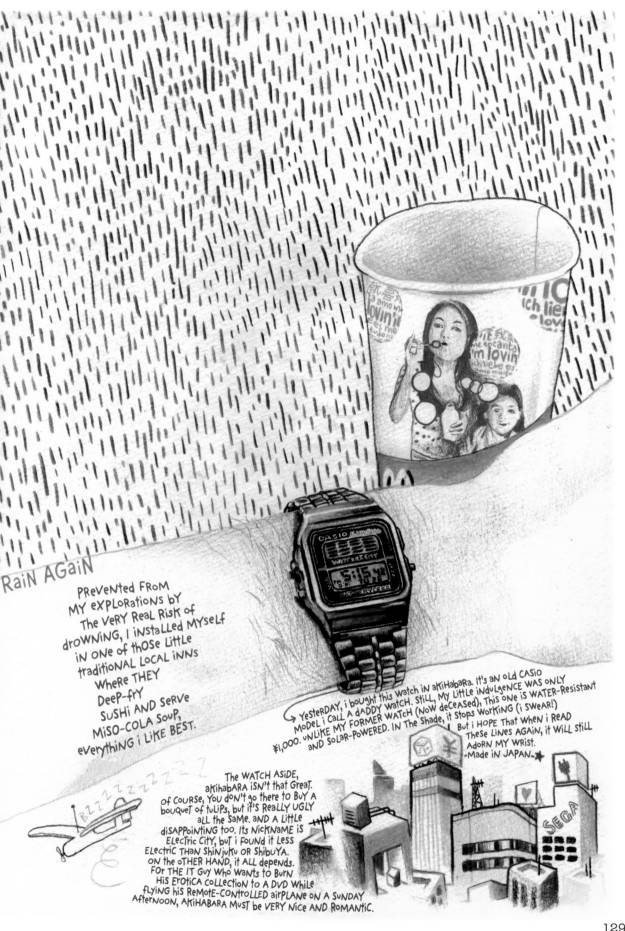

Rain Again

Prevented from my explorations by the very real risk of drowning, I installed myself in one of those little traditional local inns where they deep-fry sushi and serve miso-cola soup, everything I like best.

Yesterday, I bought this watch in Akihabara. It's an old Casio model I call a daddy watch. Still, my little indulgence was only ¥1,000. Unlike my former watch (now deceased), this one is water-resistant and solar-powered. In the shade, it stops working (I swear!) But I hope that when I read these lines again, it will still adorn my wrist.
-Made in Japan-★

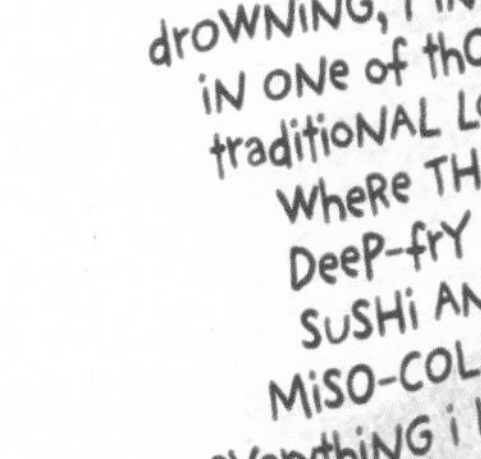

BZZZZZZZZZZ

The watch aside, Akihabara isn't that great. Of course, you don't go there to buy a bouquet of tulips, but it's really ugly all the same. And a little disappointing too. Its nickname is Electric City, but I found it less electric than Shinjuku or Shibuya. On the other hand, it all depends. For the IT guy who wants to burn his erotica collection to a DVD while flying his remote-controlled airplane on a Sunday afternoon, Akihabara must be very nice and romantic.

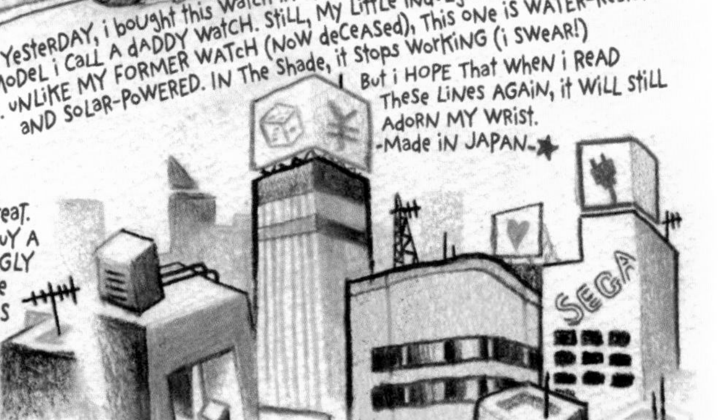

LAZY WEEKEND

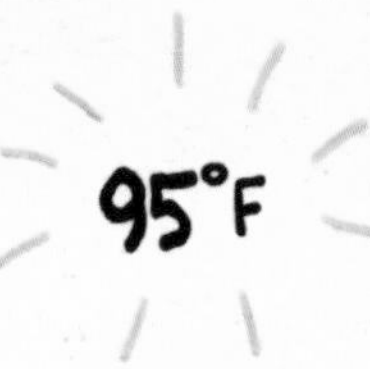

95°F

SINCE, ON TOP OF A WHOLE DAY SPENT LOUNGING ON THE LAWN IN SHINJUKU GYOEN, WE WENT TO **ODAIBA** (TOKYO BEACH), THE MEGALOPOLIS'S GORGEOUS ARTIFICIAL BEACH.

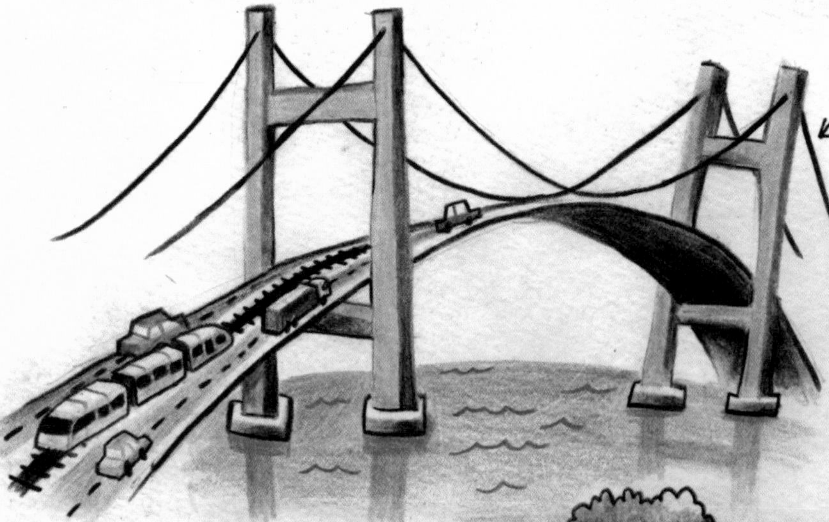

TO GET THERE, THE BEST (BUT NOT ONLY) WAY IS VIA THE RAINBOW BRIDGE, THE BIG SUSPENSION BRIDGE THAT SPANS THE BAY. ON OUR WAY OVER, WE TOOK THE MONORAIL. ON THE WAY BACK, WE TOOK OUR FEET. YES, YOU CAN WALK ACROSS IT IF YOU STAY TO THE SIDE WHILE SAMPLING THE VARIOUS EXQUISITE MUFFLER POLLENS.

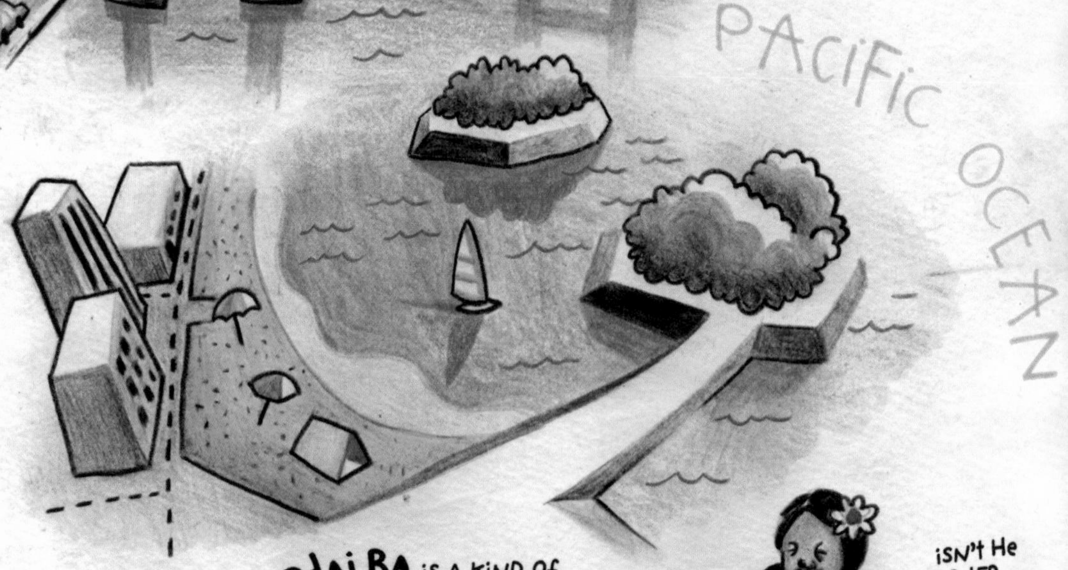

PACIFIC OCEAN

ODAIBA IS A KIND OF BEACH RESORT, WITH MALLS, OUTDOOR CAFÉS, A BEACH, AND ARTIFICIAL ISLANDS. FROM A DISTANCE, IT LOOKS NICE, ESPECIALLY WHEN THE HEAT IN THE CITY (95 DEGREES) IS UNBEARABLE. BUT WHEN YOU GET CLOSER, IT'S A LETDOWN. TOKYO BEING WHAT IT IS, THE WATER IS NOT BLUE, IT'S BROWN. THE SAND IS NOT FINE, IT'S MUD. YOU CAN'T SEE YOUR FEET EVEN IN WATER 4 INCHES DEEP. KIDS ASIDE, NO ADULTS IN THEIR RIGHT MIND WOULD THINK OF GOING IN. WELL, SAILBOARDERS DO.

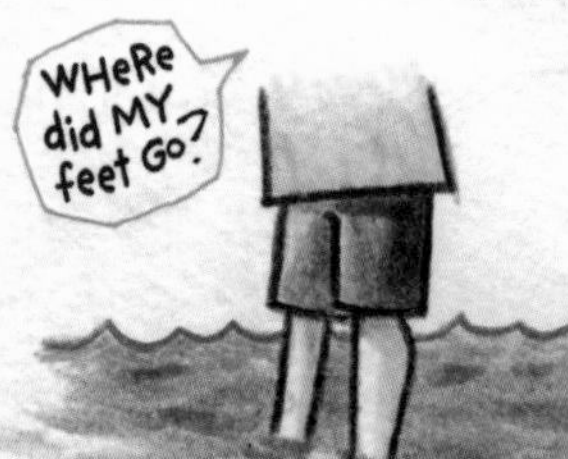

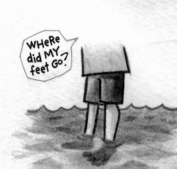

WHERE did MY feet Go?

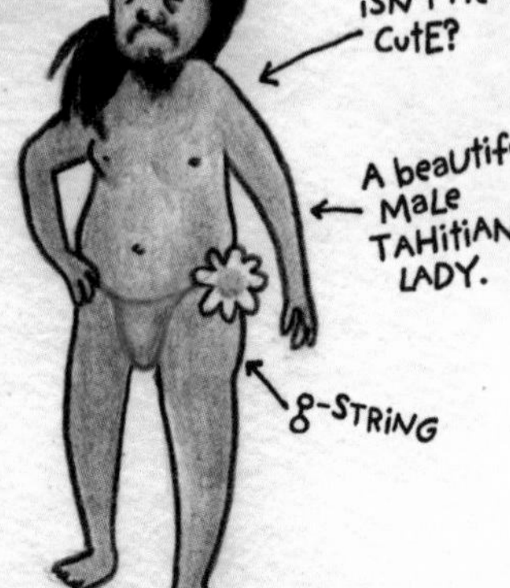

isn't He CutE?
A beautiful Male TAHITIAN LADY.
g-STRING

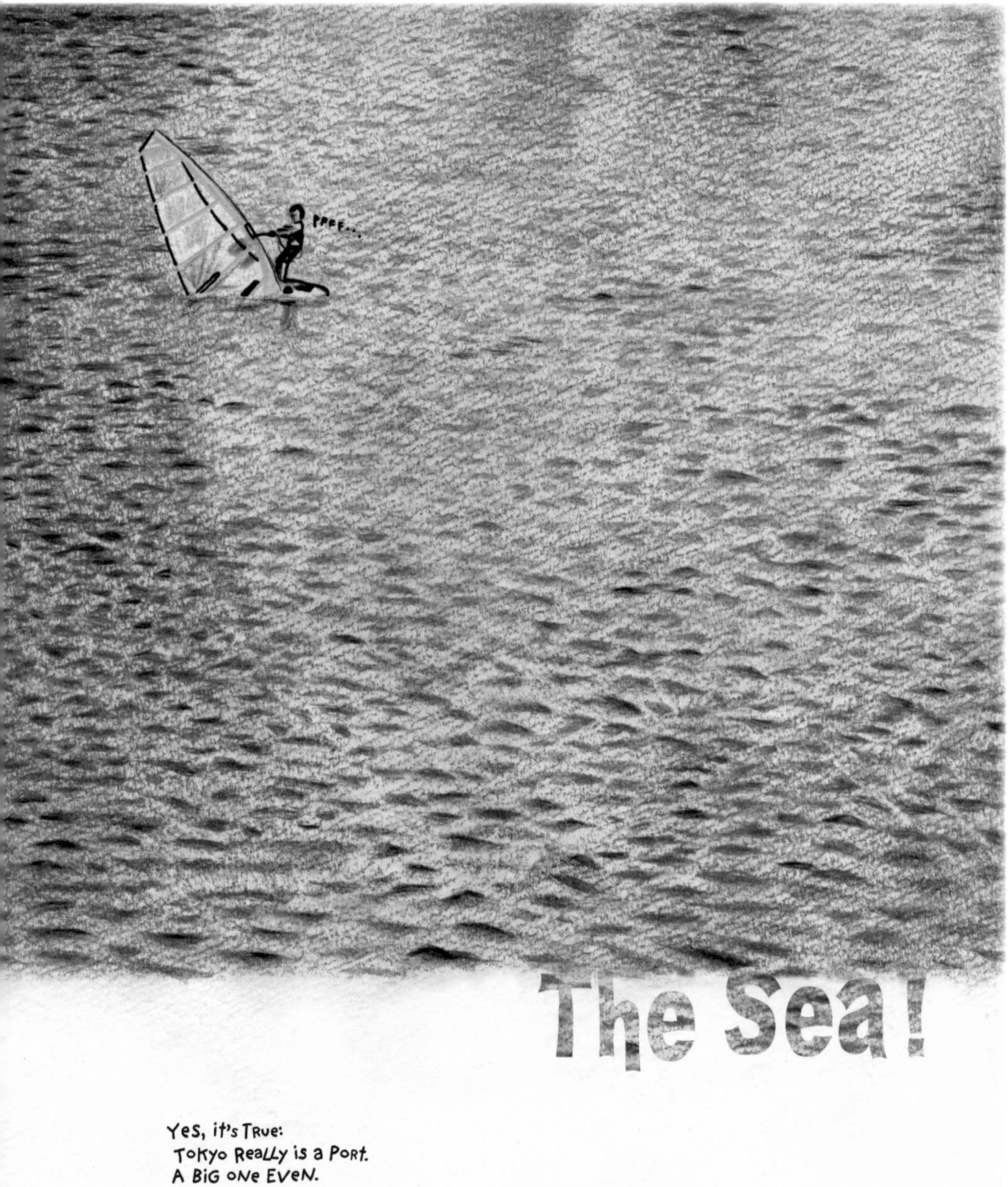
PFFF...

The Sea!

Yes, it's True:
Tokyo Really is a Port.
A Big one Even.
But No French-Fry Vendors
Like Back Home.

interlude

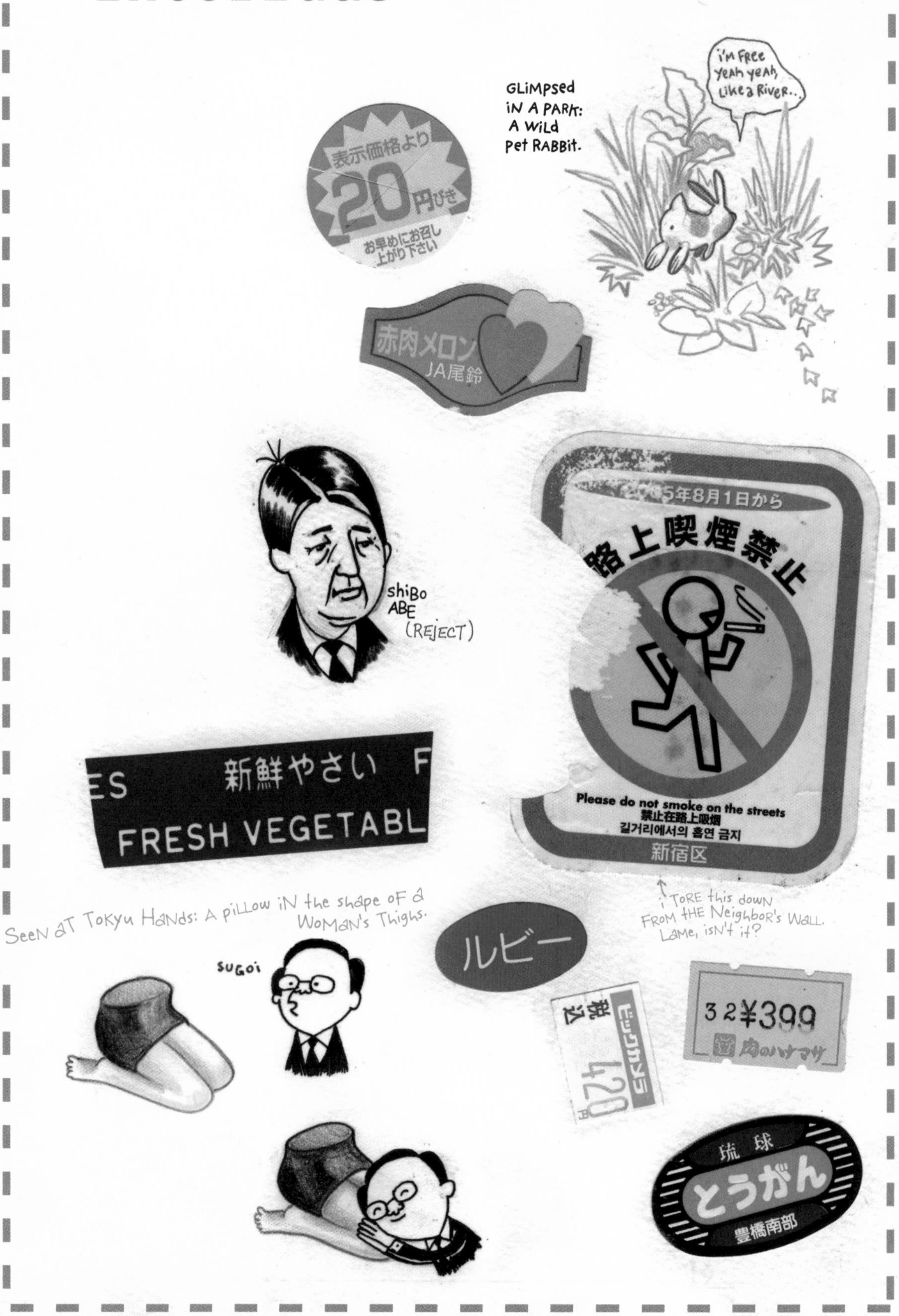

i'm Free
yeah yeah,
Like a River...
GLimpsed
iN A PARK:
A WiLd
Pet RABBit.
表示価格より
20円びき
お早めにお召し
上がり下さい
赤肉メロン
JA尾鈴
shiBo
ABE
(REJECT)
2005年8月1日から
路上喫煙禁止
Please do not smoke on the streets
禁止在路上吸烟
길거리에서의 흡연 금지
新宿区
ES 新鮮やさい F
FRESH VEGETABL
Seen at Tokyu Hands: A pillow iN the shape of a
Woman's Thighs.
i TORE this down
FROM the Neighbor's WaLL.
Lame, isn't it?
ルビー
SUGoi
税込
ビックカメラ
420円
32¥399
肉のハナマサ
琉球
とうがん
豊橋南部

yoyogi harajuku

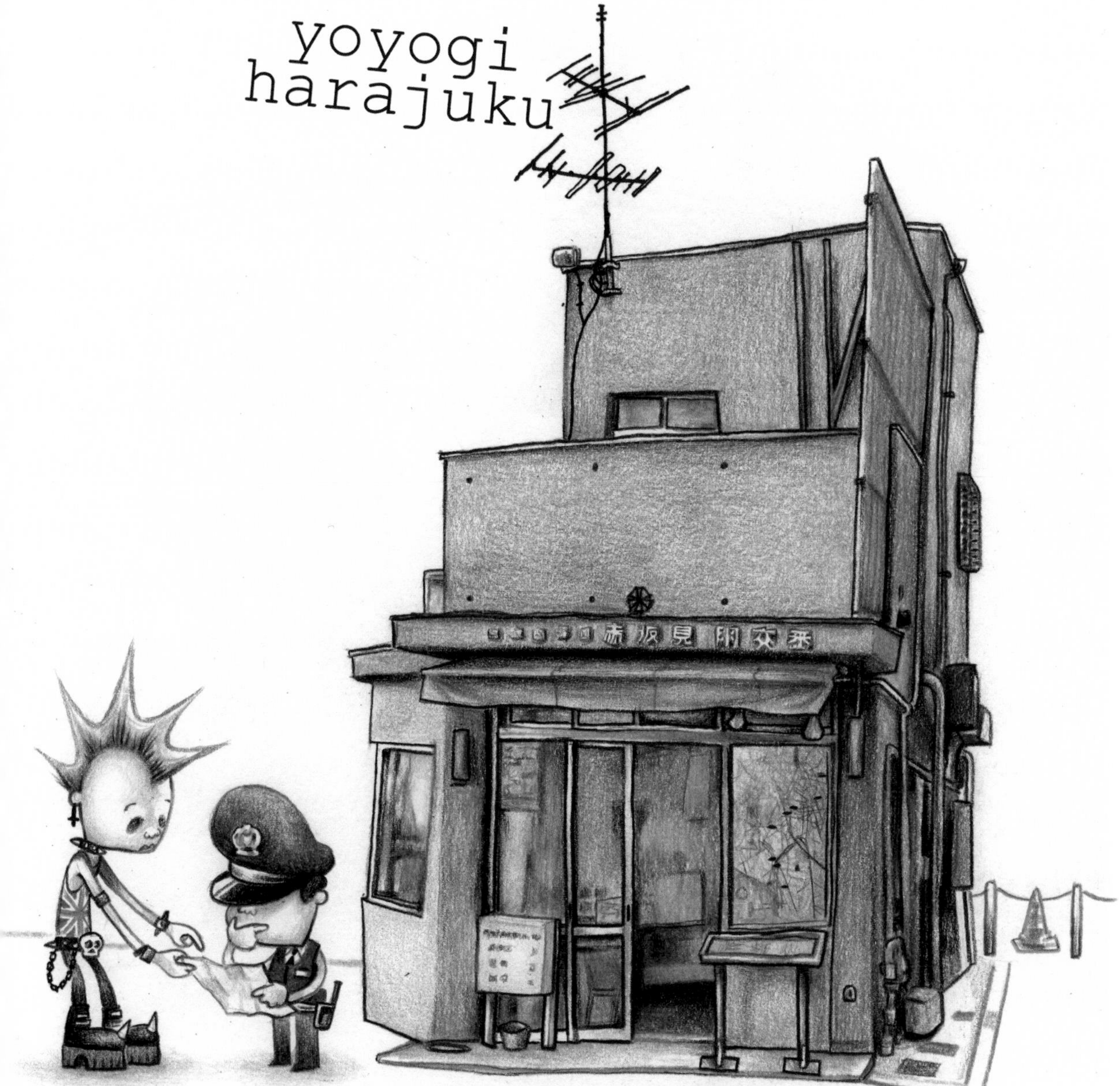
赤坂見附交番

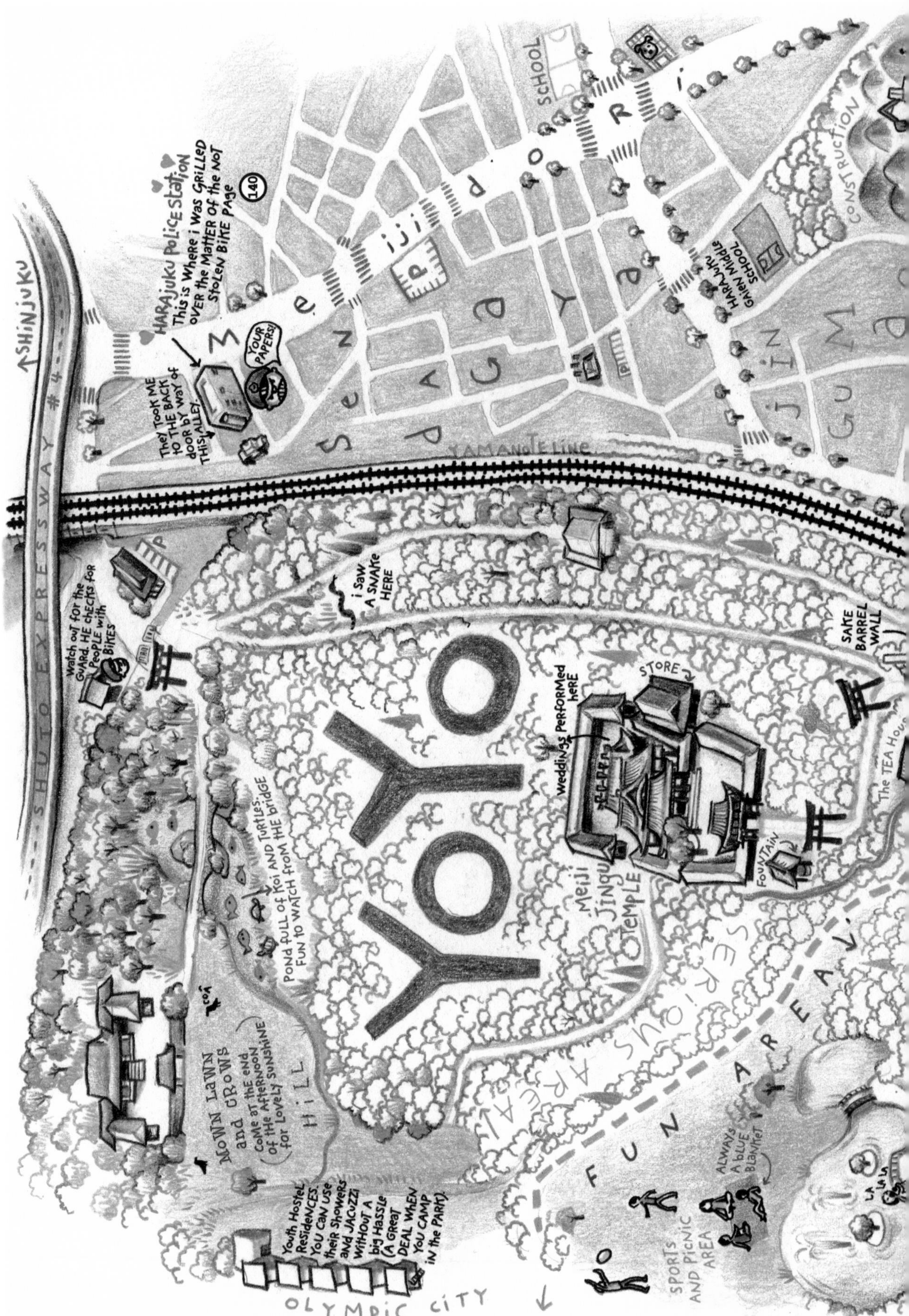
SHINJUKU
SHUTO EXPRESSWAY #4
HARAJUKU POLICE STATION
This is where i was GRILLED OVER the MATTER of the NOT STOLEN BIKE PAGE
140
They took ME to THE BACK door by way of THIS ALLEY.
YOUR PAPERS!
SCHOOL
CONSTRUCTION
YAMANOTE LINE
Watch out for the GUARD. HE checks for PEOPLE with BIKES
i SAW A SNAKE HERE
YOYO
SAKE BARREL WALL
STORE
Weddings Performed here
The TEA House
FOUNTAIN
Meiji Jingu TEMPLE
POND full of Koi AND TURTLES. FUN TO WATCH from THE bridge
MOWN LAWN and CROWS
Come at the end of the afternoon for lovely sunshine
HiLL
Youth Hostel Residences. You can use their showers and Jacuzzi without a big Hassle (A GREAT DEAL WHEN YOU CAMP in the PARK)
OLYMPIC CITY
SERious AREA
FUN AREA
ALWAYS A BLUE BLANKET
SPORTS AND PicNic AREA
LA LA LA

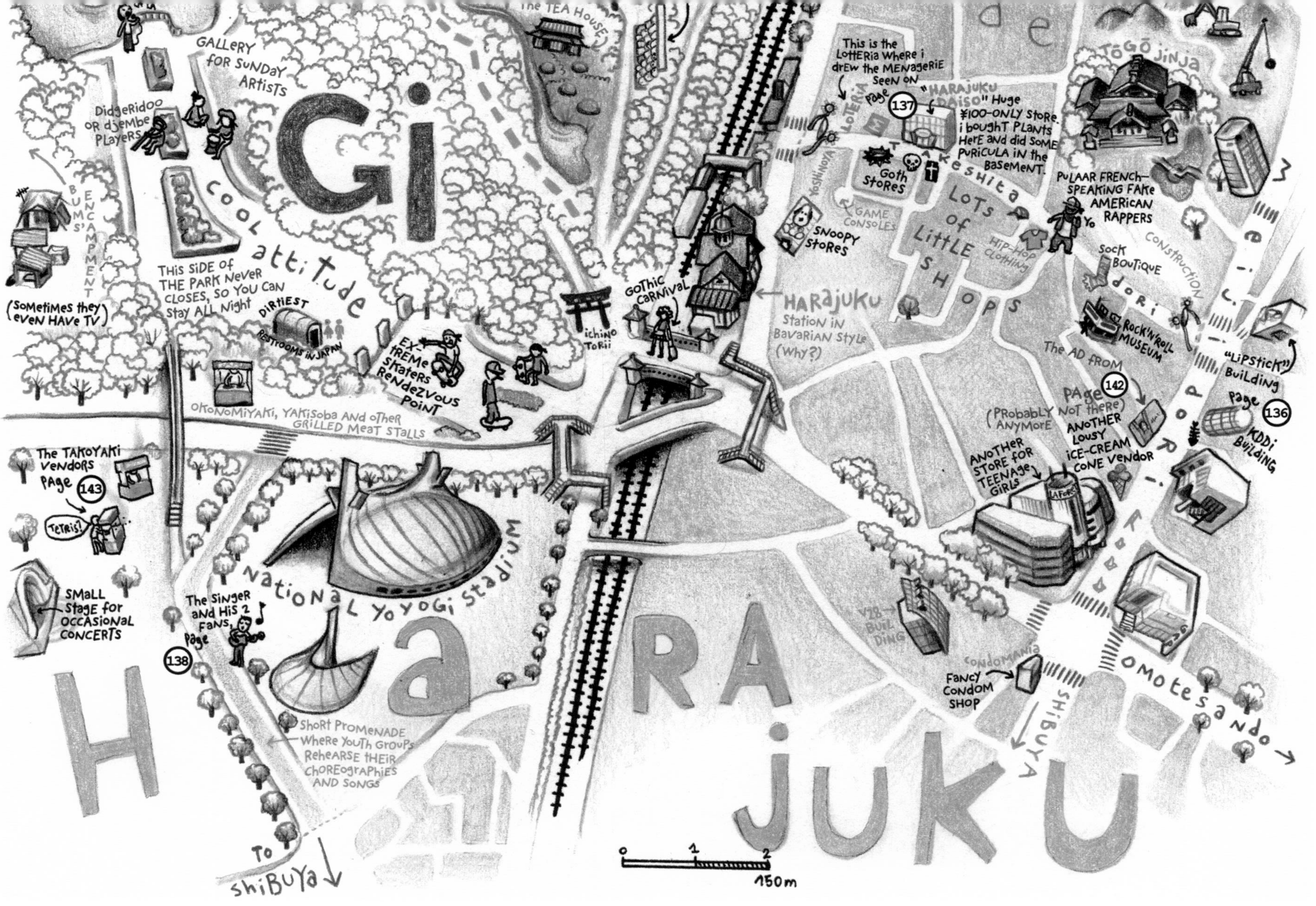
GALLERY FOR SUNDAY ARTISTS
Didgeridoo or djembe PLAYERS
BUMS' ENCAMPMENT
(Sometimes they even HAVE TV)
COOL attitude
This SIDE OF THE PARK NEVER CLOSES, SO YOU CAN Stay ALL Night
DIRTIEST RESTROOMS IN JAPAN
EX-TREME SKATERS RENDEZVOUS POINT
OKONOMIYAKI, YAKISOBA AND OTHER GRILLED MEAT STALLS
The TEA HOUSE
ichino Torii
GOTHIC CARNIVAL
HARAJUKU Station in BAVARIAN STYLE (Why?)
The TAKOYAKI VENDORS Page 143
TETRIS!
SMALL Stage for OCCASIONAL CONCERTS
The Singer and His 2 Fans, Page 138
NATIONAL YOYOGI STADIUM
SHORT PROMENADE WHERE YOUTH GROUPS REHEARSE THEIR CHOREOGRAPHIES AND SONGS
TO SHIBUYA
This is the LOTTERIA where i drew the MENAGERIE seen on Page 137
LOTTERIA
"HARAJUKU DAISO" Huge ¥100-ONLY STORE. i bought PLANTS HERE and did SOME PURICULA in the BASEMENT.
YOSHINOYA
Goth Stores
GAME CONSOLES
SNOOPY STORES
TAKESHITA DORI
LOTS of LITTLE SHOPS
HIP-HOP CLOTHING
TŌGŌ JINJA
PULAAR FRENCH-SPEAKING FAKE AMERICAN RAPPERS
Yo
SOCK BOUTIQUE
CONSTRUCTION
ROCK'N'ROLL MUSEUM
The AD FROM Page 142 (PROBABLY NOT THERE ANYMORE)
ANOTHER LOUSY ICE-CREAM CONE VENDOR
ANOTHER STORE FOR TEENAGE GIRLS
LAFORET
"LIPSTICK" BUILDING Page 136
KDDI BUILDING
MEIJI DORI
V28 BUILDING
CONDOMANIA
Fancy CONDOM SHOP
SHIBUYA
OMOTESANDO
HARAJUKU
0 1 2
150m

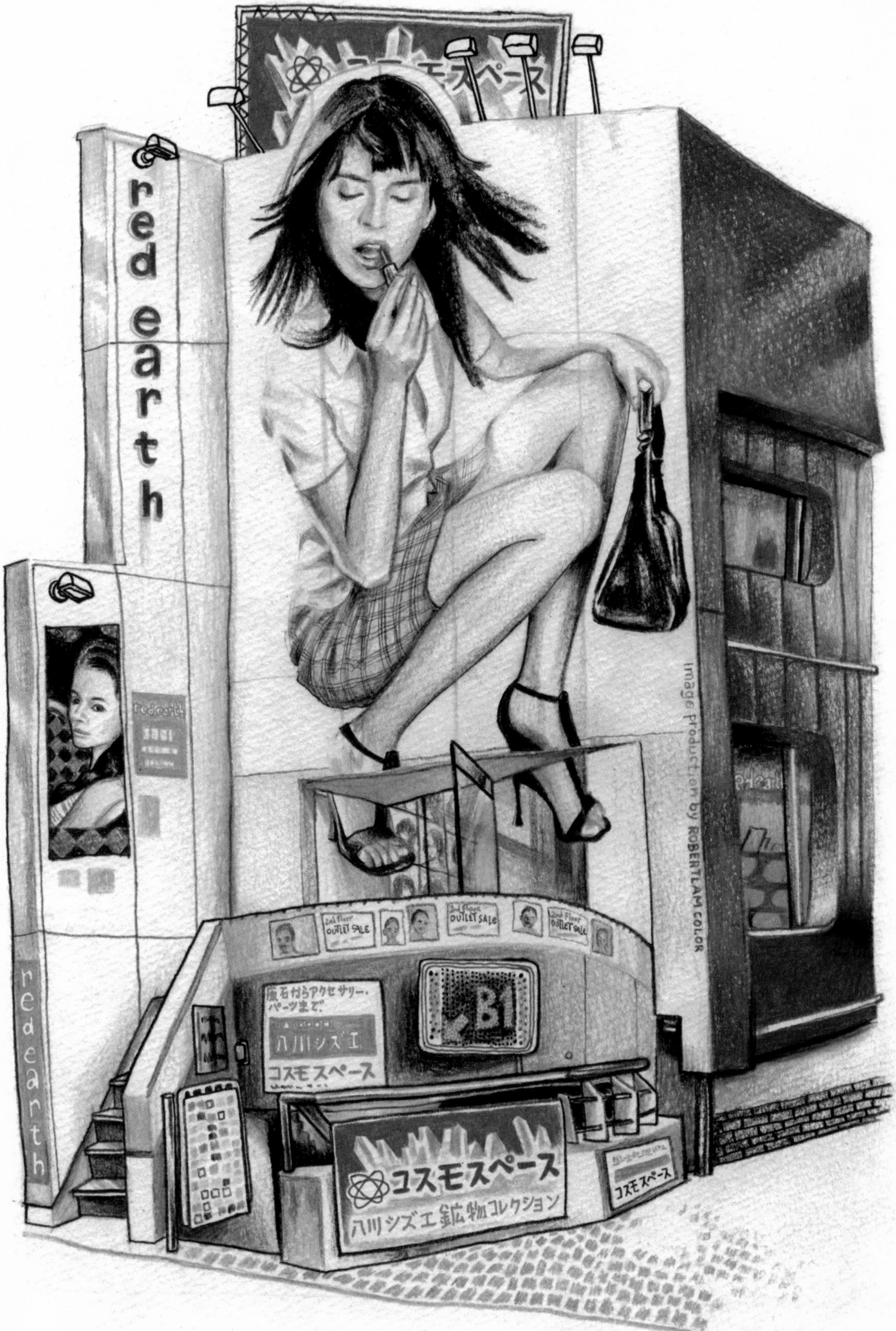
red earth
コスモスペース
image production by ROBERTLAM COLOR
2nd Floor OUTLET SALE
原石からアクセサリー・パーツまで
八川シズエ
コスモスペース
B1
コスモスペース
八川シズエ鉱物コレクション
コスモスペース
red earth

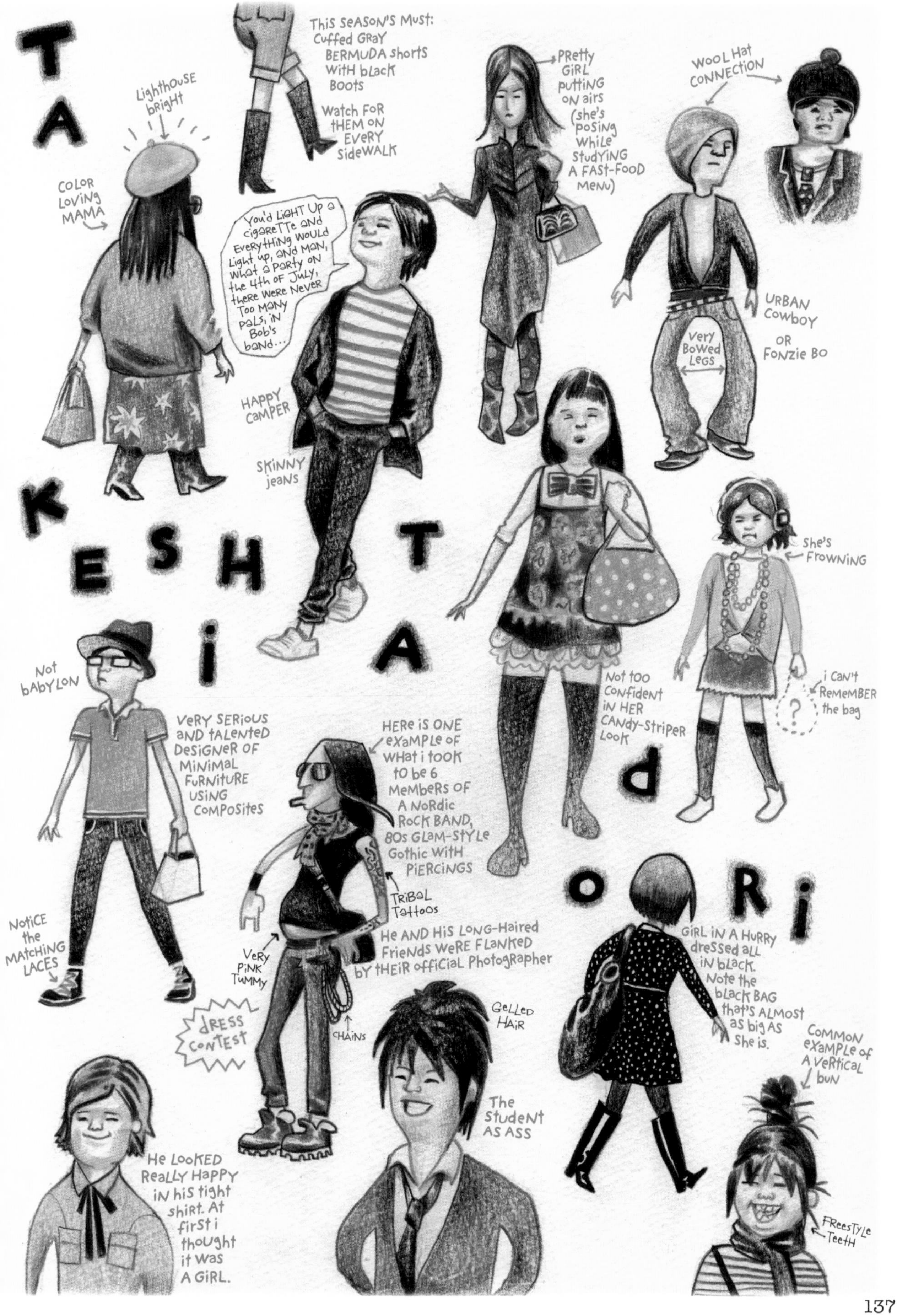

TA
KESH
i TA
d
o Ri
Lighthouse bright
COLOR LOVING MAMA
This SEASON'S Must: Cuffed GRAY BERMUDA shorts WITH black Boots
Watch FOR THEM ON EVERY SideWALK
Pretty GIRL putting ON airs (she's posing while studying A FAST-FOOD menu)
WOOL Hat CONNECTION
You'd Light Up a cigarette and everything would light up, and man, what a party on the 4th of July, there were never too many pals, in Bob's band...
HAPPY CAMPER
SKINNY jeans
URBAN COWBOY OR FONZIE BO
Very Bowed Legs
She's FROWNING
i can't Remember the bag
?
Not babylon
VERY SERIOUS AND TALENTED DESIGNER OF MINIMAL FURNITURE USING COMPOSITES
HERE IS ONE EXAMPLE OF WHAT i TOOK TO BE 6 MEMBERS OF A NORDIC ROCK BAND, 80s GLAM-STYLE Gothic WITH PIERCINGS
Not too Confident in HER CANDY-STRIPER LOOK
TRIBAL Tattoos
Notice the MATCHING LACES
Very PINK TUMMY
He AND HIS LONG-Haired Friends WERE FLANKED BY THEIR official Photographer
CHAINS
dRESS CONTEST
GIRL IN A HURRY dressed ALL IN black. Note the black BAG that's ALMOST as big AS She is.
Gelled HAIR
COMMON EXAMPLE of A VERTICAL bun
The Student AS ASS
He LOOKED REALLY HAPPY IN his tight shirt. At first i thought it was A GIRL.
FReesTyLe TeeTH

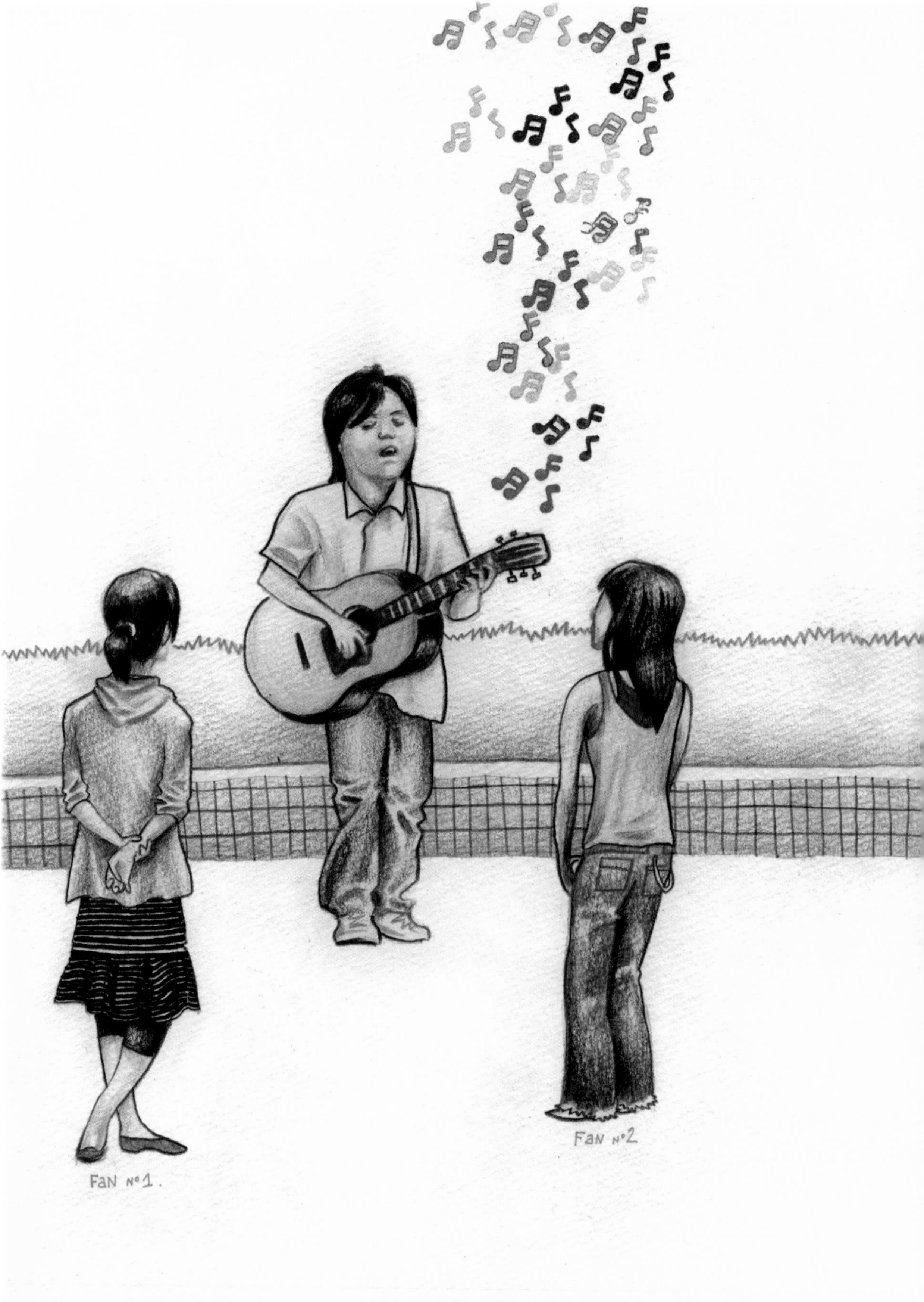
FaN No1.
FaN No2

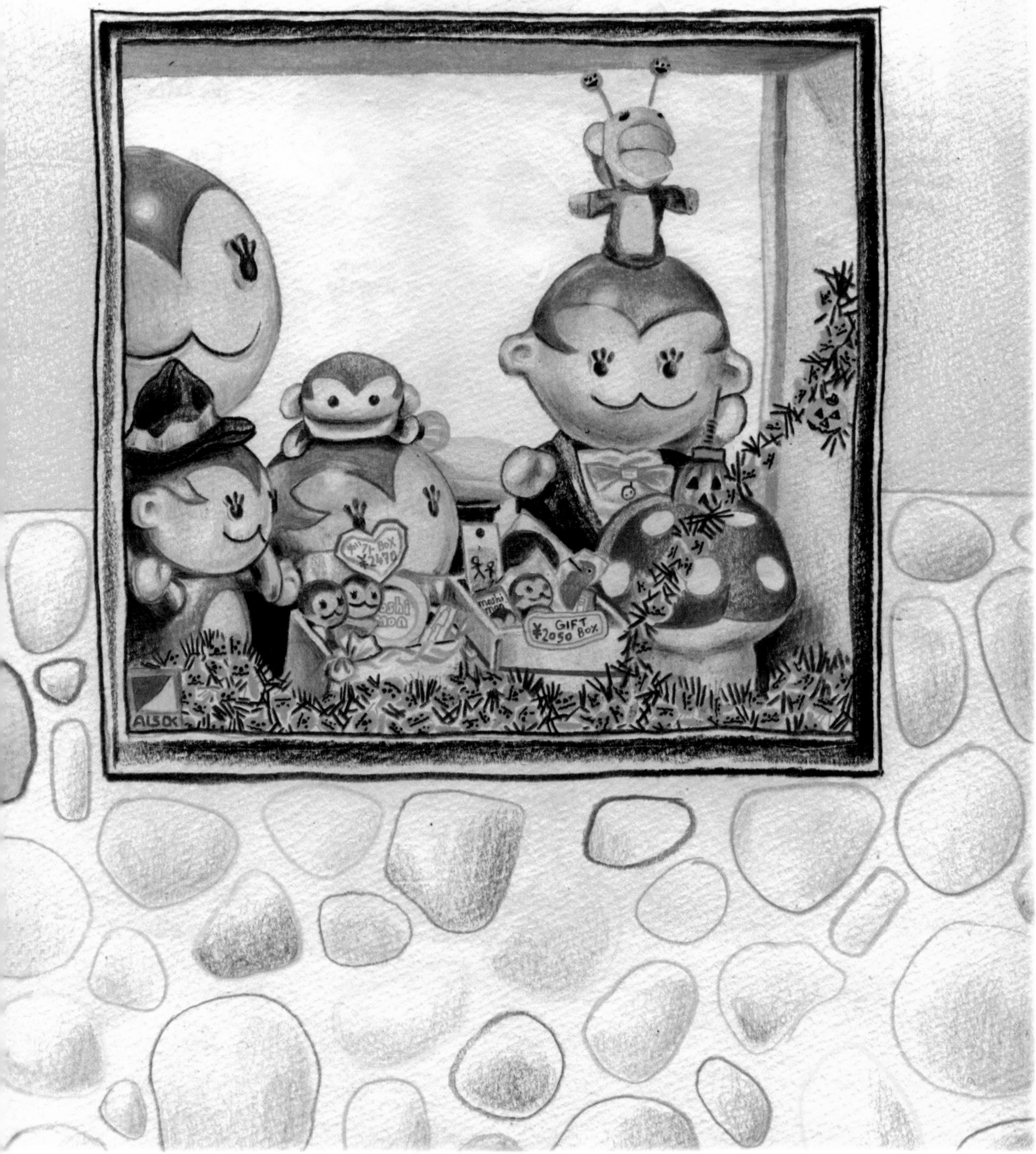
ギフトBOX ¥2490
meshi mon
GIFT ¥2050 BOX
ALSOK

HOW did I GeT HeRe?

OR
HOW to BeCOME HOMesicK FoR YOUR DeAR FAtHeRLAND

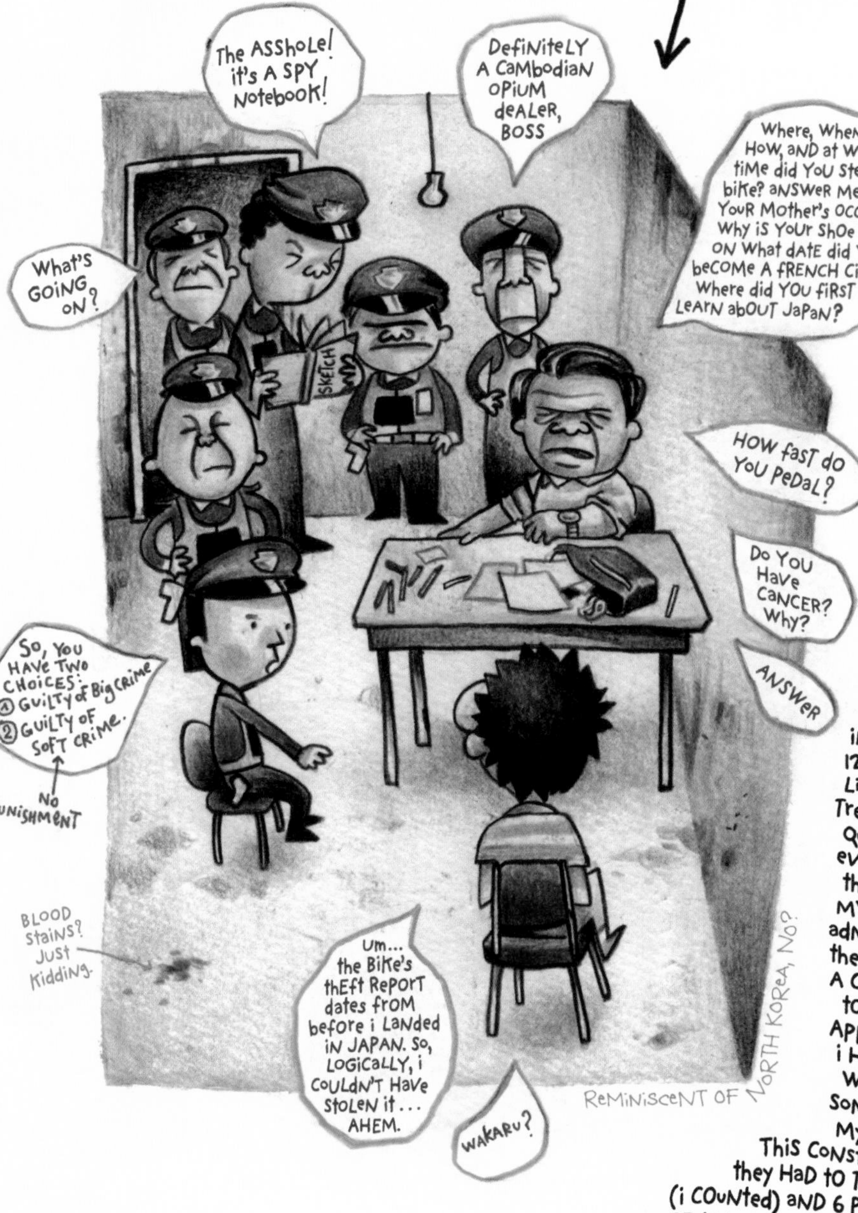

The ASSHOLE! it's A SPY Notebook!
DefiNiteLY A CamBodian OPiUM deALeR, BOSS
What's GOiNG ON?
SKETCH
Where, WheN, HOW, AND at What tiMe did YOU steAL This bike? ANSWeR Me. What is YOUR Mother's OCCUpation? Why is YOUr ShOe Size 9? ON What date did YOU become A FRENCH Citizen? Where did YOU fiRST Learn about JaPaN?
HOW fasT do YOU PeDaL?
Do YOU Have CANCER? Why?
ANSWeR
So, YOU HAVE TWO CHOICES: ① GUILTY of Big CRIME ② GUILTY OF SOFT CRIME.
No PUNISHMENT
BLOOD STAINS? JUST Kidding.
Um... the Bike's theft Report dates from before i Landed iN JAPAN. So, LOGiCaLLY, i COULDN'T Have stoLEN it . . . AHEM.
WAKARU?
ReMiNiSceNT OF NORTH KORea, No?

WHAT FOLLOWED WAS aN iNTERROGATiON LASTiNG 90 to 120 MiNUTES iN A DiNGY LiTTLe ROOM Where i WAS TReATED TO a STRiNG OF WACKO QUESTiONS. FOR The eNTIRE eveNING i WAS the FOCUS OF the whoLe PoLice StatiON. MY iNTeRROGATORS fiNaLLY admitted That i HADN'T STOLEN the biKE (WHICH BeLONGed to A CeRTAiN Mr. iCHi, ACCORDiNG to their fiLES) BuT HAD APPROPRiated iT. iN Short, i HAD bORROWED A Bike THAT WAS aLReady STOLEN, SOMEThING i'd fiGURED OUT fOR MYSELf, ACTUALLY. FOR THEM, ThiS CONSTiTUTED A CriMe SO HEiNOUS they HAD TO Take 24 fiNGERPRiNTS (i COUNTED) AND 6 PiCTURES Of Me adORNED With SERiAL NUMBERS (À LA Hugh GRANT). NOW i'M ON fiLE, aNd they WARNED Me that aT The first SCREW-UP i'd Have to LEAVE JAPAN.

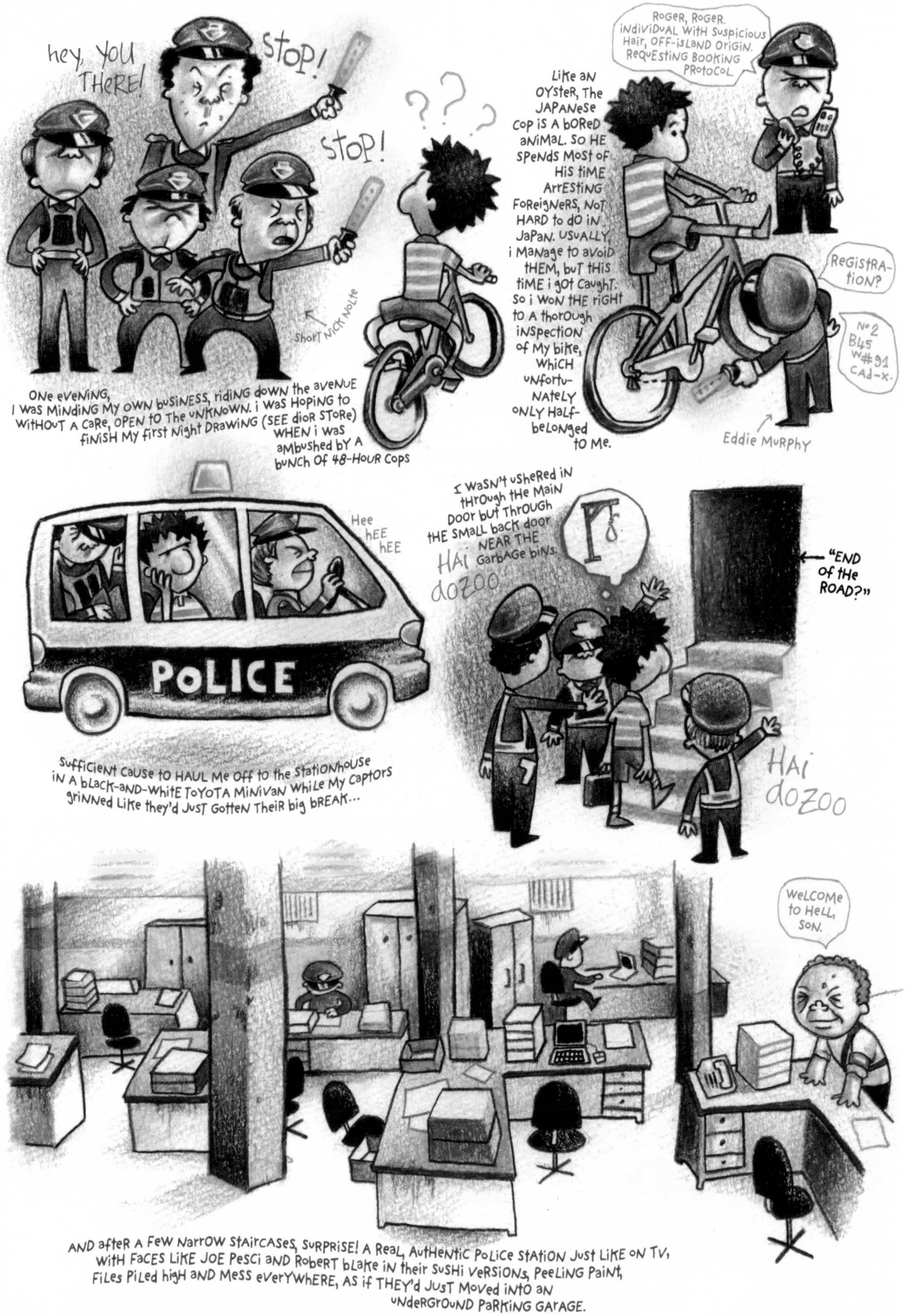
hey, YOU THERE!
STOP!
STOP!
Short Nick Nolte
ONE evening, I was minding my own business, riding down the avenue without a care, open to the unknown. i was hoping to finish my first night drawing (see dior store) when i was ambushed by a bunch of 48-Hour Cops
Like an oyster, the Japanese cop is a bored animal. So he spends most of his time arresting foreigners, not hard to do in Japan. Usually, i manage to avoid them, but this time i got caught. So i won the right to a thorough inspection of my bike, which unfortunately only half-belonged to me.
Roger, Roger. Individual with suspicious hair, off-island origin. Requesting booking protocol
Registration?
No 2 B45 W#91 CAd-x.
Eddie Murphy
Hee hEE hEE
Hai dozoo
Sufficient cause to haul me off to the stationhouse in a black-and-white Toyota minivan while my captors grinned like they'd just gotten their big break...
POLICE
I wasn't ushered in through the main door but through the small back door near the garbage bins.
"END of the ROAD?"
Hai dozoo
Welcome to Hell, son.
And after a few narrow staircases, surprise! A real, authentic police station just like on TV, with faces like Joe Pesci and Robert Blake in their sushi versions, peeling paint, files piled high and mess everywhere, as if they'd just moved into an underground parking garage.

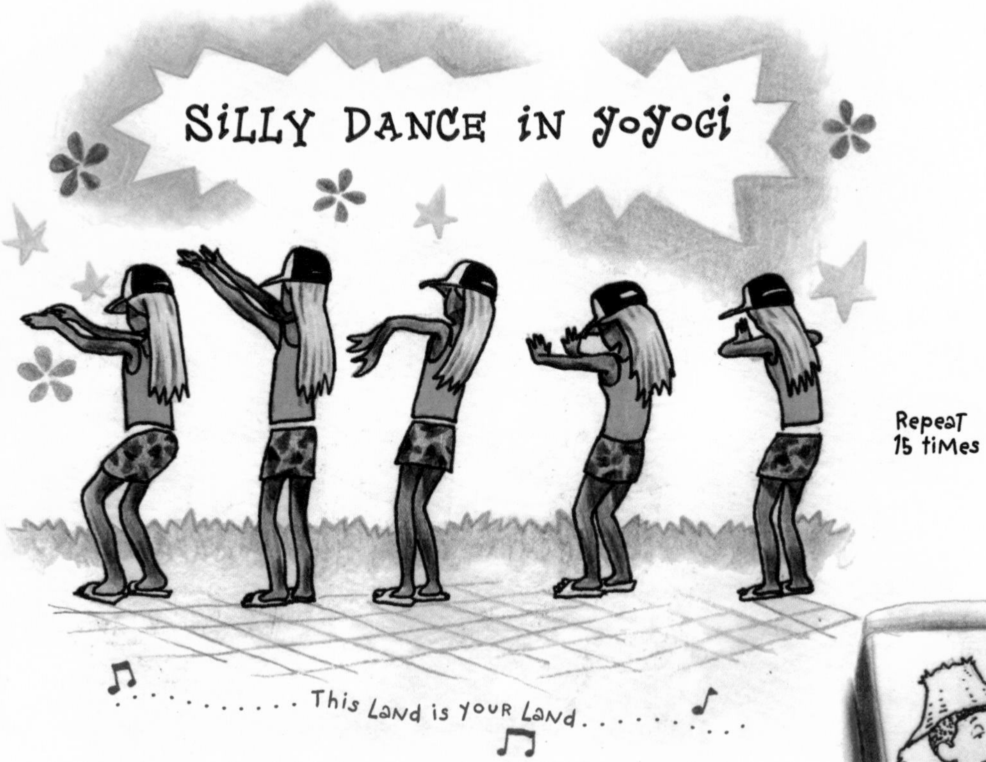
SiLLY DANCE iN YoYoGi
Repeat 15 times
This Land is your Land

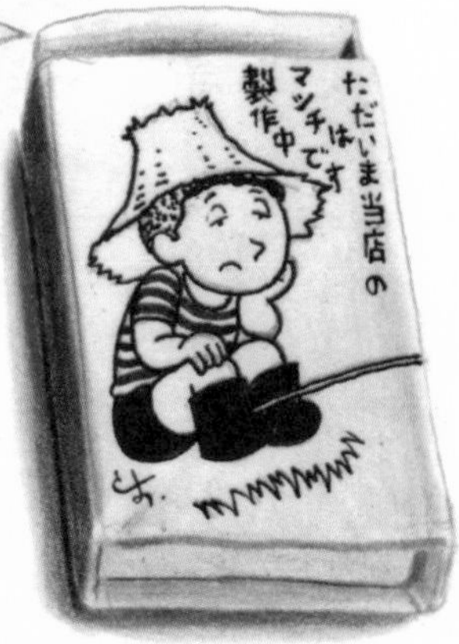
ただいま当店のマッチは製作中です

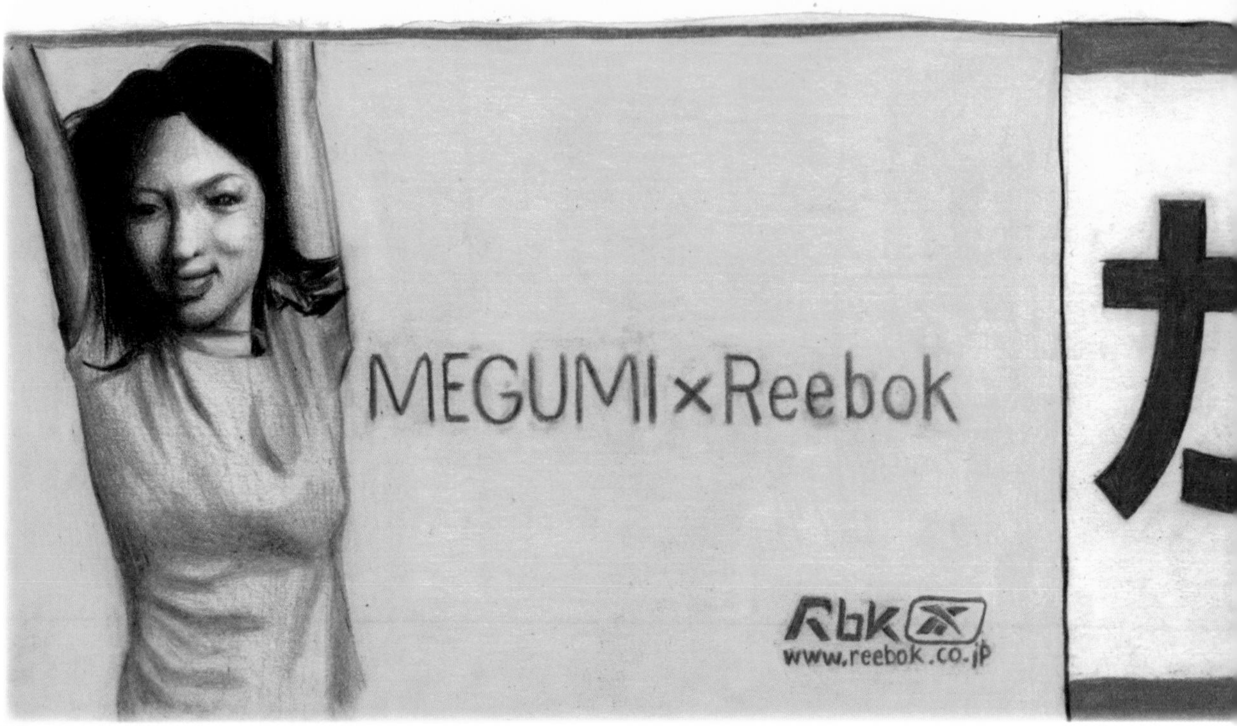
MEGUMI×Reebok
Rbk
www.reebok.co.jp

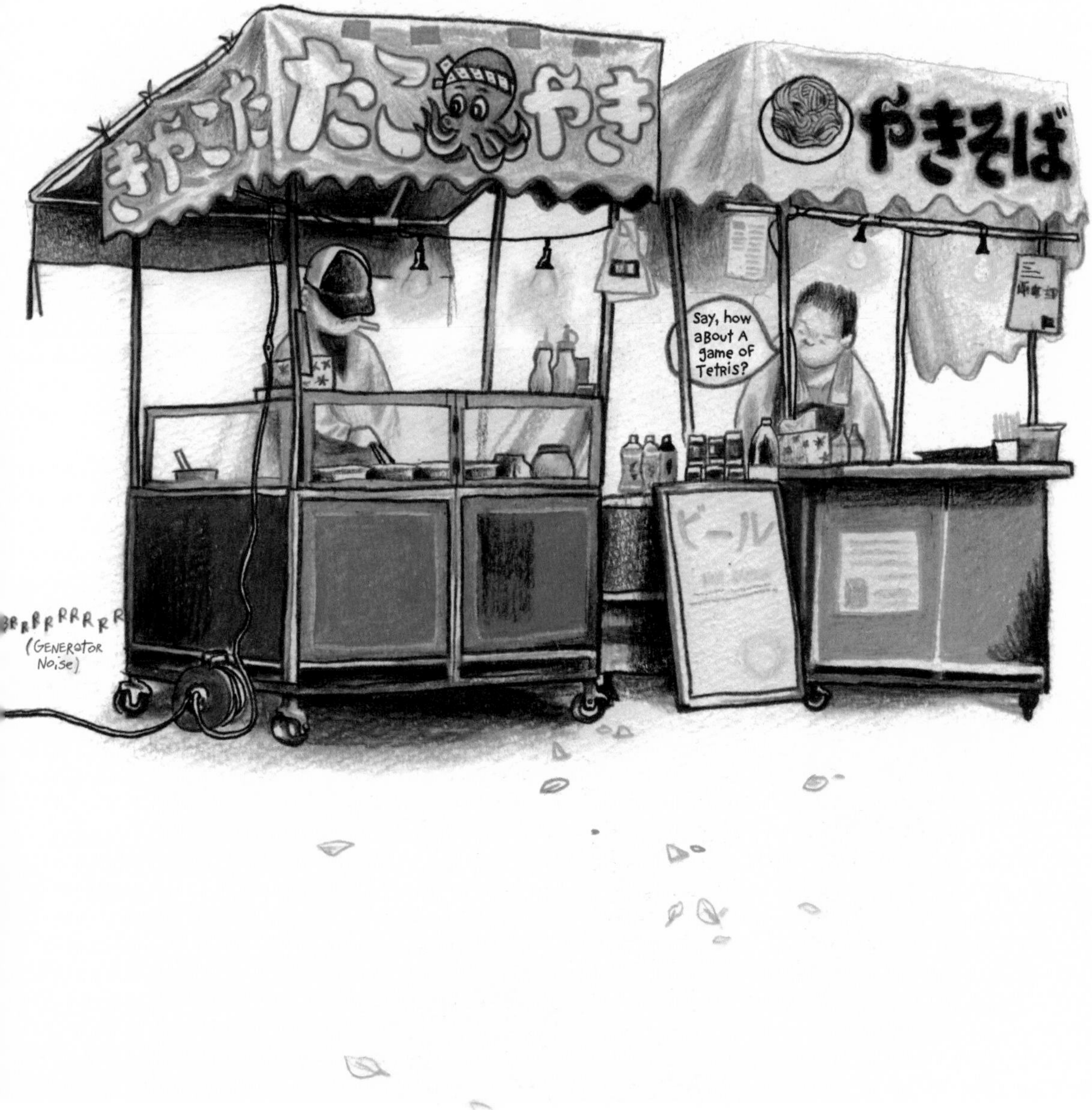

たこやき
やきそば
Say, how about A game of Tetris?
ビール
BRRRRRRRRRR
(GENERATOR Noise)

interlude

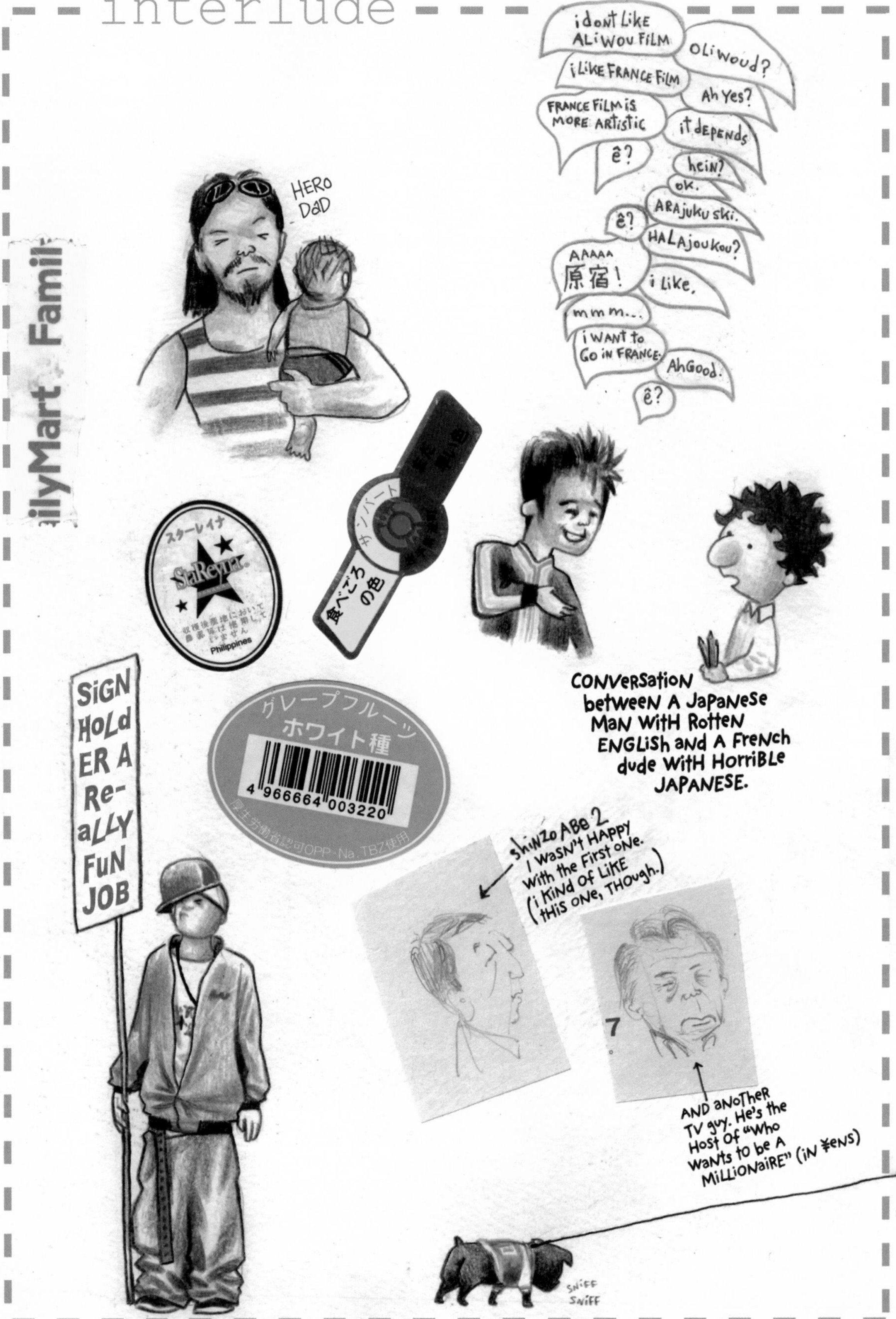
i dont Like ALiWOU FILM
OLiwoud?
i Like FRANCE FiLM
Ah Yes?
FRANCE FiLM iS MORE ARtiStic
it depends
ê?
hein?
ok.
ARAjuku ski.
ê?
HALAjoukou?
AAAAA 原宿!
i Like.
mmm...
i WANT to Go in FRANCE.
AhGood.
ê?
HERO DaD
ilyMart Famil
スターレイナ
StaReyna
Philippines
サンパート
食べごろの色
グレープフルーツ
ホワイト種
4 966664 003220
厚生労働省認可OPP-Na,TBZ使用
CONVERSATION between A JapaNese MaN WitH RotteN ENGLiSh and A French dude WitH HorribLe JAPANESE.
SiGN HOLdER A Re-aLLY FuN JOB
ShiNZO ABE 2 I WASN't HAPPY With the First oNe. (i KiNd Of LiKE tHiS oNE, THough.)
7
AND aNOTHER TV guy. He's the Host of "Who wants to be A MiLLiONaiRE" (iN ¥eNS)
SNiFF SNiFF

interlude

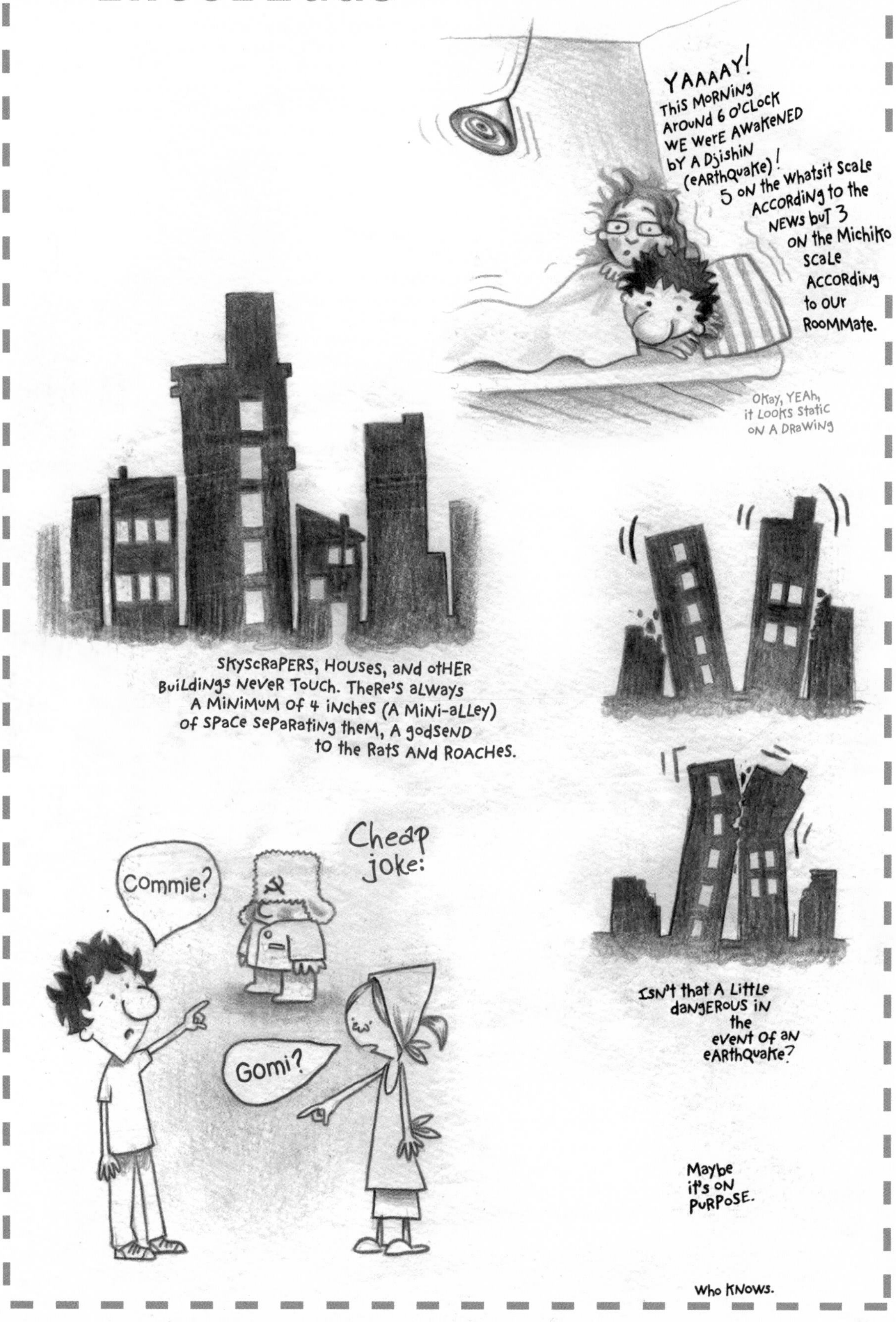
YAAAAY! This MORNING AROUND 6 O'CLOCK WE WERE AWAKENED by A Djishin (eARThquake)! 5 on the Whatsit Scale According to the NEWS buT 3 ON the Michiko Scale ACCORDING to OUr RooMMate.
Okay, YEAh, it Looks Static ON A DRAWING
SKYSCRAPERS, HOUSES, AND OTHER BUILDINGS NEVER TOUCH. THERE'S ALWAYS A MINIMUM OF 4 INCHES (A MINI-ALLEY) OF SPACE SEPARATING THEM, A GODSEND TO THE RATS AND ROACHES.
ISN'T THAT A LITTLE DANGEROUS IN THE EVENT OF AN EARTHQUAKE?
Cheap joke:
Commie?
Gomi?
Maybe it's ON PURPOSE.
Who KNOWS.

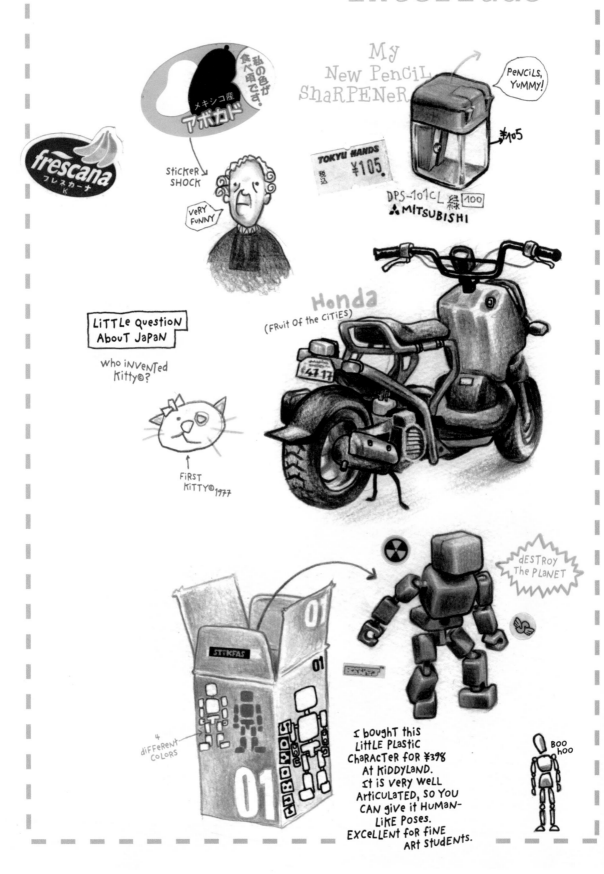

frescana
フレスカーナ
K

メキシコ産
アボカド
私の色が
食べ頃です。

StickeR
SHOCK

VeRY
FUNNY

My
New PenciL
SHaRPENeR

PeNCiLS,
YUMMY!

TOKYU HANDS
税込 ¥105.

¥105

DPS-101CL 緑 100
MITSUBISHI

LiTTLe QuestioN
AbouT JapaN

who iNVeNteD
Kitty©?

Honda
(FRuit Of the CiTiES)

47 17

FiRST
KiTTY© 1977

STIKFAS

01

01

CUBOYDS

01

4
diFFeReNt
COLORS

dESTRoy
The PLaNeT

I boughT this
LiTTLe PLastiC
ChaRacTeR FoR ¥398
AT KiDDYLAND.
It iS VeRY WeLL
ARtiCULATED, SO YOU
CAN give it HUMAN-
LiKe PoseS.
EXCELLeNt FoR fiNe
ARt StudeNts.

BOO
hoo

146

omotesando aoyama

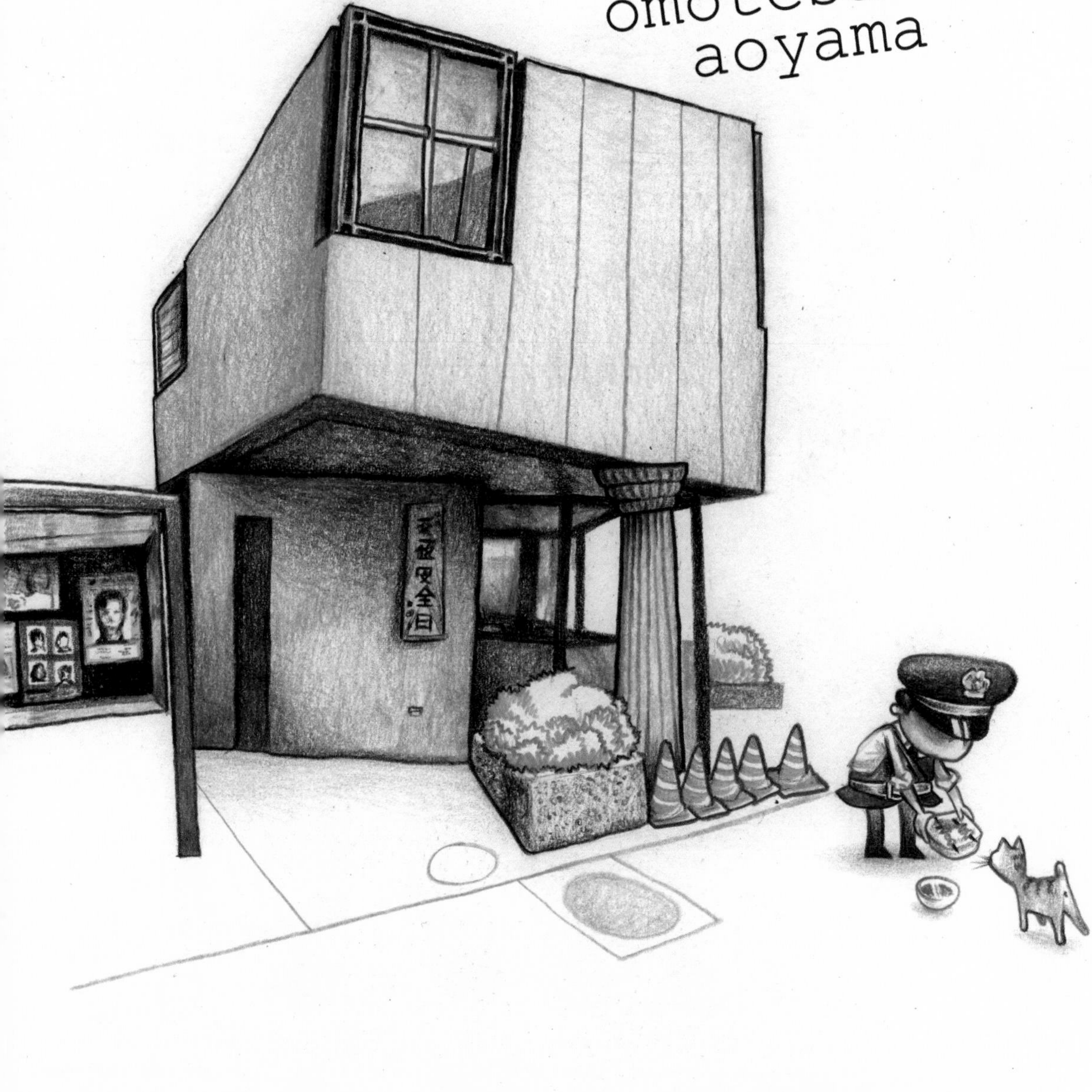

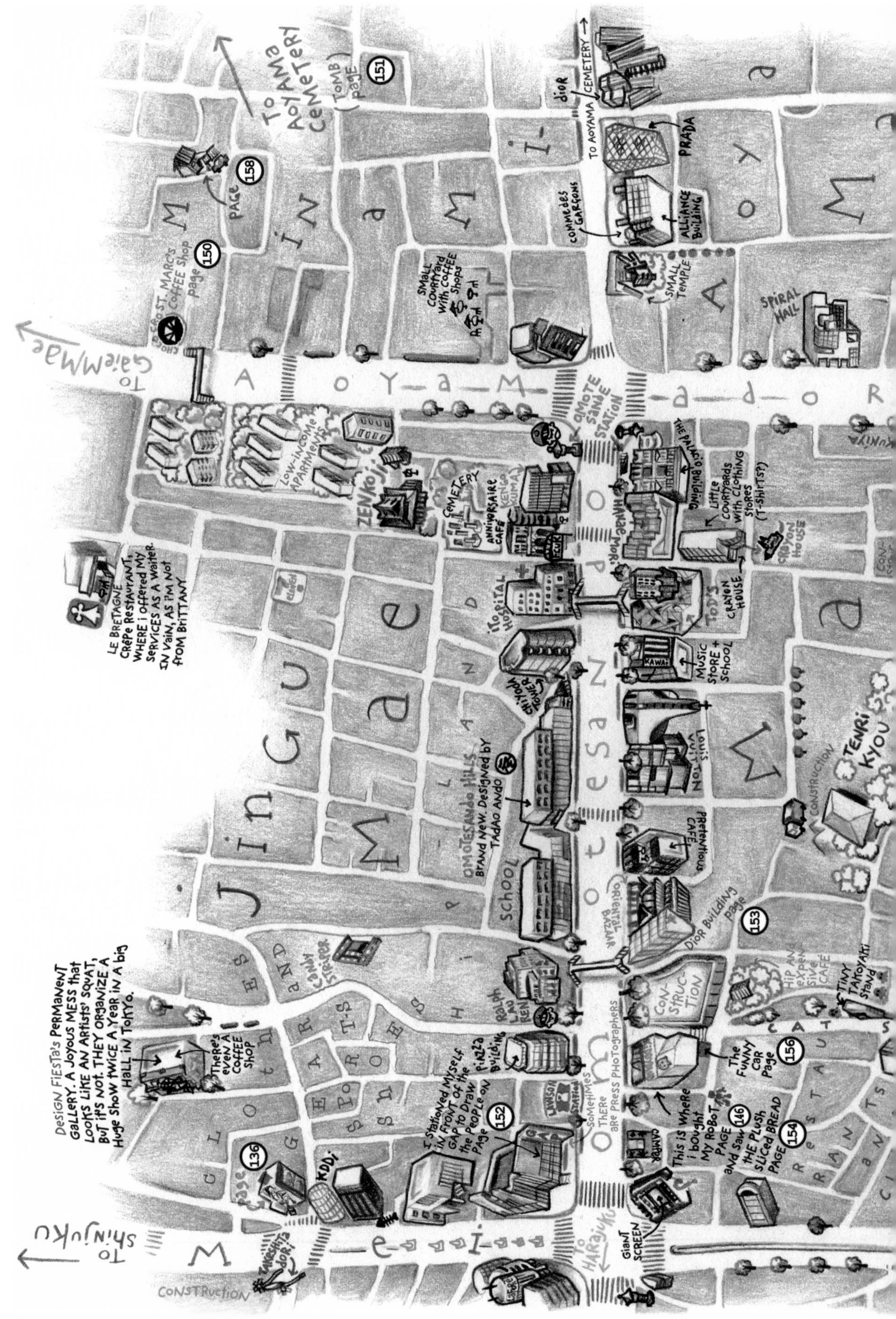

To Gaiemmae
To Shinjuku
To Harajuku
To Aoyama Cemetery
Tomb page 151
Page 158
St. Marc's Coffee Shop page 150
Le Bretagne crêpe restaurant, where i offered my services as a waiter. In vain, as i'm not from Brittany
Design Fiesta's permanent gallery. A joyous mess that looks like an artists' squat, but it's not. They organize a huge show twice a year in a big hall in Tokyo.
There's even a coffee shop
Page 136
KDDi
Takeshita dori
Construction
I stationed myself in front of the Gap to draw the people on page 152
Piazza Building
Ralph Lauren
Candy Stripper
School
Omotesando Hills Brand new. Designed by Tadao Ando
Chiyoda Tower
Ito Hospital
Anniversaire Café
Kengo Kuma
Cemetery
Zenkoji
Low-income apartments
Omotesando Station
Small courtyard with coffee shops
Dior
To Aoyama Cemetery
Prada
Comme des Garçons
Alliance Building
Small Temple
Spiral Hall
The Palace
Hanae Mori Building
Little courtyards with clothing stores (T-shirts?)
Crayon House
Tod's
Music store + school
Kawai
Louis Vuitton
Tenri Kyou
Construction
Pretentious Café
Oriental Bazaar
Dior Building page 153
Con-struc-tion
Hip and expensive café
Tiny Takoyaki stand
The funny car page 156
This is where i bought my robot page 146 and saw the plush sliced bread page 154
Camper
Giant screen
Sometimes there are press photographers
Lawson
Station
Aoyama Dori
Omotesando
Meiji Dori
Jingumae
Minami Aoyama
Cat Street
Restaurants

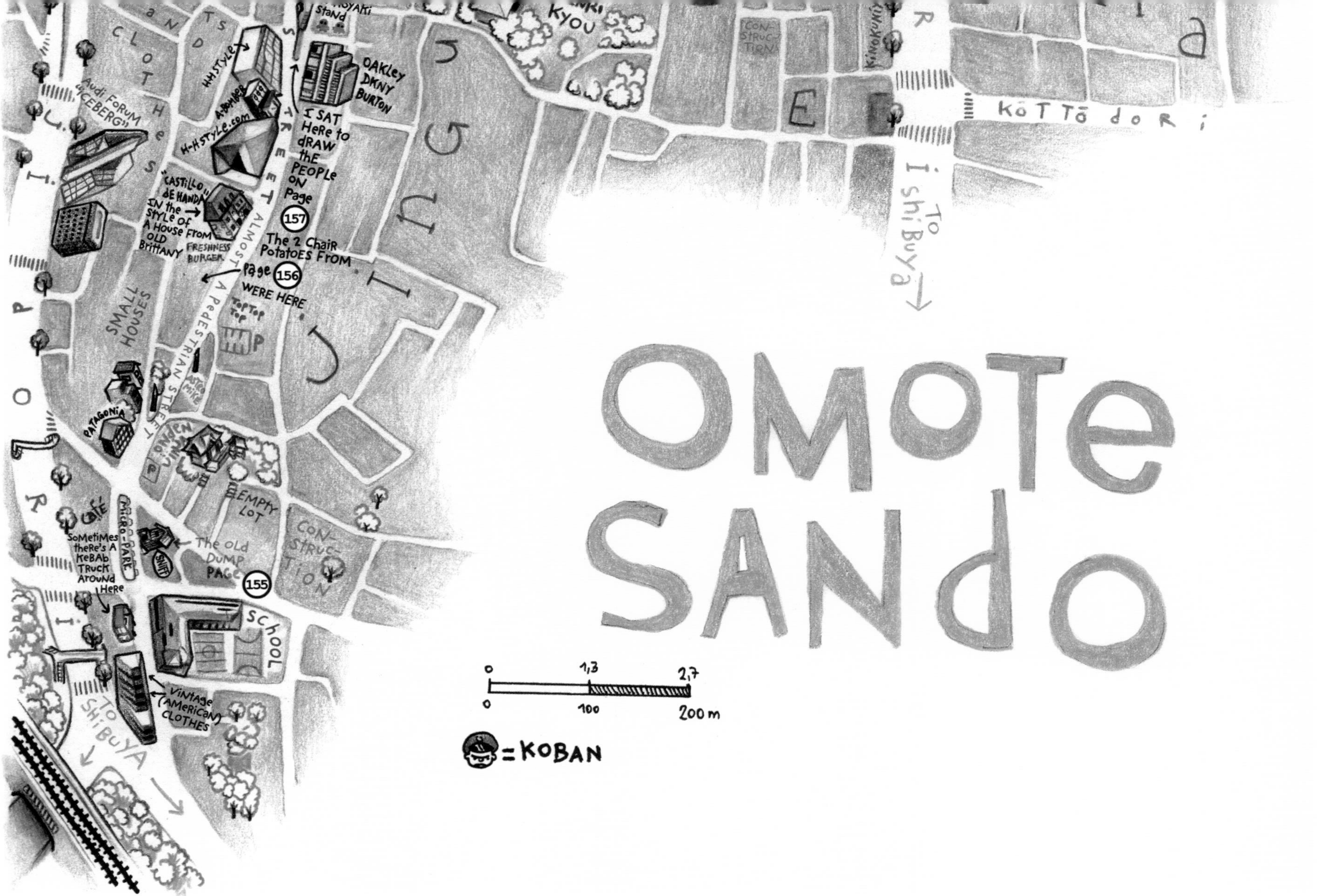
OMOTE SANDO
KŌTTŌ DORI
TO SHIBUYA →
KINOKUNIYA
CONSTRUCTION
OAKLEY
DKNY
BURTON
I SAT HERE TO DRAW THE PEOPLE ON PAGE 157
THE 2 CHAIR POTATOES FROM PAGE 156 WERE HERE
ALMOST A PEDESTRIAN STREET
H-HSTYLE
H-HSTYLE.COM
A-BOMBER
"CASTILLO DE HANDA" IN THE STYLE OF A HOUSE FROM OLD BRITTANY
FRESHNESS BURGER
AUDI FORUM "ICEBERG"
SMALL HOUSES
PATAGONIA
TOP TOP TOP
ASTRO MIKE
EMPTY LOT
CONSTRUCTION
THE OLD DUMP PAGE 155
SNIFF
MICRO-PARK
CAFÉ
SOMETIMES THERE'S A KEBAB TRUCK AROUND HERE
SCHOOL
VINTAGE (AMERICAN) CLOTHES
TO SHIBUYA
0 1,3 2,7
0 100 200 m
= KOBAN

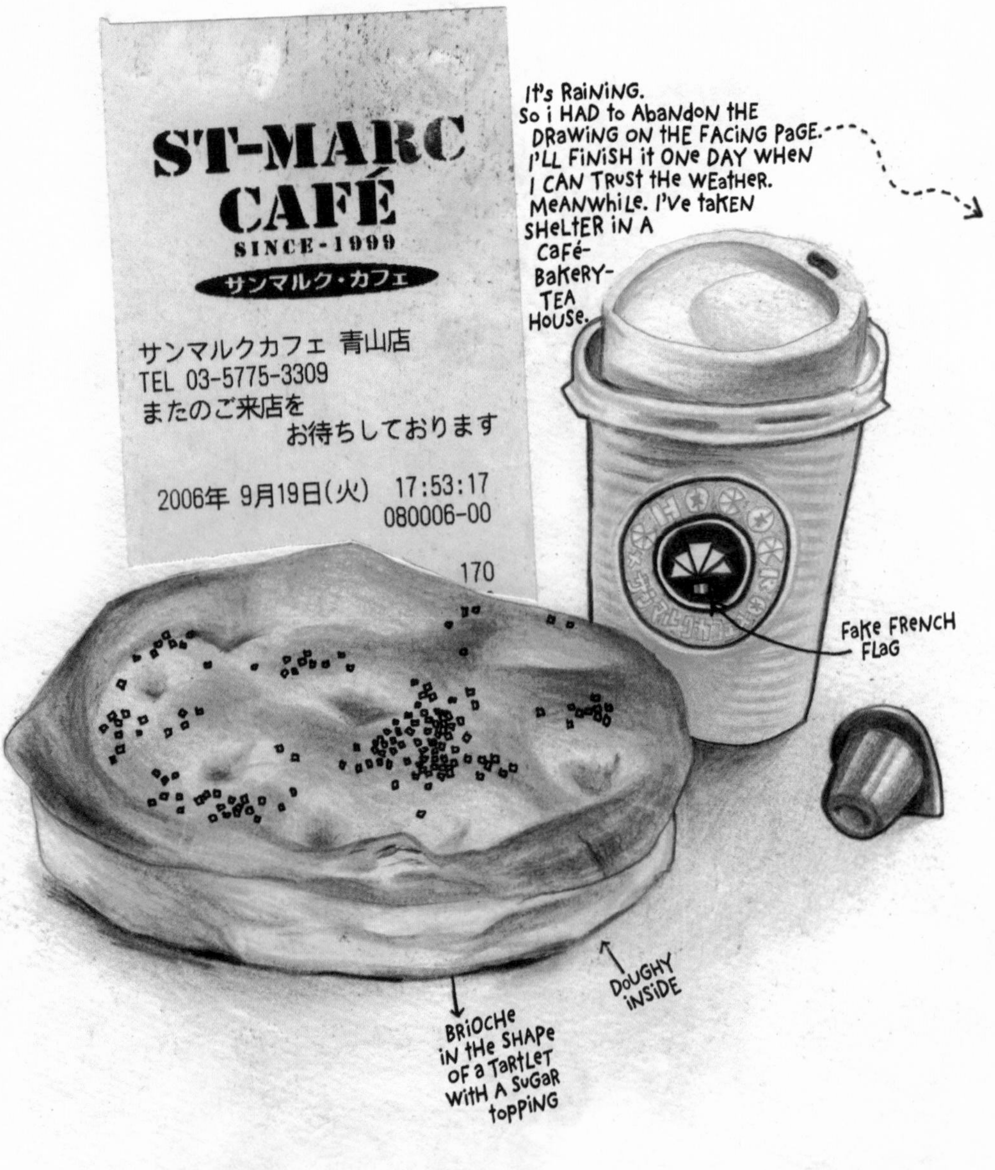
ST-MARC
CAFÉ
SINCE-1999
サンマルク・カフェ
サンマルクカフェ 青山店
TEL 03-5775-3309
またのご来店を
お待ちしております
2006年 9月19日(火) 17:53:17
080006-00
170
It's RaiNiNG.
So i HAD to Abandon tHE DRAWING ON THE FACiNG PaGE.
I'LL FiNiSH it ONE DAY WHEN I CAN TRust tHE WEatHER.
MEANWHiLE. I've taKEN SHELtER IN A CaFé-BaKERY-TEA HOuSE.
Fake FRENCH FLaG
DOUGHY iNSIDE
BRiOCHE iN tHE SHAPe OF a TaRtLEt WitH A SuGaR topping

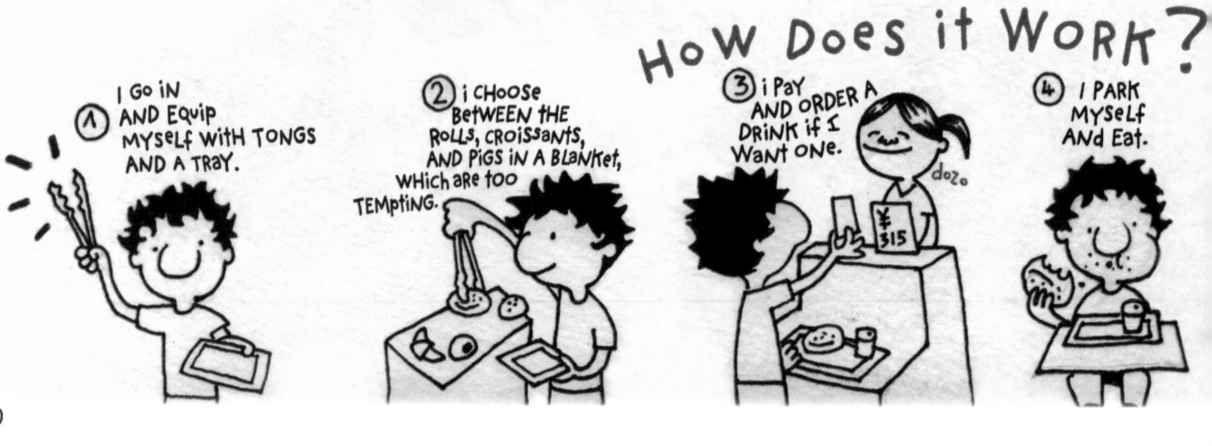
How Does it WORK?
1 I Go iN AND Equip MYSelf WitH TONGS AND A TRaY.
2 i CHOOSE BetWEEN THE ROLLS, CROiSSANTS, AND PiGS IN A BLaNKet, WHiCh are too TEMPtiNG.
3 i PaY AND ORDER A DRiNK if I Want ONE.
dozo
¥315
4 I PARK MYSelf ANd Eat.

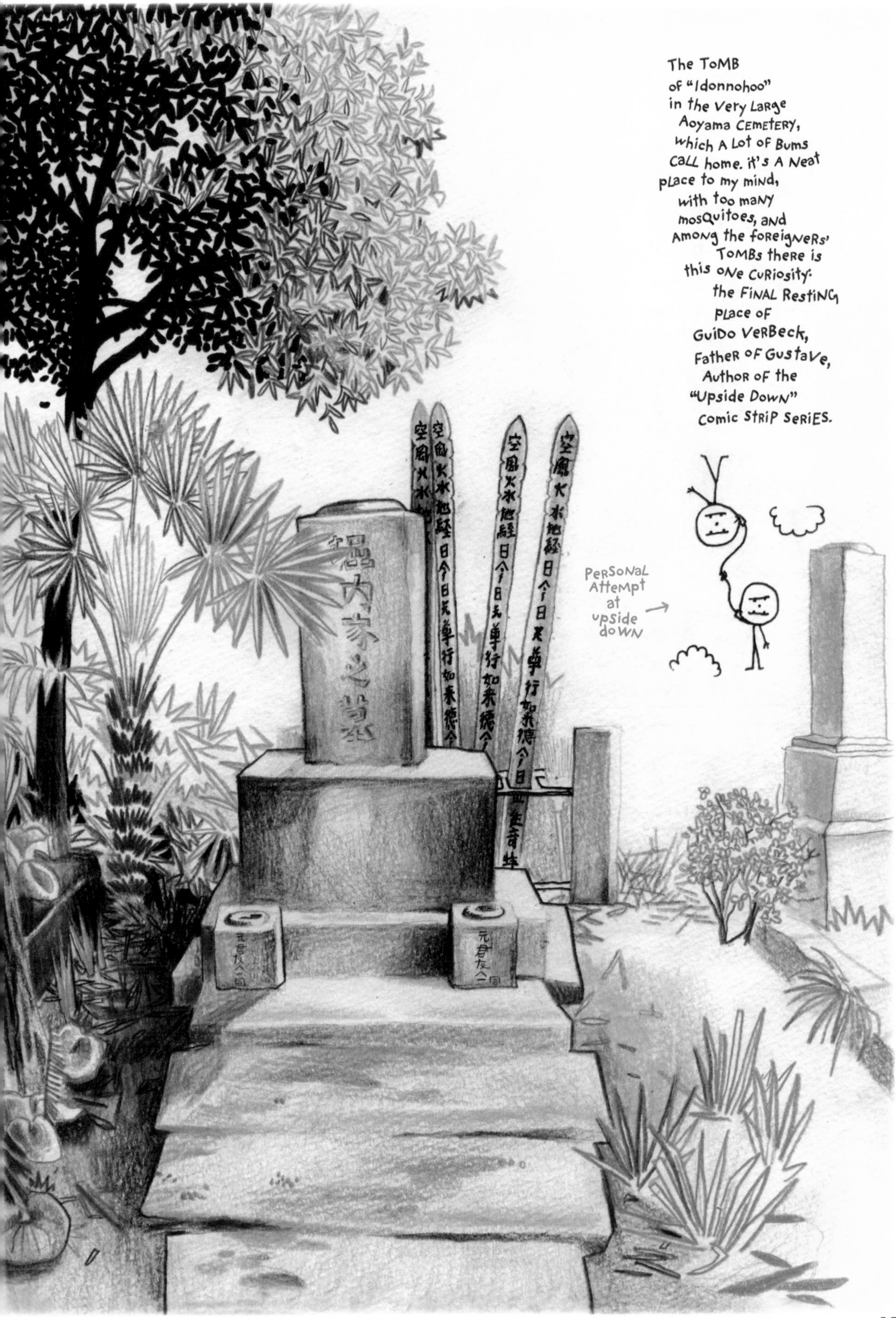
The ToMB of "Idonnohoo" in the Very Large Aoyama CEMETERY, which A Lot of Bums CALL home. it's A Neat place to my mind, with too maNY mosQuitoes, and Among the foreigNeRs' TOMBs there is this oNe CuRiosity: the FINAL RestiNG PLace of GuiDo VeRBeck, FatheR OF Gustave, AuthoR of the "Upside DowN" Comic STRiP SeRiES.
PeRSONaL AttemPt at upside doWN

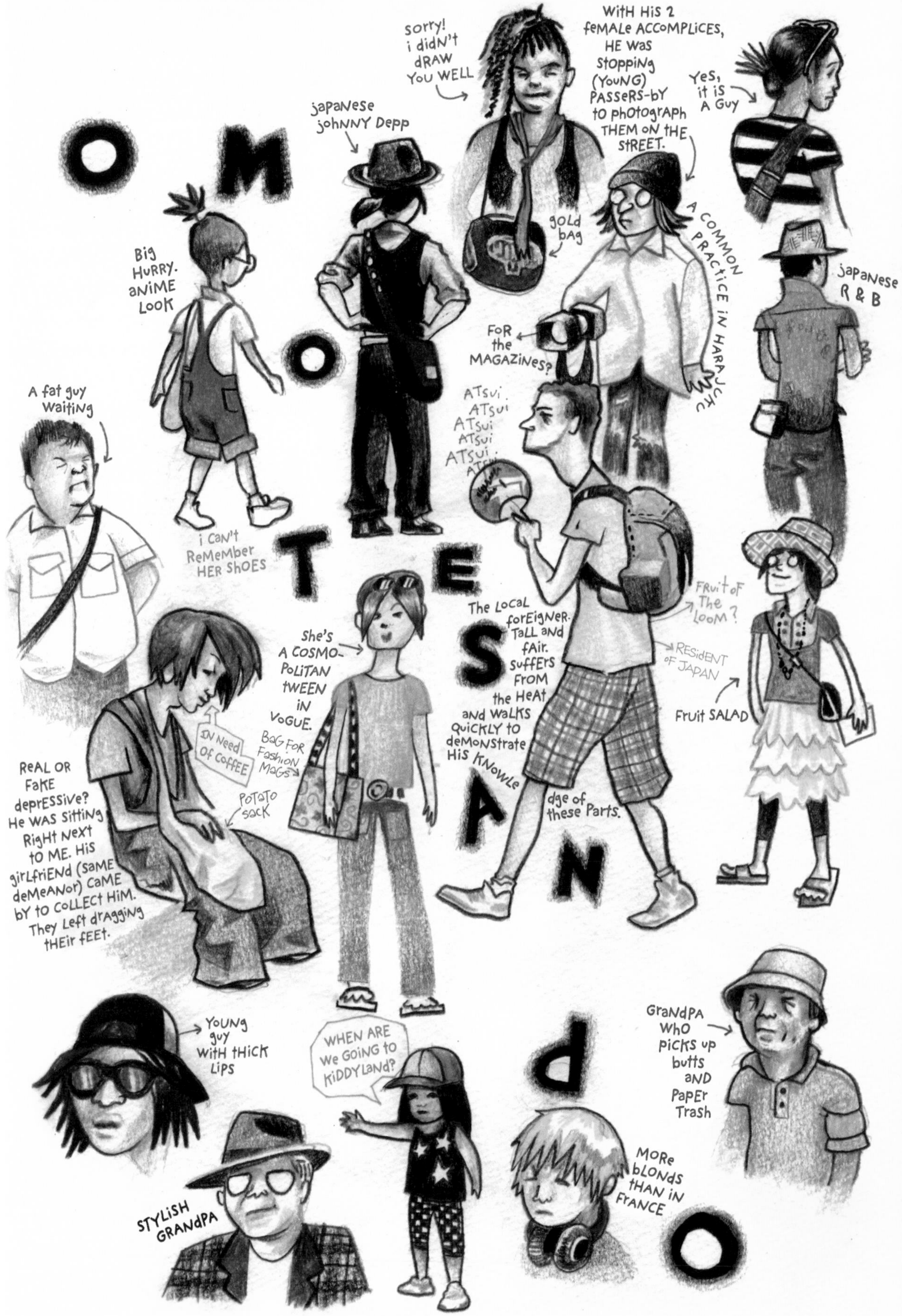
O M O T E S A N d O
Sorry! i didn't draw You WELL
With His 2 female accomplices, HE was stopping (YOUNG) PASSERS-bY to photograph THEM ON THE STREET.
Yes, it is A Guy
japanese johnNY Depp
gold bag
A COMMON PRACTICE IN HARAJUKU
Big HURRY. aNiME LOOK
japanese R & B
FOR the MAGAZINES?
A fat guy waiting
ATsui ATsui ATsui ATsui ATsui
i can't ReMember HER SHOES
Fruit of The Loom?
RESident of JAPAN
The Local foreigner. TALL and fair. suffers FROM the HEAT and WaLKS QUICKLY to deMONstrate His KNOWLEdge of these Parts.
She's A COSMO-POLITAN TWEEN iN VOGUE.
Fruit SALAD
IN Need Of COFFEE
BaG FOR Fashion MaGs
POTaTO SaCK
REAL OR FaKE depressive? He WAS sitting Right Next to ME. HiS girlfriEND (saME deMeANor) CaME bY to COLLECT HIM. They Left dragging their feet.
YOUNG guy WITH THICK LIPS
WHEN ARE WE GOING to KIDDYLAND?
GRANDPA WHO PiCKS up butts and PaPEr Trash
MORE bLONDS THAN IN FRANCE
STYLISH GRANDPA

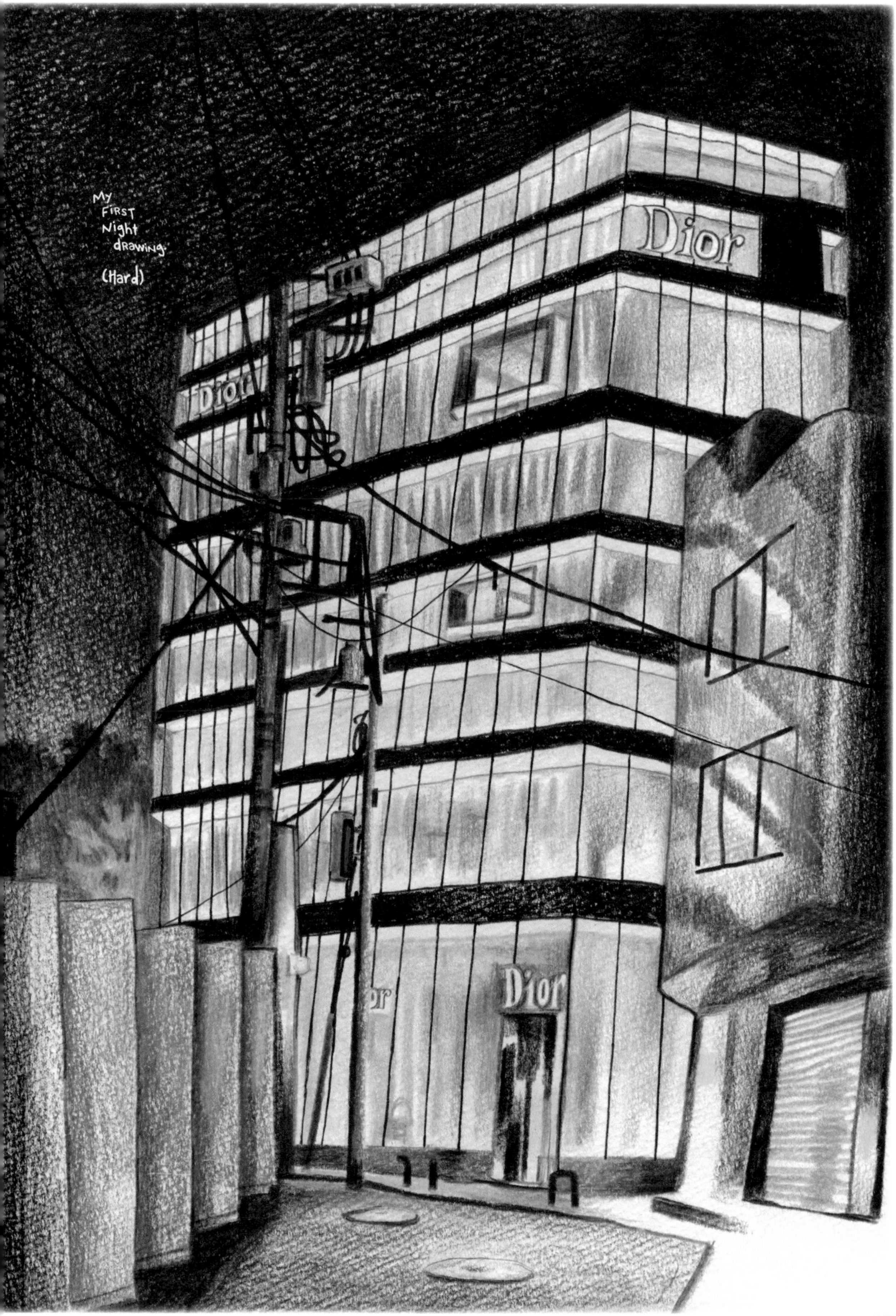

My FIRST Night drawing.
(Hard)
Dior
Dior
Dior

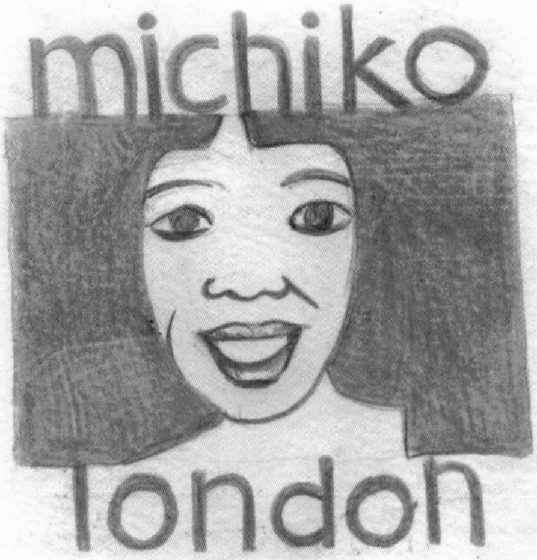

michiko
london

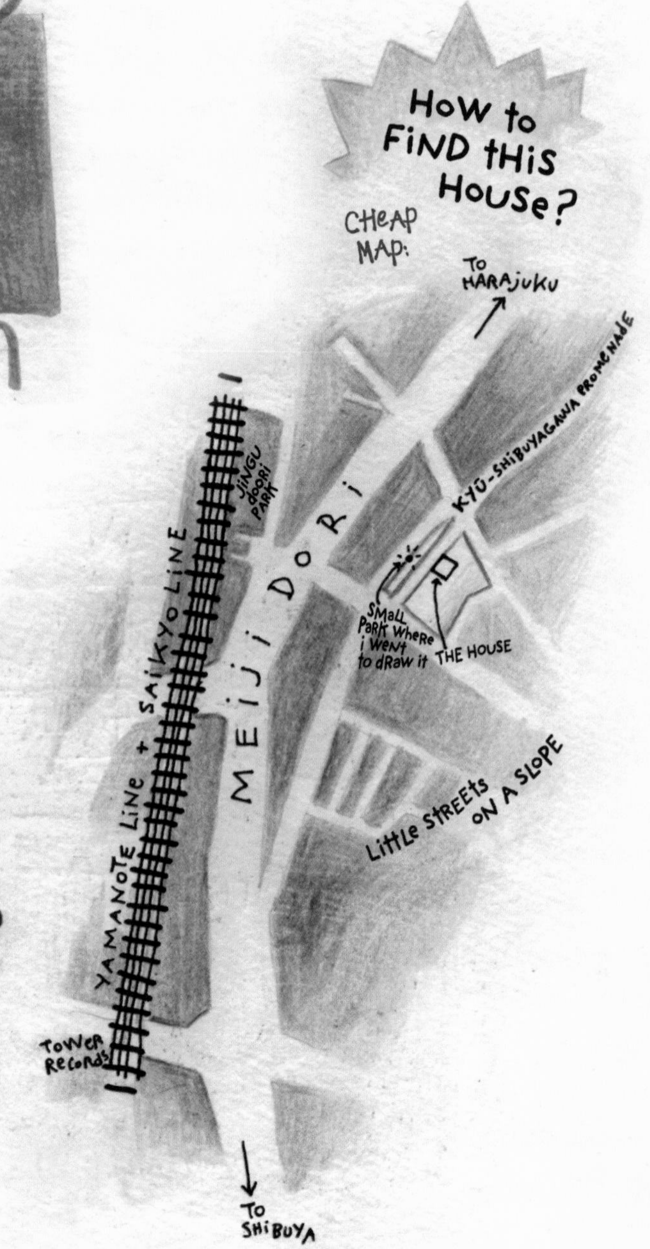

How to FIND tHIS HOUSE?
CHeAP MAP:
TO HARAJUKU
KYŪ-SHIBUYAGAWA PROMENADE
JINGU DOORI PARK
MEIJI DORI
SMALL PARK where i went to draw it
THE HOUSE
Little STREETS ON A SLOPE
YAMANOTE LINE + SAIKYO LINE
TOWER RECORDS
TO SHIBUYA

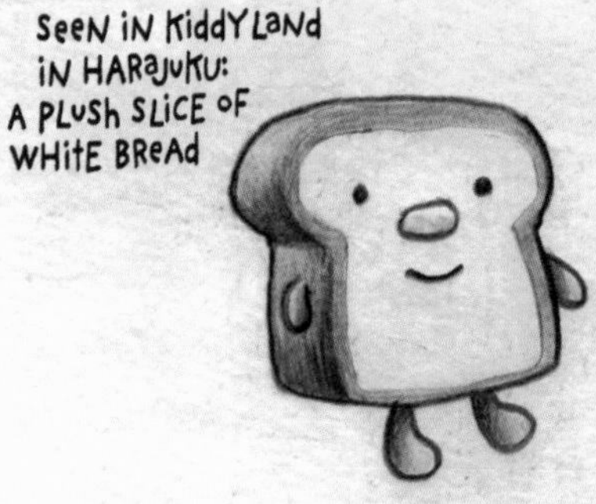

SeeN IN KiddYLaNd
IN HARAJUKU:
A PLUSh SLICE OF
WHITE BREAd

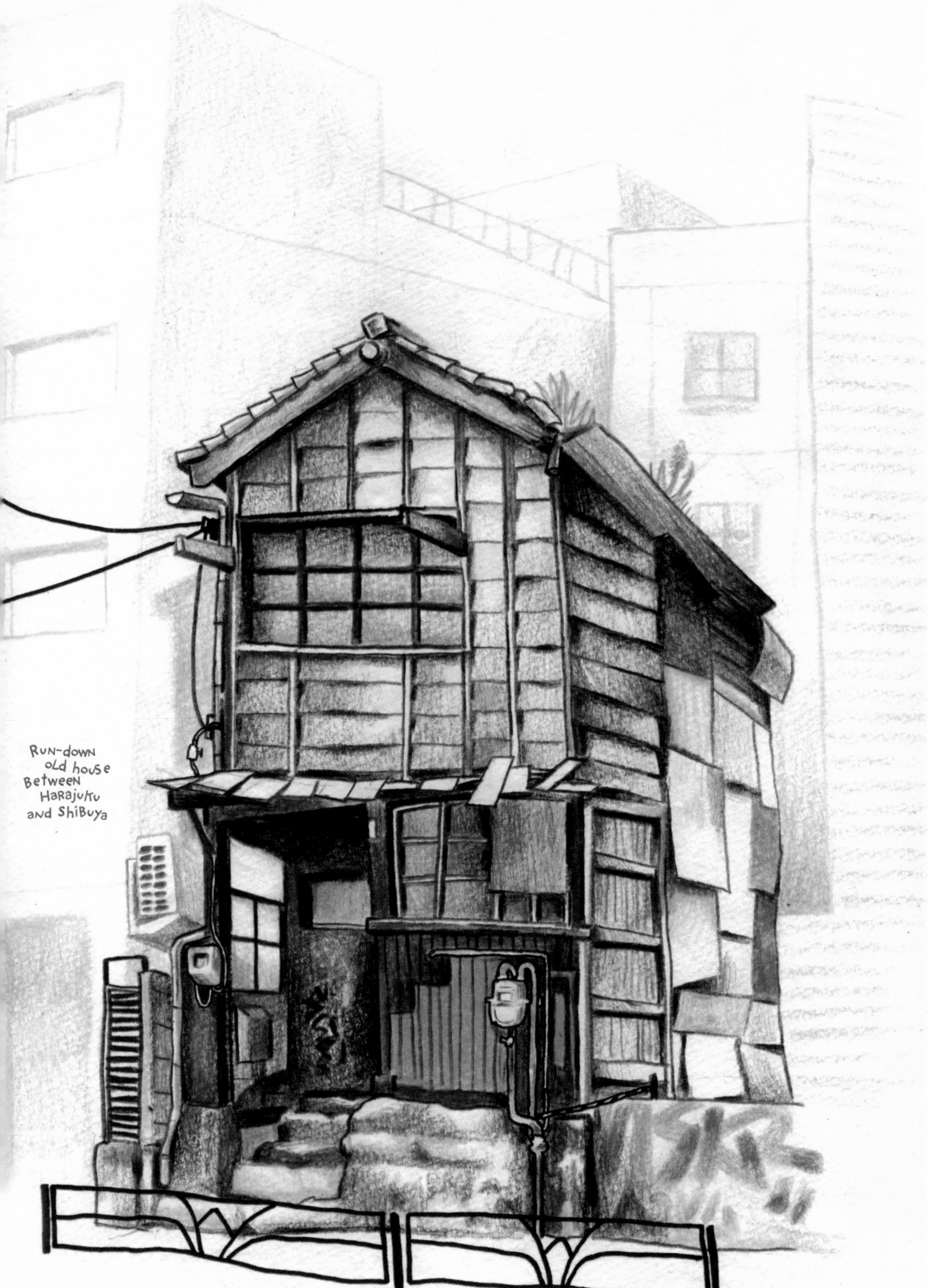
Run-down old house Between Harajuku and Shibuya

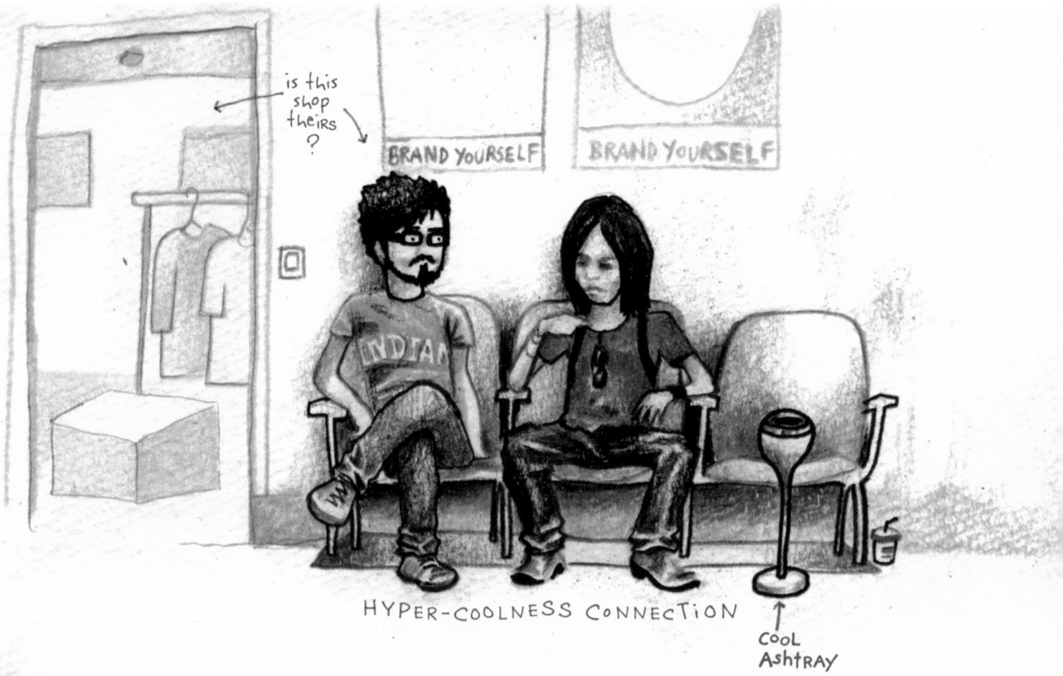
is this shop theirs ?
BRAND YOURSELF
BRAND YOURSELF
INDIAN
HYPER-COOLNESS CONNECTION
COOL Ashtray

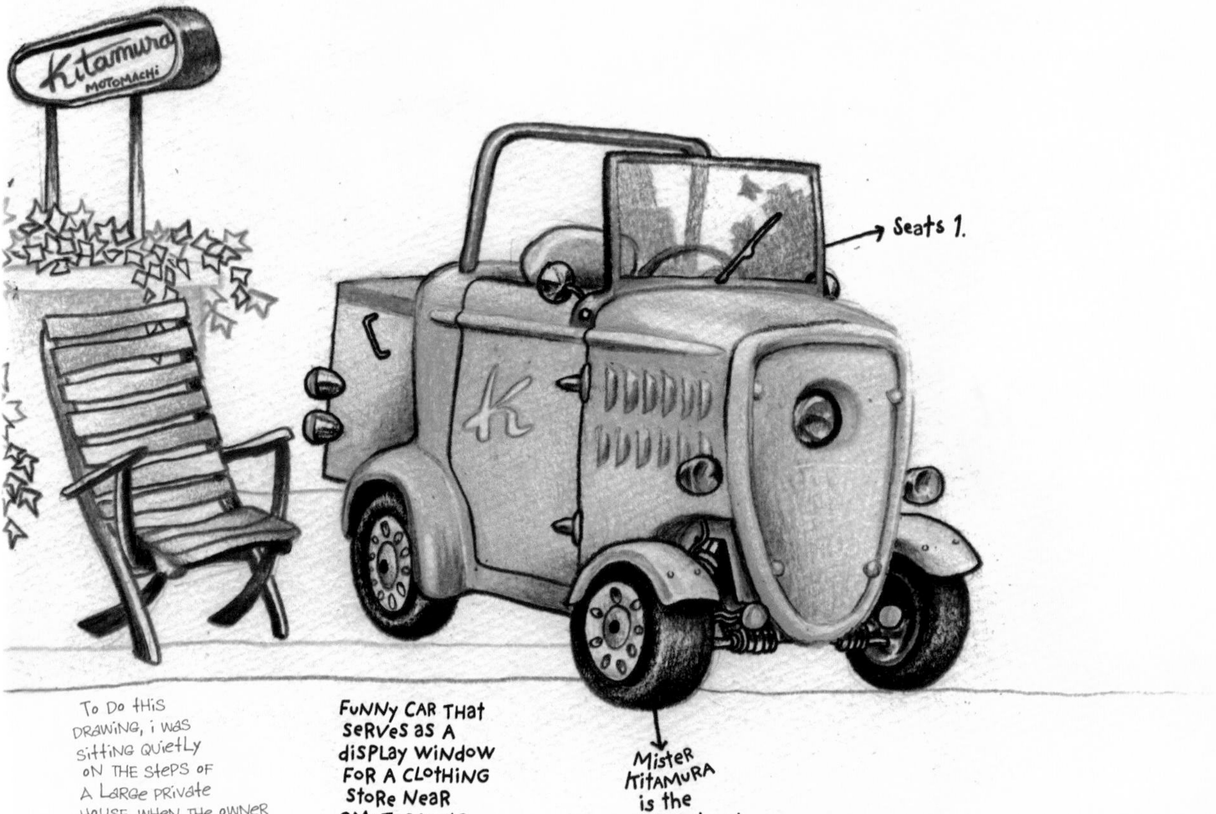
Kitamura
MOTOMACHI
Seats 1.
K
To Do this drawing, i was sitting quietly on the steps of a large private house, when the owner came out and asked me to leave because his "house is not a bench."
Funny car that serves as a display window for a clothing store near Omotesando.
Mister Kitamura is the person who built it.

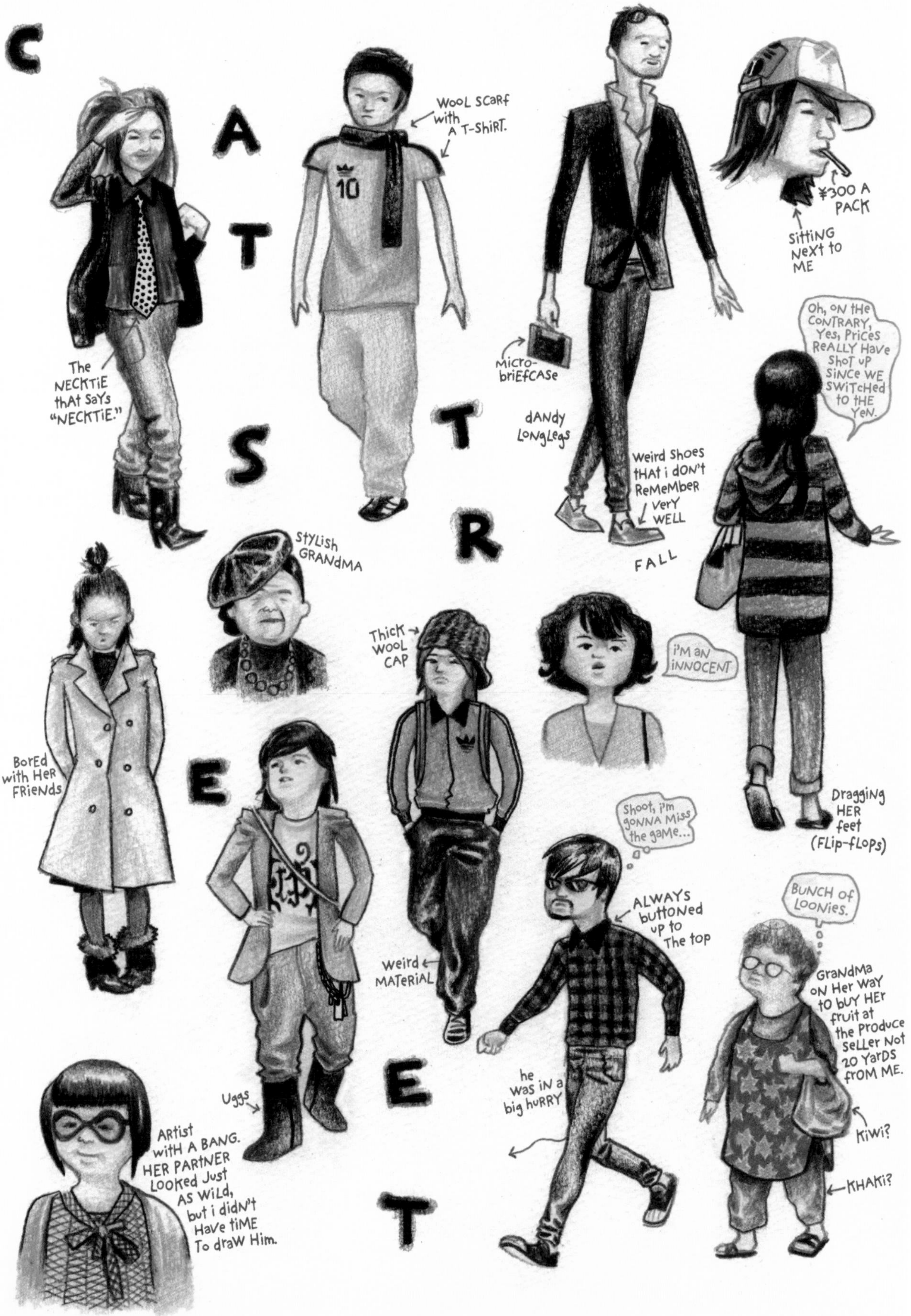
CAT STREET
The NECKTiE thAt SaYs "NECKTiE."
WOOL SCarf with A T-SHiRT.
10
Micro-briEfCASE
dANdy LONgLegs
Weird Shoes THAt i dON't ReMeMBer VerY WELL
FALL
¥300 A PACK
SittiNG NeXt to ME
Oh, ON the CONTRARY, Yes, Prices ReALLY Have Shot UP SiNCe WE SWiTChed to THE YeN.
STYLiSh GRANdMA
Thick WOOL CAP
i'M aN INNOCENT
BorEd with Her FRiENds
Dragging HER feet (FLip-fLOPS)
Shoot, i'm gONNA Miss the gaME...
ALWAYS buttoned up to The top
BUNCH of LOONiES.
Weird MATERiAL
GraNdMa ON Her WAY to BUY HEr fruit at the Produce SeLLer Not 20 YaRDS FROM ME.
Uggs
he was iN a big hURRY
Kiwi?
KHAKi?
Artist with A BANG. HER PARTNER Looked Just AS WiLd, but i didN't Have tiME To draw Him.

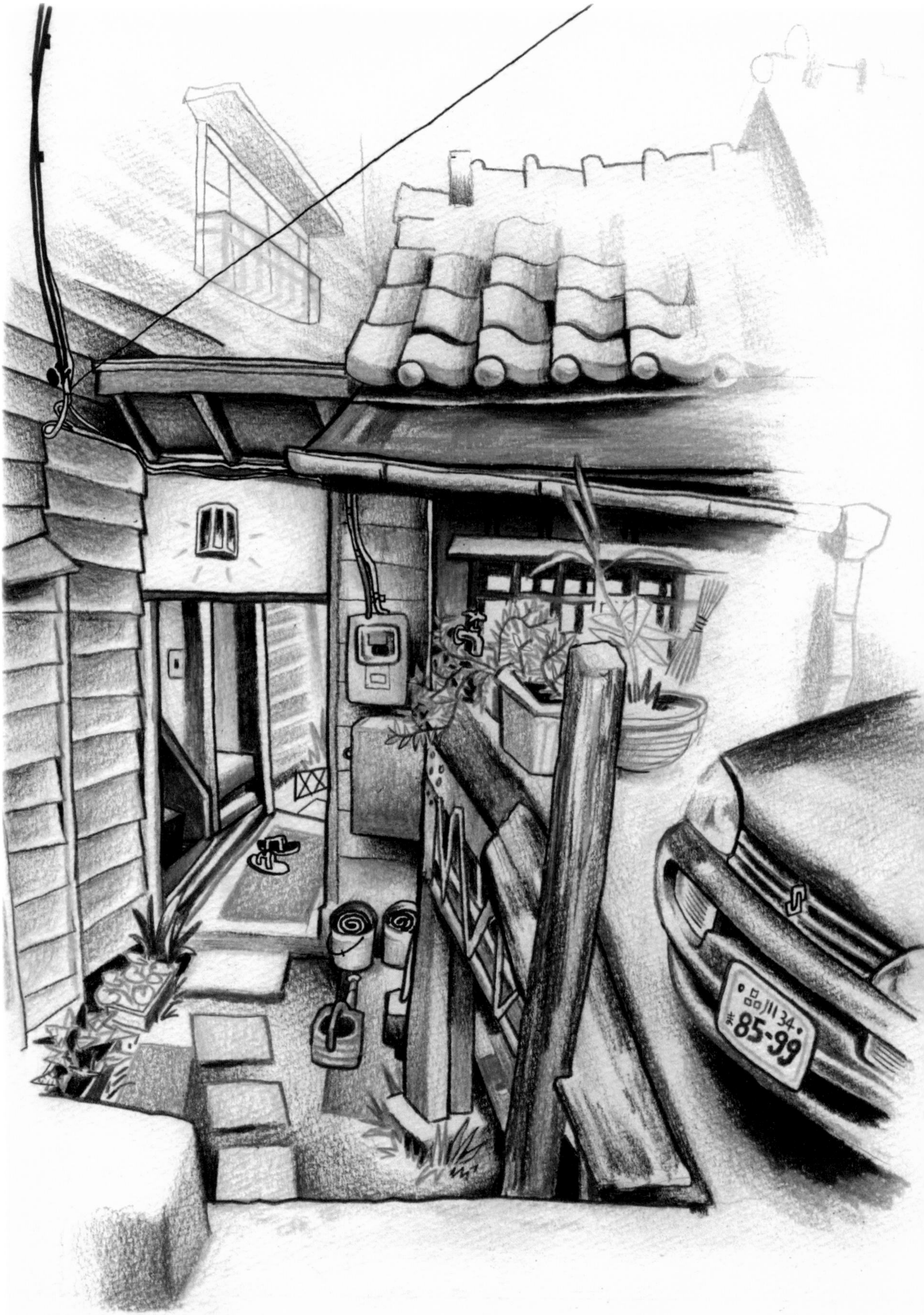
品川34
85-99

STORE
WINDOW

irony

Near
(OMOTESANDO)

interlude

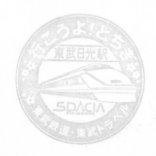

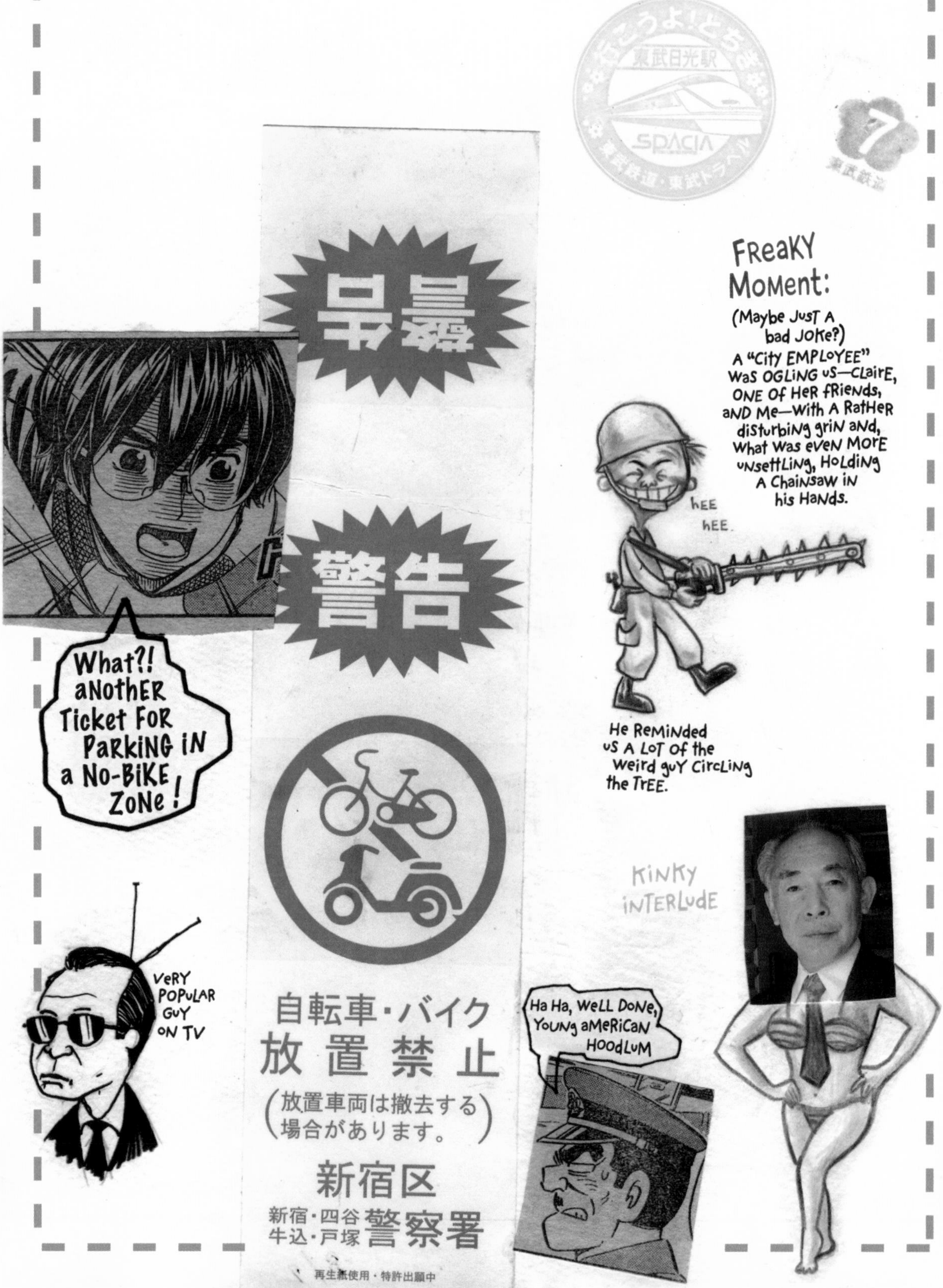
東武日光駅
SPACIA
東武鉄道・東武トラベル
東武鉄道
警告
警告
自転車・バイク
放置禁止
(放置車両は撤去する場合があります。)
新宿区
新宿・四谷 牛込・戸塚 警察署
再生紙使用・特許出願中
What?! another Ticket For Parking in a No-Bike Zone!
Freaky Moment:
(Maybe just a bad joke?)
A "City Employee" was ogling us—Claire, one of her friends, and me—with a rather disturbing grin and, what was even more unsettling, holding a chainsaw in his hands.
hee hee.
He reminded us a lot of the weird guy circling the tree.
Kinky interlude
Very popular guy on TV
Ha ha, well done, young American hoodlum

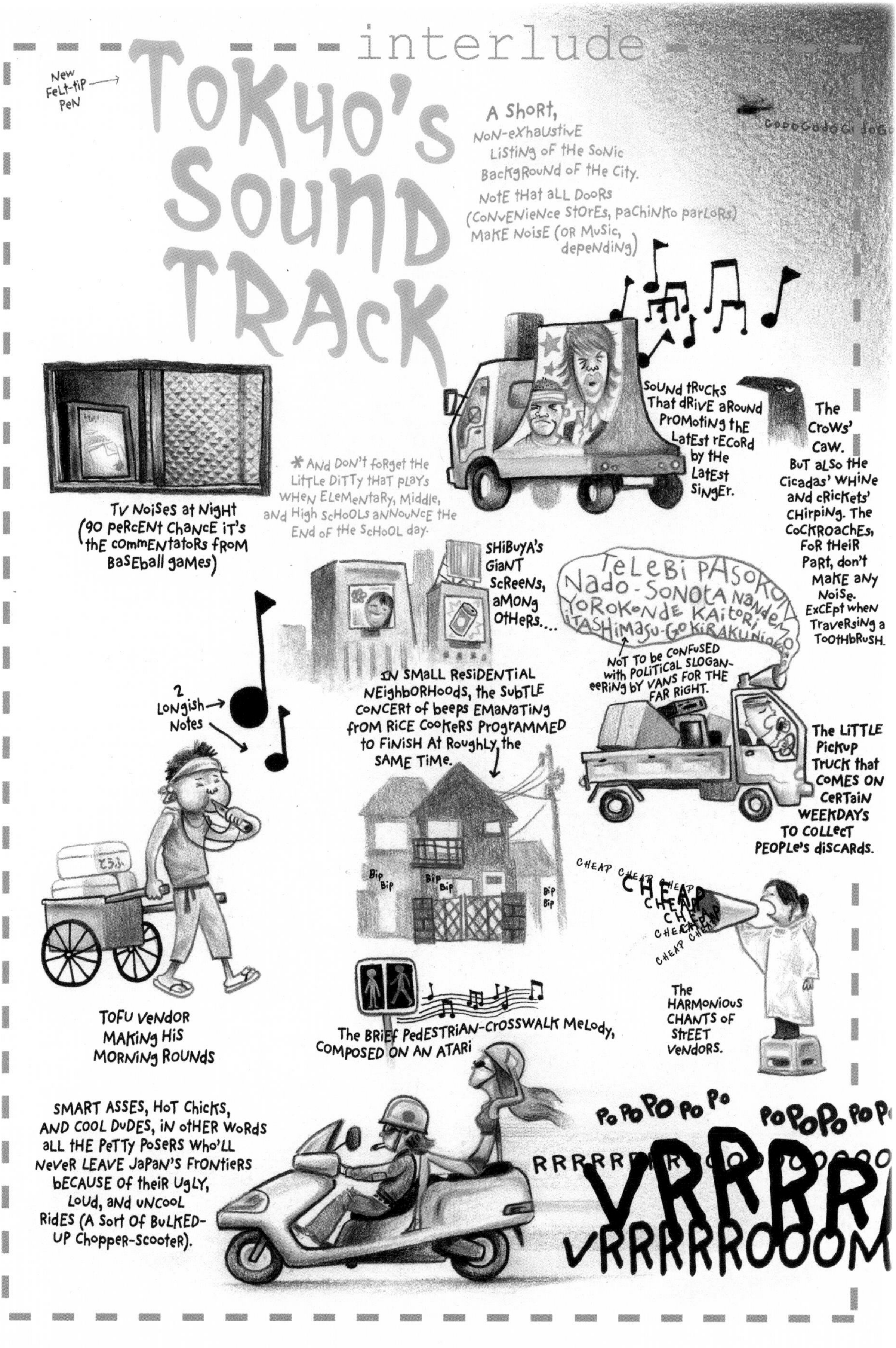
interlude
New Felt-tip Pen
Tokyo's Sound Track
A Short, non-exhaustive listing of the sonic background of the city.
Note that all doors (convenience stores, pachinko parlors) make noise (or music, depending)
GoGoGoGoGoGoG
Sound trucks that drive around promoting the latest record by the latest singer.
The crows' caw. But also the cicadas' whine and crickets' chirping. The cockroaches, for their part, don't make any noise. Except when traversing a toothbrush.
TV noises at night (90 percent chance it's the commentators from baseball games)
* And don't forget the little ditty that plays when elementary, middle, and high schools announce the end of the school day.
Shibuya's giant screens, among others....
Telebi pasokon nado - sonota nandemo yorokonde kaitori itashimasu - gokirakuni...
Not to be confused with political sloganeering by vans for the far right.
2 Longish notes
In small residential neighborhoods, the subtle concert of beeps emanating from rice cookers programmed to finish at roughly the same time.
Bip Bip
Bip Bip
Bip Bip
The little pickup truck that comes on certain weekdays to collect people's discards.
CHEAP CHEAP CHEAP CHEAP CHEAP CHEAP CHEAP CHEAP CHEAP
とうふ
Tofu vendor making his morning rounds
The brief pedestrian-crosswalk melody, composed on an Atari
The harmonious chants of street vendors.
Smart asses, hot chicks, and cool dudes, in other words all the petty posers who'll never leave Japan's frontiers because of their ugly, loud, and uncool rides (a sort of bulked-up chopper-scooter).
Po Po Po Po Po
PoPoPoPoPoP
RRRRRRROOOOOOO
VRRRR
VRRRRROOOM

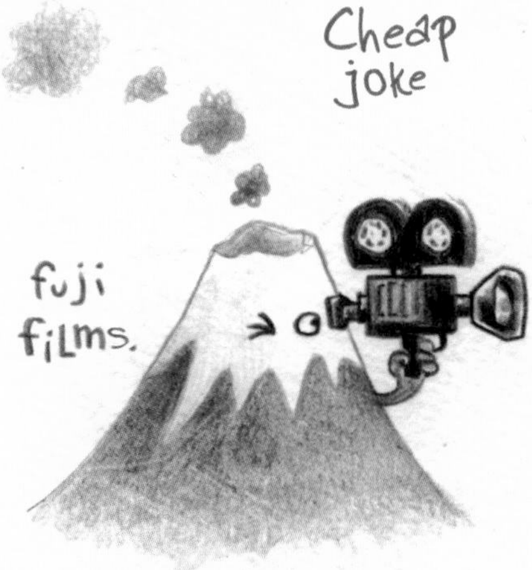
Cheap joke
fuji films.

Japanese Facial Hair

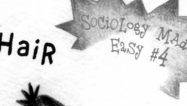

Sociology Made Easy #4

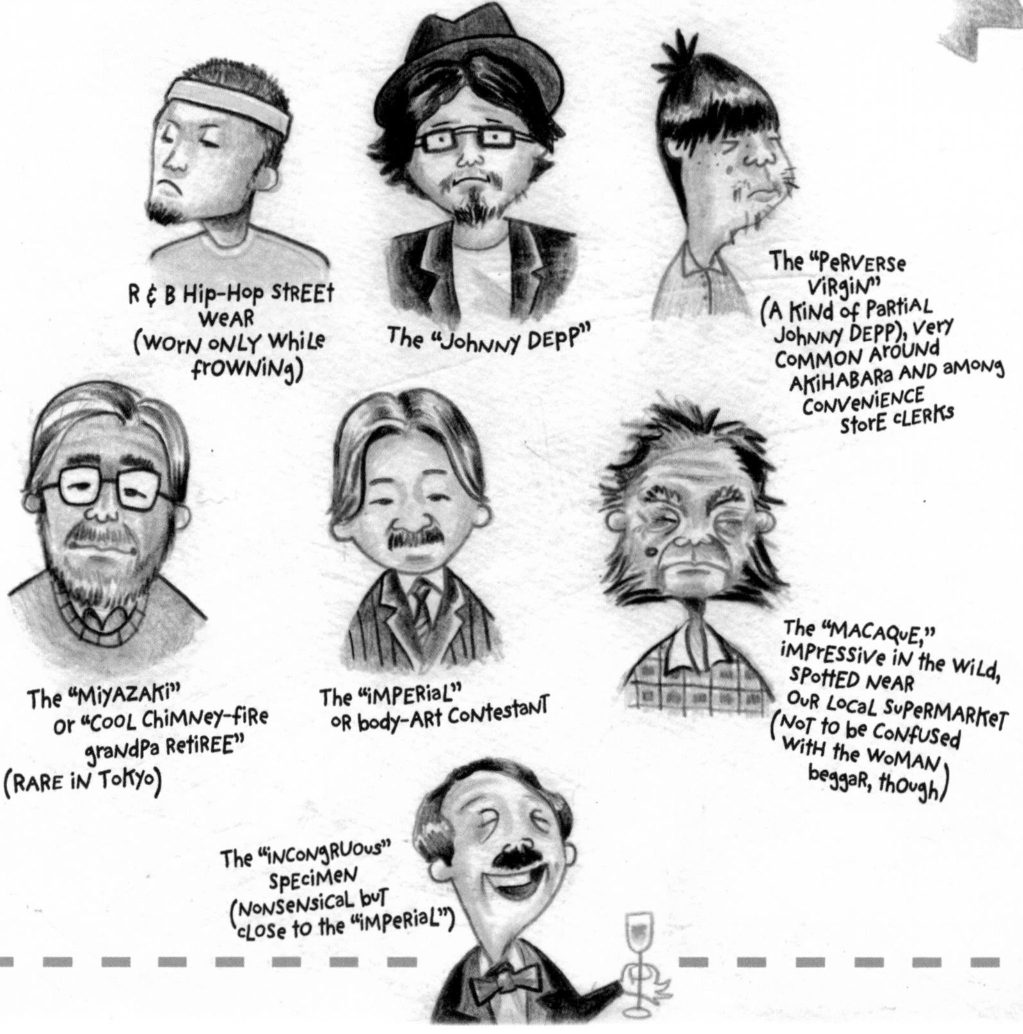
R & B Hip-Hop street wear (worn only while frowning)
The "Johnny Depp"
The "Perverse Virgin" (a kind of partial Johnny Depp), very common around Akihabara and among convenience store clerks
The "Miyazaki" or "Cool chimney-fire grandpa retiree" (rare in Tokyo)
The "Imperial" or body-art contestant
The "Macaque," impressive in the wild, spotted near our local supermarket (not to be confused with the woman beggar, though)
The "incongruous" specimen (nonsensical but close to the "Imperial")

roppongi

KOBAN
POLICE

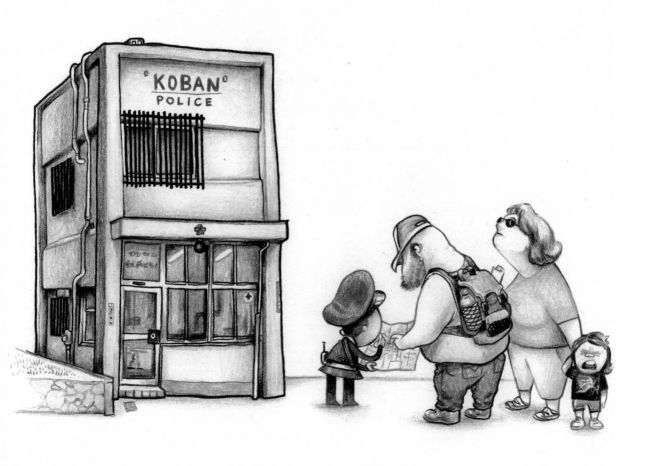

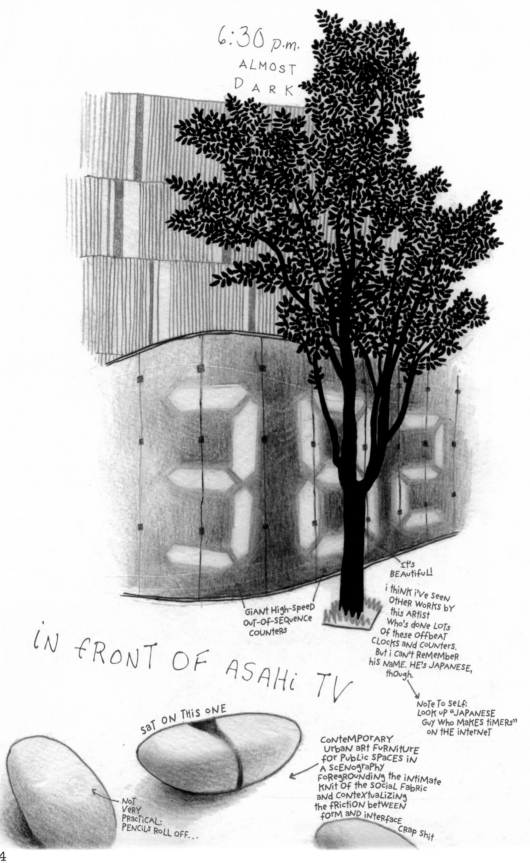

6:30 p.m.
ALMOST DARK

IN FRONT OF ASAHi TV

GiANT High-SpeeD OuT-OF-SEQUENCE COUNTERS

It's BEAUTiFUL!

i thiNK i've seeN OTHER WORKS by this ARTist Who's doNE LOTs Of these offbeAT CLOCKS aNd COUNTERS. But i CAN't ReMeMbER hiS NaME. HE's JAPaNESE, though.

NOTE TO SELF: LOOK UP "JAPANESE Guy Who MaKES tiMERs" ON THE iNTERNET

SAT ON THIS ONE

NOT VERY PRACTiCAL: PENCiLS ROLL OFF...

CONTEMPORARY URbaN aRT FURNiTURE FOR PUbLiC SPACES iN A ScENOgRaPHY FOREgROUNDiNG the iNtiMate KNit Of the SOCiAL FAbRiC and CONTEXTuaLiZiNg the FRictiON betwEEN FORM aNd iNTERFaCE

CRap Shit

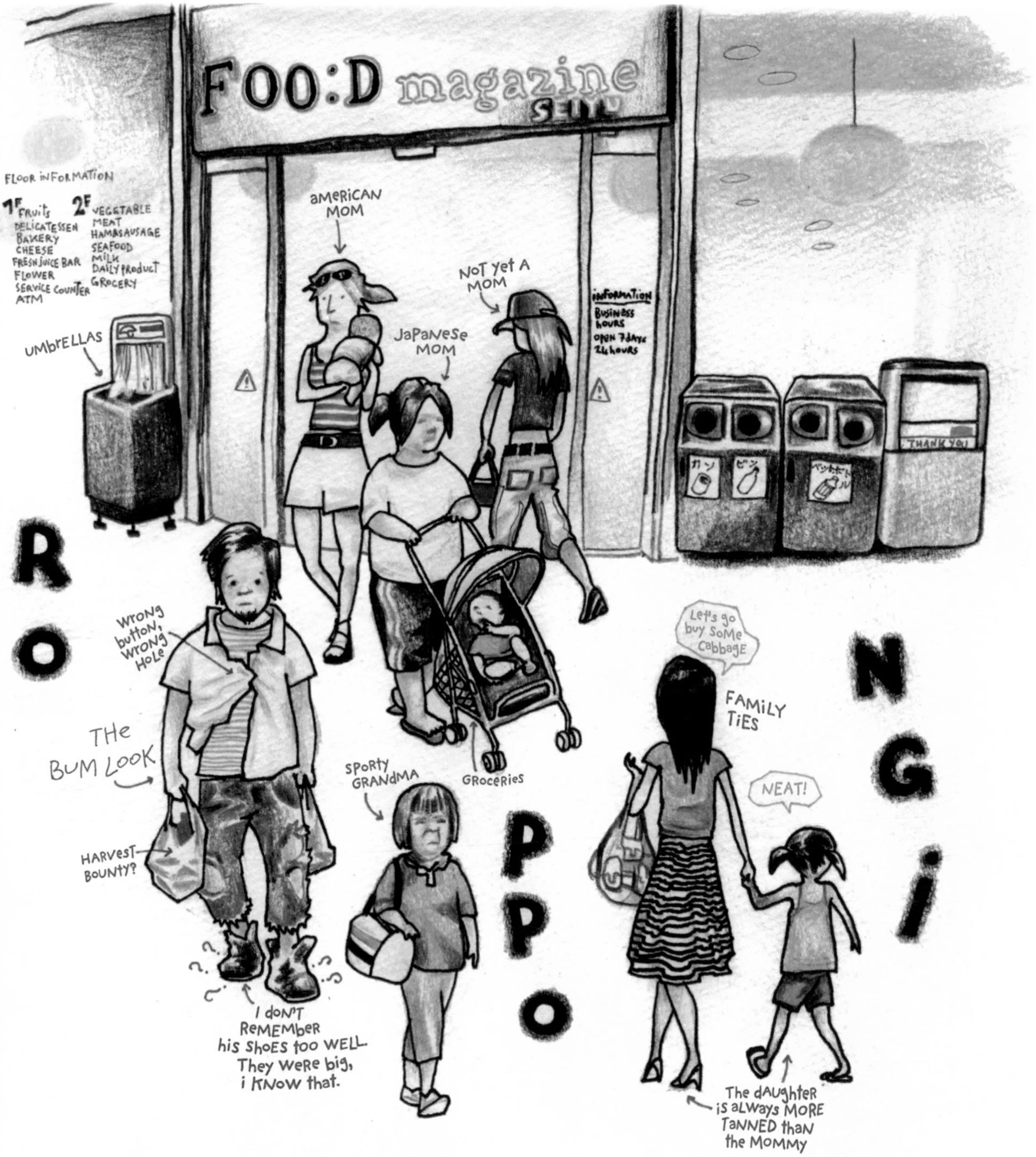
FOO:D magazine
SEIYU
FLOOR iNFORMATiON
1F FRuits DELICATESSEN BAKERY CHEESE FRESH JUiCE BAR FLOWER SERViCE COUNTER ATM
2F VEGETABLE MEAT HAM&SAUSAGE SEAFOOD MILK DAiLY PRODUCT GROCERY
UMbRELLAS
aMeRiCAN MOM
JaPaNeSe MOM
NOT yet A MOM
iNFORMATiON
BUSiNESS HOURS
OPEN 7DAYS 24 HOURS
THANK YOU
カン
ビン
ペットボトル
ROPPONGi
WRONG buttoN, WRONG HOLE
THe BUM LOOK
HARVeST BOUNTY?
I doN'T REMEMbeR his SHOES too WELL. They WeRe big, i KNOW that.
SPORTY GRANdMA
GROCeRies
Let's go buy SoMe Cabbage
FAMiLY TiES
NEAT!
The dAughteR is aLWays MORE TANNED than the MOMMY

interlude

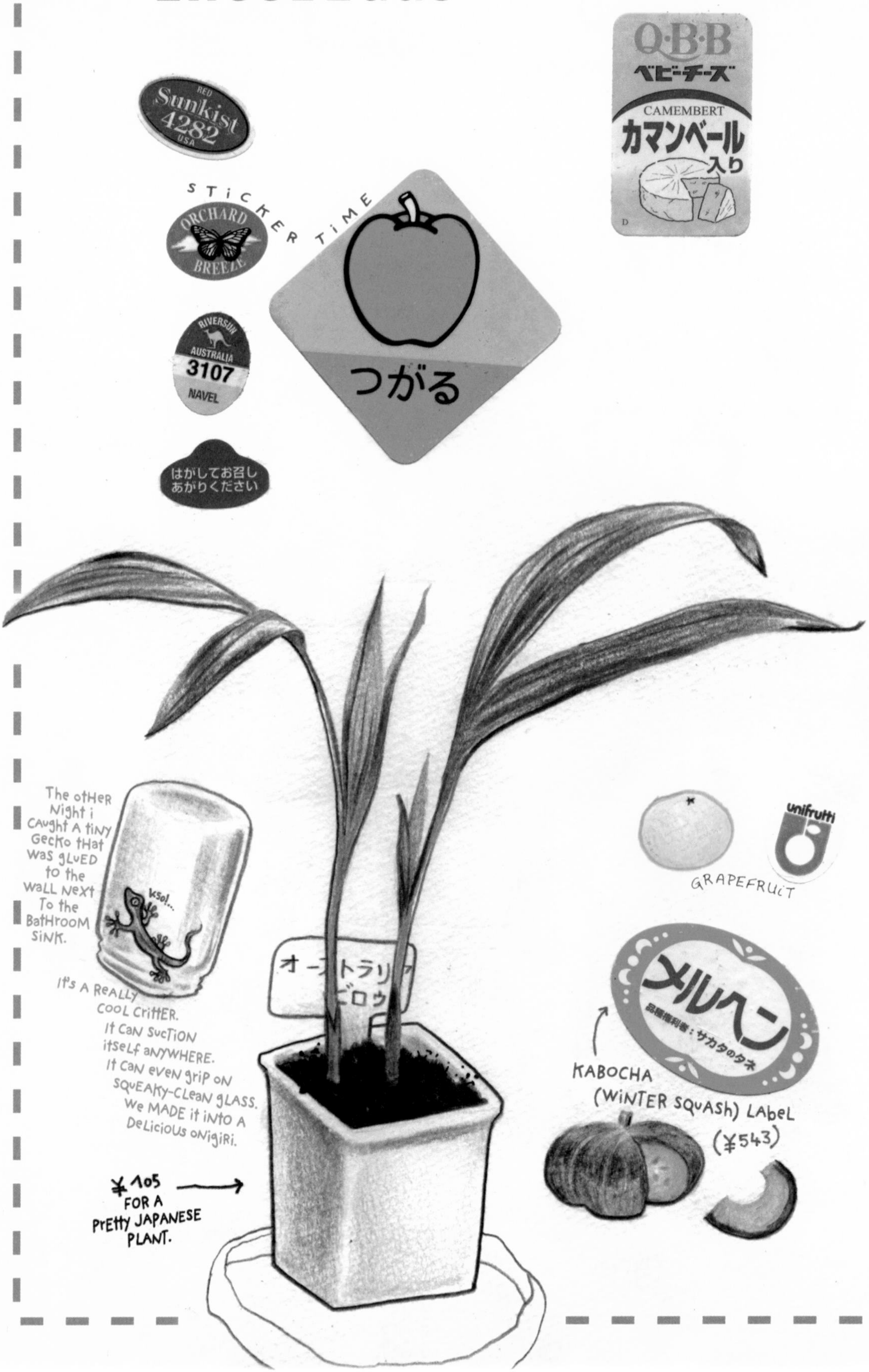
RED Sunkist 4282 USA
STICKER TIME
ORCHARD BREEZE
RIVERSUN AUSTRALIA 3107 NAVEL
はがしてお召しあがりください
つがる
Q·B·B ベビーチーズ CAMEMBERT カマンベール入り
D
The other night i caught a tiny gecko that was glued to the wall next to the bathroom sink.
ksol...
It's a really cool critter. It can suction itself anywhere. It can even grip on squeaky-clean glass. We made it into a delicious onigiri.
オー トラリ
ビロウ
¥105 FOR A pretty JAPANESE PLANT.
unifrutti
GRAPEFRUIT
メルヘン
品種権利者：サカタのタネ
KABOCHA (WINTER SQUASH) LABEL (¥543)

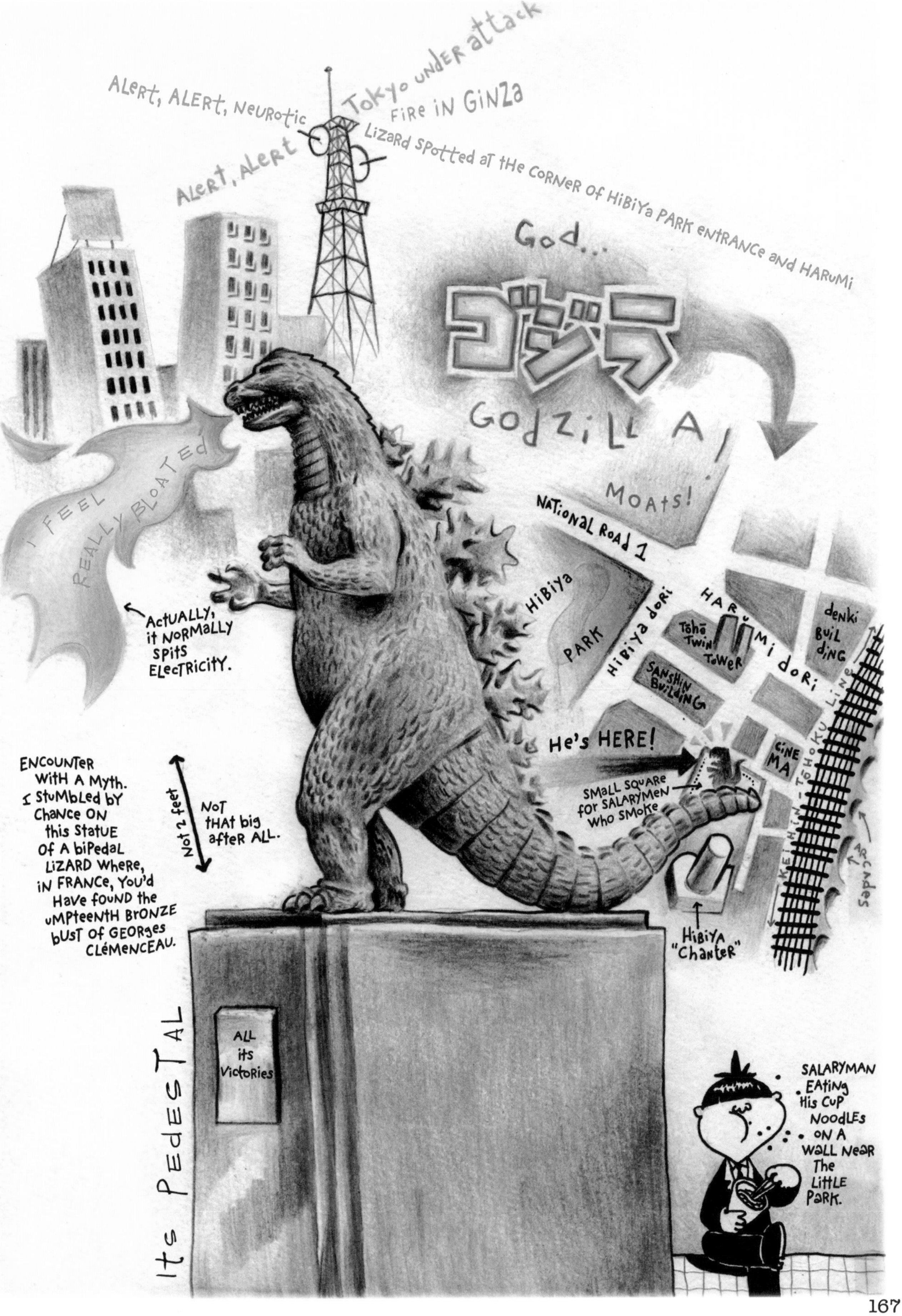

ALERT, ALERT, NEUROTIC
ALERT, ALERT
Tokyo under attack
Fire in GINZA
LIZARD SPOTTED AT THE CORNER OF HIBIYA PARK ENTRANCE AND HARUMI
God...
ゴジラ
GODZILLA!
MOATS!
I FEEL REALLY BLOATED
Actually, it normally spits electricity.
NATIONAL ROAD 1
HIBIYA PARK
HIBIYA DORI
HARUMI DORI
TŌHŌ TWIN TOWER
SANSHIN BUILDING
DENKI BUILDING
He's HERE!
CINEMA
SMALL SQUARE FOR SALARYMEN WHO SMOKE
KEIHIN-TŌHOKU LINE
ARCADES
HIBIYA "CHANTER"
ENCOUNTER WITH A MYTH. I STUMBLED BY CHANCE ON THIS STATUE OF A BIPEDAL LIZARD WHERE, IN FRANCE, YOU'D HAVE FOUND THE UMPTEENTH BRONZE BUST OF GEORGES CLÉMENCEAU.
Not 2 feet
NOT THAT BIG AFTER ALL.
ITS PEDESTAL
ALL its Victories
SALARYMAN EATING HIS CUP NOODLES ON A WALL NEAR THE LITTLE PARK.

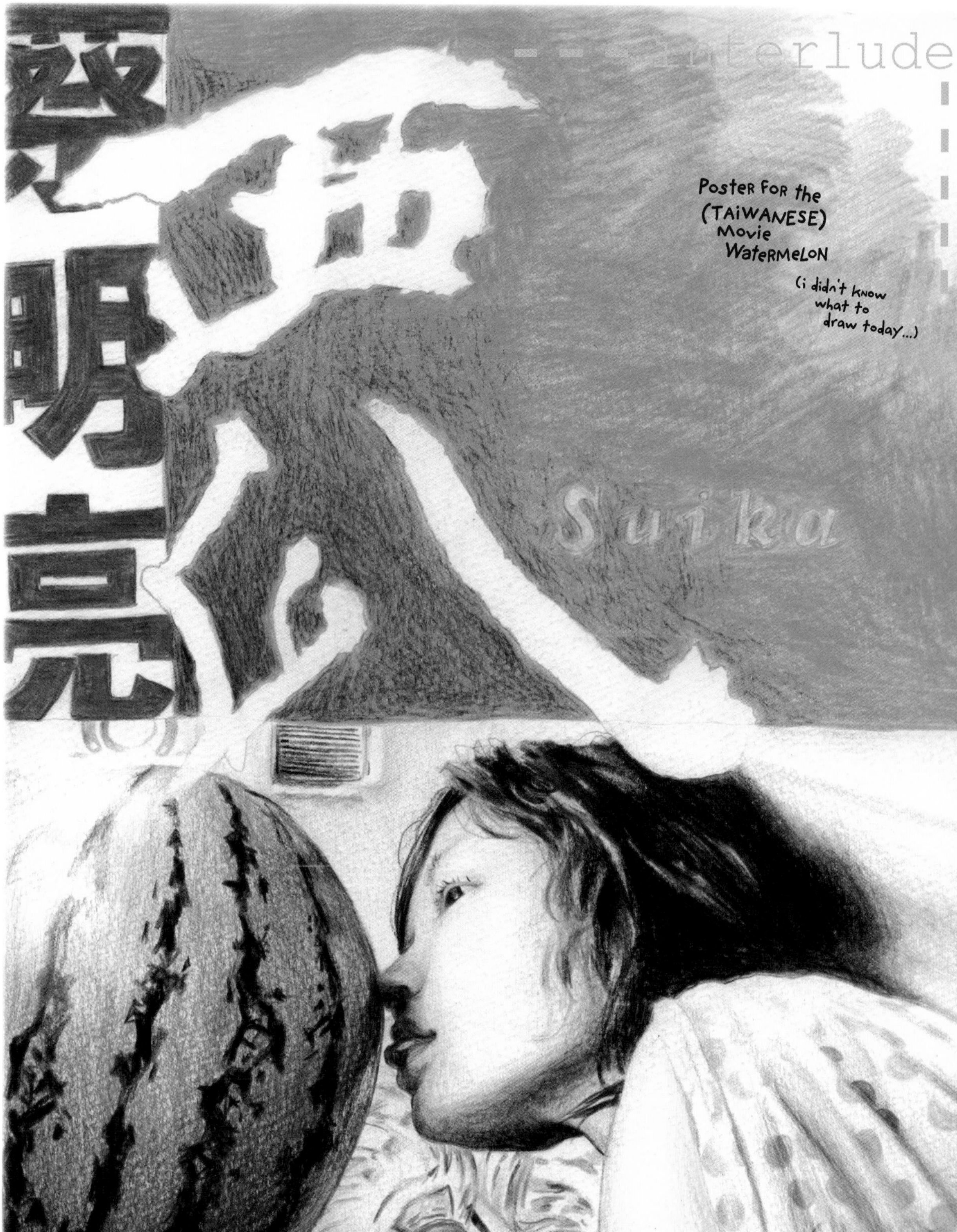
Poster for the (TAIWANESE) Movie WaterMELON
(i didn't know what to draw today...)
Suika

shibuya

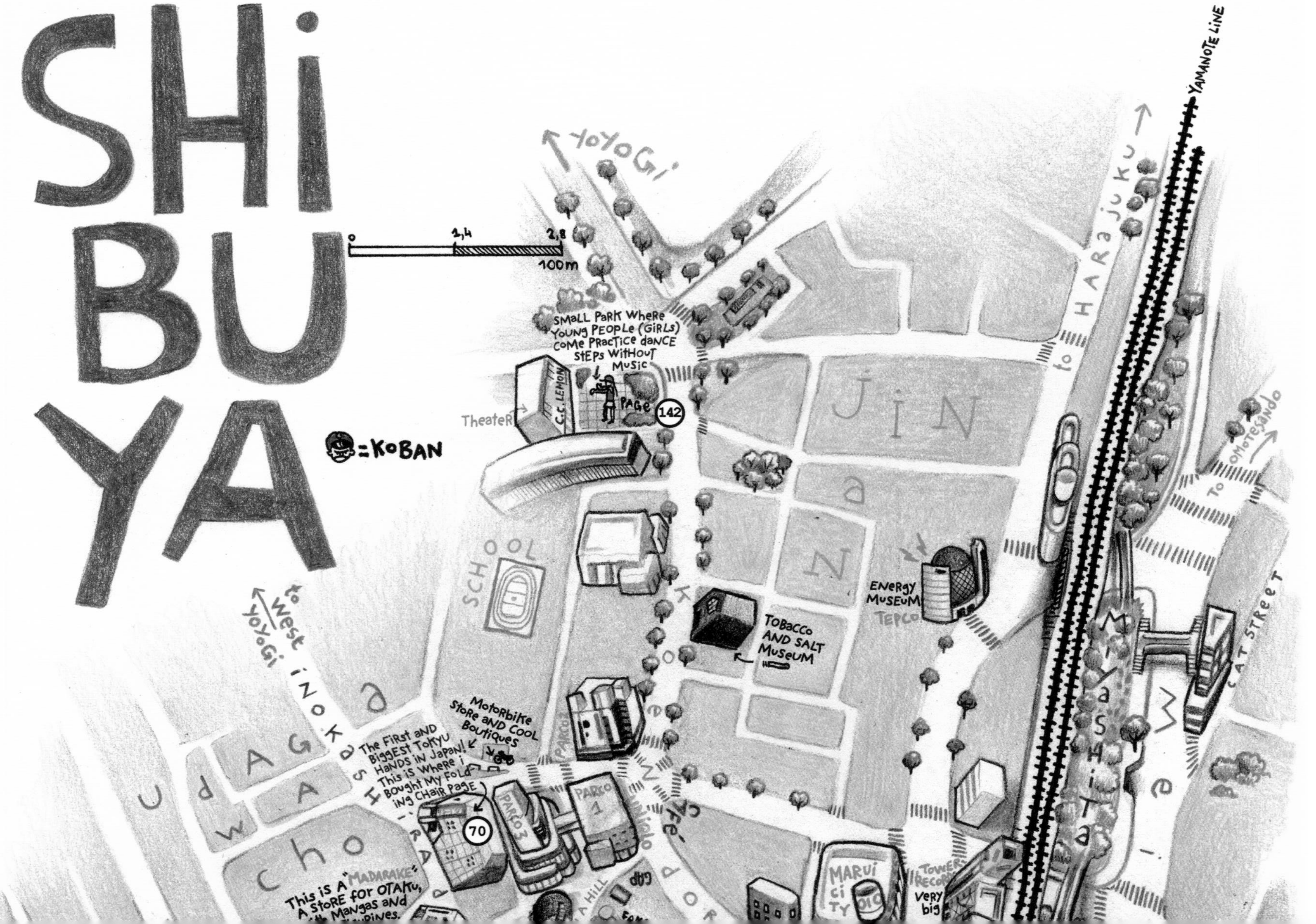
SHiBUYA
0 1,4 2,8 100m
=KOBAN
YAMANOTE LINE
to HARAJUKU
to OMOTESANDO
CAT STREET
MiYASHiTA
YOYOGi
SMALL PARK WHERE YOUNG PEOPLE (GIRLS) COME PRACTICE DANCE STEPS WITHOUT MUSIC
PAGE 142
C.C. LEMON
TheateR
JiNNAN
ENERGY MUSEUM
TEPCO
TOBACCO AND SALT MUSEUM
SCHOOL
KOEN
to west YOYOGi
iNOKASHiRA
UdAGAWAcho
Motorbike Store AND COOL Boutiques
The First AND BiGGEST TOKYU HANDS IN JAPAN! This is WHERE i Bought My FOLDiNG CHAiR PAGE 70
This is A "MADARAKE": A STORE for OTAKU,
PARCO
PARCO 1
PARCO 3
Café
uniqlo
MARUi CiTY
TOWER RECORD
VERY big

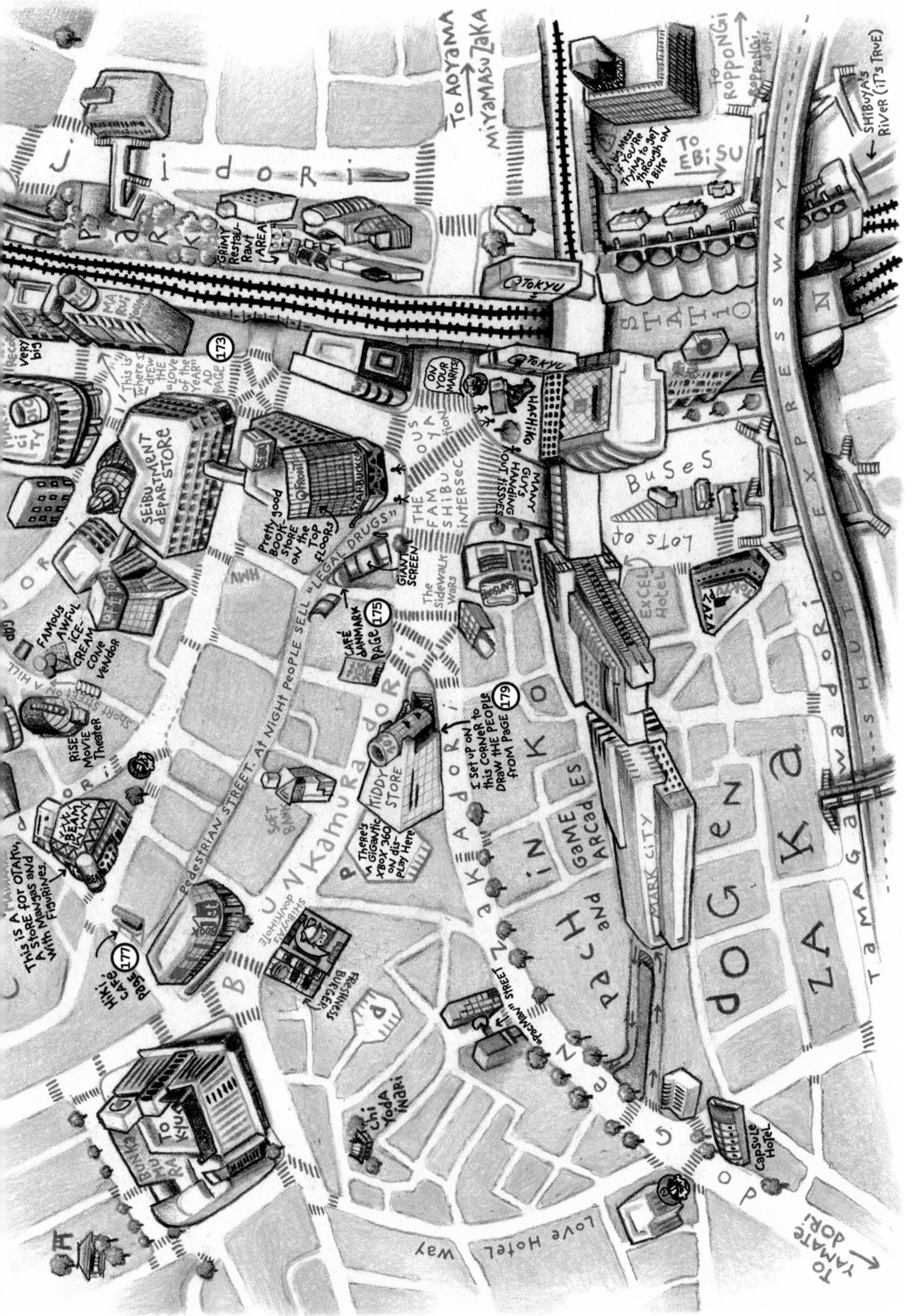
TO AOYAMA
MIYAMASU ZAKA
TO ROPPONGI
ROPPONGI DORI
SHIBUYA'S RIVER (IT'S TRUE)
A big Mess if you're trying to get through on A Bike
TO EBISU
GRIMY Restau-Rant AREA
TOKYU
STATION
SHUTO EXPRESSWAY
ON YOUR MARKS!
HACHIKO
MANY GUYS HANDING OUT TISSUES
THE FAMOUS SHIBUYA INTERSECTION
BUSES
lots of
EXCEL HOTEL
SEIBU DEPARTMENT STORE
Pretty good BOOK-STORE ON the Top FLOORS
STARBUCKS
GIANT SCREEN
The Sidewalk Wars
CAFÉ DANMARK PAGE 175
HMV
FAMOUS AWFUL ICE-CREAM CONE Vendor
SHORT STREET ON A HILL
RISE MOVIE Theater
This is where I drew THE "Love of the YEAR" AD PAGE 173
very big
Pedestrian STREET. At NIGHT PEOPLE SELL "LEGAL DRUGS"
BUNKAMURA DORI
KIDDY STORE
I set up on this CORNER to draw THE PEOPLE from PAGE 179
GAME ARCADES
PACHINKO
MARK CITY
DOGENZAKA
TAMAGAWA DORI
There's A Gigantic XBOX 360 on display Here
SOFT BANK
This is A store for OTAKU, A store with Mangas and with Figurines.
HIKI CAFÉ PAGE 177
FRESHNESS BURGER
SHIBUYA'S DONKIHOTE
"PACMAN" STREET
CHIYODA INARI
BUNKAMURA
TOKYU
CAPSULE HOTEL
Love Hotel way
TO YAMATE DORI

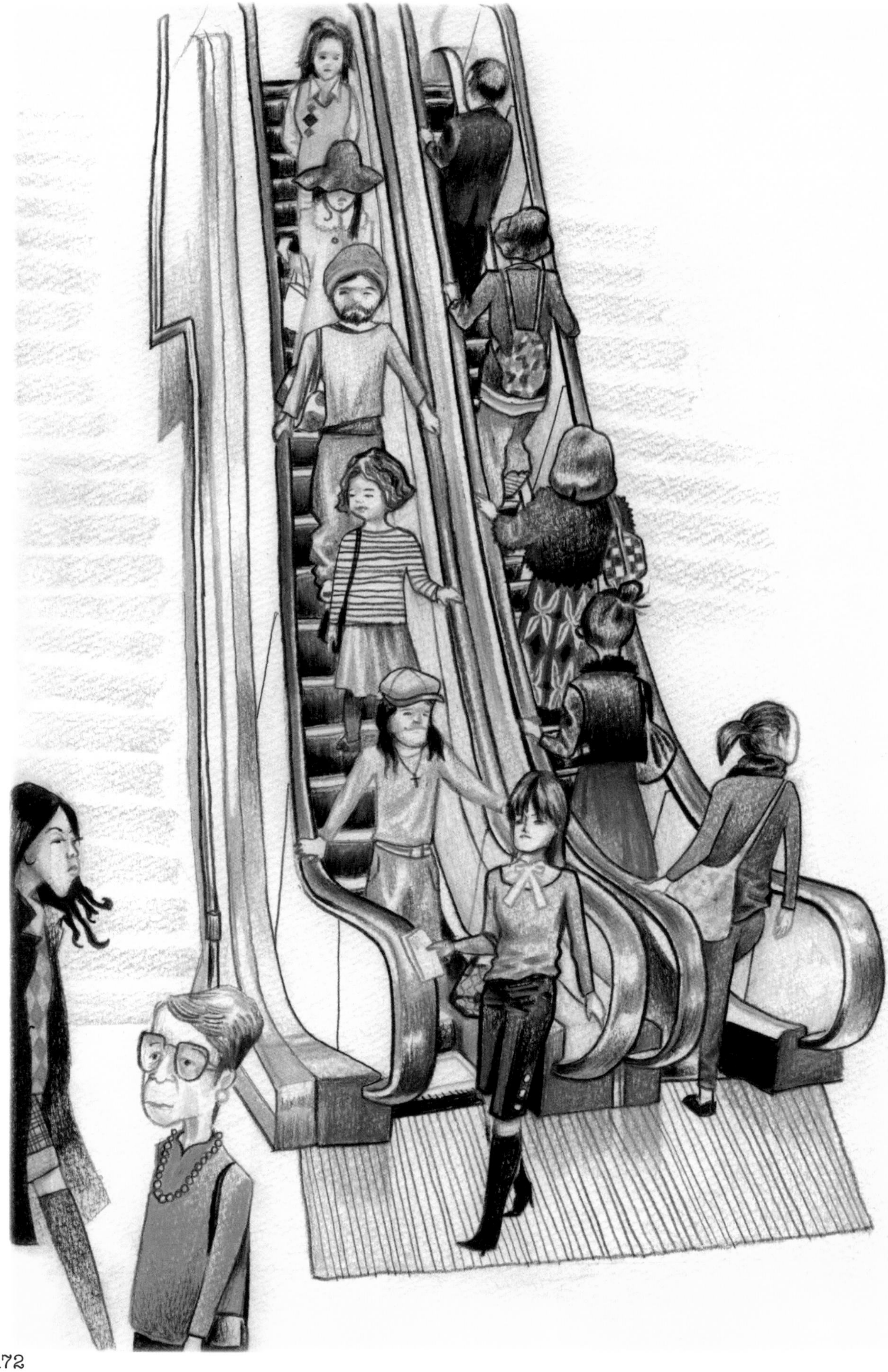

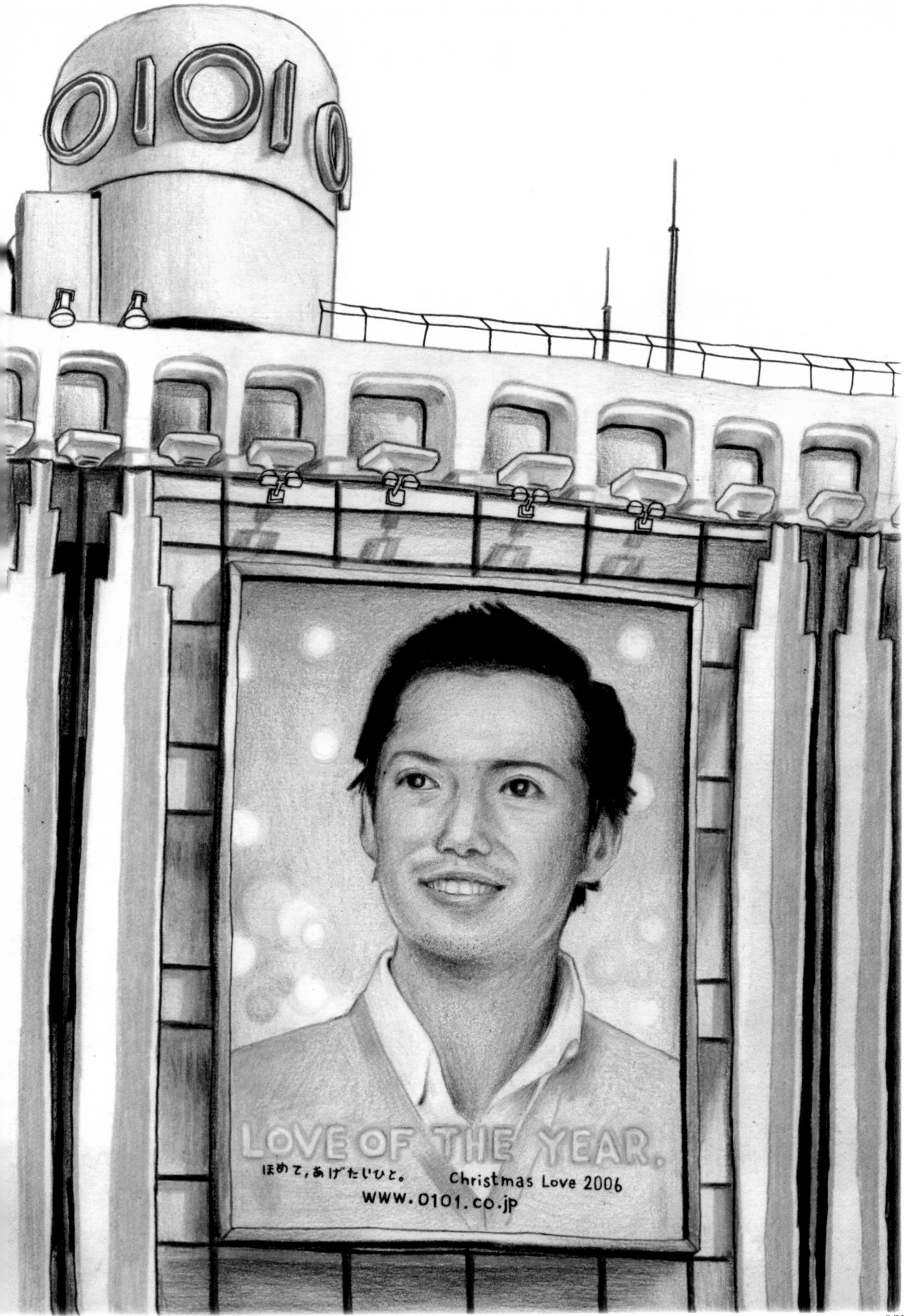
0101
LOVE OF THE YEAR.
ほめて，あげたいひと。
Christmas Love 2006
www.0101.co.jp

A BIT OF SHIBUYA

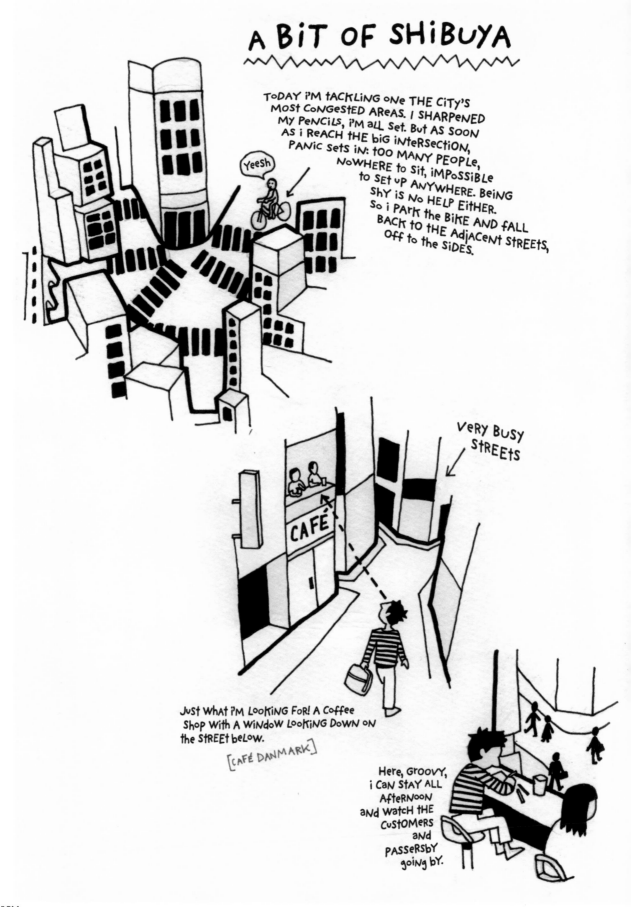

TODAY i'M TACKLING ONE THE CITY'S MOST CONGESTED AREAS. I SHARPENED MY PENCILS, i'M ALL SET. BUT AS SOON AS i REACH THE big INTERSECTION, PANIC SETS IN: TOO MANY PEOPLE, NOWHERE TO SIT, iMPOSSIBLE TO SET UP ANYWHERE. BEING SHY IS NO HELP EITHER. SO i PARK THE BIKE AND FALL BACK TO THE AdjACENT STREETS, OFF TO THE SiDES.

Yeesh

VERY BUSY STREETS

CAFÉ

Just WHAT i'M LOOKING FOR! A COFFEE SHOP WITH A WINDOW LOOKING DOWN ON THE STREET beLOW.

[CAFÉ DANMARK]

Here, GROOVY, i CAN STAY ALL AFTERNOON AND WATCH THE CUSTOMERS AND PASSERSbY GOING bY.

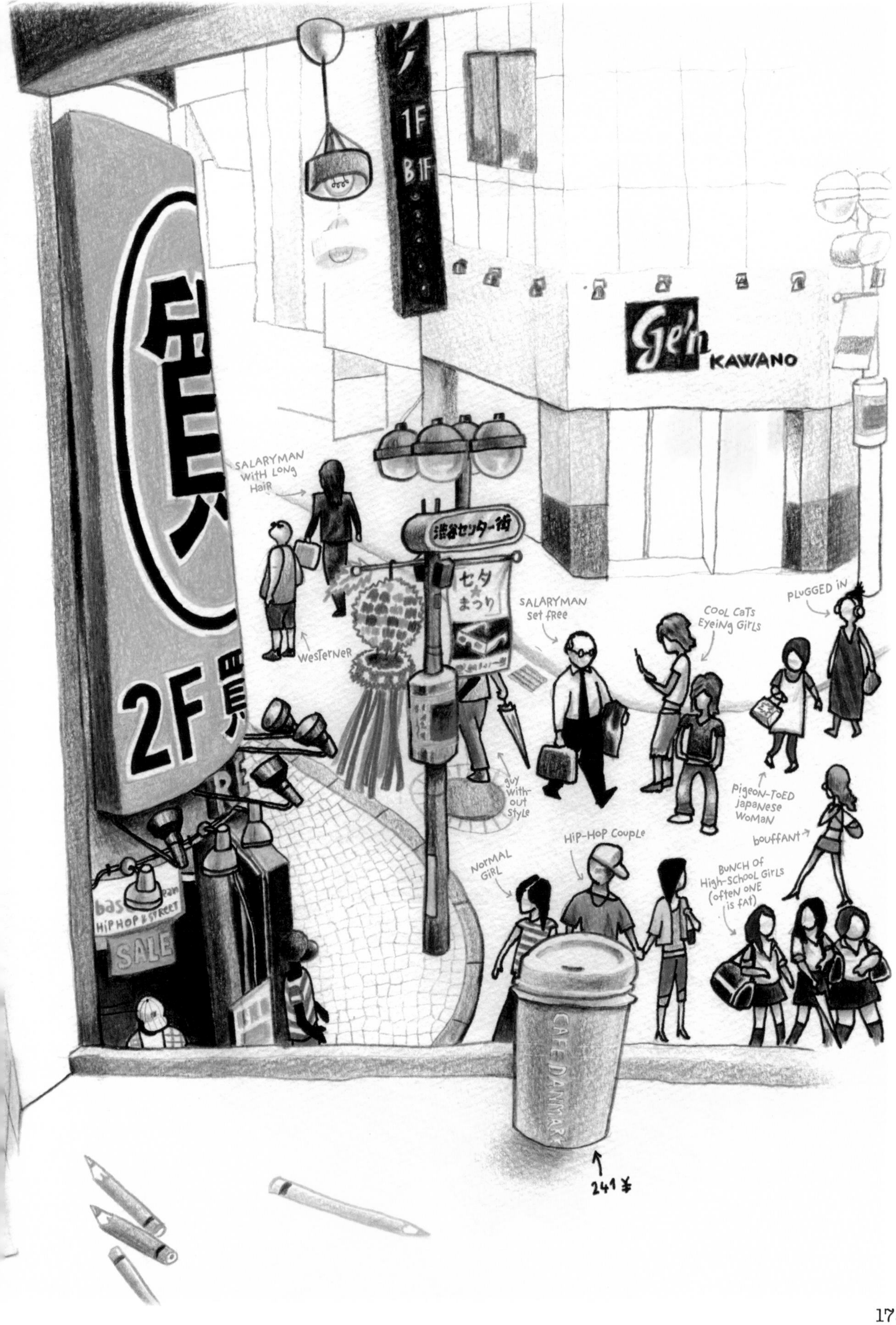
1F
B1F
Ge'n KAWANO
SALARYMAN WITH LONG HAIR
渋谷センター街
セタ まつり
SALARYMAN set free
COOL CATS EYEING GIRLS
PLUGGED IN
WESTERNER
2F
guy without style
PIGEON-TOED JAPANESE WOMAN
bouffant
HIP-HOP COUPLE
NORMAL GIRL
BUNCH OF HIGH-SCHOOL GIRLS (often ONE is fat)
HIPHOP & STREET
SALE
CAFE DANMARK
241 ¥

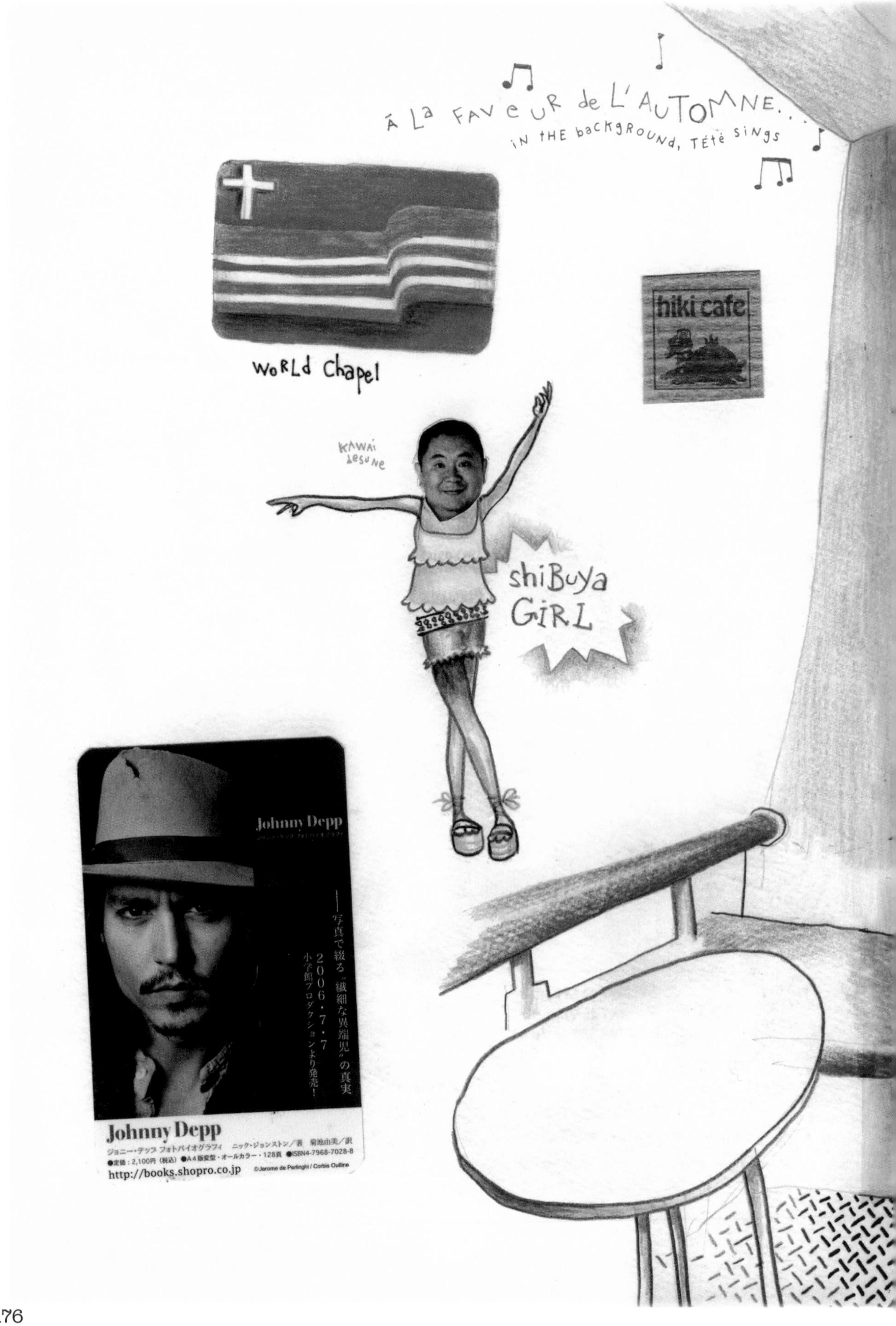
À LA FAVEUR DE L'AUTOMNE...
IN THE BACKGROUND, TÊTE SINGS
WORLD Chapel
hiki cafe
KAWAI desune
shiBuya GIRL
Johnny Depp
ジョニー・デップ フォトバイオグラフィ
——写真で綴る"繊細な異端児"の真実
2006・7・7
小学館プロダクションより発売!
Johnny Depp
ジョニー・デップ フォトバイオグラフィ ニック・ジョンストン/著 菊池由美/訳
●定価:2,100円(税込) ●A4版変型・オールカラー・128頁 ●ISBN4-7968-7028-8
http://books.shopro.co.jp
©Jerome de Perlinghi / Corbis Outline

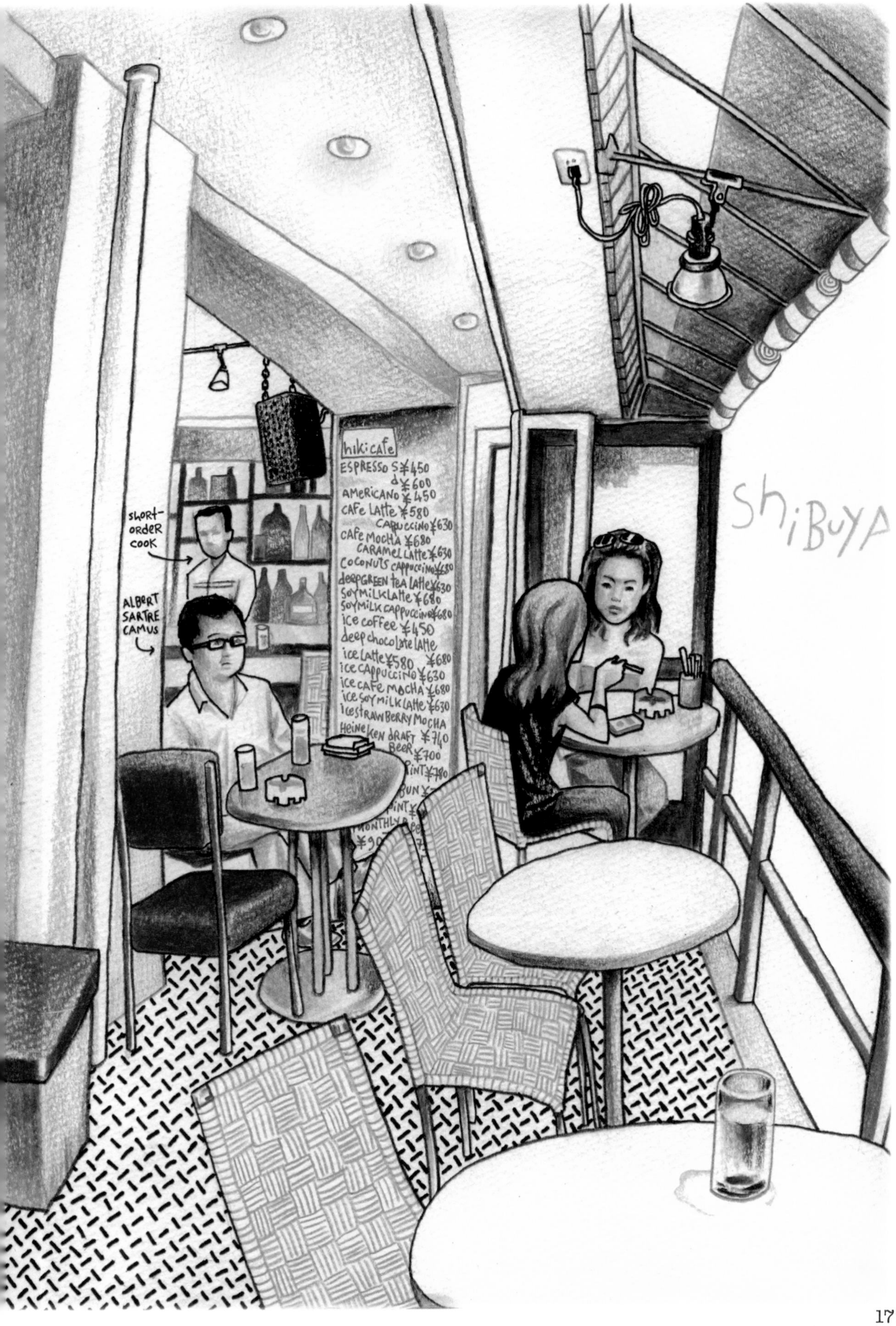

hiki:cafe
ESPRESSO S ¥450
d ¥600
AMERICANO ¥450
CAFe LATTe ¥580
CAPPUCCINO ¥630
CAFe MOCHA ¥680
CARAMEL LATTe ¥630
COCONUTS CAPPUCCINO ¥680
deepGREEN TEA LATTe ¥630
SOYMILK LATTe ¥680
SOYMILK CAPPUCCINO ¥680
ice coffee ¥450
deep chocolate latte
ice latte ¥580 ¥680
ice CAPPUCCINO ¥630
ice CAFe MOCHA ¥680
ice SOYMILK LATTe ¥630
ice STRAWBERRY MOCHA
HeineKEN DRAFT ¥740
BEER ¥700
short-order cook
ALBERT SARTRE CAMUS
ShiBuYA

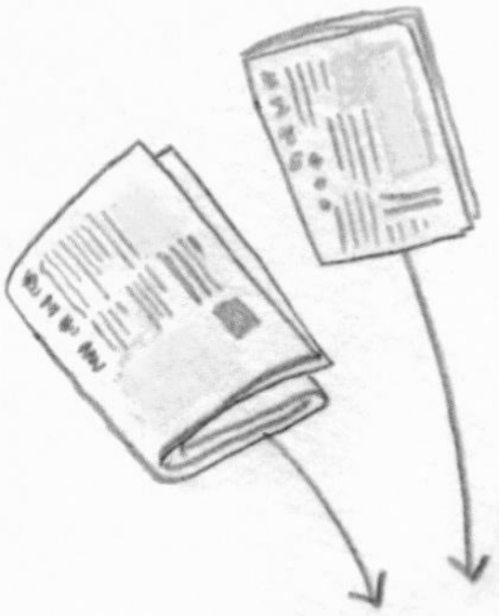

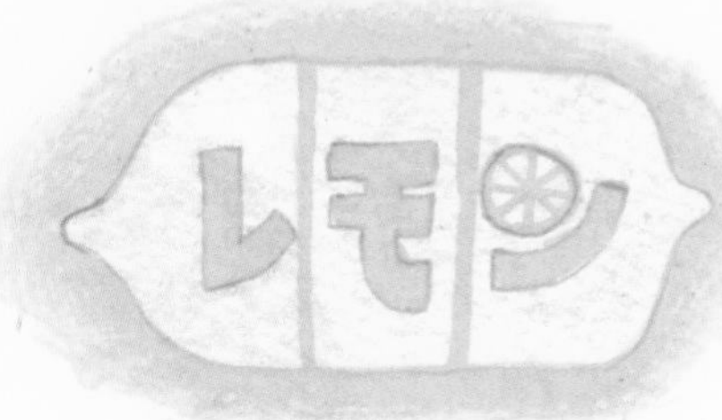
レモン

The Moped used By NEWSPAPER Boys

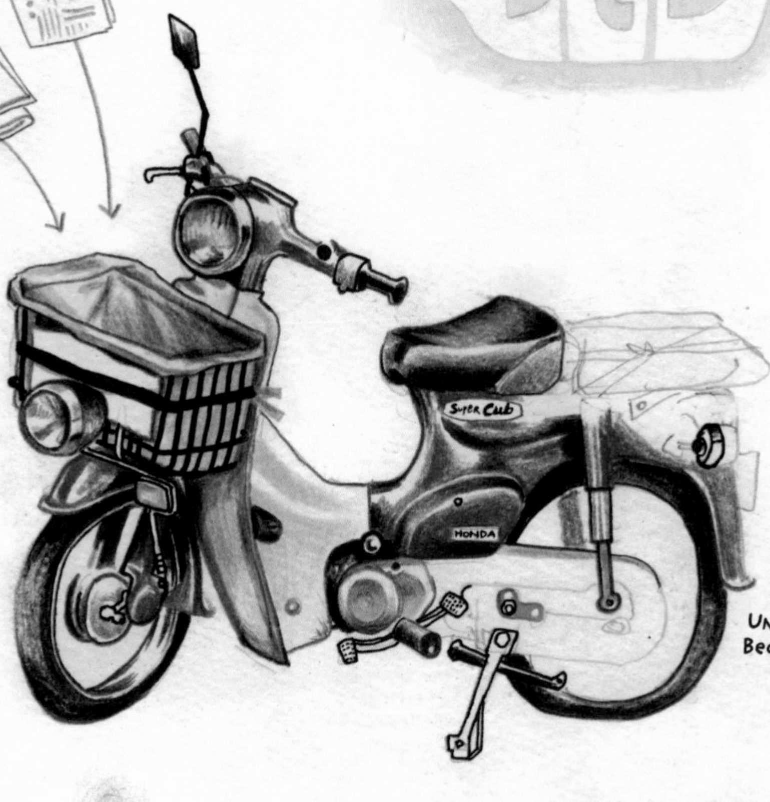
Super Cub
HONDA

UNFiNished Because Moped goNE

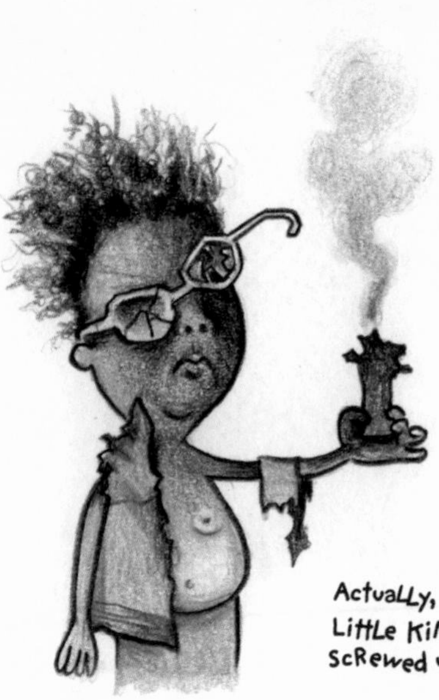

Actually, Little KiM screwed up his BOMB.

i Set up iN FRONT of the ENtrance to tHiS FAMOUS SHiBuYA Store to draw the Catalog of FashioN Opposite.

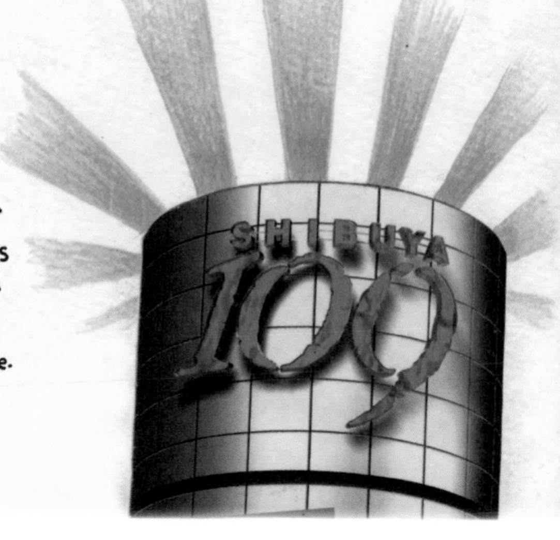
SHIBUYA
109

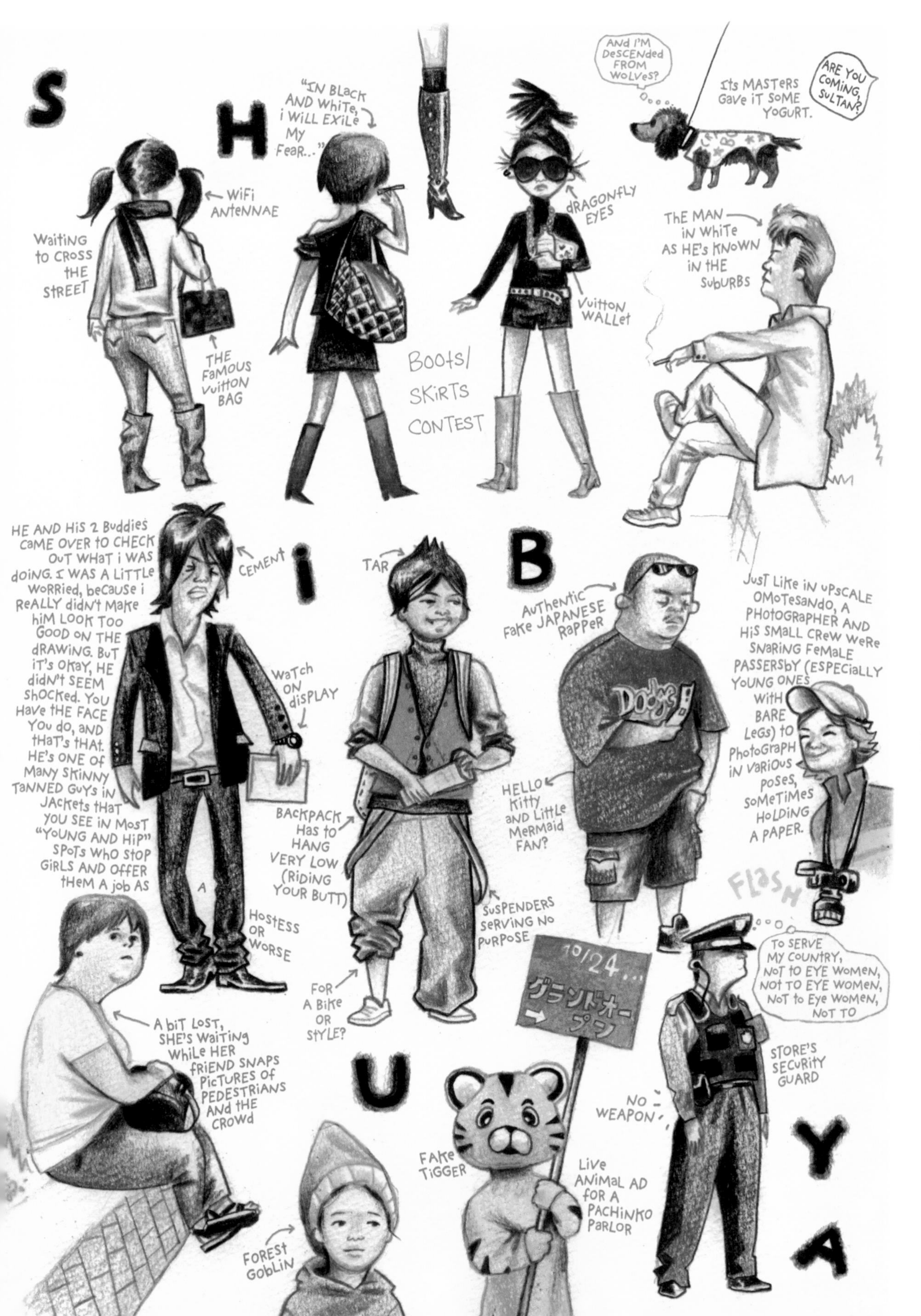
S
H
i
B
U
Y
A
Waiting to CROSS the STREET
WiFi ANTENNAE
THE FaMOUS vuitton BAG
"IN BLacK AND WhiTe, i WiLL EXiLe My Fear..."
Boots/ SKiRTS CONTEST
dRAGONfLY EYES
Vuitton WALLet
And I'M DeSCended FROM WOLves?
ARE YOU COMING, SULTAN?
Its MASTERS Gave iT SOME YOGURT.
THE MAN in WHiTe AS HE's KNOWN iN THE SuBURBS
HE AND His 2 Buddies CaME OVER TO CHECK OUT WHAT i WAS doiNG. I WAS A LiTTLe WORRied, because i ReALLY didn't Make hiM LOOK TOO GOOD ON THE dRAWiNG. BuT iT's OKay, HE didn't SEEM SHOCKed. YOU Have tHE FACE You do, and tHAT's THAT. HE's ONE OF Many SKiNNY TANNED GUYS iN JACKets THAT YOU SEE iN MOST "YOUNG AND HiP" SPOTS WHO STOP GiRLS AND OFFER THEM A job AS A HOSTESS OR WORSE
CEMENT
Watch ON diSPLAY
TAR
BACKPACK Has to HANG VERY LOW (RidiNG YOUR BUTT)
SuSPENDERS SERViNG NO PURPOSE
FOR A Bike OR STYLE?
AuThentic Fake JAPANESE RaPPeR
Dodge
HELLO Kitty and LittLe MeRMaid FAN?
JuST Like iN uPSCALE OMOTeSANdO, A PHOTOGRAPHER AND HiS SMALL CREW WeRe SNARiNG FeMALE PASSERSBY (ESPECiaLLY YOUNG ONES WiTH BARE LeGs) to PHOTOGRaPH iN VaRiOUS POSES, SOMeTiMES HOLdiNG A PAPER.
FLasH
TO SERVE MY COUNTRY, NOT TO EYE WOMEN, NOT TO EYE WOMEN, NOT to Eye WOMEN, NOT TO
10/24...
グランドオープン
A biT LOST, SHE's WaiTiNG WHiLe HER FRiEND SNAPS PiCTURES OF PEDESTRIANS AND THE CROWD
FOREST GOBLIN
FaKe TiGGER
Live ANiMAL AD FOR A PACHiNKO PARLOR
NO WEAPON
STORE'S SECURiTY GUARD

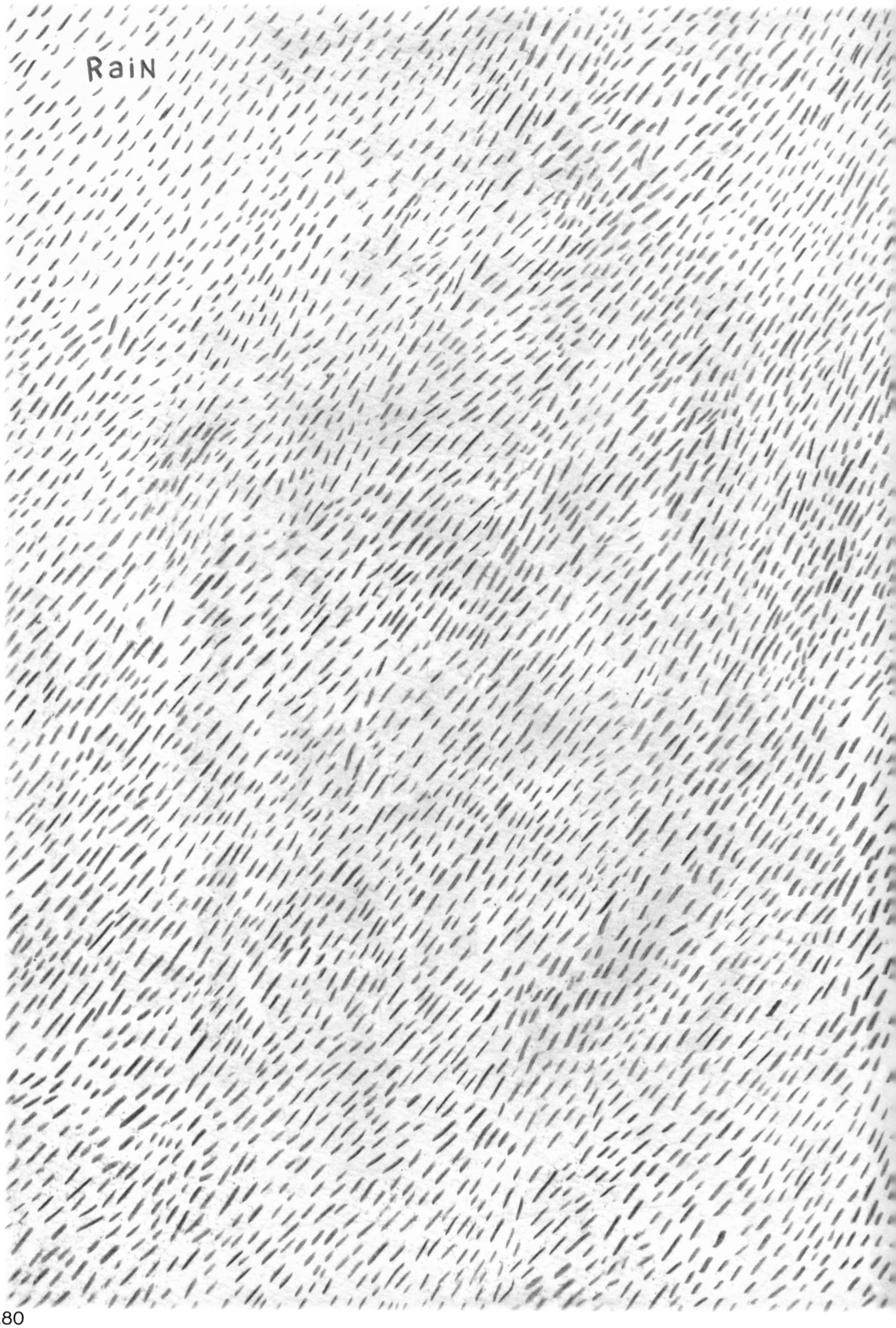
Rain

SANWA

FAKE TOKYO TOWER →

Build Your Own Japanese Street

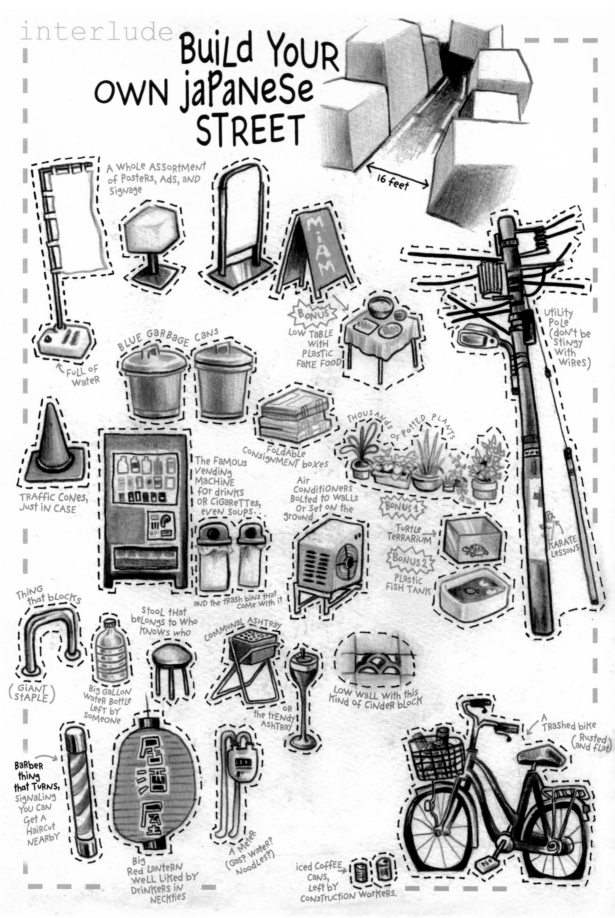

16 feet

A Whole Assortment of Posters, Ads, and Signage

MiAM

BONUS! LOW TABLE WiTH PLASTiC FAKE FOOD

UtiLiTY POLE (don't be stingy with wiRes)

← FULL OF WATER

BLUE GARBAGE CANS

FOLDABLE CONSIGNMENT boxes

THOUSANDS OF POTTED PLANTS

TRAFFiC CONES, JUST iN CASE

The FAMOUS VENDiNG MACHiNE for drinks OR CiGaReTTes, even SOUPS...

AiR CONDiTiONERS BOLTED TO WALLS OR SET ON the ground

BONUS 1 TURTLE TERRARiUM

KARATE LESSONS

BONUS 2 PLASTiC FiSH TANK

AND the tRASH biNS that COME WiTH it

THiNG that bLOCkS

STOOL tHAT beLONGS to WHO KNOWS WHO

COMMUNAL ASHTRAY

LOW WALL WiTH this KiND OF CiNDER bLOCK

(GiANT) STAPLE

Big GALLON WaTeR BOTTLE LeFT bY SOMEONE

OR the tRENDY ASHTRAY

A TRASHED bike Rusted (and flat)

BARBER thing that TURNS, SiGNALiNG YOU CAN GeT A HaiRCUT NEARbY

Big Red LANTERN WeLL LiKed bY DRiNKeRS iN NECKTiES

A MeTeR (GAS? WaTeR? NOODLeS?)

iced COFFEE CANS, LeFT bY CONSTRUCTiON WORKeRS.

daikanyama

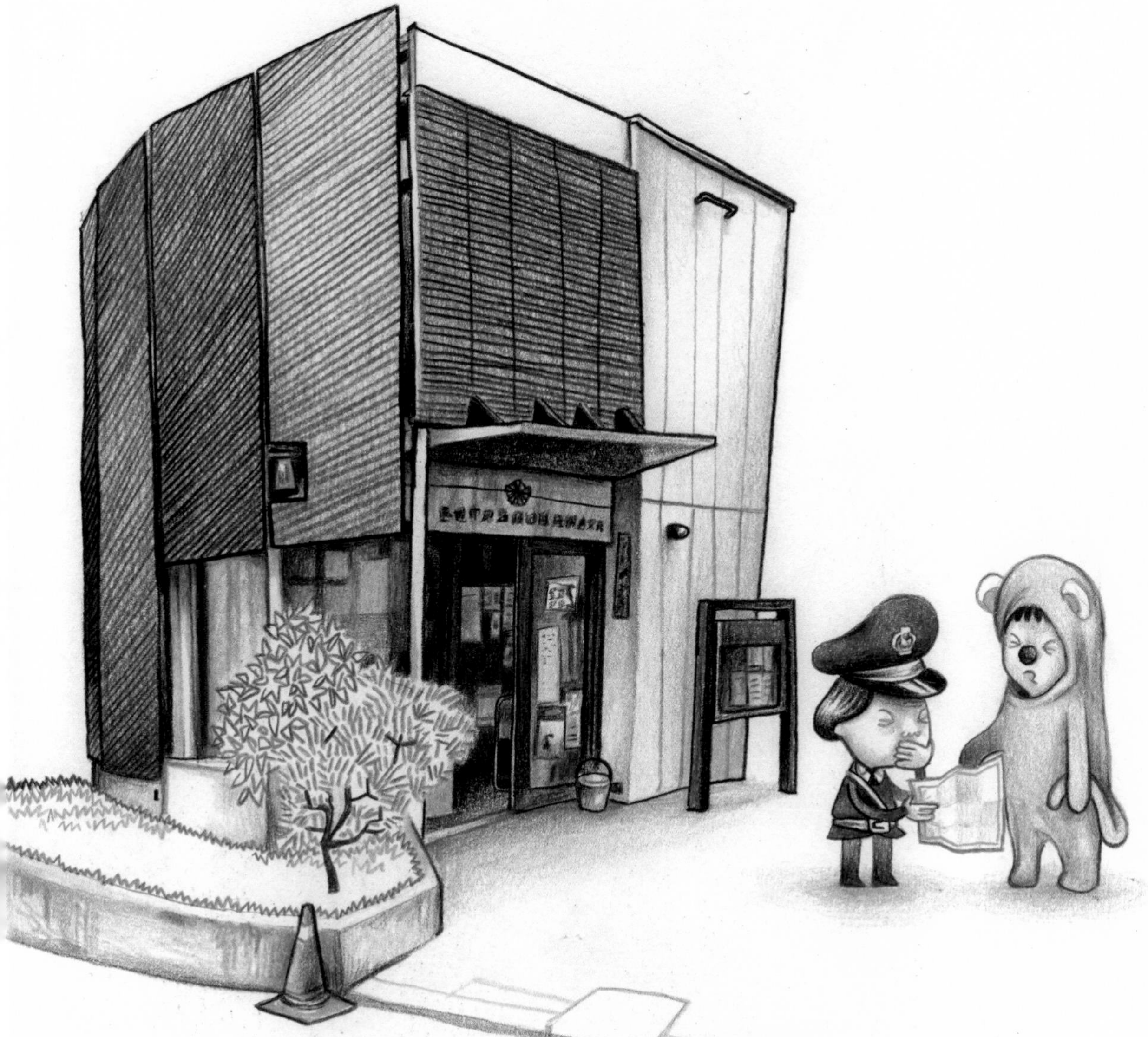

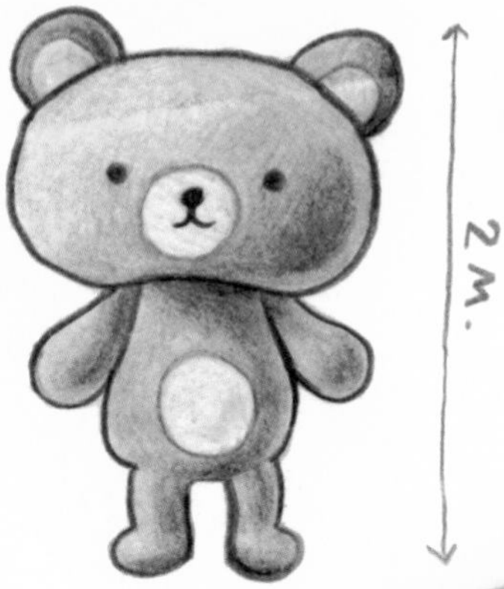
2 M.

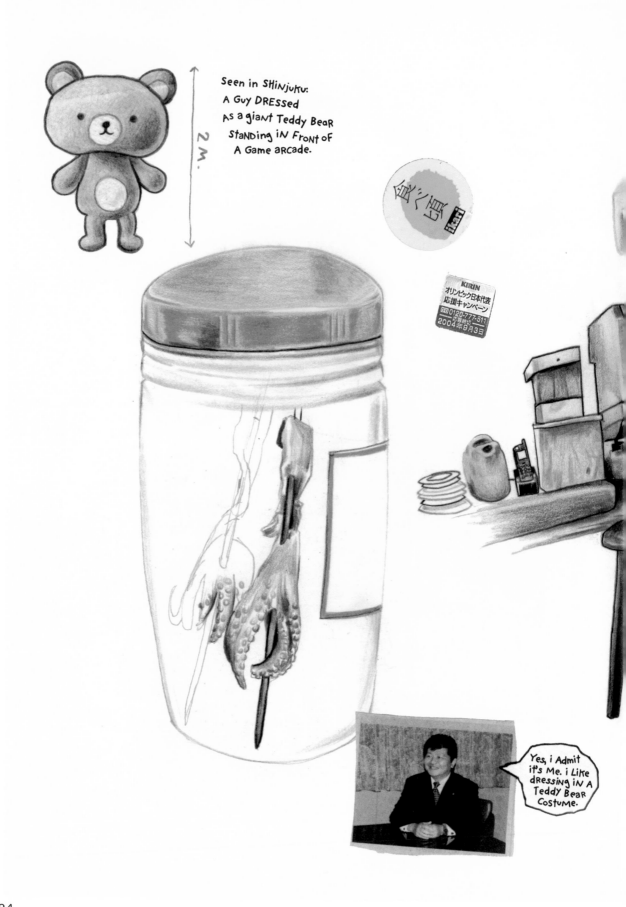

Seen in SHINJUKU:
A Guy DRESSed
As a giant Teddy Bear
standing in Front of
A Game arcade.

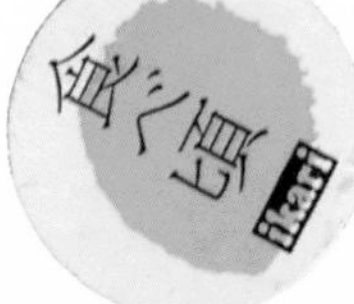

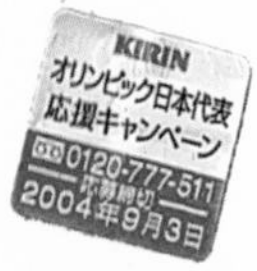
KIRIN
オリンピック日本代表
応援キャンペーン
0120-777-511
2004年9月3日

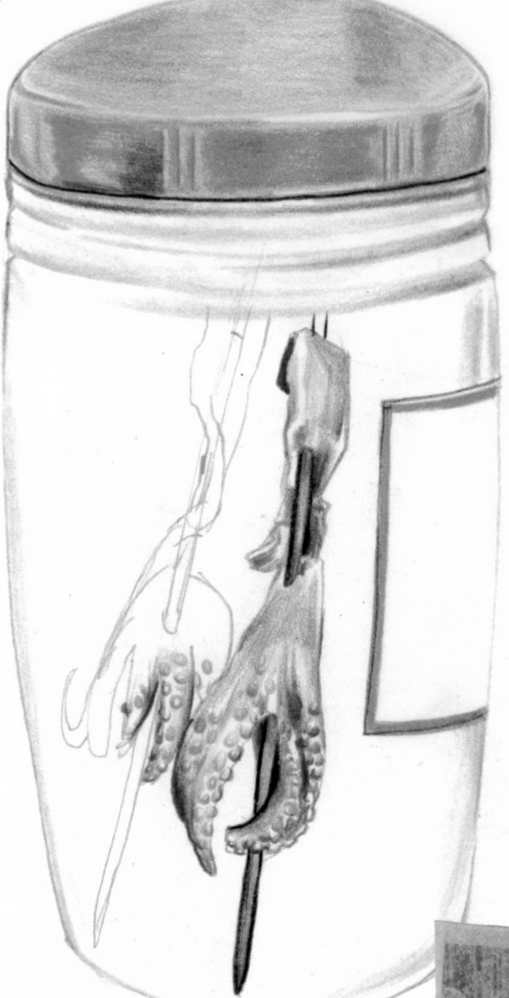

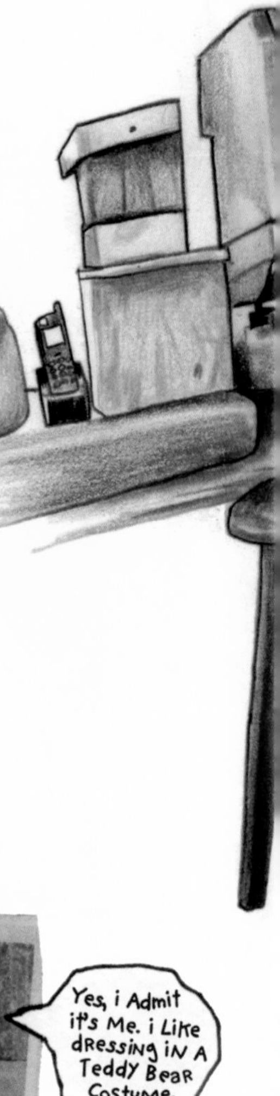

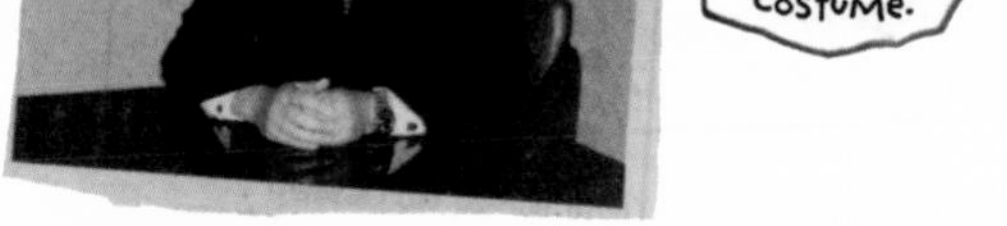
Yes, i Admit it's Me. i Like dressing in A Teddy Bear Costume.

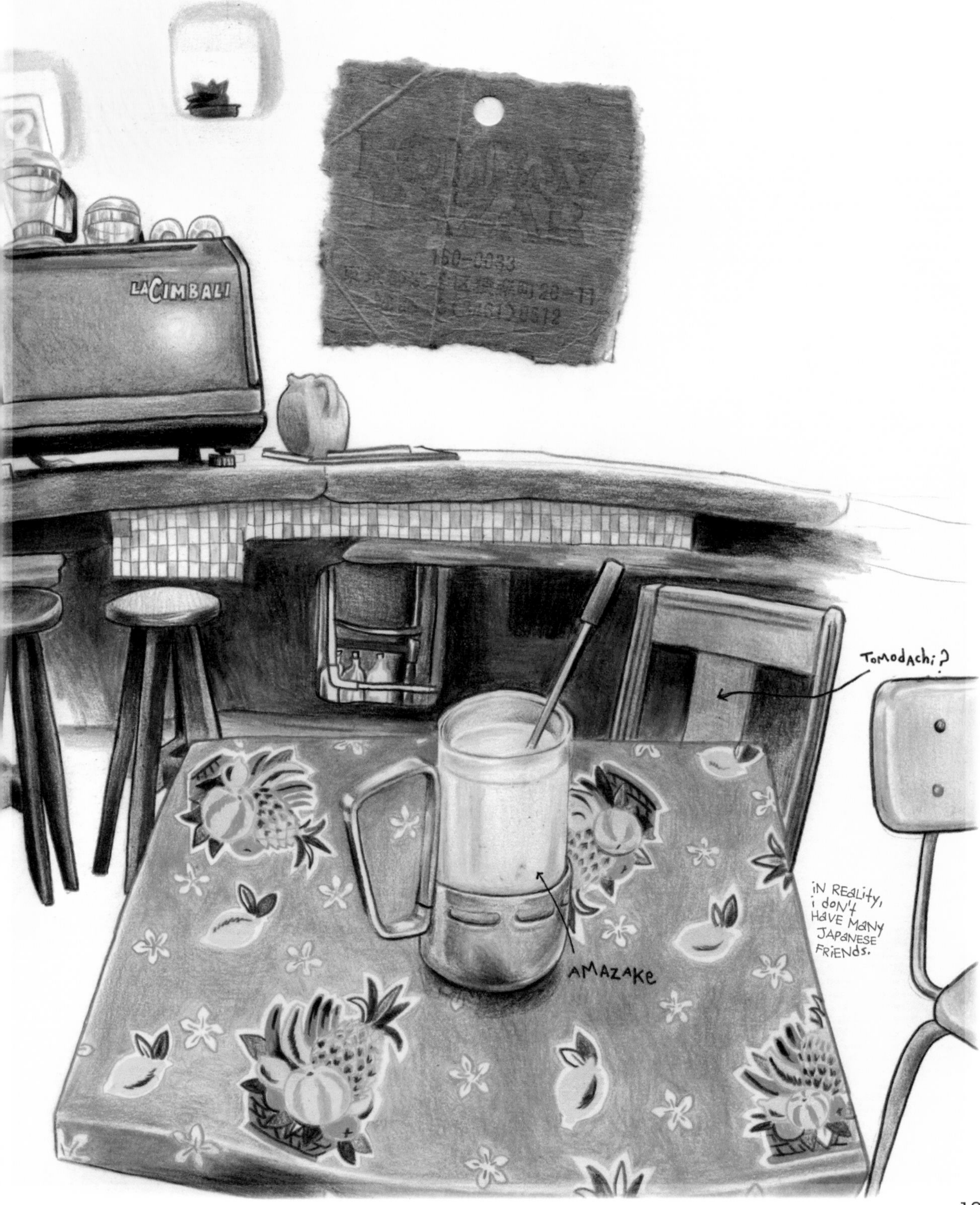
LACIMBALI
TOMODACHI?
AMAZAKE
IN REALITY, I DON'T HAVE MANY JAPANESE FRIENDS.

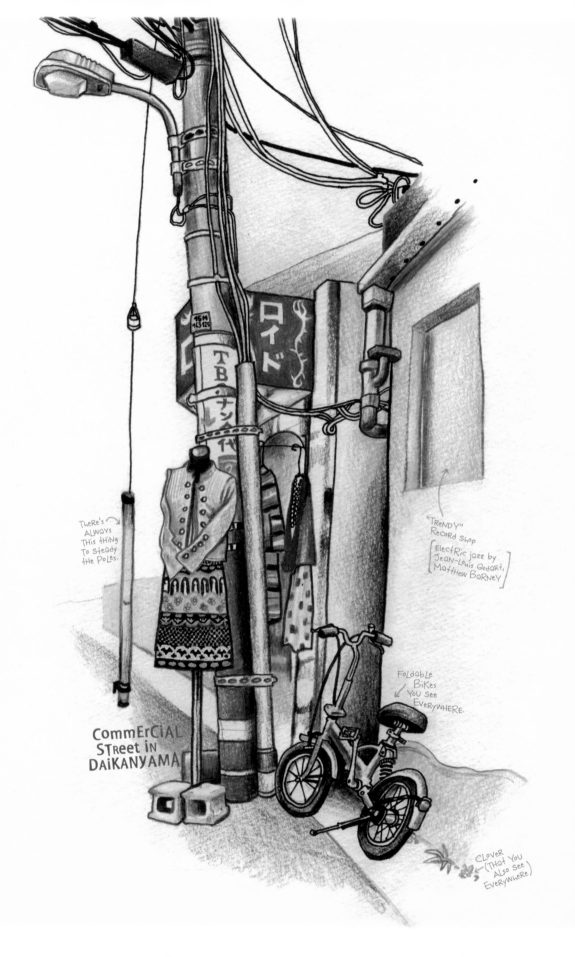

There's always this thing to steady the poles.

"Trendy" Record shop
[Electric jazz by Jean-Louis Godart, Matthew Barney]

Foldable Bikes you see everywhere.

Commercial Street in Daikanyama

Clover (that you also see everywhere)

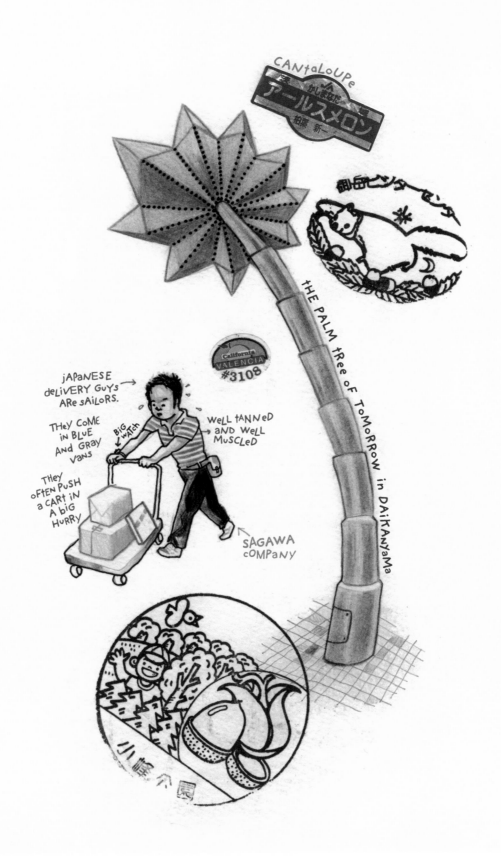

CANtaLoUPe

アールスメロン

THE PALM tRee of ToMoRRoW in DAiKAnyaMa

JAPaNESE
deLiVERY GuYs
ARe sAiLoRs.

THey CoME
in BLUE
And GRay
Vans

BiG
WATch

WeLL tANNeD
AND WeLL
MuScLeD

They
oFtEN PUSH
a CARt iN
A biG
HURRY

SAGAWA
coMPany

California
VALENCIA
#3108

187

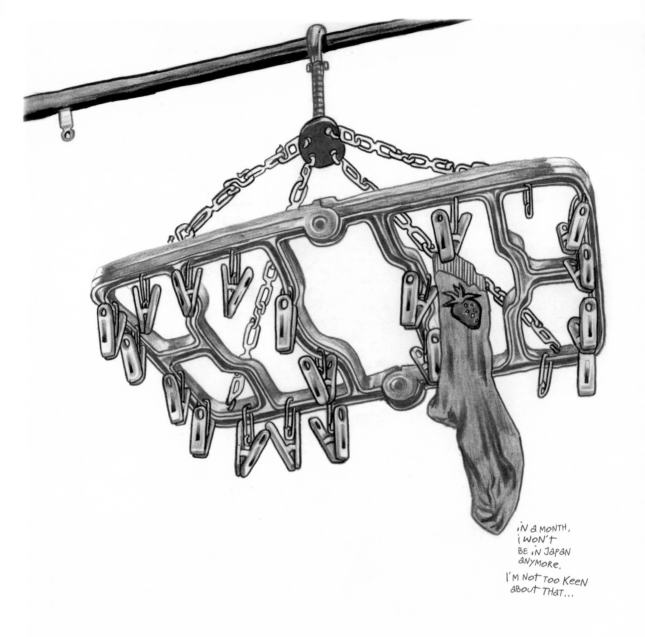

IN A MONTH,
I WON'T
BE IN JAPAN
ANYMORE.

I'M NOT TOO KEEN
ABOUT THAT...

- - interlude - - - - - - - - - - -

SOCioLOGY made easY 5

 SURVEY of tHE KoBaN PopuLation: THE KoBaNeSE.

THE OLd HAND **THE YOUNG VETERAN** **THE FReSH ReCRuit**

	THE OLd HAND	THE YOUNG VETERAN	THE FReSH ReCRuit
SYMPATHY	★★	★★★	★
COMMUNiCAtioN	★	★★★	★
DANGeRouSNeSS	★★	★	★★★

BeWARe: beNeatH his Wise oLd GRaNdPa AppeARaNCe HAS RetAiNed SoMe of tHE ReFLeXeS oF HiS GLoRY DAYs WHeN He PuRSUeD and rAN DoWN THe SNatcHeRS oF SACKS oF RiCe. Has A SuRpLus oF MoRal RectitUDe ("it iS foRbiDDeN tO CROSS WHeN tHe LiGHT iS Red.")

SMiLes the MoSt OF ALL AND iS tHE MOST TALeNTed at GiViNG DiReCtioNS. SoMetimeS HESitateS tO uTiLiZe the ENGLiSH He LeARNeD duRiNG A WeeK-LoNG CAMPiNG tRiP iN New ZEALAND ONCE. He's tHE ONe WhO dRiVes THE CAR.

VeRY PROUD Of HeR iLLuMiNATeD bAToN. FANtASizeS AbOut AL-QaEdA KoReAN terrOrists and CHoMpS At tHE bit WHiLe WaitiNG FoR HeR big bReAK (THe theFt OF tHE DAiLY eARNiNGS FRoM A dRiNKs VeNDiNG MACHiNe)

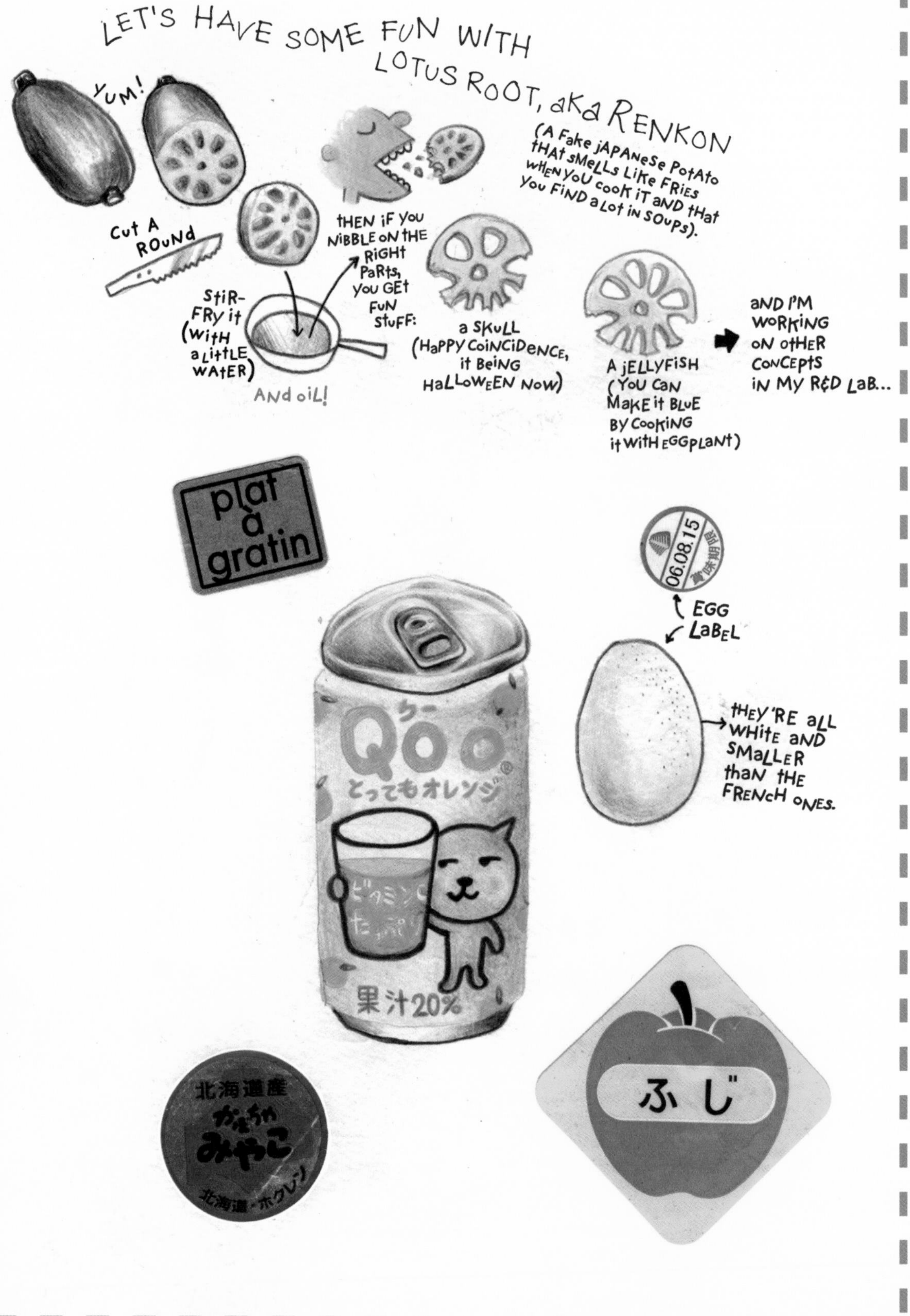
LET'S HAVE SOME FUN WITH LOTUS ROOT, aKa RENKON
(A Fake jAPANese PotAto tHAt sMeLLs LiKe FRies wHeN YoU cooK iT AND tHat you FIND a Lot in SOUPs).
YUM!
Cut A ROUNd
StiR-FRy it (WitH a LittLE WAtER)
AND oiL!
tHEN iF YoU NIBBLE oN tHE RiGHt PaRts, you GEt FUN StuFF:
a SKuLL (HaPPY CoiNCiDENCE, it BeiNG HaLLoWEEN Now)
A jELLyFiSH (YoU CaN MaKe it BLUE BY CooKiNG it With EGGPLANt)
AND I'M WORKiNG ON otHER CoNCEPtS iN MY R&D LaB...
plat à gratin
06.08.15
賞味期限
EGG LaBEL
tHEY'RE aLL WHitE aND SMaLLER than tHE FRENcH oNES.
クー
Qoo
とってもオレンジ
果汁20%
北海道産
みやこ
北海道・ホクレン
ふじ

ebisu

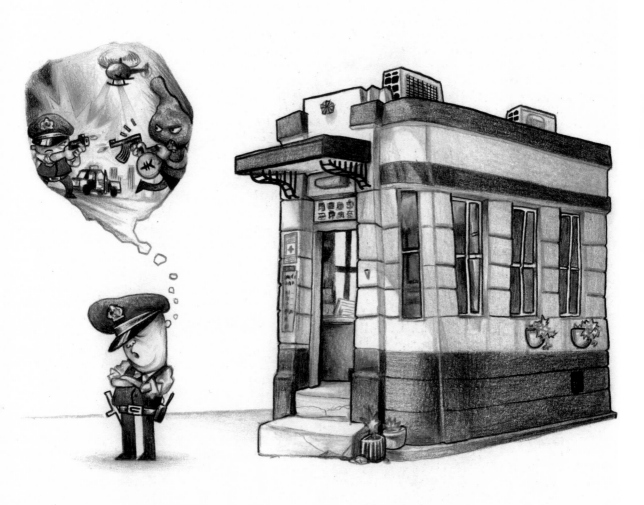

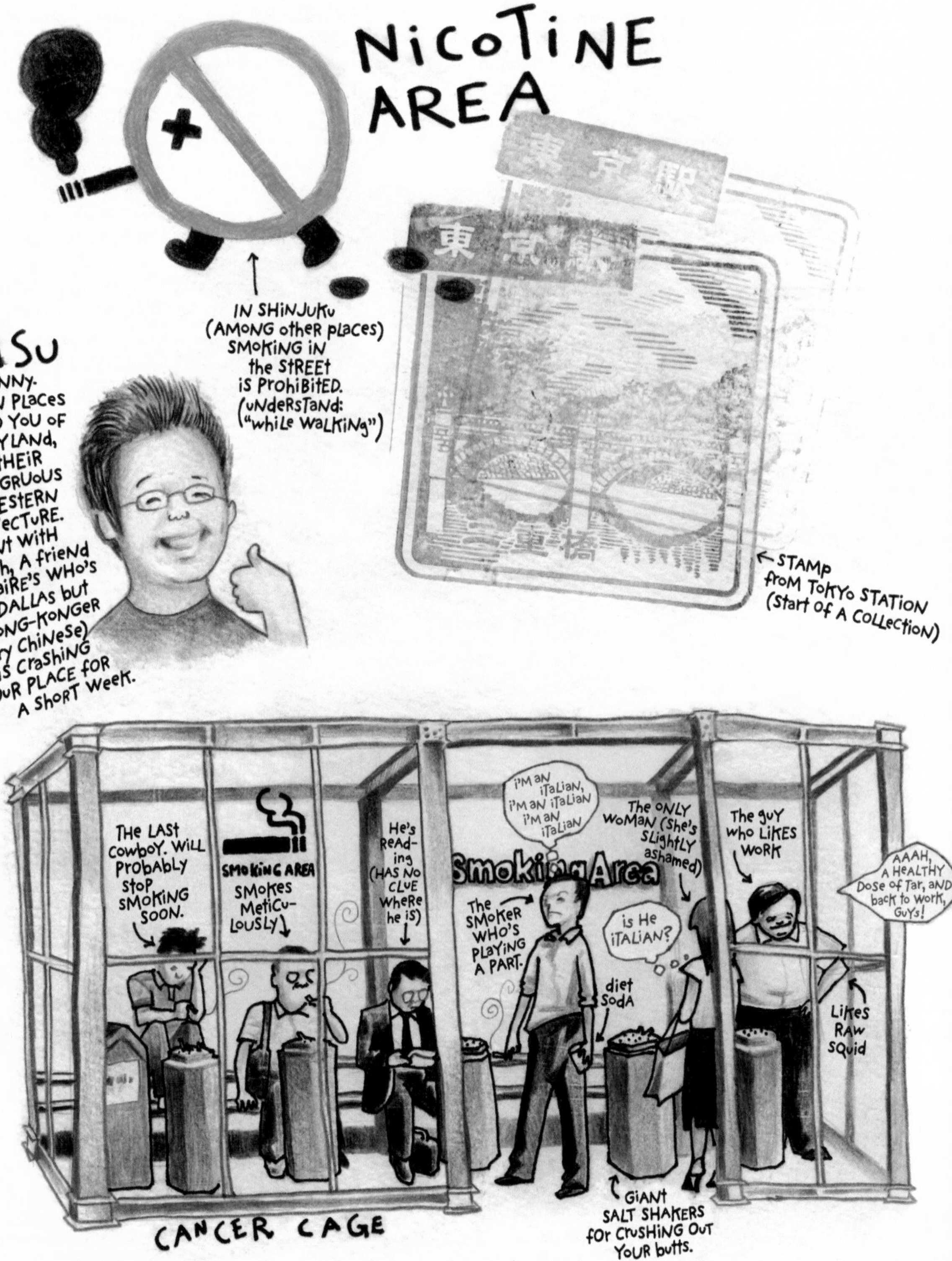
NICOTINE AREA
IN SHINJUKU (AMONG other places) SMOKING IN the STREET is ProhiBITED. (UNDERSTAND: "While WALKING")
東京駅
東京駅
二重橋
← STAMP from TOKYO STATION (Start of A COLLECTION)
EBISU
It's FUNNY. Certain PLACES REMIND YOU of disNEYLAND, With THEIR iNCONGRUOUS WESTERN ArchiTECTURE. i WENT WITH KENNeth, A friend of CLAIRE's WHO's from DALLAS but is A HONG-KONGER (and very ChiNESE) AND is CrAShiNG at OUR PLACE FOR A SHORT WEEK.
The LAST cowboy. WILL Probably stop SMOKING SOON.
SMOKING AREA
SMOKES METICULOUSLY
He's Reading (HAS NO CLUE where he is)
I'M an iTaLian, I'M an iTaLian I'M an iTaLian
SmokingArea
The SMOKER WHO's PLAYING A PART.
The ONLY WOMAN (She's SLightLY ashamed)
is He iTALIAN?
diet SodA
The guy who LIKES WORK
AAAH, A HEALTHY Dose of Tar, and back to work, GUYS!
LIKES RAW SQuid
GIANT SALT SHAKERS for CRUSHING OUT YOUR butts.
CANCER CAGE

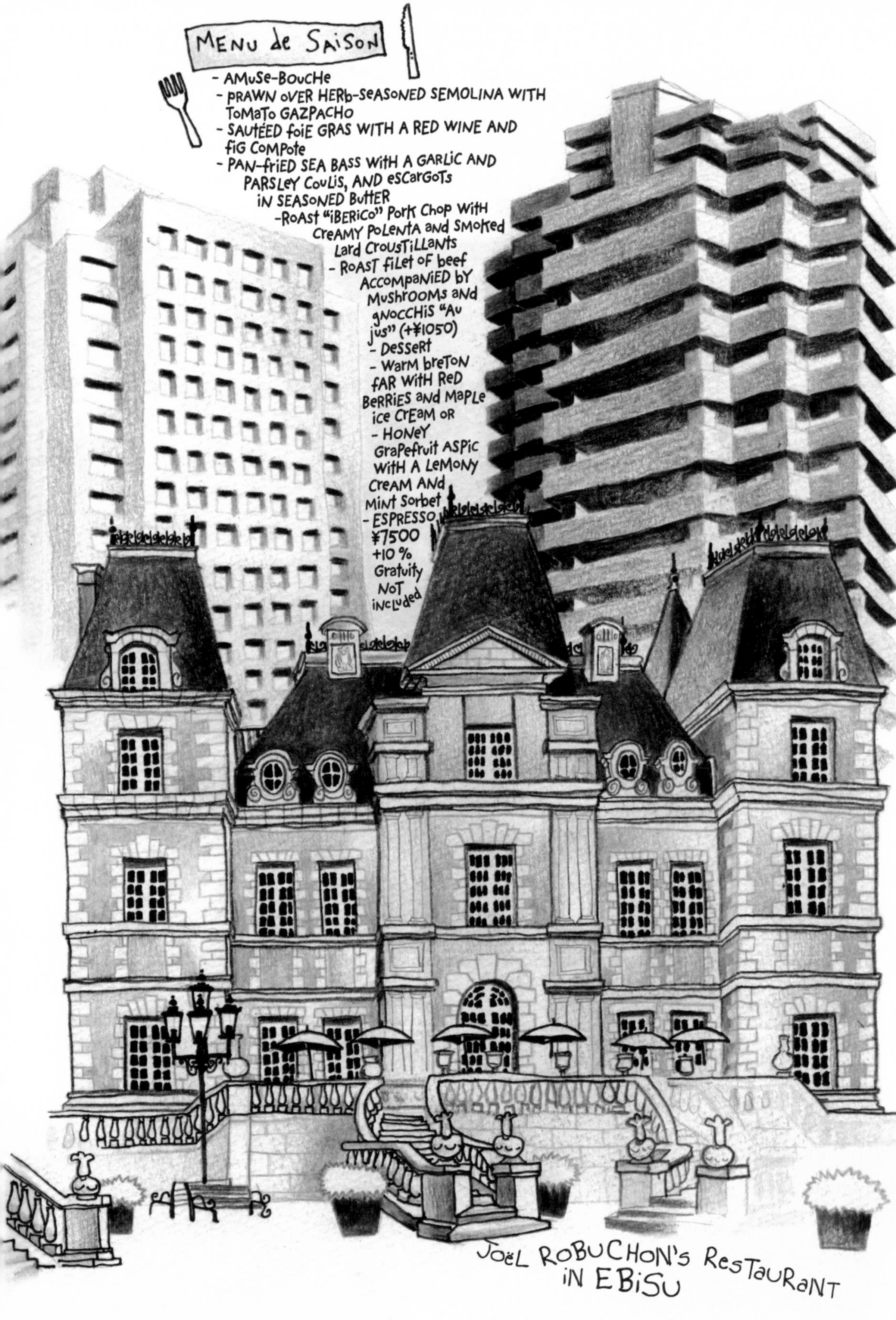

Menu de Saison
- Amuse-bouche
- Prawn over herb-seasoned semolina with tomato gazpacho
- Sautéed foie gras with a red wine and fig compote
- Pan-fried sea bass with a garlic and parsley coulis, and escargots in seasoned butter
- Roast "iberico" pork chop with creamy polenta and smoked lard croustillants
- Roast filet of beef accompanied by mushrooms and gnocchis "au jus" (+¥1050)
- Dessert
- Warm breton far with red berries and maple ice cream or
- Honey grapefruit aspic with a lemony cream and mint sorbet
- Espresso
¥7500 +10 % gratuity not included
Joël Robuchon's Restaurant in Ebisu

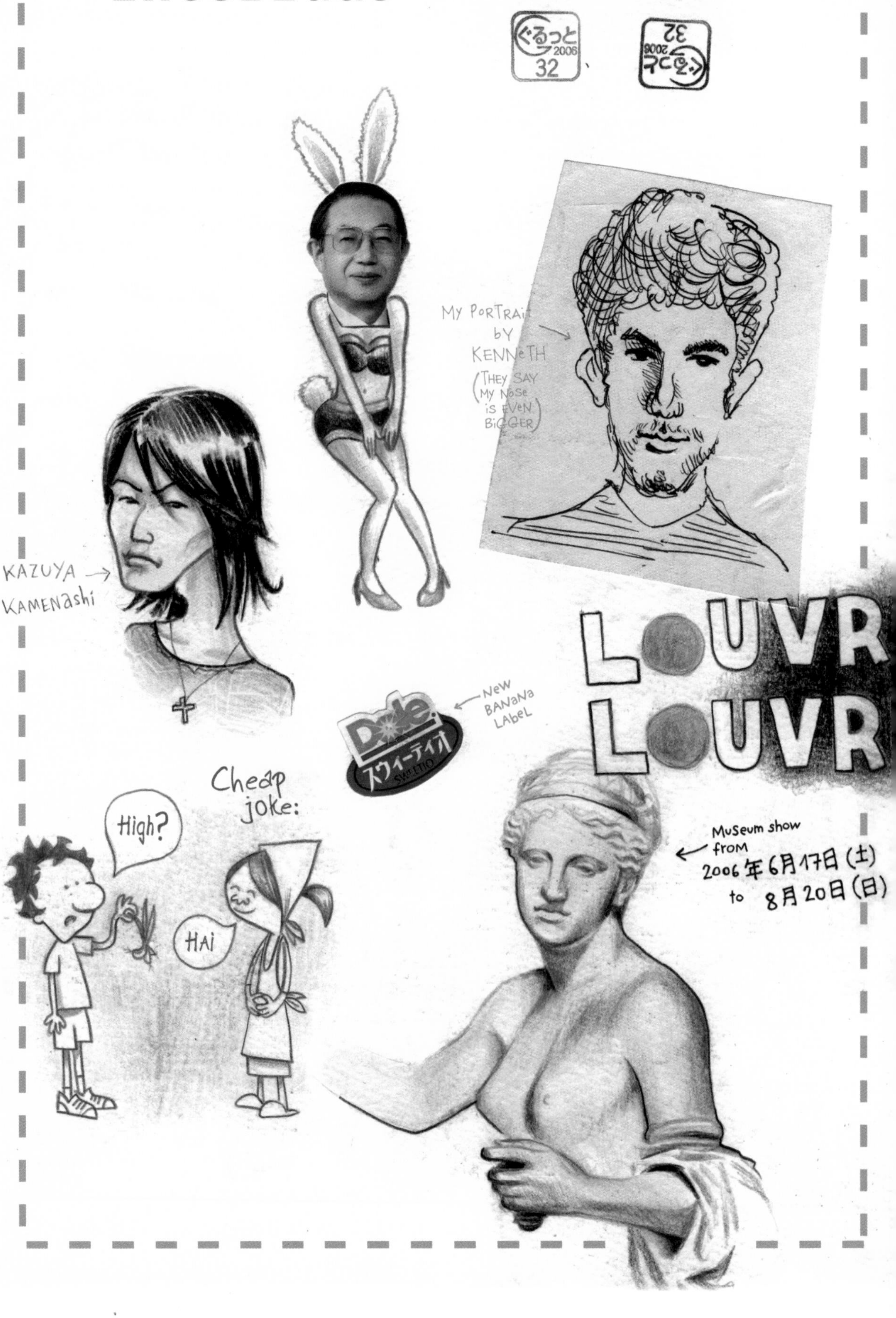
ぐるっと 2006 32
ぐるっと 2006 32
MY PORTRAIT BY KENNETH
(THEY SAY MY NOSE IS EVEN BIGGER)
KAZUYA KAMENASHI
LOUVR
LOUVR
Dole スウィーティオ SWEETIO
NEW BANANA LABEL
Cheap joke:
High?
HAi
Museum show from 2006年6月17日(土) to 8月20日(日)

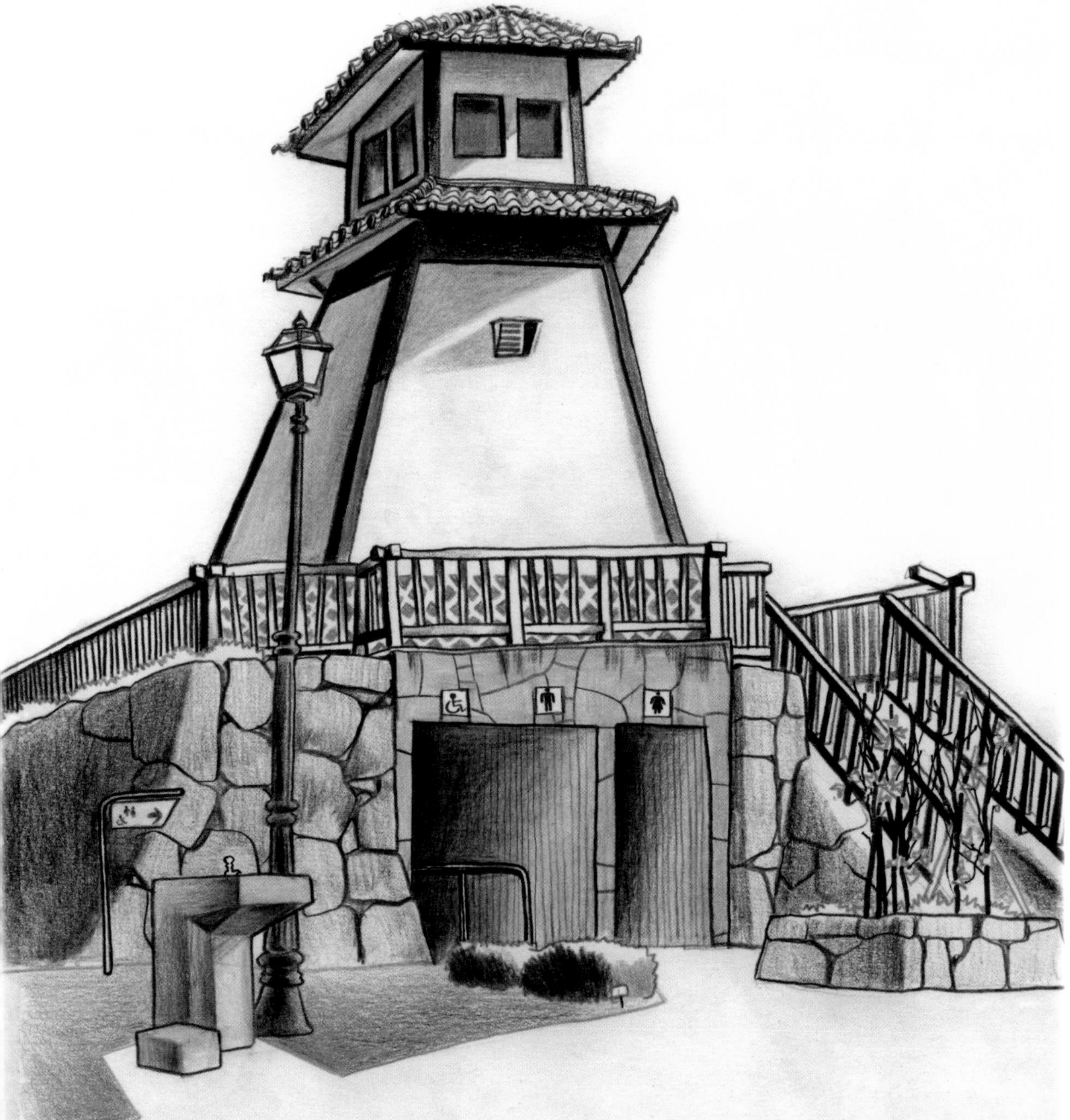

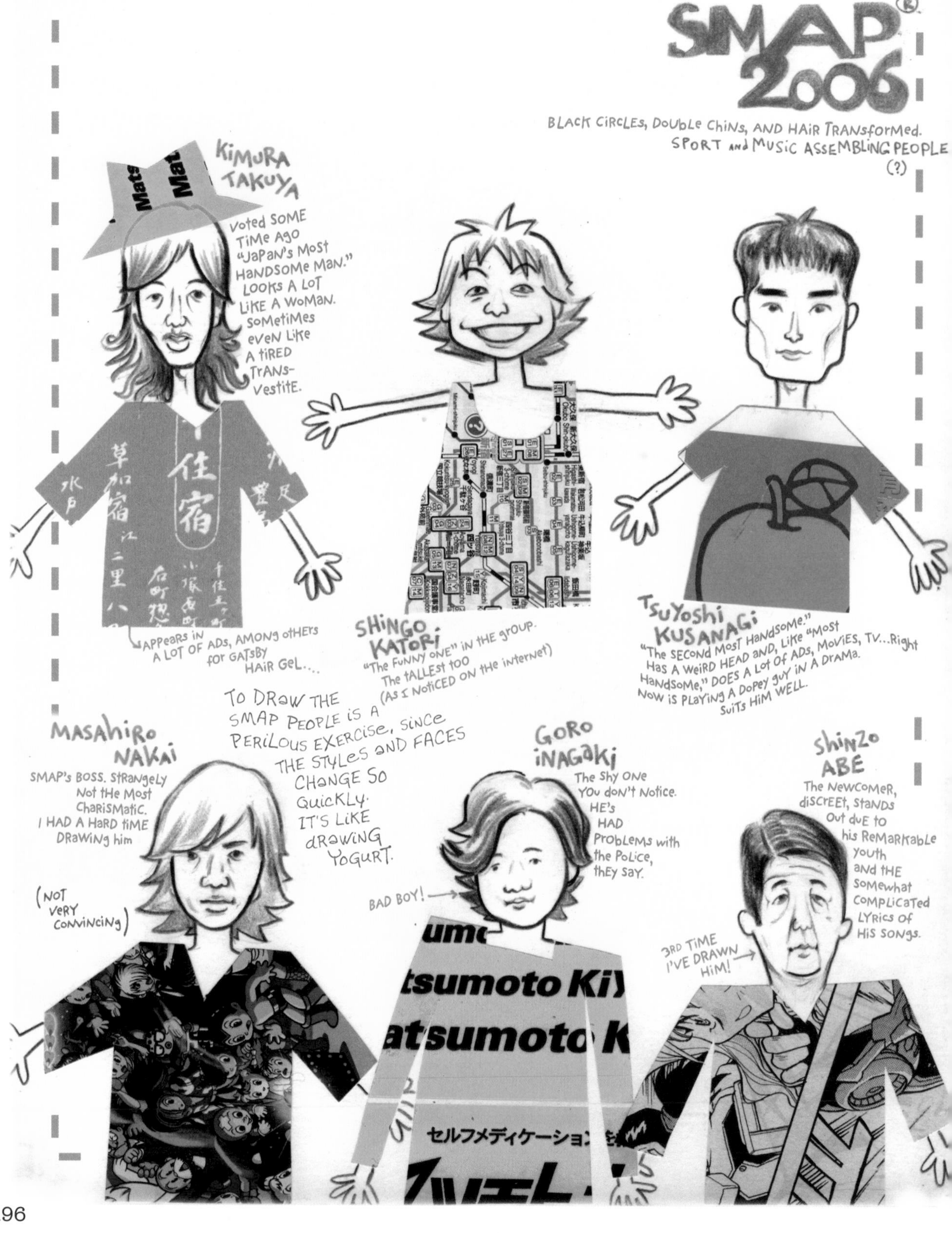
SMAP®
2006
BLACK CIRCLES, DOUBLE CHINS, AND HAIR TRANSFORMED.
SPORT AND MUSIC ASSEMBLING PEOPLE
(?)
KIMURA TAKUYA
Voted SOME TIME AGO "JAPAN'S MOST HANDSOME MAN." LOOKS A LOT LIKE A WOMAN. SOMETIMES EVEN LIKE A TIRED TRANS-VESTITE.
APPEARS IN A LOT OF ADS, AMONG OTHERS FOR GATSBY HAIR GEL....
SHINGO KATORI
"The FUNNY ONE" IN THE GROUP. The TALLEST too (AS I NOTICED ON THE INTERNET)
TSUYOSHI KUSANAGI
"The SECOND MOST HANDSOME." HAS A WEIRD HEAD AND, LIKE "MOST HANDSOME," DOES A LOT OF ADS, MOVIES, TV...Right NOW IS PLAYING A DOPEY GUY IN A DRAMA. SUITS HIM WELL.
TO DRAW THE SMAP PEOPLE IS A PERILOUS EXERCISE, SINCE THE STYLES AND FACES CHANGE SO QUICKLY. IT'S LIKE DRAWING YOGURT.
MASAHIRO NAKAI
SMAP's BOSS. STRANGELY NOT THE MOST CHARISMATIC. I HAD A HARD TIME DRAWING HIM
(NOT VERY CONVINCING)
GORO INAGAKI
The SHY ONE YOU DON'T NOTICE. HE'S HAD PROBLEMS WITH THE POLICE, THEY SAY.
BAD BOY!
SHINZO ABE
The NEWCOMER, DISCREET, STANDS OUT DUE TO HIS REMARKABLE YOUTH AND THE SOMEWHAT COMPLICATED LYRICS OF HIS SONGS.
3RD TIME I'VE DRAWN HIM!
tsumoto Ki
atsumoto K
セルフメディケーション

tsukiji

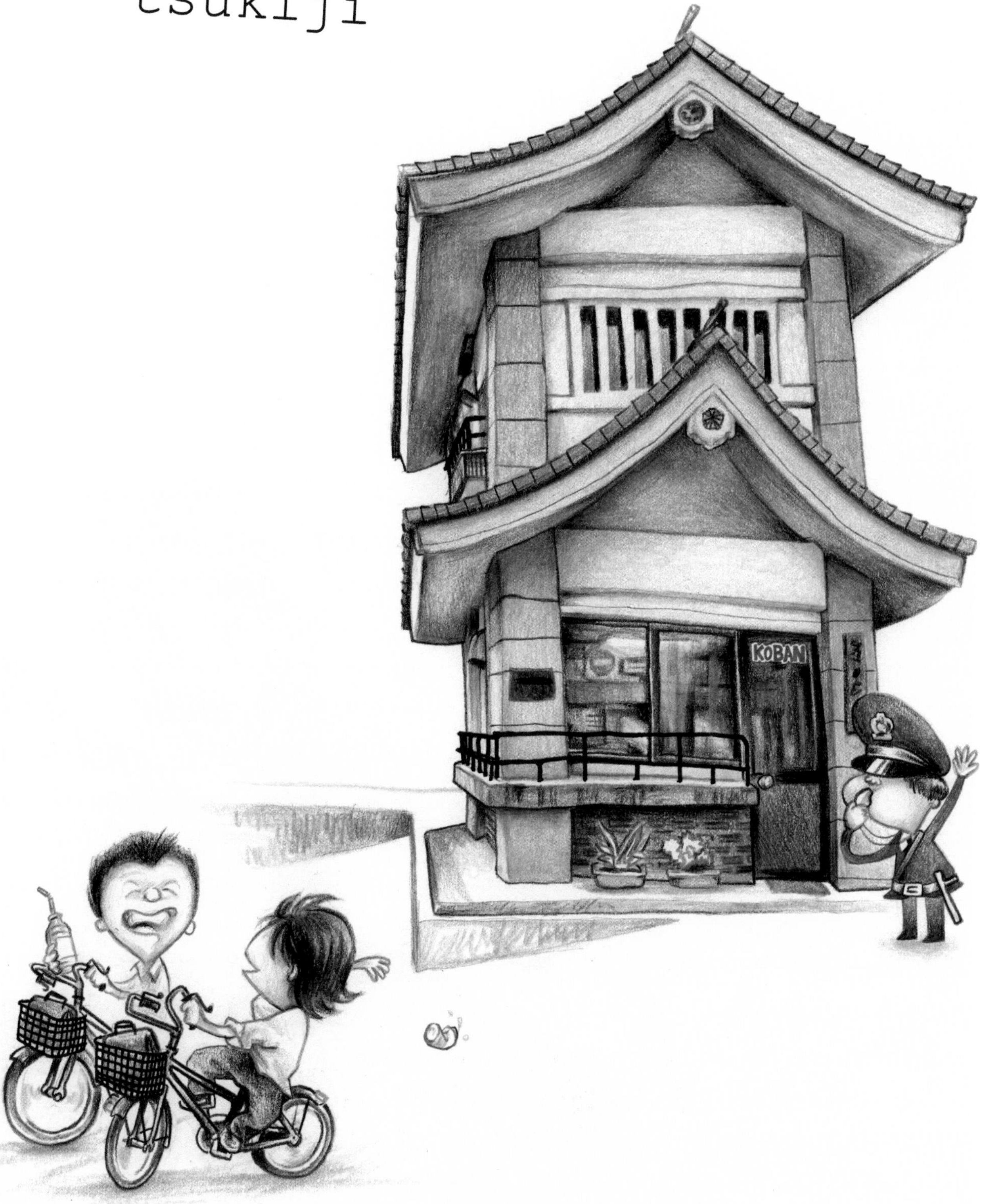
KOBAN

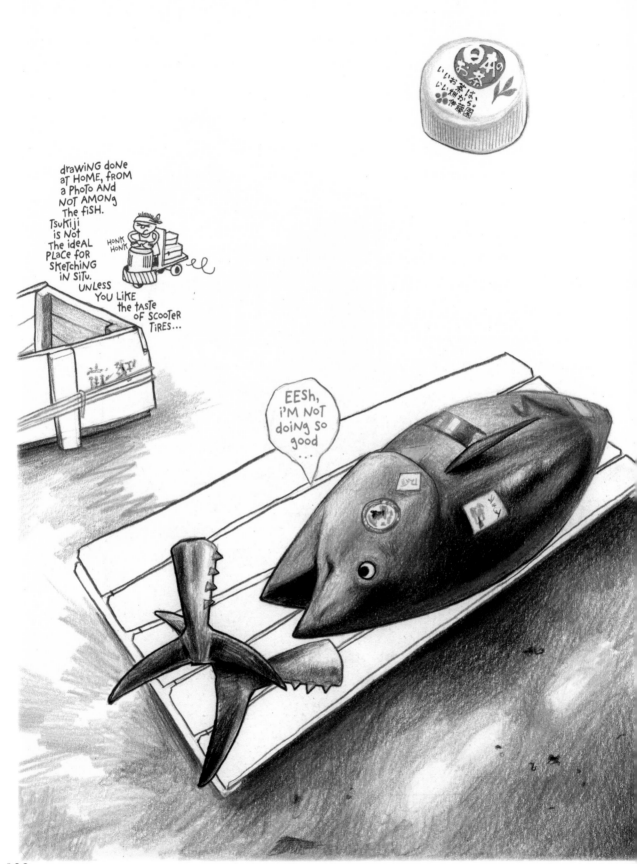

drawING doNE at HOME, froM a Photo AND NOT AMONG The fiSH. TsuKiJi is NoT The ideAL PLACE FOR SKETCHING IN SiTu. UNLESS YOU LIKE The TASTE OF SCOOTER TIRES...

HONK HONK

EESh, i'M NoT doiNG So good ...

198

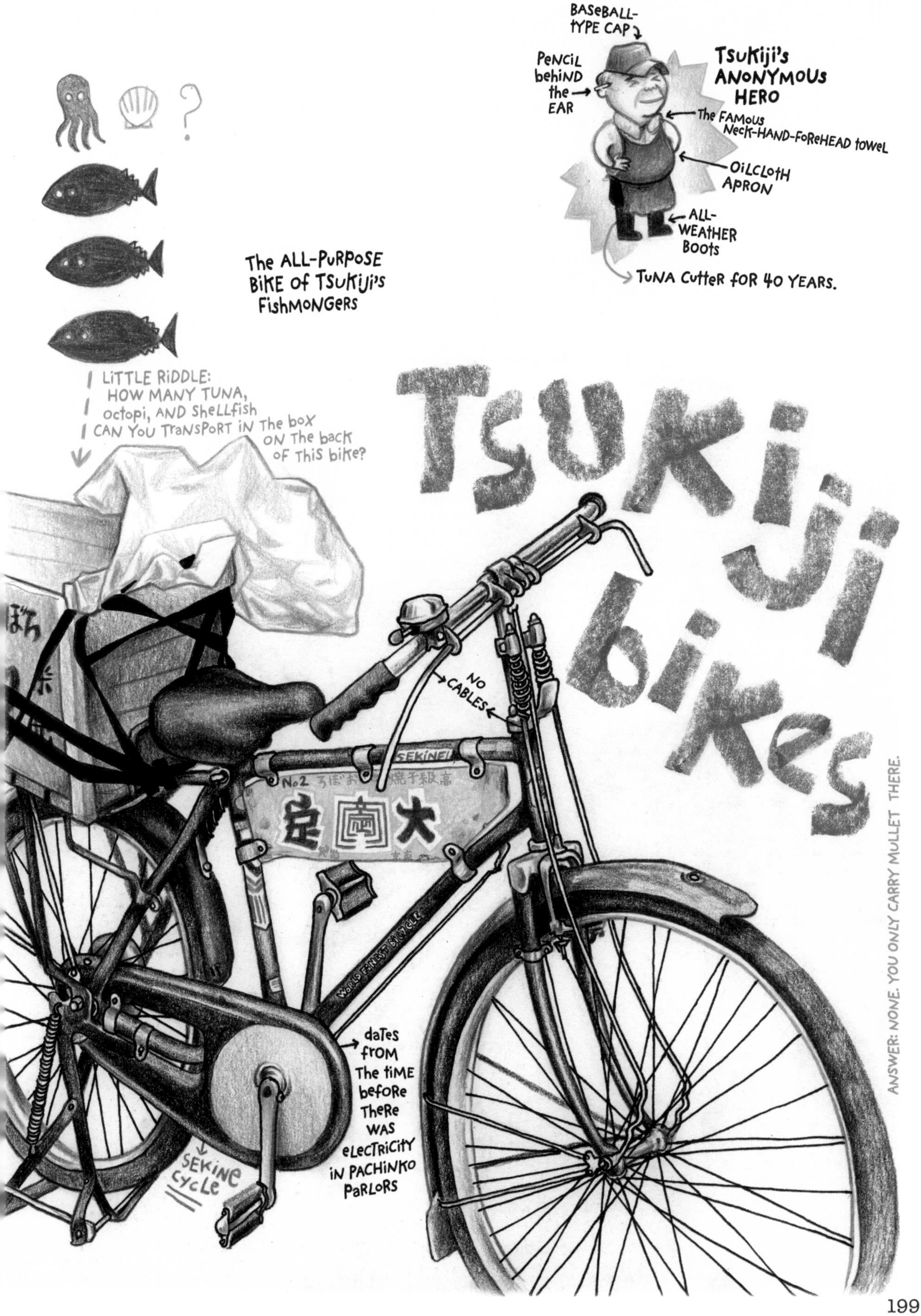

BASEBALL-TYPE CAP
PENCIL behind the EAR
TSUKIJI'S ANONYMOUS HERO
The FAMOUS Neck-HAND-FOREHEAD towel
OILCLOTH APRON
ALL-WEATHER Boots
TUNA Cutter FOR 40 YEARS.
The ALL-PURPOSE BIKE of TSUKIJI'S FishMONGERS
LITTLE RIDDLE: HOW MANY TUNA, octopi, AND Shellfish CAN YOU TRANSPORT IN The box ON The back of This bike?
TSUKIJI bikes
NO CABLES
SEKINE
WORLD FINEST BICYCLE
dates from The time before There WAS electricity in PACHINKO PARLORS
SEKINE cycle
ANSWER: NONE. YOU ONLY CARRY MULLET THERE.

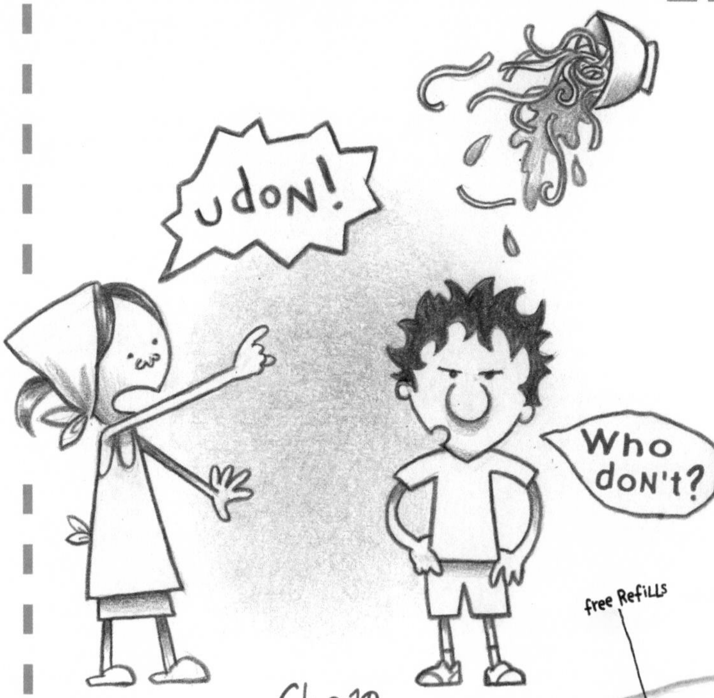
udon!
Who don't?

Cheap joke:

START OF A List of POLICEMEN WHO DETAINED ME →

NA 120
OH 116
OH 246
MA 305
MA 352
MA 061

Hi 108
Hi 100
KA 058
ji 204
To 193

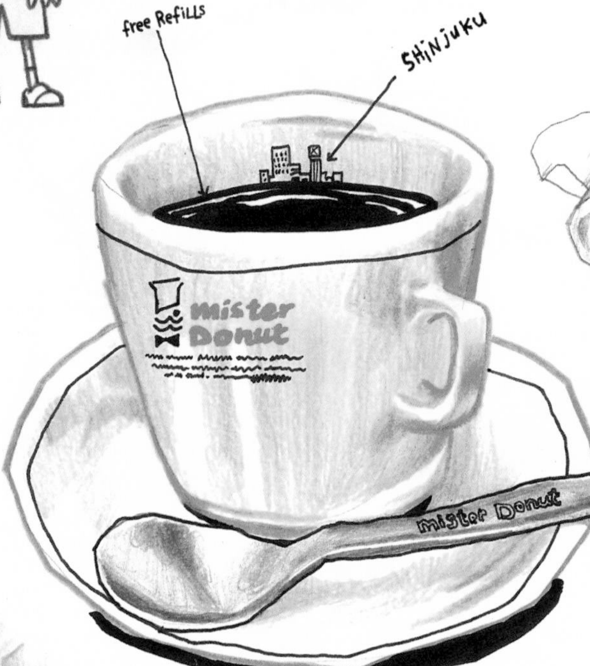
free Refills
SHINJUKU
mister Donut
mister Donut

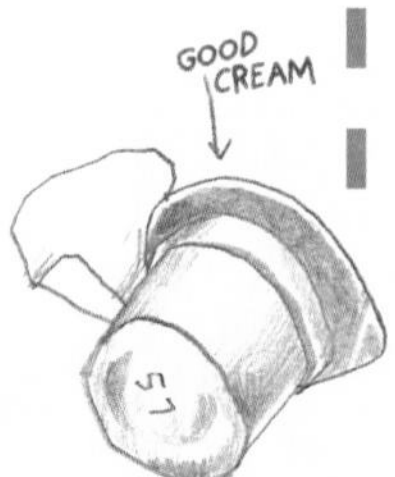
GOOD CREAM

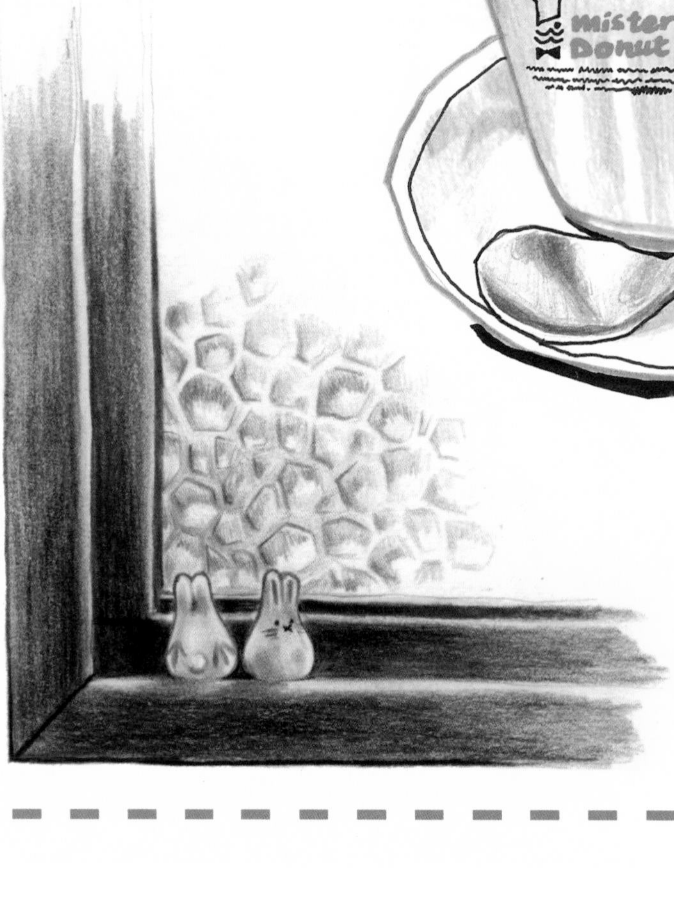

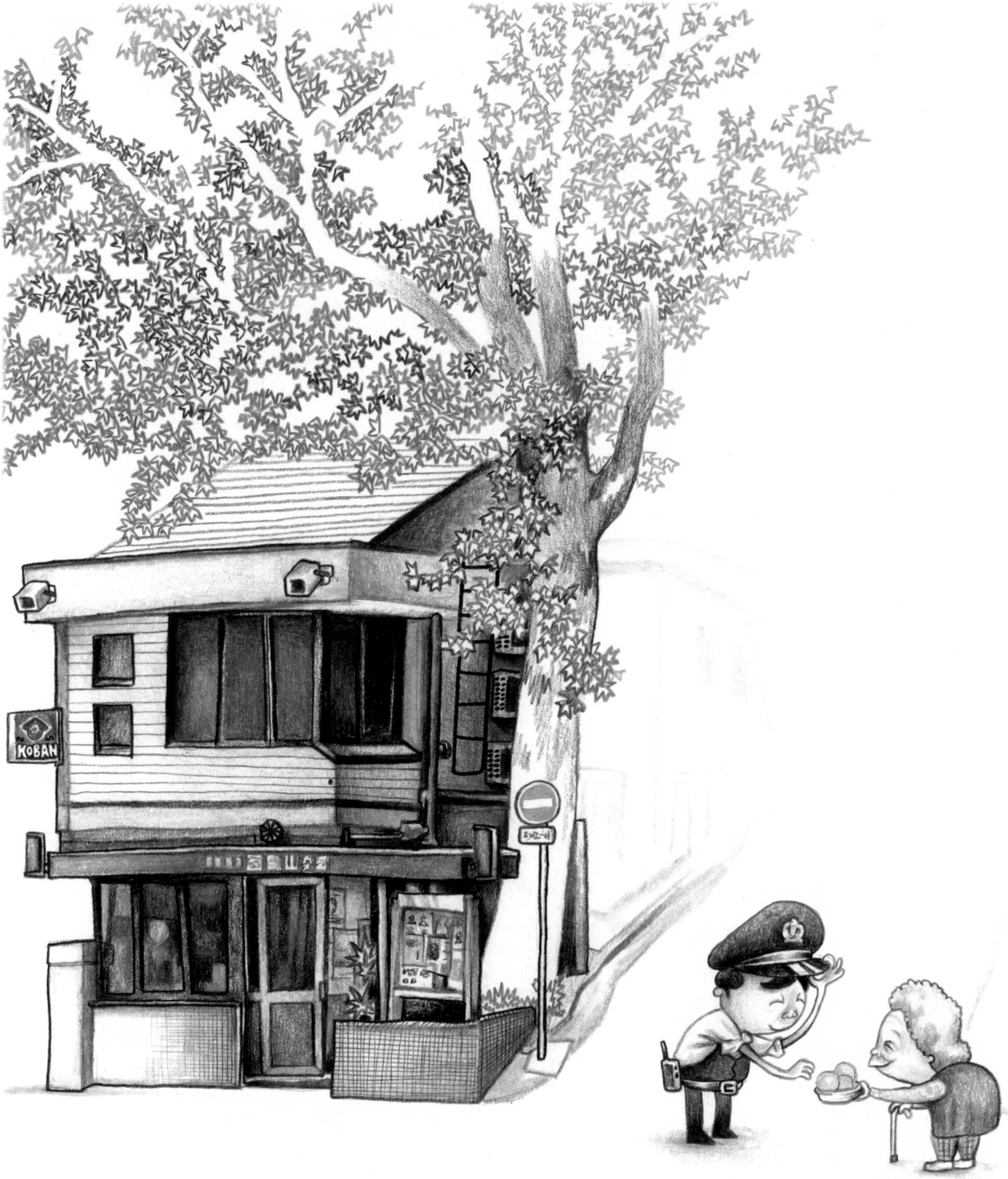
KOBAN

points south

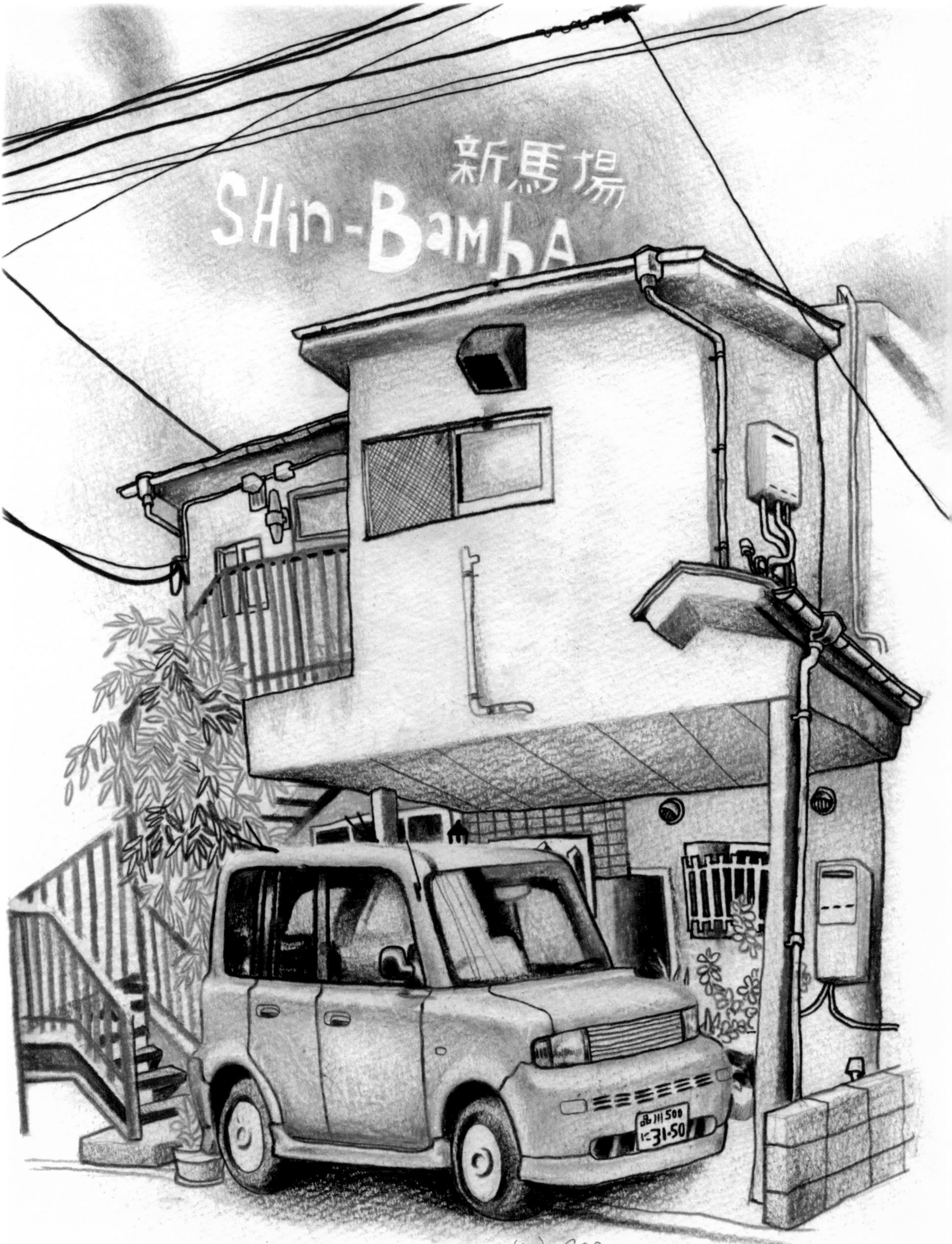
新馬場
SHin-BambA
品川500
に 31-50
CUBE(ic) CaR
-Nissan-

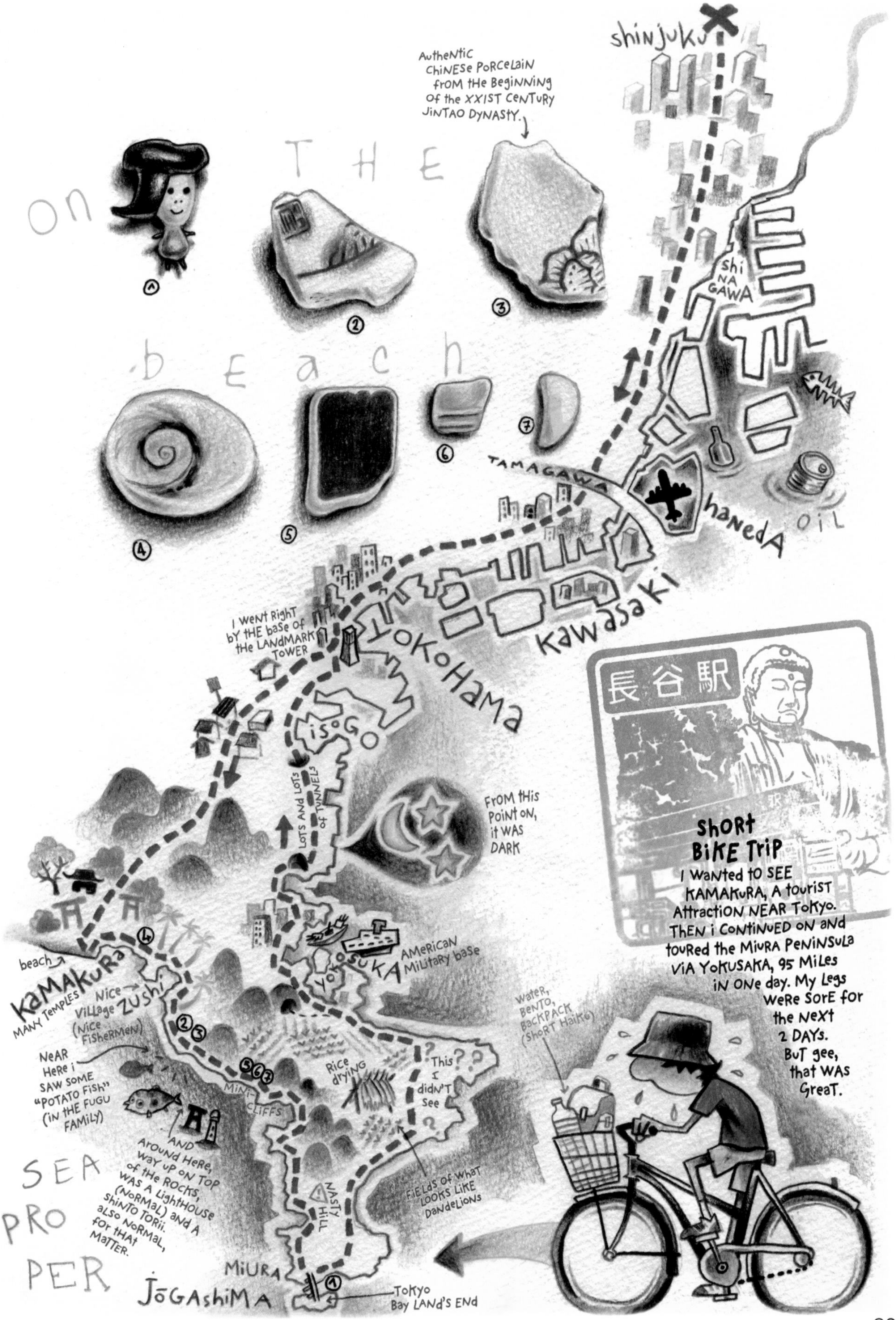

Authentic CHINESE PORCELAIN FROM THE BEGINNING OF THE XXIST CENTURY JINTAO DYNASTY.
On THE beach
1
2
3
4
5
6
7
shinjuku
shi NA GAWA
TAMAGAWA
hanedA
OIL
KAWASAKI
YOKOHAMA
I WENT RIGHT BY THE BASE OF THE LANDMARK TOWER
ISOGO
LOTS AND LOTS OF TUNNELS
FROM THIS POINT ON, IT WAS DARK
長谷駅
SHORT BIKE TRIP
I WANTED TO SEE KAMAKURA, A TOURIST ATTRACTION NEAR TOKYO. THEN I CONTINUED ON AND TOURED THE MIURA PENINSULA VIA YOKUSAKA, 95 MILES IN ONE DAY. MY LEGS WERE SORE FOR THE NEXT 2 DAYS. BUT GEE, THAT WAS GREAT.
beach
KAMAKURA
MANY TEMPLES
Nice Village ZUSHI (Nice FISHERMEN)
YOKOSUKA
AMERICAN MILITARY BASE
NEAR HERE I SAW SOME "POTATO FISH" (IN THE FUGU FAMILY)
MINI-CLIFFS
Rice drying
This? I didn't see
Water, BENTO, BACKPACK (SHORT Haiku)
AND AROUND HERE, WAY UP ON TOP OF THE ROCKS, WAS A LIGHTHOUSE (NORMAL) AND A SHINTO TORII. ALSO NORMAL, FOR THAT MATTER.
SEA PRO PER
NASTY HILL
FIELDS OF WHAT LOOKS LIKE DANDELIONS
MIURA
JŌGASHIMA
TOKYO Bay LAND'S END

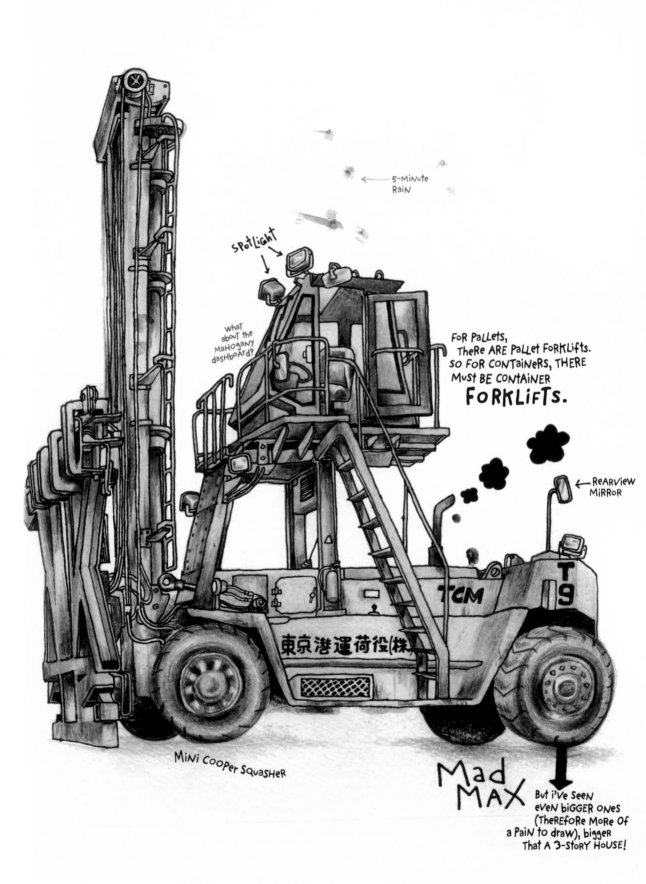

5-Minute Rain

Spotlight

What about the mahogany dashboard?

For pallets,
there are pallet forklifts.
So for containers, there
must be container
FORKLIFTS.

Rearview Mirror

Mini Cooper Squasher

TCM

東京港運荷役㈱

T9

Mad MAX

But I've seen
even bigger ones
(therefore more of
a pain to draw), bigger
that a 3-story house!

Japan in Cards

but NOTHING ON CRedit

MY GEO VideO CLUB MEMbership card. ALLOWed Me to KiLL time SOME eveNiNgs AND broadeN the Scope of My KNOWLedGE of OLD FreNCh fiLMS. JAPAN iS WHERE i SAW ZAZie iN tHE MeTro for the FiRST time

Merde alors!

They ALSo Have Video GaMes, Music...

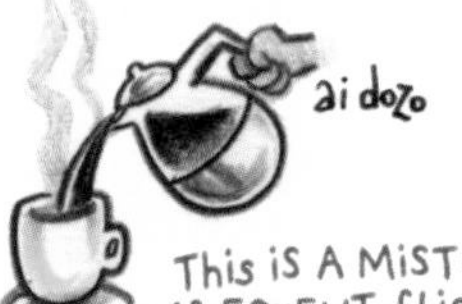
ai dozo

This iS A MiSTeR DONUT (frEQUENT fLieR?) CArd. ONe of My HaUNTS WHEN it Was RaiNiNG. NOT THAT I'M A big doNUT FaN, buT iN tHESe PLaces tHERE ARE UNLiMiTed frEE ReFiLLS of CoFFee (aMeriCaN STyLe, buT iT's OKAY). A Kind WaitreSS WOULD CoMe over aNd RePLeNiSH My SUPPLY ReguLarLy WHiLE i CoNtiNued drAWiNG iN A WARM, drY ENViroNMeNt.

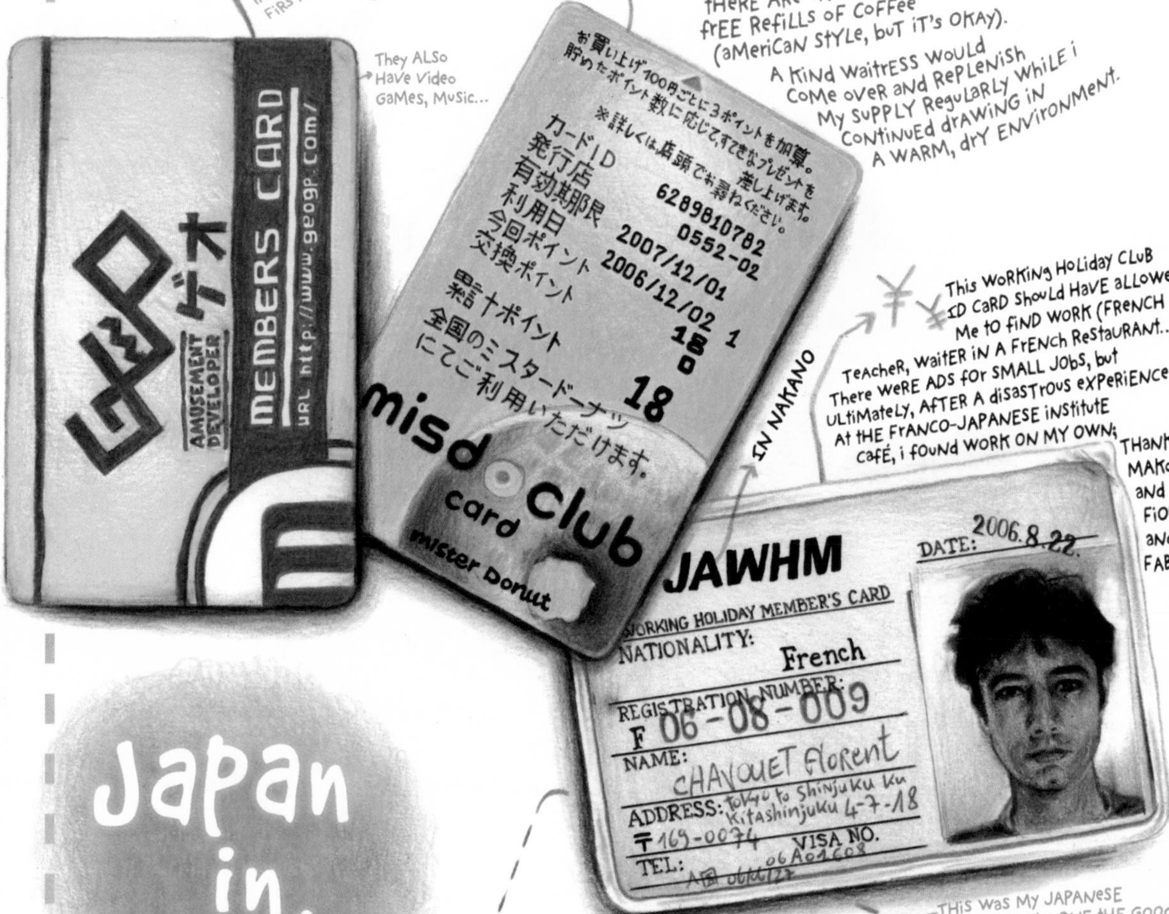

GEO ゲオ
AMUSEMENT DEVELOPER
MEMBERS CARD
URL http://www.geogp.com/
お買い上げ100円ごとに3ポイントを加算。貯めたポイント数に応じて、すてきなプレゼントを差し上げます。
※詳しくは店頭でお尋ねください。
カードID 6289810782
発行店 0552-02
有効期限 2007/12/01
利用日 2006/12/02 1
今回ポイント 15
交換ポイント 0
累計ポイント 18
全国のミスタードーナツにてご利用いただけます。
misdo club card
mister Donut
JAWHM
DATE: 2006.8.22.
WORKING HOLIDAY MEMBER'S CARD
NATIONALITY: French
REGISTRATION NUMBER: F 06-08-009
NAME: CHAVOUET Florent
ADDRESS: Tokyo to Shinjuku ku Kitashinjuku 4-7-18
〒169-0074
VISA NO. 06A01608
TEL:

IN NAKANO

This WORKiNg HoLiday CLUB ID CaRD ShouLd HaVE aLLowed Me to fiND WORK (FRENCH TeacheR, WaiteR iN A FreNch ResTauRANT...). There WeRE ADS for SMALL JObS, but ULtiMateLy, AFTER A disasTrous exPeRiENCE At tHE FrANCO-JAPANESE iNstitute café, i fouNd WORK ON MY OWN; THANK YOU MAKoTo and FiORiNA and FABieNNE!

THis Was My JAPANeSE ID CaRD. The ONE tHE Good GENtLeMEN FROM tHe PoLiCE WouLd ALWAys ASK to SEE.

I.d.

I WaNTED to CaRRY it Back to FraNCe With Me buT it ENdED uP BetWeeN the SciSSORS of ONE of tHoSe COUNTLeSS PEOPLe iN UNiFORM Who HaNG OuT iN AirPORTS.

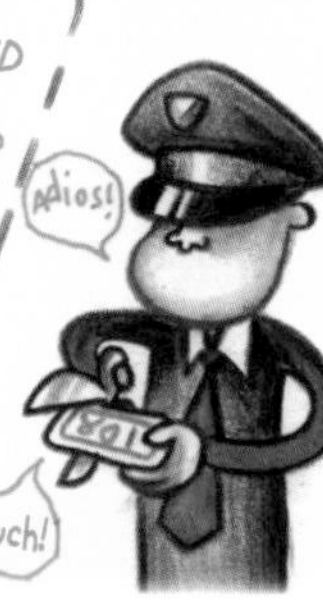

Adios!
Ouch!

i CONGRaTuLaTE MYSeLf
ON HaViNG Subsisted ON LeSS
THAN ¥900 per day.

i do NOT CONGRatuLate MySeLf
ON KNOWiNG AS Many
JaPaNeSe WORDS AS theRe ARE
JAPANESE cheeses.

It's aLReadY OVeR?

WeLL, Yeah.

Bah, i'LL BE BACK . . .

Boarding Pass
氏名 Name
CHAVOUET/FLORENTM
FFP番号 FFP Number
TOKYO/NARITA
PARIS/CHARLES DE
クラス class 日付 Date
便名 Flight
JL 405 Y 20DEC
Boarding Time 座席 Seat
95 1035
46G
0009 Q
JAL

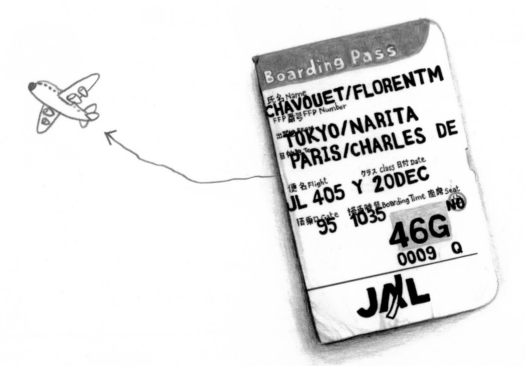